The Italy of Garibaldi's Campaigns

FRANCE

Geneva

Chambéry

P I E D M O N T

Grasse

Nice

San Remo

MARSEILLE

St.Tropez

Bandol

Biella

Navara

Chivasso

Vercelli

TURIN

Mortara

Casale

R. Ticino

Lake Maggiore

Arona

Varese

Lugano

Como

Bergamo

Lovare

Monza

Magenta

MILAN

Salo

Trento

Riva

Brescia

Lake Gardia

Solferino

Peschiera

Verona

Legnago

LOMBARDY

A U

VEN

R. Po

Mantova

PARMA

MODENA

Bologna

ROMAGNA

GENOA

Chiavari

T U S C A N Y

Viareggio

Lucca

Pisa

FLORENCE

Leghorn

ELBA

Talamone

San Stefano

Orbetello

Civita Castellano

RO

Civita Vecchia

CORSICA

La Maddalena

CAPRERA

S A R D I N I A

CAGLIARI

Isles of Aegades

Marsala

THE LION OF CAPRERA

Giuseppe Garibaldi in 1865. This photograph was autographed by his daughter, Clelia, shortly before her death

THE
LION
OF
CAPRERA

❖❖❖❖❖❖❖❖❖❖❖

A Biography of Giuseppe Garibaldi

by

JOHN PARRIS

Garibaldi had the true lion nature in him, all dignity and gentleness, the sudden flash of anger, the forgiveness, the absence of all rancour, malice or uncharitableness.

'THE TIMES' OBITUARY 1882

Probably a human face so like a lion, and still retaining the image of its Maker, was never seen.

MARTINENGO CESARESCO 1890

'Have you ever noticed the face of a lion? Don't you think it is a very stupid face? Well that is Garibaldi.'

MAZZINI TO JOHN MORLEY 1864

DAVID McKAY COMPANY, INC.

NEW YORK

PRINTED IN GREAT BRITAIN

Dedicated with gratitude
and affection to
JULIA WARD

CONTENTS

＊＊＊＊＊＊＊＊＊＊

CONTENTS

I

THE PERSECUTED APOSTLES

◆◆◆◆◆◆◆◆◆◆◆

O N THE 23rd March 1833, the lighthouse on the sea wall of
Marseilles harbour was still swinging its beam across the
night sky as a party of thirteen men made their way along the
quay to take a small boat out to a two-masted brig that lay at
anchor in the port. Although it was three o'clock in the morning,
they had to pass through a crowd so dense that there was scarcely
room for them to move. All Marseilles had turned out to watch
their departure; even the merchants of the port were assembled
outside the Bourse. Torches and lanterns bobbed amidst the
throng; the vessels in the port were gay with bunting; and as the
men walked they sang a song with a lilting air, which was taken
up by the crowd and echoed back from the rocks:

> Compagnons de la Femme,
> Si sa voix nous réclame,
> De coeur, de bras et d'âme,
>   Soyons prêts;
> Que nul effort ne côute,
> De fleurs semons sa route,
> Et que la terre écoute,
>   Nos chants de paix.

After the repeated refrain *Vive la femme, c'est l'ange de la
liberté*, there was applause and cheers and shouts of 'Le Père! La
Mère!'.[1]

The thirteen 'Companions of the Woman' presented a striking
appearance even for an age when costumes were more colourful
and personal idiosyncrasies more common than they are today.
Although they were all young men, each wore his hair long
and had a beard of Socratic length. A tight-fitting garment of

vermilion covered the whole of the body and disappeared into gauntlets and kneeboots of black leather. Over this, each wore a loose white tunic open over the chest which, frock-like, ended in the middle of the thighs, and was clasped in tightly at the waist by a broad, black belt. A long, black scarf, wound round the neck with one end tucked through the belt, completed their attire.[2]

They were St Simonian apostles on their way to find, in some city of the Bosphorus, *la femme libre* who was divinely ordained to be acknowledged as the Mother of Humanity, to establish the equality of the sexes, and by union with the Father of Humanity, their leader Enfantin, to unite East and West in the cause of peace. There was not one person in the crowd who had not heard of them long before they appeared in Marseilles; for the previous year several of the leaders of the sect had appeared as defendants in two trials which attracted attention not only in France but throughout Europe. Of the principal trial, Thomas Carlyle wrote to John Stuart Mill: *The Simonian trial was better than any Drama I have read for years . . . a chimera and a truth*[3]. With that latitude which the French legal processes allow to defendants to introduce issues which other jurisdictions would regard as extraneous and irrelevant, the defendants had used the Court as a pulpit to proclaim their gospel; and the effect of the proceedings had been to discredit the authorities and the Court, to arouse sympathy for the defendants and to publicize their ideas in a manner they could never have achieved without them.

The adherents of the sect had supported the revolutionaries of 1830, who in July of that year had driven out the despotic Charles X and had installed Louis Phillipe on the throne amid a chorus of protestations of democratic rights, and with a constitution which purported to guarantee them. Less than two years after that, the soldiers of His Majesty Louis Phillipe had surrounded a hall in Paris in which the sect was holding a service. The hall was crowded and for a moment it looked as if the unarmed Frenchmen would exercise their traditional right of setting about the military. But Emile Barrault, who was preaching, quietened the crowd by telling them: 'You come here to seek a gospel of peace. Prove yourselves now to be peaceful.' And he and the other leaders went docilely off to prison.

Louis Phillipe had been annoyed by a proclamation of the sect: *Suppose there were taken away from France three thousand or so of the men of science and industrial workers . . . it would be a catastrophe which would rob France of its very soul; but suppose you took away all the richest people in France . . . the brother of the King, duchesses, the landed proprietors . . . the state would not suffer at all. For in our society it is the idle who are the best rewarded.* His Majesty had been offended by the reference to his brother; but instead of leaving the cult to live and die in obscurity, he conferred on them the privilege of martyrdom.

The Apostles had been brought to trial on patently trumped-up charges of raising money by false pretences, endangering the security of the State and public morality, and, on the basis of the Proclamation, of conspiring to kill the King's brother. When the trial began, Enfantin, to the fury of the Court and the delight of the spectators, took a seat on the Bench beside the Presiding Judge, from which he had to be ejected with much unseemly disorder. None of the defendants would give testimony without first asking leave of the 'Father of Humanity'; and when his own turn came, he was silent for so long that the President had to adjourn the Court with the tart observation: 'We are not here to await the fruits of your meditation.' Enfantin eventually gave his evidence, in the form of a long dissertation on the tenets of the sect, which concluded with the information 'I judge but cannot be judged'. The Court thought otherwise. He was sentenced to twelve months' imprisonment.[4]

The whole of Europe had as a result learned that they were the posthumous followers of the aristocratic Count Henri Claude de Rouvroy de Saint-Simon, who had claimed to be a direct descendant of Charlemagne, and was the author of *Le Nouveau Christianisme*; though in reality the conduct and beliefs of the sect bore even less relationship to the philosophy of its founder than do those of most religions.

The Father of Humanity was still in prison when the Companions of the Woman arrived in Marseilles and the cartoonists were having great fun with 'Our Father which art in Sainte-Pélagie' but the leader of the party bound for the East was none other than the Emile Barrault who had stilled the crowd when the arrests took place and who came to the city fresh from his prison martyrdom. Formerly Professor of Rhetoric of the College at Sorèze, he was a playwright and poet as well as an accomplished orator, of whom a well-qualified judge was to say that he 'never heard a voice so eloquent or a poetry of language so harmonious'. For several hours the previous day he had moved a crowd of five hundred to fervour, alternating with tears, as he proclaimed the new gospel.

As he led the Companions into the rowing-boat, the crowd seized every small vessel around the harbour to accompany them out to the brig awaiting them, until the surface of the basin was covered with bobbing lanterns like a swarm of fireflies. When the Companions had clambered on board the 250-ton brig, *La Clorinda*, there was a moment of silence as Barrault blessed the vessel in the name of God, the Father and Mother. Then the crowd began to swarm on board until the ship was like *a citadel under assault*[5] and the songs continued:

> *Qui féconde la terre?*
> *Qui plante bois et vignes?*
> *Qui sème les moissons?*
> *Qui pour chacun prépare*
> *L'habit et la parure,*
> *La chair, le pain, le vin?*
>   *PEUPLE FIER, PEUPLE FORT*
> *C'est toi!*[6]

The crew of *La Clorinda* must have cursed these interlopers as they set about their task of preparing the vessel for sea, but one at least of their number was fascinated by the St Simonians and the scenes of enthusiasm they aroused. He was the twenty-six-year-old mate, whose own russet locks fell almost to his shoulders. *I knew of them only as the persecuted apostles of a new religion,* he wrote later.[7]

Before the twenty-five days of the voyage to Constantinople were over, Giuseppe Garibaldi had learned a great deal more about them and their faith.

II

THE COURSE TO MARSEILLES

❖❖❖❖❖❖❖❖❖❖

THE YOUNG mate of the brig had been born in Nice on the 4th July 1807[1] in a small house, heavy lidded with shutters, in a passage-way on the north side of the inner basin of the harbour only a few yards from the water's edge. In all the official records of this period, the place of residence of his family is given only as *Le port de Lympia*—the old name of Nice harbour—and it would appear that neither the house nor the street ever had an official designation. The alley was, however, known locally as the 'Cuoù de Buoù,' in the Nice *Patois* 'the tail of the ox'. Even the site has long since disappeared, for it was excavated in 1897 to enlarge the harbour; it was situated some two hundred yards in front of the church on what is today the place *Ile de Beauté*.[2]

In one version of his autobiography, Garibaldi professed to have been born not only in the same house but in the same room as that in which Napoleon's famous Marshal Massena first saw the light of day. There were no civil records in 1758 when Massena was born but, quite apart from the inherent improbability that two famous soldiers of fortune should have reported for duty in this world in the very same room, there are other good reasons for considering this as no more than an attempt to give a romantic touch to a birth that was otherwise completely undistinguished.[3]

Garibaldi was the second son and the third child[4] of a couple who both came from farther along the Ligurian coast. His father Domenico Garibaldi, was a sailor, who had moved with his own father, Ange, from Chiavari near Genoa when he was a small boy. His mother, formerly Rosa Raimondi had been born in Loano. Both parents, therefore, could properly claim to be of Italian stock, though the paternal surname and the physical characteristics of their children both suggest some distant teutonic origin.[5]

The boy was christened with names of Joseph Marie. That he received the French form of the Christian names, and not the Italian, was due to the fact that Nice, which had belonged to the House of Savoy since the fifteenth century, had been taken from the Kingdom of Piedmont by Napoleon in 1793. Garibaldi was therefore born a French citizen and a subject of the great Emperor, but since Nice reverted to Piedmont in 1815 and his parents were Italian, it is not without justification that he always regarded himself as of that nationality; though his patriotism no doubt gained an added element of intransigence as the result of his nationality being marginal and precarious, as did his anger when he was once more made of alien birth by the cession of Nice to France in 1860.

In the civil records of his birth his father is described as *capitain au gran cabotage*. Domenico Garibaldi in fact owned a 29-ton ship *La Santa Reparata* which he used for voyages along the Ligurian coast with wine and oil, as his father had before him with the same vessel. It was a poor living and at no time did the Garibaldi family ever achieve the distinction of a house of their own. At the time of Giuseppe's birth, the family, with their two children, were huddled in with the grandfather, Ange, in the house of Rosa's uncle, Gustavin, with his wife and children. In 1815, when one of the Gustavin boys got married and brought his bride home, Domenico and Rosa, with four children by then, had to move out. They went to rooms in a tenement house, *Maison Aburaram*, on the east side of the port which remained their home until Domenico died in 1841 and Rosa in 1852. It was a rabbit warren of a place which occupied three numbers on *quai Lunel* and had work-rooms and shops on the ground floor.

It was probably there that Giuseppe received the first steps of his education from a Father Giaume, who he wrote, *lived in our house and was, in a way, one of the family*. This man can be identified as a former monk of the Augustin order who taught from 1807 to 1811 at *l'école centrale des Alpes-Maritimes* and later took private pupils. The other teacher specifically named by Garibaldi was a M. Arena. *To him I owe the little I know,* he wrote, *above all, eternal gratitude for having grounded me in my mother tongue . . . and Roman history.* This tutor, too, can be identified in records of Nice as a retired army man who had a small private school up to 1815, when it was dissolved by the authorities and who subsequently also took private pupils.

Garibaldi belittled his knowledge unnecessarily. He could read and write French and Italian with equal facility; he had learned Latin and had a knowledge of the classics unusual for a sailor; and he was well versed in algebra, geometry and mathematics. So much so, that one of his close friends often asked him where he had acquired his knowledge. The only reply she got was: 'By applying myself to their study. I set to work with books by myself.'[6] There may have been a good deal of truth in that reply, but he was always so vague about his education and early life that the apparent lacuna in his account of it may conceal a secret which he preferred not to have revealed; it is a matter about which one may be permitted to speculate, particularly as he once told Gladstone in an unguarded moment that he had been to school in Genoa.[7]

Of his boyhood little is recorded and nothing specific except by himself. He claimed to have rescued, at the age of eight, a washerman from drowning. Another incident has a greater ring of authenticity: *One day,* he wrote, *I found a cricket which I took to my room; there, while playing with it I clumsily broke one of the feet. My grief was such that I shut myself up for several hours, weeping bitterly.* It is a picture consistent with his character as a man; there was always honey in the lion. Apart from an occasion on which he and some other boys attempted to steal a boat and sail to Genoa, his early life is passed over by him with the comment: *Nothing unusual happened to me in my childhood.* The picture he gave of it was of a youth in a red woollen shirt and blue trousers, running wild amid the vessels of the harbour and spending his time clambering their rigging.[8]

He claimed to have gone to sea as a *mousse* (cabin-boy apprentice) when he was *about fifteen.* His biographers have usually stated that it was in fact in 1821, when he was thirteen, or in the following year. As it happens, the Register of *Mousses* of Nice is still extant with the detailed record of all his early voyages. The first entry relates to the vessel on which he himself says he first sailed, the *Constanza,* and the voyage, which was to Odessa, also corresponds with his own account. The date on which he signed on that vessel is given as the 29th January 1824—less than six months before his seventeenth birthday; it seems an extraordinary long time for a boy of working class parents to have been kept at home doing nothing in those days.

II

The voyage to Odessa on the *Constanza* was one he remembered with pleasure all his life. *Oh, beautiful Constanza,* he wrote, *thy stout sides, thy rigging, lofty and light, thy wide decks, even the figurehead of thy prow will remain ever engraved on my memory by the tool of youthful imagination.* Although he never served in her again after he was paid off on 28th July 1824, for many years he was writing letters to her skipper, Angelo Pesante, as to an old friend; and from him he gratefully acknowledged he had learned all his practical seamanship.

On 11th November 1824, he was signed as *mousse* on board his father's smaller vessel and made a few coasting voyages to Bandol and St Tropez. On the 26th March of the following year, *La Santa Reparata* set off on a trip in which business was being combined with pleasure and piety. Instead of the usual crew of five, eight were shown on the books, including Giuseppe Deideri, a youth of nineteen, whose family also lived in the *Maison Aburaram*, and there were two passengers. They were carrying a cargo of wine but Domenico also had some litigation in Rome to attend to, and it was a Holy Year—the first to be held since 1775.

La Santa Reparata docked in Fiumicino on the 12th April and the party made their way to Rome. To see Rome for the first time was an experience for the excitable youth comparable with his first voyage at sea. It was not the city of the Popes that inspired him, but that of the ancient Romans and, sharing the spirit of romanticism that was abroad in art and literature, he dreamed of a revival of the glories of former days. Thereafter, the city exercised a fascination for him which was almost irrational. *What joy to go to Rome,* Garibaldi wrote of that first visit. *Rome! What else was this city to me but the centre of the world, of the universe. A dethroned queen? Yes; but from her ruins, immense and sublime, emerges the memory of all that was great in her past. The Rome that I saw in my youth was not only the Rome of the past but also the Rome of the future . . . to me, holy and dear beyond all else. I loved her with all the fervour of my soul . . . Rome to me was Italy . . . Rome to me was the one and only symbol of Italian unity.*[9]

It needed the eye of a poet to see all that in the Rome of his youth, for it was a city of narrow streets into which the sun barely penetrated, horse-drawn *carrozze,* swarms of flies, and hundreds of shrines; and the population of Romans, regarded as heavy and brutish by the rest of Italy, had many more than their fair share of cut-throats and pickpockets. Yet in this most urban of all cities, the fingers of the countryside stretched almost into the heart. There were vineyards in Laterano, and farms and grass-lands reaching even the Ripetta. Through the streets moved half-starved peasants driving their scraggy cattle.

Garibaldi was not there long enough even to glimpse political conditions in the city and there is no reason to believe that at the age of eighteen he had the slightest interest in them; but it was a critical period in the history of the temporal power of the Papacy, and the policy then being shaped by the new Pope, Leo XII, and implemented after his brief reign by his successors, Pius VIII and Gregory XVI, was to have a drastic effect on his life. In 1825, the reign of terror and oppression throughout the Papal States, which was to lead to the explosions of 1830 and 1848, was just beginning. The Holy Year itself was sanctified by two waves of executions in Ravenna, when large numbers of men suspected of liberal sympathies were hanged after farcical trials, and their bodies left to decompose on public gibbets; and the prisons all over the Pope's domains were filled with similar suspects who, without trial or charge, were chained to the walls and left to rot in their own excreta.[10] After the return from Rome, Garibaldi continued sailing with his father and in a vessel called the *Enea*[11] until the following year, most of which he spent as a *mousse* in a vessel named as *Il Giovanni Francesco*. It is a ship that he never mentioned in any edition of his autobiographies, although the names of the others are given.

His own version of events subsequent to the voyage on the *Enea* is: *Next, I began a series of journeys in the Levant, during which we were three times captured and robbed by the same pirates. This happened twice on the same voyage.*[12]

Strangely enough, that is exactly the experience which befell the *Constanza*, in which Garibaldi had made his first voyage, in the year 1826. Greece had rebelled against Turkish domination in 1821 and for nearly a decade afterwards the Greek Archipelago swarmed with pirates, so that no merchantman went unarmed. In the early part of 1826, the *Constanza* set out from Marseilles on a voyage for Taganrog but she returned in March, having been pillaged by pirates. She sailed again and was twice, on 10th June and 21st June, boarded and robbed by the same pirates.[13] These facts have led some historians to suppose that Garibaldi was on the ship in 1826 when this happened; but his sailing records show that from 13th February until 4th December of that year, when he was discharged at Gibraltar, he was in the *Il Giovanni Francesco*.

In versions of his autobiography in which the episode figures, it precedes a voyage which, for him, ended in Constantinople; but the exact record of all his voyages up to that is available. He was in the *Conte des Geneys* (he gives the name of the vessel as the *Coromandel* but the name of the captain, Giuseppe Galleono, the same as the Register) for a voyage to the Canaries from the 5th January 1827 to the 15th May of the same year; and in the *San Giuseppe* from the 26th May until the 23rd August. On the 12th September he sailed on the *Il Cortese* on a voyage to the Black Sea. As he seems to date the attack by pirates as taking place before that voyage, it is difficult not to believe that these adventures in reality happened to his friend, Captain Pesante. It would not be the first time that a raconteur with a romantic disposition attributed to himself adventures that in fact befell another.

In his voyages to the East it is more than probable that he had some brush with pirates. After his death there was found amongst his papers a record, written in pencil in his own hand,[14] of every engagement he was in up to 1871 and it commences with: *1831 Fight in the Archipelago with Greek pirates. Wounded slightly in the right hand*. Since it appears to be a list made for his own edification and not for publication, it may well be reliable; but even so it is difficult to reconcile, as will be seen, with the maritime records and his own published accounts.

III

By the autumn of 1827, Garibaldi had made such progress as a sailor that he was shipped in the 191-ton brig *Il Cortese*, according to the records *come secondo*—as mate. He was only twenty and had been going to sea for barely three and a half years. It is some tribute to his ability as a sailor that at that age, and while he was still entered in the Register of *mousses*, he was entrusted with such a post, involving as it did responsible duties such as navigation.

He was so much of a man by now that he proposed to get married. When he sailed again in the same vessel, he was engaged to a Nice girl named Francesca Roux and they had arranged that they should be married as soon as the vessel returned to Nice.

After a voyage delayed in Smyrna, as the result of being in a storm, *Il Cortese* returned to Nice, but Garibaldi was not on board. He had been taken ill in Constantinople and left there on the 24th August 1828. His illness lasted longer than he had expected, with the result that he became destitute. When he was recovered, through the good offices of his doctor he was found employment as a teacher. How long he remained in Constantinople is uncertain, but war between Turkey and Russia delayed his return home.

He left Constantinople by signing on the brigantine *Nostra Signora della Grazie,* according to his own accounts, *in which vessel I obtained my first command as Captain on a voyage to Port Mahon and Gibraltar.* There is no entry in the maritime records of Nice of either of these voyages but Garibaldi reappears in the Register of Captains, Second Class, and the first entry shows that he signed on *La Clorinda* as mate on the 20th February 1832. Above this is a date without explanation, 18th May 1831, and a note 'Released from Genoa 20th February 1832.' It may well be, therefore, that the documents relating to those voyages were amongst the maritime records of that latter port. Perhaps the brush with the Greek pirates occurred on the voyage from Constantinople.

Whenever it was that he returned from the East to Nice, he found that things had not remained the same in his absence. After a brief visit to his parents, he rushed round to the house where Francesca Roux lived. In front of it was a small garden surrounded by a wall and the gate was closed. With the impatience he was to show in many greater ventures later in life, he vaulted the wall. Francesca was not alone. In her arms was a child and on her finger was a wedding ring. When she saw him she was overcome with confusion and tried to stammer out an explanation. 'Don't bother to say anything,' he said to her. 'I understand. I wish you every happiness.' And he kissed her and left.[15]

As he once exclaimed to a friend when he was discussing somebody who had committed suicide after being disappointed in love: 'Why on earth should a man kill himself for a woman? Why? When there are so many women in the world. When a woman takes my fancy, I say to her "You like me? I like you. You don't like me? Too bad for you".'[16]

Four days after the issue of his master's ticket in Nice, he sailed as mate in *La Clorinda*. His younger brother, Michel, was signed on the same vessel as a hand. They made two voyages, one to Taganrog[17] and one to Odessa, before that momentous day in his life, when he leaned over the side of the brig and watched the strange scene of the embarkation of the St Simonians.

III

A STRANGE LIGHT

❖❖❖❖❖❖❖❖❖❖❖

As the *La Clorinda* ploughed her way eastward through the Mediterranean, Emile Barrault found that he had in the mate an eager listener.

Both men belonged to that rare strain which runs like a vein of quicksilver through the clay of humanity, the ones whose mental stability is so finely balanced that they are excitable by new ideas; men, the molecules of whose minds dance perceptibly. They are invariably those whose fine balance of mind is matched by an equally delicate poise of emotion; they know the deep tempests of sensation and the swirling intensity of dreams; their lives are lit by vivid flashes of delight and clouded by the dark growlings of disappointment. Creatures of fire and air, they are creatures also of paradox: the Garibaldi who could weep over the broken limb of a cricket was the Garibaldi who, without taking the cigar out of his mouth, could order one of his own men to be shot; the one who could pause in the midst of battle to listen to the song of a nightingale was the same who could, without a qualm, make protestations of love to four different women in the same week. Psychopaths, hypermaniacs, and saints; ludicrous charlatans to their foes and omniscient prophets to their followers; faithful to causes and faithless to women; they are gods amongst men. None truly comprehends them unless he be one of them, and when they meet together there is a communication that is beyond language, and as they walk together their hearts burn within them.

Garibaldi's road to Emmaeus lay along the deck of the *La Clorinda*. As he paced it with Barrault, with the two masts above them peering up to the skies and the square-rigged sails filled and bellowing, against the swell of the sea and the rattle of the gaff in the wind, they talked. *During those translucent Eastern nights, which are not darkness but only the absence of light, beneath a sky sprinkled with stars, sailing across the sea . . . we discussed the great questions of the human race,* wrote Garibaldi.[1] In the sentence that follows he tries to give the essence of what he learned but he hurries on to the record of his actions, as if fearful that the reader will be bored by a discussion of abstractions. *Firstly,* he says, *the apostle showed me that a man who defends his own country or attacks another's, is no more than a soldier . . . but he who, by becoming an internationalist . . . offers his blood and his sword to every people struggling against tyranny, is more than a soldier; he is a hero.*

In subsequent editions of his autobiography he omitted all reference to the St Simonians; but to neglect the influence of them over him is to lose the key to his whole life and conduct.

At first sight, the St Simonian beliefs are a tangled skein of economics, religion, sociology, dusted with the glittering sparkles of the bizarre and the ridiculous. Untangle them, and they present long strands which reach out to the present day.

In economic theory, the movement was essentially a revolt against the extreme individualism of the French Revolution and against the anarchy of unrestrained capitalism. It has been termed 'the first, the most eloquent, the most profound expression of socialism in the nineteenth century'. Marx was early familiarized with the tenets of the sect through his father-in-law, von Westphalen, who was an adherent, and many of the maxims which pass as communist principles today are but variants of those invented by the St Simonians:

> *From each according to his capacity, to each according to his works.*
> *The end of the exploitation of man by man.*
> *The abolition of all privileges of birth*

appeared first in the pages of their first journal, *Le Producteur* in 1825–26.[2] It is, however, just as true to say that they were the precursors of enlightened capitalism.

The common ground is to be found in the view taken by the St Simonians of the purpose of industry; that it must be used to serve the people and not to enrich a privileged few by the exploitation of the majority. As they declared: *All social institutions must have as their object the improvement, moral, intellectual, and physical, of the most numerous class.* That is a view of society that carries almost universal assent in the twentieth century and to the economic aspects of which both communism and capitalism pay at least lip service. The real controversy between the two systems, on this point, is limited simply to which is the best means of achieving that end. The communist says that capitalism only functions when there is an excess of demand over production and that it breaks down into chaos when there is an excess of production over demand; that it is rooted in scarcity, so that the starvation of millions in India is the price paid for the prosperity of the American farmer. The modern capitalist says that communism does no more than to take caviare from kings and give it to commissars, and that without the incentive of individual advantage, it cannot produce to fulfil the demand; and that, even if it can, the price in the surrender of personal liberty is too high to pay. But both systems are agreed upon the end; that the purpose of commerce and industry, and one of the objects of society itself, is to produce the maximum number of goods for the greatest number of people.

In that, the St Simonians were the forerunners not so much of communism or of enlightened capitalism, but of the ideals of the twentieth century; if it were socialism (and it was) it was a socialism that has percolated into the thinking of thousands who would indignantly reject that description of their beliefs.

The echo of all these ideas is to be found in Garibaldi's thoughts, particularly those expressed in the later years of his life when he was disillusioned about the nature of the unified Italy that he had done so much to bring about. *It was a different Italy than I had dreamed of all my life*, he wrote two years before he died. The communists may claim him as one of their heroes, but there is no more justification for that than there was for the similar claims that were made by the Italian fascists. He was also reproached in his own day for the inconsistency of his ideas. All these false judgements can only be avoided if it be realized that he was in his beliefs about the purpose and organization of society essentially a St Simonian, albeit an unacknowledged one, to the end of his days; and, above all, that the unification of Italy was, for him, never more than a means to an end.

Commonplace as the economic ideas of the St Simonians are to us in the twentieth century, at the beginning of the nineteenth they were startling and dangerous innovations. While it is true that as early as 1758, Rousseau had been speaking of 'men so abominable that they dare to have more than enough while others die of starvation' and there were those in the French

Revolution who believed that political equality without economic equality was no more than a tantalizing illusion, the Revolution proceeded on the assumption that liberty meant unfettered free enterprise and no limit to property rights, and even executed those like Babeuf who taught otherwise. Free enterprise as a result was really free; free to dump a cargo of rice in the sea in Marseilles in a time of famine to maintain extortionate prices; free to engineer scarcity and starvation to make profits.

With the restoration of 1815, it became the fixed policy of governments to keep the poor poor; as Robert Owen, the English social thinker, whose mind worked on parallel lines to those of the St Simonians, discovered to his amazement when he attended the Congress of Sovereigns at Aix-la-Chapelle in 1817. The restored rulers understood perfectly well that for the first time in history, industrial progress enabled all men in Europe to be properly fed, housed and educated. It was just that they did not want that to happen; for if the masses became independent how were they to be governed? The beliefs of the St Simonians therefore challenged not only the conceptions of the Revolution but those of the Restoration.

The St Simonians did more than proclaim the brotherhood of men and that the purpose of any society was to serve all its members. They had a specific programme for achieving it. It included such details as: a planned economy; education of all children together without regard to rank or colour or fortune; an organization of the nations into United Nations; and many a scheme for immediate social amelioration ranging from municipal drains and municipal pawnshops to the extension of railways on a scale that at the time seemed wildly impracticable. They are classed by some amongst those reformers who are incapable of organizing anything except the future, but an astonishing number of their schemes came to fruition. The first railway line, from Paris to St. Germain, was organized at a funeral of a St Simonian saint; the *Crédit Mobilier* is theirs; so also is the *Compagnie Générale Transatlantique,* all of whose ships originally bore the names of their saints; and it was they who first mooted the idea of both the Suez and the Panama canals.

II

There were at least four reasons why they adopted *la couleur théologique* and cast their beliefs in a religious form. The first was that they still lived in an era, although towards the end of it, when it was obligatory to cast all philosophical thought in a theological form. Secondly, they had not only to challenge the secular order, but also the established Church, which was welded, and to all appearances inseparably welded, to it; the third, because they genuinely found their inspiration in the teaching of Jesus and, although Saint-Simon himself was in reality an agnostic, or at best a non-theistic Christian, it was the starting point of his argument; the fourth was because they consciously adopted the forms of religion as the media of communication.

The second was necessary because in the abuse of property rights the Church was not merely a silent observer but an active accomplice. At the end of the eighteenth century, Clement XIV, who as a Cardinal had opposed the use of the famous treasure of Sixtus V to buy corn in time of famine, as Pope was in league with the profiteer Bischi who controlled Rome's food supplies and who used to create profits by restricting supplies.[3] Even Pius VII, when he returned in 1815 from his abduction and imprisonment by Napoleon, in a time of famine squandered the resources of the theocracy on selling up obelisks, adding the vast Chiaramonte wing to the Vatican, and embellishing Rome with ornate fountains, so that the populace of that unhappy city who had no bread could console themselves with water from a work of art.[4]

The Church was the ally of the monarchs in their determination to keep the poor starving and submissive; and, in fact, persisted in that view when the secular rulers of men were on the way to abandoning it. As late as 1860, Pius IX was complaining bitterly that the peasants of North Italy, and Piedmont in particular, were no longer satisfied with 'the food of their forefathers', maize, and were demanding luxuries like bread and meat that were unknown to their brethren in the South; wicked demands, that he could only ascribe to their being led astray by foreign agents.[5]

Whoever challenged the right of rulers to keep their subjects bound to poverty and misery, challenged therefore the authority of the Church.

Religion, the St Simonians believed, *must direct society towards the great end of the most rapid improvement of the condition of the poorest classes.* In this they opposed the authority of Jesus to that of the Church. *God had said that all men ought to live together as brothers; this sublime principle comprehends all that is divine in religion.* As others have done before and since them, they sought for return to the simple teachings of Jesus, before those teachings became overlaid with successive layers of superstition that conceal them. *Love thy neighbour as thyself* was the first, and only, article of their creed.

No doubt their costumes, their ritual, their 'Father of Humanity' invited immediate ridicule; but they were intrinsically no more absurd than the religious accessories existing to this day. Dressing up in fancy clothes was no innovation in religious practice; the symbolism of a waistcoat that could not be unfastened save with another person's help was no more fanciful than the symbolism of the chasuble, and its meaning was more immediately apparent; and Enfantin was as well (or as little) qualified as any other man to be an infallible father. And if the sincerity of agnostics who adopt religious forms to propagate their message is called into question, it was no different in essence to the members of another hierarchy who, to this day, tolerate fraudulent miracles and idolatrous objects of devotion 'to assist the faith of the weak'.

What the St Simonians did they did with a clear mind; they adopted colourful garments, songs and ritual as powerful instruments to stir the minds of others, and engender enthusiasm for their cause. *When we shall have three hundred men, properly robed, carrying symbols, when they shall have been taught to sing as the chorus of Greece, not a single soul will be unmoved,* declared Enfantin; and if there is a touch of the charlatan about such a conscious striving for effect, it is wise to bear in mind what John Stuart Mill wrote to Carlyle about them: *The Enthusiast no wise precludes the Quack; nay rather . . . it presupposes him.*

This was one of the lessons Garibaldi learned from his mentor; and most thoroughly applied. Vestments inspired the coloured garments and trick waistcoats and they in turn inspired the red shirts and the Moor galloping behind on a black horse. From Gregorian chants came the hymns of the St Simonians; from them in turn came the songs of nation-making campaigns; and many a touch of flamboyancy in his speech and gesture and garment came from a calculated desire not to leave a soul unstirred.

III

The influence of the St Simonians continued long after the cult as such had disappeared and Enfantin had become a staid director of the P.L.M. railway line, which he did much to bring into existence. In philosophy, it persisted in positivism, for Auguste Comte was secretary to Saint-Simon, and though he later despised his former master as 'a depraved charlatan', he in fact owed to him the whole of his ideas; and the essence of their economic teaching had found a new exponent in the twentieth century in the person of Thorstein Veblein. Their ideas still reverberate in the modern world.

But at the moment we are concerned only with their influence, as wielded by Barrault, over one man; and two other aspects are worthy of notice. One is their teaching about marriage and sex; the other, more important, is what they believed about leadership in society.

The St Simonians believed, although they were almost alone in doing so in their time, in the equality of the sexes and the emancipation of women. Marriage, they believed, *was ordained to make life more agreeable, but the contrary was not infrequently the result.* Therefore, once the fundamental object had failed, there was no reason why a marriage should continue to exist. As Enfantin put it: *Let those whose affections are constant adhere to one companion throughout life, but it is not desirable to impose such an obligation universally.* They preached, too, what they termed *The Rehabilitation of the Flesh*: that there was nothing inherently unclean about the sexual act and that the gratification of the senses belonged to the same realm as the appreciation of beauty in art or music.

It is almost inconceivable that as Barrault and the young mate paced the deck, they did not discuss the relationship between men and women; and in the latter's subsequent conduct it is possible to discern not only the prompting of undisciplined instinct but also the dim outline of a theory.

But the influence of the St Simonians over Garibaldi is most clearly seen in their doctrine of leadership in society. For they did not believe that all men were born equal; they believed in a hierarchy of talents in which all contributed what they could, in accordance to the *Principle of Association*, to the common good. *We believe in the natural inequality of man and look on this inequality, divorced from heredity, as the basis of Association . . . We want all the*

instruments of labour, land and capital which now form . . . the in-
heritance of private owners to be united in one social fund. This fund
should operate on the principle of Association . . . so that each will be
given a task according to his ability and each will be rewarded according
to his needs.

The expression of this inequality was to culminate in a leader,
under whom all would serve. In that, they were not the first (or
the last) to believe, but the distinctive feature of their faith lay in
the character of the despot. He was to live as an ascetic and rule
in love and for the people; to be selected by them and deposable
by them; and in his manner of life he was to be of them. In 1832
Enfantin had taken forty of his disciples off to live a monastic life
in manual labour at Menilmontant, believing: *We have too white*
skins to be able to claim to save the people. When the proletariat presses
our hands they will feel that they are calloused like their own. We are
injecting ourselves with proletarian nature. The idea of philosophers,
scientists and scholars so engaged aroused some amusement
elsewhere. *Figure Duveyrer with waiter's apron emptying slop-pails*
for the salvation of man, wrote Carlyle to Mill. Yet they had a perfectly valid point, the necessity of identification with the people
they aspired to lead; a lesson that labour leaders who dine off
silver plate and ride around in expensive motor-cars might do
well to ponder.

The whole idea of Caprera, where Garibaldi was to devote
much of his life in an unrewarding effort to till a barren soil
with his own hands, surely found its inspiration on the deck
of *La Clorinda*; as did his renunciation of all the prizes that a
monarch was willing to shower upon him for the gift of a new
kingdom.

The young sailor who listened to these theories might, as
Bandi later said, have had dictatorship in his blood because every
venture in which he was engaged called for prompt and unques-
tioned decisions and blind faith in a leader; but quite apart from
the instinct of his nature and the necessities of his manner of life,
it is clear that he had learned to formulate them as principles; and
a letter he wrote to a young lady of noble birth that he was contemplating marrying, shows that he had an acute perception of
the truth that the St Simonians were attempting to express: *By*
uniting myself to you . . . I would be renouncing that character of
abnegation, the fruit of which is some popularity which I prize and
which may be valuable for my country . . . They will say 'He has

*done himself well' and has set himself apart from the people that he so
often swore he would serve until death.*[6]

In later years, Garibaldi's mother was wont to exclaim: 'The
St Simonians ruined my son.' From her point of view, that of a
pious daughter of the Church, she was right; but it would be
more correct to say that they made him. For he received their
message with all the fervour of a religious conversion. *A strange
light broke in on my mind, by the aid of which I saw a ship no longer as
just a means of carrying goods from one country to another, but as a
winged messenger bearing the Word of the Lord and the Sword of the
Archangel.*

La Clorinda docked at Constantinople on the 15th April 1833 and
Emile Barrault and Garibaldi parted, never to meet again. Before
long the St Simonians were dispersed; they were too impracticable
to change society fundamentally and too practical to live out the
rest of their lives in a wilderness alienated from other men; they
submerged, were assimilated and forgotten. But their message
lived on not only in the memory of the young sailor, but on the
printed page. In the room adjoining the one in which he died at
Caprera is still to be found a slim volume of *Le Nouveau Christianisme*, in the French edition of 1825, inscribed in a large spidery
hand: *E. Barrault*. It is difficult to believe that it had accompanied
Garibaldi through all vicissitudes of his wandering life, but it is not
impossible that he was given it on this voyage and left it in his
parents' home in Nice until he reclaimed it.

It is unlikely that Barrault and Garibaldi parted without the
prophet passing on to the new disciple the dying words of the
Master. For with his last breath, the apostles believed, Saint-
Simon had said: 'Nothing great is achieved without passion'.
It was a maxim which the young recruit was by temperament
disposed to accept anyway. *I parted from Barrault,* he wrote,
*yearning for emotions, eager for new ventures and wondering whether
there was not for me . . . some horizon not yet visible, of which I
thought I caught a glimpse through the mists of time.* Before the year
was out, the horizon had loomed up, still vague and indistinct,
but discernible.

IV

THE GOD OF GOOD MEN

◆◆◆◆◆◆◆◆◆◆

THERE WAS a group of young sailors in a corner of the rough drinking dive near the waterfront of Marseilles when Garibaldi entered. He was just back from a further voyage in *La Clorinda* and, as they were talking Italian, he went across and joined them. One of the company was holding forth to his companions, boasting that he was only one of a multitude who had enrolled in a new organization called 'Young Italy' led by a young man named Mazzini; but he was not having it all his own way.

'Italy? What do you mean by Italy?' exclaimed another youth scornfully. 'Do you mean the kingdom of Naples? Or the kingdom of Piedmont? Or what?' He pointed to another man at the table and added sarcastically. 'Perhaps you mean the Duchy of Modena, where he comes from!'

There was a guffaw at this, for Modena was a pocket-handkerchief size state.

'I mean the new Italy . . . the united Italy of all the Italians,' replied the first speaker.

The impressionable Garibaldi, newly converted from having no greater ambition than to be the master of a ship sailing the seven seas, caught a glimpse of the horizon for which he sought. *I felt*, he wrote later, *as Columbus must have done when he first sighted land.* He rose and clasped the hand of the youth who was advertising the new organization.[1]

II

There was some point in the objection raised by the sceptic at the table, for in the year 1833 even the idea of a united Italy

existed only in the dreams of a handful of visionaries. The numerous royal despotisms, and the few city republics, which existed in
the Italian peninsula before the French Revolution, had been
swept away by the invasions of Napoleon. He had ended up by
incorporating Piedmont and the north of the western seaboard in
the French Republic and creating a separate Kingdom of Italy
stretching across from Milan to Venice and as far south as Ancona;
below that the Kingdom of Naples was ruled by his Marshal,
Murat.

When the statesmen of the victorious allies assembled in Vienna,
and the flurry of the Hundred Days was over and Waterloo won,
they solemnly sat down to restore it all as if nothing had happened
in all those twenty weary years. Legitimacy was the watchword of
the Congress of Vienna, but like another much-publicized principle, on which a century later Europe was remade after a similar
cataclysm, it was strictly subordinated to the interests of the great
powers.

Because Austria was the dominant power at the Congress, she
acquired all the territories of the former Republic of Venice and
the Duchy of Milan; and even though the inhabitants spoke
only Italian, they were incorporated as provinces of the Austrian
empire. The House of Savoy, in the person of Victor Emmanuel I,
were allowed to return from their unpleasant exile in the malaria-
ridden wilderness of Sardinia and their Kingdom of Piedmont
was rebuilt as a buffer state between France and Austria, enlarged
by the acquisition of the territories of the former republic of
Liguria—in spite of promises by the British that its independence
would be respected. The miniature states of Parma, Modena and
Tuscany reappeared on the map. The first was given to Napoleon's widow, Maria Louisa, an Austrian princess, to console her
for the indignity suffered by her in having to marry the usurper.
Modena, with the other minute duchies of Reggio, Massa and
Carrara, went to Austrian princes. Tuscany was given to Ferdinand III of Austria. The Papacy received back its former territories comprising Rome, the Romagna, the Marches, Umbria and
the Patrimony; and in the Kingdom of Naples in the south was
included the island of Sicily. In the end, Austria dominated the
peninsula, as thoroughly as Napoleon ever had, and Italy was no
more than a geographical name.

The Restoration aimed at undoing the territorial changes made
by Napoleon; but more than that it aimed at rooting out every

vestige of the French Revolution, by exterminating all the pernicious ideas about equality, liberty and fraternity that had unfortunately become so prevalent. The new states were to be absolute monarchies. There was to be no nonsense about constitutional government or representation of the people. 'The people? Who are they?' sneered the Austrian Emperor. 'I know only *subjects*'. The idea that human beings, apart from rulers, had any rights was to be firmly suppressed. There was to be no freedom of discussion, no freedom of the Press, no freedom of association. Despotism, autocracy and police tyranny were to be the lot of those who lived in the restored kingdoms.

Of all the unhappy people who were delivered into bondage by the Congress of Vienna, none was more miserable than those who had been restored to 'the seamless robe of Christ', as a future Pope liked to term his temporal possessions. At the Congress itself the Pope's representative, Cardinal Consalvi, was busy scheming and intrigued not only to secure a restoration of all territories formerly ruled by the Church but also to prevent anywhere even the most rudimentary forms of democracy. For the Papacy was more devoted to absolution than even Metternich. Consalvi went round France and England lecturing the restored Bourbon, Louis XVIII, and the Prince Regent, on the sin of tolerating a free Press (which he termed: *the most dangerous weapon ever put into the hands of the enemies of religion and the monarchy . . . the liberty of the Press is not merely a temporary or a limited evil*),[2] in the hope that those two countries in which, alone in Europe, the Press had some measure of freedom, would join the others in the suppression of it. England was, as he himself admitted, *an altogether exceptional kingdom*, but elsewhere the whole weight of Papal authority was thrown behind the monarchs in their attempt to ensure that their rule was absolute, and administered without the assistance or consent of the ruled. One of the first acts of Pius VII on his restoration to his kingdom was to re-establish the Society of Jesus which his predecessor Clement XIV, in exercise of his divine and infallible authority—and for good reasons—had declared was to be *for ever broken up and dissolved*.[3] The Jesuits were brought back for one reason alone: that they might be the defenders of absolute monarchies; monarchies which, if they allowed their subjects no rights, would readily surrender to the Church a monopoly of education and of the right to adjudicate in the law of status.

The implacable opposition to democratic rights which the Papacy fostered amongst the monarchs, she certainly demonstrated in her own rule in subsequent years. All the offices of state, however minor, were filled by ecclesiastics. The Napoleonic civil and criminal codes were abolished; so, too, was uniformity of weights and measures, street lighting, public drainage, even vaccination against smallpox; the wine-shops were closed; the waltz was banned at carnivals; those wicked inventions of the devil, the railway train and the telegraph, were prohibited in all the holy realm; the Jews were driven back to the ghettoes and forbidden, on pain of death, to have friendly relations with any Christian; even education was so limited that by 1837 only two out of a hundred in the country districts could read and in Rome itself fewer than one in ten. Taxes were increased, and no accounts from the Papal Government were ever published of how they were expended. Permits were required for every trivial act any man might want to do.

This suppression of liberty is something that should not be forgotten when the attitude of Garibaldi and Mazzini to the Church is considered; they opposed her not because of what she claimed to be but what she did.

In the Kingdom of Piedmont things were a little better than they were in the rest of Italy, but not a great deal. Victor Emmanuel I, who had been placed on the throne by Austria, was by instinct clerical and autocratic; and he had pledged his word to Metternich that he would make no concessions to the people; but he had the interests of the house of Savoy at heart, if not those of his subjects. When the people rebelled against him in 1820, and demanded the Spanish Constitution of 1812, he abdicated in favour of his brother, Charles Felix, rather than be unfaithful to his pledge to the Austrians. Charles Felix, in whose name the Spanish Constitution had been proclaimed, soon found excuse for repudiating it and sentencing to death on the gallows the 178 men who had been the most active in these mild and constitutional demands. He reigned as the faithful tool of the Austrians, and when he died in 1831, he was succeeded by Charles Albert, the very one who as Regent had proclaimed the Spanish Constitution in Turin but who had expiated his offence by subsequently going to fight against it in the country of its origin.

III

Giuseppe Mazzini, whose name Garibaldi heard for the first time in the café in Marseilles in the late autumn of 1833, had been born on the 22nd June 1805 in a rather grand house with finely proportioned rooms and high arched ceilings, which still exists in via Lomellini, a narrow street on the hillside above the harbour of Genoa. He was the son of a doctor who, after 1816, became a professor at the University. Both his parents were politically conscious and held radical opinions. His father had been amongst those who welcomed the eruption of the French revolution in Italy and he had held office under the Ligurian republic.

As a child of eight, Giuseppe Mazzini showed such talent that a relative was prompted to write to his mother: *This dear boy is a star of utmost brilliance, destined to shine with true light, and be admired by the scholarship of Europe.*[4] No pen-portrait of Mazzini can compete with that given by Giovanni Ruffini, who was at school and university with him in Genoa, in the guise of the fictional character 'Fantasio' in his novel *Lorenzo Benoni: He had a finely shaped head, the forehead spacious and prominent, and the eyes black as jet, at times darting lightning. His complexion was pale olive and his features . . . were set . . . in a profusion of flowing black hair. The expression of his countenance, grave and almost severe, was softened by a smile of great sweetness, mingled with a certain shrewdness. . . . He spoke well and fluently, and, when he warmed upon a subject, there was a fascinating power in his eyes, his gestures, his voice, his whole bearing that was quite irresistible. His life was one of retirement and study; the amusements common with young men of his age had no attraction for him. . . . Spare and thin in body, he had an indefatigably active mind; he wrote much and well both in prose and verse and there was hardly a subject he had not attempted. . . . A passionate lover of liberty under every shape, there breathed in his fiery soul an indomitable spirit of revolt against tyranny and oppression of every sort.*[5]

In his last year at the university Mazzini had joined the powerful secret society known as the *Carbonari*. This society, which had its origin with the charcoal burners of France, and had been spread in Italy by the soldiers of the Revolution, was rather nebulously dedicated to fighting for freedom against tyranny wherever found. They had already successfully engineered one revolution in the Kingdom of Naples in 1820 and had only been suppressed

by an Army sent from Austria; and no sooner was that over-
thrown than they staged a similar revolt in Piedmont, which the
Austrians had crushed on the 8th April 1821.

As soon as Mazzini came down from the university at the age of
twenty-three he acquired a newspaper, which he turned into a
literary periodical, and assisted by the Ruffini brothers, amongst
other like-minded radicals, in the guise of supporting the new
Romantic movement, he used it as a vehicle for political propaganda. Since political discussion of any kind was forbidden in
Piedmont, as elsewhere in Italy, the police closed the paper
down.

In 1831, he was betrayed as a member of the *Carbonari* to the
police and after a far from arduous imprisonment, he was released for want of evidence, and fled to Marseilles to exercise his
revolutionary talents in exile. Disillusioned by the failure of a
further *Carbonari* uprising the same year in parts of central Italy
and the Papal States, he had turned to organizing his own secret
society, 'Young Italy'. Mazzini's 'Young Italy' was not merely a
patriotic association set on getting rid of foreign domination, ending partition of the peninsula, and making it one united State.
Those objects were incidental. They fought first and foremost to
win for their fellow men the right to govern themselves, to exercise such religion or none as they chose, and to be free to express
their opinions, orally or in the Press, without persecution; and
above all to be free from torture, arbitrary arrest and imprisonment. In short, they fought for all the principles that are now
expressed in the Charter of Human Rights of the United Nations;
and they sought these, not for Italians alone, but for all men everywhere. In all that, they differed fundamentally from some of the
Nationalists who have appeared in the twentieth century and not
least of all from those who have traded upon their reputation to
re-establish tyranny and, in the sacred name of patriotism, to
invade the rights of other men in other countries.

It so happened, not for the last time, that the preservation of the
integrity of a nation against foreign dominion coincided with the
cause of human liberty. For one of the many aspects freedom
bears, is the right of a people who speak the same language and
who feel themselves to be a nation, to determine their own destiny. If the requirements of a later age demand a wider view, so
that the sacrifice of sovereignty to larger units, and the subjection
of national consciousness to a greater loyalty, is an imperative

need of Europe in the twentieth century, it is in no way incompatible with this idea; for it must, if it is to have any validity at all, be an expression of exactly the same principle of self-determination as justifies the existence of a nation.

'Young Italy' did not require its members to take an oath to murder traitors or assassinate tyrants, as did the *Carbonari*; but the whole purpose of the association was armed rebellion. If 'Young Italy' had little of the ferocity or terror of the *Carbonari*, it had all of its love of esoteric ritual. When two members met they were to give the secret sign of hands crossed and folded across the chest, and were to exchange the secret greeting:

'Brother, *now*'

'And always'.

By 1833, Mazzini's plans were coming to fruition. His scheme was an invasion of Savoy from France, and a landing on the Piedmontese coast, a general uprising, and the subornation of the members of the Piedmont armed forces.

But before this revolution, timed then for August, could be carried out, Charles Albert's police struck in Genoa. With three or four army sergeants who had joined 'Young Italy' and now turned King's Evidence, they went through the streets of Genoa arresting the other members. The story put out by the authorities was that two soldiers had quarrelled over a girl and in the process of investigating that quarrel, they had stumbled on the conspiracy; but there was a great deal more to it than that. The police were possessed of every secret of the organization, including those known only to the leader in Genoa, Jacopo Ruffini, and Mazzini and his close circle in France. Jacopo, Mazzini's bosom friend from his school and university days, and the David to his Jonathan, was arrested. When he realized how much the police knew, he committed suicide by opening a vein with a splinter of metal wrenched from his prison door. He died on June 19th 1833, believing that it was Mazzini who had betrayed him to the police. It was despair at this supposed treachery rather than fear of his fate that led him to take his own life.

Most of the historians of the *Risorgimento* have assumed that this belief was instilled in him as a trick played on him by the police in order to extort a confession, though some have pointed out that, since they had ample evidence, deceit was unnecessary. Without underestimating the possibility that it may have been done in spite, it is possible that the police believed so themselves or that it was a conclusion that Jacopo himself drew when he realized, from the extent of their knowledge, that it could only have come from the fountain-head; and so it may well have—but not from Mazzini. It is now known that one of the latter's most trusted aides, Michele Accursi, who shared all his secrets, was a Papal spy and from March 1833, although he was in Paris and Mazzini was in Marseilles, he was forwarding to Rome the most detailed accounts of the patriots' plans and intentions.[6] The information could readily have been transmitted to Piedmont, for, from December 1831, the Papacy and that government had been exchanging information about the underground movement. Accursi's treachery was not discovered during the lifetime of any of the actors in this drama. In fact, Accursi joined Mazzini in Geneva on 15th September 1833, sat in the republican assembly in Rome in 1849, and enjoyed his confidence to the end. It would appear that he was the inspiration of certain schemes, every detail of which he duly related to his master in Rome, or at least was in at their very conception.

Two days after the suicide of Jacopo Ruffini, his mother and a brother arrived in Marseilles and were met by Mazzini at the port. From that day, until he appeared in Geneva a week later, there is an extraordinary lacuna in his life. He disappeared, leaving his followers shaken and depressed. There have been many theories to account for where and why he went—some of them not very creditable—but the explanation is surely to be found in a postscript of a letter written to his mother on the day he arrived in Geneva, the 28th June. The postscript was written by his mistress, Giuditta Sidoli, and contained the words: *I did not write to you because I dare not tell you the whole truth about Pippo's health, because he would not let me . . . But now Pippo, although very weak, is a little better, but still is in need of much care . . . the fits of sobbing are growing less.*[7]

On the day Signora Ruffini arrived in Marseilles, Mazzini must have received from her the first intimation that Jacopo was dead, and that he had died believing he had been betrayed by his Jonathan. He must have experienced anguish and rage at the death by the enemy of one whose soul was knit with his soul, and to whom he had sworn a covenant for life; and to that agony was added the horror of knowing that his friend had died in the belief that he was delivered into their hands by the one he had trusted. It was too much for his delicately poised mind. The obvious explanation of the gap in Mazzini's life is that in that week he suffered a mental breakdown that left him incapable of rational thought; a state that he sank into after a later defeat and which he described in his own words *as passing from one delirium to another, with intermittent gleams of consciousness, which disappeared quickly into darkness again.* It is borne out by the letters he wrote when he had partially recovered. On July 8th he wrote to one: *I could not write to you. I did not know what to say,*[8] and the next day, to another: *If my silence has made you fear that I have forgotten my country, you are mistaken. . . . But I . . . cannot justify myself. Believe me I belong to my country wholeheartedly; let us leave it at that*[9], and again later: *It grieves me to have caused you sorrow. Yet it is my own affair . . . compounded of more irreparable wounds than can ever be realized by anybody who does not know everything . . . to you, all I can say is that, if you understand me at all, and realize where I was and what ties bound me, you have the key to it all.*[10] It has been assumed by some that 'the ties' were those to Giuditta Sidoli and their child, and that his disappearance was due to some undiscovered personal crisis in their lives; but that seems quite untenable in view of the date when it happened. 'The ties' were obviously those that bound him by affection to Jacopo Ruffini, who had been his closest friend from childhood.

Years later, he would awake in the middle of the night in anguish, crying: 'Jacopo, I didn't betray you. I didn't!'

IV

Garibaldi, after describing his voyage with the St Simonians, in the earlier editions of his autobiography continued: *This time the vessel on which I returned from the East had the port of Marseilles for its destination. When we arrived there, I heard of the abortive revolution in Piedmont and of the shootings at Chambéry, Alessandria and Genoa. At Marseilles I made friends with a man named Covi, who introduced me to Mazzini . . . Shortly after I had been introduced to him and had told him that he could rely on me, Mazzini . . . was obliged to leave France and flee to Geneva.*[11]

More than one patriotic print purports to show this meeting; Mazzini, frock-coated, grave, clasping with one hand his new comrade while the other points heavenward; and the sailor, a familiar bearded figure, his hand clasped over his heart, swearing fidelity to the cause of Italy; a picture of a momentous occasion, a meeting which was to shape great events. The imagination of writers has played around the event: *One sees the chief himself lift up that broad, high, wondrous brow overhung with black masses of softest, finest hair; raise his frail, slender, yet upright form; then, on learning who was his guest, spring forward with outstretched hands and eyes luminous with the fire of genius and the light of holiest passion, to welcome this bronzed, lion-featured, tawny-bearded captain, who had come so far to volunteer his services to Italy in her hour of defeat. What a contrast, yet what counterparts! Suffice it, they had met, clasped hands, exchanged their pledge and pronounced their vow . . . Would . . . victory have been won, would Italy today be living her third life of the people, honoured among the peoples, a nation peerless amongst her peers, had Joseph Mazzini and Joseph Garibaldi never met that autumn in Marseilles and parted with the 'Now* [ore] and for ever [e sempre]' as their watchword from that moment to their death-hour?*[12] wrote Jessie White Mario, who knew both of them well.

Yet there is a mystery about that alleged meeting. The shootings of fourteen patriots at Chambéry, Alessandria and Genoa was in connexion with the same wave of arrests as the result of which Jacopo Ruffini took his own life, and took place at the end of July 1833. Mazzini, as we have seen, mysteriously disappeared from Marseilles on 21st June that year and reappeared in Geneva on 28th June. Thereafter, until 1st February 1834, when preparations for the invasion of Savoy began, he resided continuously at the Hotel de la Navigation in Geneva.[13]

Where was Garibaldi after he sailed with the St Simonians on the 23rd March 1833?

La Clorinda, with him on board, landed the party in Constantinople on April 15th 1833 and the ships' papers show that she then went on into the Black Sea. She did not arrive at her final destination, Taganrog, until May 15th. She was delayed in the Black Sea and was not back in Constantinople until 9th July, when she had on board a party of passengers bound for Villefranche. She finally docked at Nice on the 17th August, when the crew—Garibaldi included—were paid off.

It follows therefore that during the only period when it would have been possible for Mazzini to have met Garibaldi in Marseilles in the year 1833 after the 23rd March 1833, the latter was in fact in the Black Sea; and it may well be, therefore, that the story of the meeting of the two, so firmly entrenched in the legends of the *Risorgimento*, is just another of those pieces of fiction which continually confound anyone who seeks to find out the real truth about these earlier events.

Certainly, it could not possibly have taken place in the autumn of 1833, which is the date ascribed to it by Jessie White Mario and most biographers[14], for by then Mazzini was in Geneva.

The account of the first meeting with Mazzini disappeared from all versions of Garibaldi's autobiography after 1859 and this has usually been ascribed to the animosity then existing between the two; but there may have been an even better reason.

On the 17th October 1833, Garibaldi shipped once more as mate on *La Clorinda,* this time for a voyage to Barletta, and he was paid off in Marseilles on the 22nd November 1833. Everything therefore points to his meeting with the 'Young Italy' enthusiast in the café in Marseilles taking place after this date; and from subsequent events it seems more than probable that it was then that he was enrolled in 'Young Italy'—but by somebody other than Mazzini.[15]

V

On the 16th December of the same year, Garibaldi was authorized by the port authorities of Nice to leave the Merchant Service in order to join the Royal Piedmontese Navy; on the 26th day of December, he was sworn in with a friend from his boyhood days, Edoardo Mutru, at the Royal Arsenal at Genoa, when he chose as his *nom-de-guerre* the name of 'Cleombroto'. He was performing his *leva* (compulsory National Service) and there has been controversy amongst historians as to whether he went as a conscript or voluntarily on a mission for 'Young Italy'. Both are probably true, for a merchant seaman of Piedmontese nationality who was in foreign waters at the age of eighteen, when his time for call-up came round, was allowed to serve his five years in the Royal Navy at any time before his fortieth birthday; but there can be little doubt that his enrolment at that particular time was prompted by the conspirators of 'Young Italy' and that his mission was, as he himself said, *to make converts to the Revolution . . . and should [it] break out, to help seize* the vessel in which he was serving and place it at the disposal of the republicans.

There can be little doubt, from subsequent events, that Garibaldi was in complete ignorance of what really was being planned, and that as a new member of the secret society was only on the fringe of its activities. Mazzini, in Geneva, was busy organizing the invasion of Savoy from Switzerland, scheduled to begin on the 2nd February 1834. Timed to support that, but due to commence later, on 11th February, there was to be a revolution in Genoa, aided by an invasion from the French coast. The organization of the latter insurrection was in the hands of Melegari in Marseilles and three leading members of the society in Genoa.[16] The plan was for members of the organization to board a Neapolitan vessel as passengers in Marseilles, seize the vessel on the high seas and put in to Genoa, which was to be the signal for the uprising in that city. Of the nature of these plans, it would appear that Garibaldi was kept in ignorance and it may be that the excess of zeal with which he went about the minor role assigned to him, helped partly to frustrate them.

He was posted to the frigate *Euridice* where he appears on the register as a seaman, third-class, with a description which is the only authentic record of his appearance at that time: *height, five feet six and a half inches; hair and eyebrows, reddish; forehead, wide; nose, aquiline; chin, round; eyes, chestnut colour*[17]*; healthy colour, no distinguishing features.* From that it would seem that the beard which was so characteristic a feature of his appearance in later years had not appeared; and possibly it was grown as a disguise shortly afterwards.[18] He was, in fact, a small man of very ordinary appearance.

In his enthusiasm for the new cause, he did not confine himself to making propaganda only amongst his shipmates. At the Café Londra in Genoa he met two sergeants of artillery and endeavoured to seduce them from their allegiance to the Crown and get them to provide arms; a few days later, on the 28th January, a lieutenant of artillery named de Medici sought him out, disclosed that he, too, was a supporter of the cause and wanted to participate in their revolutionary plans.[19] *My propaganda on the 'Euridice' was crowned with success,* was Garibaldi's comment.

Meanwhile, Mazzini had been joined in Geneva by Accursi, among others. Even though he did not know that there was a traitor peering over his shoulder all the time, it was an act of folly to persist in his plans after the failure of the attempts in May and June. He had foisted on him as military leader of the invasion of Savoy, a soldier of fortune, Ramorino, who had been a Napoleonic general. There is more than a suspicion that the latter was also in the pay of the Austrians. Whatever may be the whole truth about the affair, which is not known to this day, the expedition which began in farce ended in tragedy, with their defeat and flight at St Julien.

The day that the news of these events reached Genoa, the 4th February, Garibaldi's service in the Royal Piedmontese Navy came to an end. He was posted on the 3rd from the *Euridice* to the flagship *Des Geneys*; the next day his brief record of service with that ship is closed with the note: *A.S.L.*, meaning *Assentatosi senza licenza*, or 'Absent without leave'.

It would appear from the ship's log that he and Edoardo Mutru had gone ashore that morning under the pretext of being sick. Mutru had returned and had been arrested; but Garibaldi is shown as having been *in flight*.

As to what had happened, Garibaldi gave subsequently at least three versions which can be reconciled only with difficulty. *In my keen enthusiasm, I was not content to fill only the role assigned to me. Hearing that an uprising was to take place in Genoa, and that the barracks of the carabinieri in piazza Sarzana[20] were to be seized, I left the ship . . . and in two bounds was on the piazza Sarzana. There I waited for two hours but nobody assembled. The news got around that the affair had collapsed and that the republicans were in flight and that some arrests had just been made . . . troops began to surround the piazza . . . I took refuge in a shop of a woman fruit seller and told her of my predicament. The excellent woman did not hesitate a moment. She had me in the back of the shop, got me some peasant's clothing and in the evening about eight o'clock, just as if I was going for a stroll, I left Genoa; it was the 5th February,* was one of his earliest accounts.

In other accounts he gave, he professed to have been sleeping that night in a room with Mutru when he was awakened about six o'clock as if by an unseen hand and with a premonition of disaster. Unable to awake Mutru from a sound sleep, he had fled by himself and was told on his way to the harbour that the police had arrived at the house just after he had left and had arrested Mutru[21]. From letters he wrote subsequently, it would seem that he was still in the city on the 9th February and was sheltered that morning by one Teresa Forzano[22].

The truth of those events still lies very much *au fond du sac* but if one may hazard a guess, it is possible that he was alarmed by the sudden transfer to the flagship, and fled and hid in the city, where he learned of the failure of the Savoy invasion. While other members of the organization were being arrested he laid low, dodging from one house to another, and made his escape when he could a few days later. Natalie, Teresa and Caterina appear in various accounts he gave at different times of these events and he wrote *women are angels in that kind of a situation.* It seems, therefore, that his energies in Genoa had not been directed exclusively to the affairs of 'Young Italy' and it may well be that he was deliberately misleading about what really happened in order to protect some wives whose husbands may not have been so appreciative as he of the singular services they rendered their country.

Meanwhile, Mazzini was lying, delirious, in a hiding-place in Switzerland, and living in hopes that the rising planned for the 11th February in Genoa would take place. But by then all the conspirators were either in flight or in the hands of the police, and every detail of the plot was known. In the select band of the plotters had been numerous police spies. One of them, as appeared from the subsequent trial, was the charming young lieutenant of artillery, de Medici, who seemed so anxious to assist the cause and to whom Garibaldi had opened his heart in the Café Londra.

VI

Between Piedmont and France stretched the river Var just to the west of Nice. It was in full flood when Garibaldi reached it, but he managed to cross it higher up. So relieved to find himself outside his own country and in one which he believed to be devoted still to the cause of liberty, he went straight to the French Customs and told them who he was and why he had fled from Genoa. Much to his surprise and disgust, they arrested him.

He was taken to Grasse and then lodged in a room on the first floor. His account of what happened next is: *I went near the window, as if to have a look at the country, and leapt out through it. While the customs officers, being less agile or more careful of their legs than I were rushing down the stairs to recapture me, I had gained the highway and from there I fled deep into the mountains.*

The next evening he arrived at a village, where he entered an inn. It was empty save for a young man and woman seated at a table, waiting to be served with their dinner. In the hearth burnt a cheerful fire.

He sat down and enjoyed a good dinner and a bottle of the local wine. Relaxed and content, he began to chat to the innkeeper. He still had not learned the wisdom of reticence, and he cheerfully told the host how he had escaped death in Piedmont and imprisonment in France. Once again, he was astonished when he saw the man's face cloud over.

'What's the matter?' he asked.

'Well—after that confession, I feel in duty bound to arrest you'.

'All right—arrest me. Only wait until I've finished my fruit.'

So he continued to eat. Gradually the inn filled up with the youth of the village. Soon there was a dozen of them, playing cards, drinking, arguing. They started to sing; and when one of them sang a solo and sat down to applause, Garibaldi rose to his feet, glass in hand, and said 'Now it's my turn.' He launched into a song written by Béranger, the French radical poet. It was the *Le Dieu des Bonnes Gens* and when he came to the last line of the first verse:

> *Glass in hand I trust myself,*
> *To the God of good men,*

the company burst into the refrain.

> *To the God of good men*
> *To the God of good men.*

The verses of Béranger, the gusto with which I had sung them, the brotherly warmth of the refrain and the popularity of the poet, transported the audience. So much so that they made me repeat two or three verses and after the last, they embraced me, shouting 'Long Live Béranger! Long live France! Long live Italy!'

The rest of the night he spent drinking with them, playing cards and singing, and when dawn began to break they insisted on accompanying him on his road. Nothing more was heard from the innkeeper about his duty to arrest him.

He arrived at Marseilles, penniless, dusty and worn and had to seek hospitality with a friend.

VII

The thin sunshine of early summer was gilding the tangled rigging of the ships and the wings of wheeling gulls, when he sat outside a café on the harbour front of Marseilles and read a copy of *Le Peuple Souverain*. 'For the first time in my life I have the honour of seeing my name in a newspaper,' he remarked to his companion.

As he read the smudgy print he hastily decided to change it. For that newspaper of the 12th June 1834, recorded the fact that he had been sentenced to death, *in absentia*, by a military tribunal in Genoa nine days previously for his part in what was termed 'armed rebellion'. So when the French vessel *L'Union* of 165 tons sailed for Odessa on the 25th July, she carried on board as mate one Joseph Pane;[23] and it was Joseph Pane who dived overboard fully clothed the Sunday before she sailed and rescued a child who had fallen in the water. It was the 5th March of the following year before that vessel returned to Marseilles and the crew were paid off.

Two months later, the same Joseph Pane sailed on the maiden voyage of a new frigate, the *Eussene*, newly built in France for the Bey of Tunis. When he returned to Marseilles on another vessel, the city looked like a deserted ruin. Cholera had broken out and the inhabitants had all fled to the mountains; and Joseph Pane spent a fortnight acting as a medical orderly in a hospital.

On the 17th August, a gentleman of the same name shipped as an ordinary seaman on the 204-ton brig *Nautounier* bound for Brazil; but by this time he had so far forgotten his origins that he gave a different date and place of birth and different parents from those he had supplied when he joined *L'Union*. When he came to write his memoirs he claimed to have sailed on that voyage as mate, but another name appears on the ship's papers in that capacity. However, as they also show that he drew twice as much pay as any other ordinary seaman, he may have served as a sort of unofficial second mate.

In the month of December 1835, Joseph Pane, alias Ex-Captain Second Class Giuseppe Garibaldi (his Master's ticket had been cancelled by the Piedmontese authorities in August 1834), alias Ordinary Seaman Third Class Cleombroto of the Royal Piedmont Navy, alias 'Giovanni Borel' of 'Young Italy'[24], sailed on board that vessel through the narrow granite-walled passage into the calm waters of the bay of Rio de Janeiro and was entranced by the beauty that lay before his eyes.

V

RECOURSE TO EXTREMES

◆◇◆◇◆◇◆◇◆◇◆◇

T HE HARSH régimes of the Italian States and the endemic poverty of their landless peasants sent a stream of immigrants out from the peninsula to all parts of the world. To many of them, the American continent seemed to offer the fairest opportunities of both political freedom and commercial prosperity; and when Garibaldi arrived in Brazil, he found in Rio de Janeiro a colony of his fellow-countrymen already established there. It is possible that some news of him had already reached that port, for in the June of the same year as he had fled from the *Des Geneys*, that frigate had paid a visit to Rio and it is unlikely that his former shipmates failed to recount to the compatriots they met in the port the story of his flight and subsequent condemnation to death.

Soon after he arrived, he became very friendly with a group of Italians who were combining political activity with commercial ventures. Most of them were already members or supporters of 'Young Italy' and with the nourishment of their enthusiasm, his own interest, which appears to have been dormant during the two previous years when he had been sailing out of Marseilles, revived; and thanks to them, and in particular one Giacomo Picasso, he was quickly found the command of a small schooner engaged in coastal trade. As early as 27th January 1836, he was writing to Mazzini, describing himself as the skipper of the vessel and asking to become recognized as an Initiator for the organization *Young Europe*, which Mazzini had started in April 1834 to co-ordinate similar republican movements in various countries, so that any nation rising in insurrection should immediately find others ready to support it.[1] It is a rather naïve letter in which he made a suggestion that he should be granted letters of marque from Mazzini to seize Austrian and Piedmontese vessels on the high seas;[2] a peaceful commercial life seemed far from his mind.

The despots of Italy kept an anxious eye on the activities of their exiled subjects overseas and Garibaldi's arrival in Rio de Janeiro did not go unnoticed. Before he had been there little more than a month, the Piedmontese minister was reporting back to Turin on 1st February 1836, that *a certain Garibaldi, a subject of Your Majesty, ... has signalized his arrival in this port with an article against Your Majesty, published in the daily newspaper 'Paquet du Rio'.*[3] From the subsequent dispatches sent by the minister it is possible to gather something of what the exiles were up to. They apparently owned three small vessels which, although used in the coasting trade, bore the significant names of *Young Italy, Young Europe* and *Mazzini.* They flew the republican tricolour of Italy (today the Italian national flag), without the cross of the House of Savoy, which the minister regarded as an insult to his sovereign. The dispatches disclose that, not to be outdone by the exiles in schemes of unlawful violence, the minister was planning to have the three vessels they owned sunk in the harbour by the crew of a Piedmontese ship; it could, according to him, be done in Rio de Janeiro with impunity.

Although Garibaldi's mind was taken up with ill-formed revolutionary plans, he was condemned to spend most of the year that followed in trading up and down the Brazilian coast in the 20-ton schooner. How little to his liking this trading was may be judged from a letter he addressed to his fellow-exile, Cuneo, on the 27th December 1836. *Our trips have not been lucrative owing to our trust in seeming friends, who turned out thieves. . . . Of myself I can only say that I am not happy, tortured as I am by the thought of being unable to do anything for our cause. Preferring tempests to calm, I am impatient to have recourse to extreme measures. Write to Pippo [Mazzini], tell him to give us a recipe, and we will get it made up. This is not the first time, O brother mine, that I importune you; don't be angry. By God, I am weary of dragging on this life of a trading sailor, so useless to our country. Be sure we were destined for higher things; we are out of our element altogether. I long to plunge into it once again.*[4]

He had not long to wait. While the Italian exiles were entertaining dreams of insurrection in Europe, they were confronted with a revolution on their own doorstep. The region in the south of Brazil suddenly took to arms under Bento Gonçalvez and declared itself the independent Republic of the Rio Grande do Sol, with headquarters in the town of Porto Alegre. The merits of their cause are not immediately apparent, for in 1831 Brazil had rebelled against autocratic Don Pedro I, forced him to abdicate in favour of his five-year-old son, Don Pedro II, and was at the time a constitutional monarchy governed by a Council of Regents, with elected assembly and senate, freedom of the Press, and such an aversion to totalitarian practices that they did not even maintain a police force.

In spite of that fact, Garibaldi, thirsting for adventure, apparently saw in the rebellion the cause of liberty. Before long he was writing to Cuneo, who had left Brazil to start a newspaper in Montevideo, that it would be impossible for him to join him there, *nor can I without risk, explain the reason by letter. All I can tell you is that I am setting out on a new path, guided ever by our principles, with that goal in view which you first put before me. I trust to you to set out our work in its true light.*[5]

The need for what is today termed 'good public relations' demonstrated by that last sentence, was something that Garibaldi was acutely aware of throughout his life; but at that moment, perhaps, he was also particularly conscious that the *new path* on which he was setting out, would require more than a little ingenuity to justify.

II

On the morning of the 7th May 1837, the *Mazzini* cast off from her moorings opposite the Fish Market at Rio and moved out under sail into the causeway. According to the information supplied to the Customs officials, she was skippered by one Cipriano Alves, had a crew of five and carried one passenger, Luigi Rossetti, and a cargo of meat bound for Campos; Garibaldi had acquired yet another pseudonym.

Some hours later,[6] the schooner *Luisa*, flying the Brazilian flag and just out from the island of Grande with a cargo of coffee bound for Europe, entered the roads of Rio de Janeiro. While she was only two or three miles from that port, and almost within range of its coastal batteries, the *Mazzini* came alongside her, and broke from her mast the red, yellow and green colours of the Republic of the Rio Grande do Sol. Garibaldi could barely speak any Portuguese, but the sight of him and a villainous-looking crew of twelve[7] armed to the teeth, indicated to the captain of the *Luise*

clearly enough what their intentions were. He hove to, and
allowed his vessel to be boarded. A trembling passenger came and
offered Garibaldi, as the price of his life, a casket containing three
diamonds. *I closed the box, gave it back to him, assuring him that his
life was in no danger and that consequently, he might keep his diamonds
for an occasion when they might be more useful.*[8] *At the same time* [I]
*gave orders that the private property of the passengers and crew should be
untouched. This was my invariable practice in similar circumstances*[9]
wrote Garibaldi, in later years, proud of his virtue.

The *Mazzini* was sunk, for want of a pilot to navigate her; and
the *Luisa*, rechristened a more appropriate name, the *Farropilha*
('The Ragged Ones') hastily sailed southwards for safer waters.
The crew and passengers were put off in the ship's boat with
provisions and their personal effects, except for five negro slaves
who had elected to serve with their conquerors. On the 28th of
the same month, the schooner put into the port of Maldonado in
the Republic of Uruguay, which, Garibaldi had been told, recognized the rebels and where he expected to be safe from the
vengeance of the Brazilian authorities.

His reception was all that he could wish for and he and his
crew passed a week in one continual fête, celebrating their
exploit, *after the manner of buccaneers*, as he himself described it.
Part of the cargo of coffee, and, by a strange coincidence, *a few
jewels* which, he hastens to explain, belonged to the Austrian
owner of the vessel, were sold to a merchant of the town; but
before he could collect payment for them, Garibaldi was warned
by a friendly official that a Brazilian man-of-war was on its way
to apprehend him and that it was the intention of the Uruguay
Republic to hand him over. The information was quite accurate;
the *Imperial Pedro* was hot in pursuit and had been delayed only
by adverse winds.

There was no time to be lost. The crew were rounded up and
ordered to bring all their arms on deck and to prepare to sail.
But Garibaldi had still not been paid by the merchant, who seems
to have had some inside information and was counting on acquir-
ing the goods for the same price the vendor had paid for them.

He stuck a couple of pistols in his belt and slung his cloak over
his shoulders. It was a clear moonlight night and he found the
merchant enjoying a last cigar in front of the door of his house.
The latter signalled him to keep away, as if warning him that he
was running into danger.

c

Garibaldi walked straight up to him. He whipped out a pistol.
'My money!'

The merchant tried to stutter an explanation.

'My money!' was all Garibaldi said.

At the third repetition, the merchant took him inside and counted out the coins. Garibaldi replaced the pistol on his belt, tucked the bag under his arm and strolled back to his ship.[10]

Hastily, they took off into the teeth of a north-easterly gale.[11] The moon went down and in the darkness that night they were nearly shipwrecked amid reefs near shore as they tried to make the river Plate in the storm; the stock of arms stored in a cabin near the binnacle had affected the compass.

Even with daybreak, their troubles were not over. They had left in too much haste to take on board provisions; they dare not put into the port of Montevideo and they had no boat in which to go ashore. Eventually, Garibaldi improvised one out of a cabin table and couple of casks and with another man, also named Garibaldi, was swept through breakers to the shore. The return journey through the heavy surf, with quarters of beef dangling from an improvised mast and nothing but poles for propulsion, was a more difficult task and they were swept away from the schooner, which had to sail after them.

That night and the following day, they tacked about off the headland hoping to meet a vessel flying a red flag. Before they sailed, Rossetti had gone on alone from Maldonado to Montevideo and had agreed to bring them out provisions in some vessel carrying that insignia.

III

The appearance of two sets of sails on the horizon the next day excited hope that help had arrived; but since neither vessel showed the red flag, Garibaldi hove to in irons with full sails set and had loaded muskets ready on the forward hatch. His precautions were wise, for when the first vessel was within a stone's throw, twenty-four armed men suddenly sprang into sight, and the *Farropilha* was raked by a volley. The helmsman was killed. Garibaldi, who leapt to the tiller, was felled by a ball which entered behind one ear and lodged behind the other, and yet somehow missed both the vertebrae and the larynx; and he was also wounded in the right arm. When he came round after half an hour, they had shaken off their assailants, two gunboats of the Paraguay government;[12] but he was so weak that the crew had to carry him to the chart to indicate where they should sail to; by now it was apparent that every government would treat them as pirates in whatever port they were to put. He pointed to the town of Santa Fé, on the River Paraná, for no better reason than that it happened to be printed in big letters on the chart. Neither he, nor any member of the crew, had ever been in those waters before.

While Garibaldi lay helpless, in pain and delirium, kept alive on the only commodity they had in abundance—the remains of the cargo of coffee—the *Farropilha* was taken to Santa Fé by an unskilled comrade. The rest of the crew apparently found it not convenient to be in the vessel when she arrived there. At Santa Fé, Garibaldi did not receive the fate usually meted out to pirates. In fact the Governor of the Province of Entre Rios for Rosas, the dictator of Buenos Aires, allowed his own doctor to remove the bullet; an operation without anaesthetic which lasted about half an hour. The *Farropilha* was seized and Garibaldi was arrested, but was allowed to reside in a private house on an allowance from the government, pending word from the dictator as to what his fate was to be. Rosas was a capricious and cruel tyrant but he was also a dilatory one. No word came from him, and for six months or so Garibaldi remained an involuntary guest; during this period he read French newspapers, resumed his revolutionary correspondence with Cuneo, and wrote patriotic poetry. *I write and read*, he said in a letter to Cuneo, *ever with Italy in my heart, I cry aloud with rage:* quoting himself:

> I would rather see her desert
> And her palaces in ruins. . . .
> Than watch her trembling
> Beneath the Vandal's rod.[13]

Cuneo had apparently raised with him the question of escaping, for the same letter contained the sentence: *About an escape, it is enough to say that I am here on my word of honour.*[14]

But his word of honour was not enough to hold him the day after orders were received that he was to be transferred to the provincial capital of La Bajada.[15] That night Garibaldi took flight and had covered fifty-four miles on horseback before he was recaptured. He was brought back with his feet tied together under the horse's belly and his hands bound; and the mosquitoes made of his face and hands what he described as *one continuous sore*. He was taken before the local governor who demanded to know who had assisted in his bid for freedom and was struck across the face with a whip for refusing to answer. He was then strung up by his arms from a beam for two hours. The governor visited him. As wrote Garibaldi in the earlier editions of his memoirs: *I was unable to do anything except spit in his face and I gave myself that pleasure*. By the time he was cut down, he was unconscious.

Two months of imprisonment in La Bajada followed and then, suddenly, he was released and told he could go where he liked. He made his way to rejoin Cuneo and Rossetti in Monte-video.

IV

The distinction between what he had been doing and piracy for Garibaldi lay in a piece of paper he had received three days before he sailed from Rio de Janeiro in the *Mazzini*.[16] They were letters of marque, authority to employ an armed ship in the capture of enemy merchant vessels, signed by one 'General' Lima on behalf of the president of the Republic of Rio Grande do Sol. The President himself, Bento Gonçalvez, was scarcely in a position to sign them himself; at that particular moment he was in the hands of the Brazilians and incarcerated in a prison at Rio de Janeiro. Garibaldi did not meet him at that time, but he probably had met the President's Italian secretary, Livio Zambeccari, who was in the same predicament.[17]

Even without that document, what Garibaldi had done was not piracy, in the international law of the period (or indeed even in that of our own day), for the distinction lies in the object of the seizures of other vessels. If they are seized pursuant only to private ends and for private gain, then it is piracy; if there is some public end in view, even though the buccaneers profit by their seizures, it is not. That Garibaldi had convinced himself that he was helping the cause of liberty can be seen by his subsequent conduct; though the authority he had received filled him with naïve delight . . . *a feeling of happiness and pride* . . . *like an eagle hovering at a height* . . . . *the Ocean was mine and I entered into possession of my domain* was how he described his feelings on that first day the *Mazzini* sailed.

Not content with the hardships and ordeals he had so recently endured, Garibaldi spent only one month in Montevideo before he set off to rejoin the forces of the Republic of the Rio Grande do Sol. By this time, Gonçalvez had managed to escape from his imprisonment in Brazil and rejoin his army; but the affairs of the republic were in a sorry state. Gonçalvez was reputedly a man whose simplicity of life and devotion to the ideals of republicanism commended him strongly to his followers; but he had one unfortunate trait for a rebel general: he was incapable of ever winning a battle. When Garibaldi arrived back in Brazil, the republic had lost all the towns on the coast and the so-called Government was reduced to the status of guerillas with headquarters in the mountain village of Piratinim.

Before long, Garibaldi was entrusted with the command of two small vessels that the rebels had built for the purpose of operating on the great sea lagoon of Dos Passos. There was a motley crew of about sixty men, half of them escaped negro slaves, and with seven Italians; one of whom was his old friend Edoardo Mutru who had been condemned to death in Genoa, had been pardoned after only four months in prison, and had completed his five years of military service. They were delighted when, on the 4th September 1838, they were able to capture a richly laden Brazilian vessel, the *Mineira*, and everyone had a share of the booty; but the Brazilians struck back early in the following year when they surprised Garibaldi and a handful of his men and surrounded them in a storehouse with a troop of about 100 cavalry. Eleven republicans, singing the battle hymn of the republic, managed to beat off the enemy;[18] but the lagoon had become sealed by enemy vessels at both ends and the rebels were being hunted by something like thirty ships. Less than three months later, they moved out of the lagoon by carrying their vessels[19] overland, a distance of fifty-four miles, on wheels pulled by 200 oxen, until they could be launched into other waters which communicated with the Atlantic.

But their immense labours were in vain; no sooner had they reached the open sea than Garibaldi's ship, heavily overladen with stores and armaments, was wrecked in a storm. Sixteen of the crew perished, amongst them every other Italian, including his old friend Mutru.

It was a disconsolate and lonely man that moved northward to join the rebel forces which had just captured the port of Laguna, and founded yet another new republic on Brazilian territory, that of Santa Caterina. There, he was given command for a time of a captured vessel, the *Itaparica*.

V

What happened after that is best told in his own words[20] not only because there is no other account available, but because it is an extraordinary revelation of his mind at the time when the events happened and also later when he wrote the words . . . *The loss of . . . my countrymen had left me utterly isolated; I felt quite alone in the world. Of all the friends who had made those desolate regions like home to me, not one was left . . . Moreover, the change in my position had come about in a manner so unexpected and so horrible that it was long before I could recover from the blow . . . In short, I needed a human heart to love me, one that I could keep always near me. I felt that unless I found one immediately, life would become intolerable . . .*

Walking up and down the quarter-deck of the 'Itaparica', wrapped in my own gloomy thought, I came, after trying every species of argument, to the conclusions that I would look out for a woman, so as to escape from a position of intolerable weariness and discomfort.

By chance I cast my eyes towards the houses on Barra—a tolerably high hill on the south side of the entrance to the lagoon, where a few simple and picturesque dwellings were visible. Outside one of these, by means of the telescope I usually carried with me on deck, I espied a young woman[21] and forthwith gave orders for the boat to be got out, as I wished to go ashore. I landed and made for the houses where I expected to find the object of my excursion. I had just given up all hope of seeing her again, when I met an inhabitant of the place, whose acquaintance I had made soon after our arrival.

He invited me to take coffee in his house; we entered, and the first person who met my eyes was the damsel who had attracted me ashore. It was Anita . . . We both remained enrapt and silent, gazing on one another like two people who meet for the first time and seek in each other's faces something which makes it easier to recall the forgotten past. At last I greeted her by saying 'You must be mine!'[22] I could speak but little Portuguese and uttered the bold words in Italian. Yet my insolence was magnetic. I had formed a tie, pronounced a decree, which death alone could annul. I had come upon a forbidden treasure, but yet a treasure of great price.

If guilt there was it was mine alone. And there was guilt. Two hearts were joined in an infinite love but an innocent existence was shattered ... I sinned greatly but I sinned alone.

When Garibaldi sailed from Laguna on the night of the 23rd October 1839, for another buccaneering expedition, Anita was on board. If it were shortly after the shipwreck in July that he met her, as would appear from his narrative, a good few months had elapsed and as to what happened in that period, he is silent.

A great deal of ingenuity[23] was expended by Garibaldi's friends in denying the inferences which were inevitably drawn from the passage quoted above; but it is now generally accepted that *the forbidden treasure* was the wife of a humble fisherman named Manuel Duarte, to whom she had been married for four years.[24] He it was who had invited Garibaldi in for a cup of coffee in his house; and his was the *innocent existence* that *was shattered* when Anita was carried off.

A veil of obscurity remains to this day over the whole incident, but the terms of Garibaldi's confession in his autobiographies have led some to suppose that he carried her off by force of arms; if so, she was not an unwilling victim.[25] The inhabitants of Laguna had received the republicans as brothers and liberators; Garibaldi may have had his own conduct in mind when he passed the comment *it was a title we did nothing to justify during our stay amidst this friendly population*. It is not a comment which invites dissent.

Anna Maria de Jesús Riveiro da Silva, as she had been christened, was, according to a British Admiral who met her later, a Creole but with the charming manners of a lady of ancient Spain; a spirited creature, who rode a horse as if she had been born in the saddle. In what purports to be a portrait from life [26] a miniature shows her with an oval, olive and slim face, big timid brown eyes, a petite mouth and black hair sleekly parted in the middle. There must have been more verisimilitude in another picture painted shortly after her death by an artist[27] who had seen her in the flesh. In that she appears as a big-busted peasant wench, with coarse black greasy hair flowing over her shoulders and down to her waist, and a large nose; a virago of a woman. If only half of Garibaldi's stories about her were true she was indeed, as he termed her, a *Brazilian Amazon*.

Little more than a week after he had sailed away with her, the three republican vessels under his command were trapped in a small bay by enemy ships. In the fierce engagement that ensued, while their boat was repeatedly raked with artillery- and musket-fire, Anita fought, sword or carbine in hand, with the rest of the crew.

In the middle of the battle, Garibaldi was agonized to see her struck down with two men by a cannon-ball. He leapt towards her. She rose unhurt, but the two men were dead.

He begged her to go below.

'Yes—I will—but only to drive out the cowards who are skulking there.'

Down the hatch she disappeared. Shortly afterwards three sailors appeared, whipped on deck by her tongue.

If gossip be right, Garibaldi subsequently was not spared the lashes of the weapon she had employed to drive on deck in her first battle the reluctant combatants.

Soon after that Garibaldi was ordered to sack and ravage a small town, the inhabitants of which had sided with the government forces. It was a day of what he termed *hideous foulness and wickedness*, when his men, like *unchained wild beasts, disbanded and drunken*, pillaged and raped. *The worry and fatigue experienced on that miserable day in trying to restrain them were unspeakable*, he wrote later.

The buccaneers returned to their base on the lagoon of Laguna and there the three republican vessels under his command were again attacked, this time by twenty-two enemy ships. Anita it was who loaded and fired the first cannon against them. By night-fall the three republican vessels had gone down in flames, fired by their occupants, and all the republicans were in retreat over-land.

It was the 15th November, twenty-four days since Anita had joined her destiny to his, and they were in disordered retreat, without money, with only the clothes they wore, and with an enemy pressing hard on their heels. She must have been a very remarkable woman if she did not regret leaving the security of her husband's simple home.

VI

For a month the defeated republicans fled before the government forces, but on the 14th December, they were engaged near the junction of the Rivers Pelotas and Uruguay with another enemy body which had been sent to cut off their retreat. The battle took place near the banks of the river near a ford known as Santa Vittoria; the enemy commander was cut down crossing the stream, his troops routed or captured.

When the day's bloody work was over, Garibaldi flung down his sword and made love to Anita.[28]

There was a triumphant entry into the town of Lages; but sweet fruits of victory were not to be theirs for long. After a defeat in an action in a clearing of the forest and four days' march without food through a jungle so dense that there were not even footpaths, the republicans were turned out of Lages. There followed seven months of confused wandering and inconsequential battles in jungle and on the sierras, of forced marches and privation. All serious military effort came to an end when on the 17th July 1840 the republicans made an effort to retake their former capital Porto Alegre and were repulsed and scattered with horrifying casualties. Anita, now pregnant, performed prodigious feats of valour. Captured by the enemy, she managed to escape on horseback with no more injury than a bullet-hole through her hat and the loss of some hair from her head; and she was in the thick of the last battle.

Thereafter, in scattered bands the republicans began a disorderly retreat across the sierra, harried and assailed from all sides. On the 16th September 1840, Anita gave birth to a son, Menotti; and, recalled Garibaldi, he had not the means to get so much as a single handkerchief for her or the child.

Months later, the futility of the struggle and the fact that the cause was irretrievably lost sank into his stubborn mind. He had spent more than five years of his life in the dangerous and futile pursuit of a chimera, without ever receiving one penny of pay.

Now he set off for Montevideo with a herd of 900 bullocks to pay his expenses; presented to him, so he said, by the grateful republicans, though it may be permissive to wonder whether they had not in fact 'liberated' the beasts from some of their enemies. Owing to his inexperience in cattle-droving and the intrigues of his hired hands, he arrived in Uruguay with no more than the hides of a few of the animals.

He was forced to take up some sort of an occupation to maintain himself and became, to start with, a commercial traveller in spaghetti, later graduating to silk goods. Then he secured a post in a school, teaching mathematics and history. It may well have been the necessity for some sort of respectability imposed by the latter occupation that led him to go through a ceremony of marriage with Anita at the Church of S. Francisco d'Asis in Montevideo on the 26th March 1842. One of the witnesses was the schoolmaster who was employing him, an ex-priest; none of these three participants had any particular respect for the forms of the Holy Church.

Was it a bigamous ceremony?

It is to be feared so.[29]

Although it has been asserted by some that by then her husband was dead, in fact Anita gave her single name and did not disclose her previous marriage; the ceremony took place without the banns being called in the bride's home parish; and a special dispensation had been secured to dispense with the second and third publication of banns in the parish in which it took place.[30]

But Garibaldi's period of outward respectability in a commonplace occupation was not destined to last long.

VI

THE RED SHIRT

❖❖❖❖❖❖❖❖❖❖

THE Republic of Uruguay in which Garibaldi now made
his home had achieved and preserved, not without difficulty,
its independence from its two larger neighbours, Argentine and
Brazil; but before long it was embroiled in a protracted struggle
between two sets of politicians calling themselves Federalists and
Unitarians respectively, which in their claims at any rate, professed two different constitutional ideals. In 1834, the first President of the republic, Ribera, resigned in favour of one of his own
staff, Oribe, a general who had taken part in many of the battles
which had secured for the republic its independence. The following year, across the water of the River Plate, the dictator Rosas
seized power in Argentina. A flood of refugees from Buenos
Aires arrived in Montevideo and in due course Rosas demanded
that they should be expelled. Oribe was thought by some too
subservient to his demands, and in 1836 Ribera staged a revolt,
Oribe was driven out, and began a military campaign to recover
power.

This confused and turbulent picture of local politics, crossed
as it was with strands of personal ambition and financial corruption, was not such as to invite Garibaldi's participation; but it
became for him part of the larger battle for liberty when the
tyrant of Argentina, Rosas, chose to intervene in the struggle on
behalf of Oribe. For Garibaldi the cause was luminous and clear:
it was the defence of the infant republic against a despot; the
puny Uruguay against the powerful Argentina, and for him it
was particularly a meritorious struggle because the older states of
Europe, and the Vatican, gave moral support to the tyranny.
There is no reason to believe that his judgement of these events
was anything but fundamentally sound, though there is every

reason to believe that Ribera and some of his associates were at
least as venal as those on the other side.

On the 23rd June 1842, Garibaldi sailed away from Montevideo
in command of a small fleet of three vessels entrusted to him by
the Republic of Uruguay. The mission assigned to him was to sail
up the waters of the River Paraná some 600 miles to carry provisions and assistance to the town of Corrientes, so as to secure it
for Uruguay. It was an errand so foolhardy and dangerous that
when he looked back on it he could only conclude that *the real
motive of the expedition . . . was to get rid of me*. The waters of the
Rio Plate were swept by an efficient fleet commanded by Admiral
Brown (an Englishman) for the Argentinians; both banks of the
river were firmly in enemy hands and they had numerous forts
and batteries mounted along it; even worse than that was the fact
that the river was not navigable that year as far as Corrientes for
vessels drawing, as did his own, eighteen feet of water. But all
these things were more likely due to the ignorance and stupidity
not unknown amongst those who sit in offices in Defence
Ministries rather than malice; there was no real reason why
anybody should want to get rid of him, particularly as the three
vessels under his command comprised the whole of the Uruguayan
Navy; and had he in fact been able to reinforce Corrientes it might
well have had a decisive effect on the war.

At the meeting of the waters of the Uruguay and Paraná rivers
there was an island fort, manned by the enemy, which commanded the only navigable channel. As they entered the channel,
Garibaldi's small fleet were raked by its guns. One Italian officer
had his head blown off; several other men were wounded. Soon
after that Garibaldi's flagship ran aground on a sandbank. In an
effort to refloat her, her guns were transferred to another vessel,
encumbering her decks so that her own guns could not be fired.
While they were in that predicament, Admiral Brown's fleet
sailed up to them. Just as Brown was about to fire a broadside,
his ship ran aground. While they both wrestled with the problem
of getting afloat, thick fog descended on the estuary; and in the
ensuing confusion, Garibaldi and his three vessels passed right
through the enemy fleet and entered the waters of the Paraná. The
next day, Brown, confident that nobody but a lunatic would
attempt to sail up the Paraná, went chasing in pursuit of him up
the Uruguay.

At San Nicola, Garibaldi picked up a pilot who was so unwill-

ing to assist the invaders that he had to be intimidated throughout the voyage with a drawn sword. The main body of Oribe's
army was mustering at Paraná (La Bajada, as it was then called).
Luckily a following wind enabled Garibaldi to sail past without
any worse result than being raked by musketry. At Cerrito a
cannonade of forty guns awaited him but he replied in kind and
got past without serious damage; but at Costa Brava, he found
that his course was barred, not by the enemy, but by sandbanks
that precluded any further advance. He was forced to anchor and
awaited the inevitable arrival of the Argentina fleet; he was
trapped.

Brown caught up with him on the 14th August 1842. For three
days the battle raged until Garibaldi had used up all his balls and
was reduced to firing broken-up chains, nails and any ironmongery
he could find. His own vessel was shattered, one of the other
ships was sinking, the third was unseaworthy, and most of his
guns were out of action. On the morning of the third day,
Garibaldi had all the wounded carried on shore, evacuated the
able-bodied, and having laid four charges in each of his three
vessels, fired them himself.

The next few months he spent wandering from town to town
ashore in futile skirmishing until, after the defeat and dispersal of
the Uruguayan army on the 6th December at Arroyo Grande, he
was able to gather together a few of the stragglers from the
defeated and, as the year was drawing to its close, make his re-
appearance in Montevideo. By that time, the President of the
republic who had ordered the assault up the Paraná had fled to
the safer regions of Europe, taking with him in gold pieces most
of the republic's treasury; and the enemy were gathering their
resources for a final assault on the capital.

II

After the annihilation of the Uruguayan Army, Oribe and
Rosas not unnaturally concluded that, in the fashion of South
America, Montevideo would capitulate and there would be the
usual scramble to adhere to the winning side. But in those days
the population of the city amounted to some 30,000, of whom
more than two-thirds were foreigners, most of them exiles for
political reasons from their own countries. There were also a
large number of slaves in the city.

The independence of Uruguay was preserved by a stroke of genius.[1] Seven days after the defeat at Arroyo Grande, the abolitionists of Europe were gratified to learn that the Republic of Uruguay had become the first in the Americas to abolish slavery. So they had—provided the released slaves joined the army; those that were not able-bodied were to remain, for the time being, 'wards of their masters'. With that stroke, Montevideo provided herself with a conscript army of some 5,000, all of whom had the greatest incentive to fight since they were in fact fighting for their own liberty; and she put such a fair face on the struggle that she enlisted the sympathies of reformers throughout the world. Henceforth, the war became, in the eyes of world opinion, no longer a sordid little squabble between rival politicans but a fight for principle; and at the same time, Uruguay was fortunate enough to find two men, Paz and Pacheco, who were free from the corruption that had tainted Ribera and his party.

The foreign exiles, too, had the greatest incentive to fight since most knew well that defeat meant for them, if not certain death, further flight and possible bondage. It was on these that the burden of the defence of Montevideo fell. The majority were Frenchmen and they formed the largest corps, amounting in all to about 3,000 men. The French entertained some doubts of the valour of the Italians who were the next numerous contingent in the city, and one of them was heard to exclaim publicly: 'Italians are only good for stabbing in the dark or from behind; resources expended on them will be thrown away.'

There were some amongst the Italians who wished to challenge the defamer of their nation to a duel, but when Garibaldi heard of it, he declared:

'No! If one of us were to kill him in a duel, what would that prove? We have the chance of proving the Frenchman a liar; let us profit by it!'

On the 10th April 1843, the new Minister of War, Pacheco, signed a decree authorizing the formation of an Italian Legion in defence of Montevideo.

The first engagement of this legion was on the 2nd June, in a skirmish outside the city. From that most of the Italians fled, and were received with jeers from the French and the populace on their return. *I am ready to die of shame and grief*, wrote Garibaldi to his old friend, Cuneo, shortly afterwards.[2]

Up to that point, he had undertaken the task of trying to

organize the nucleus of a fleet for the republic. Now, perceiving that something more than the security of Montevideo was at stake, he turned to organizing the Italian Legion. A month after that ignominious reverse, the Italian Legion paraded to be presented with colours: a black flag with a volcano in the middle, symbolizing the sorrows of Italy and the hidden fire that raged in her heart. It was a flag that was to be raised in triumph less than twenty years later over another battlefield. For the first time, too, the Italian Legion paraded in what might be termed a uniform. In a merchant's stock had been found a supply of red shirts destined for the workers in the slaughter-houses of Buenos Aires;[3] exports frustrated by the outbreak of war, they served to give the Legion a distinctive garment which, if it advertised their whereabouts vividly to the enemy, also prevented its members fading gently away in the midst of battle as had been the custom of some Italians as long as they wore ordinary civilian clothes. Not the least of Garibaldi's achievements was the ability to create a will to fight in a people who, perhaps wisely, have no stomach for warfare. Indeed, it is difficult to think of any one victory in a century won by Italian arms other than those which were under his command; unless, of course, it were over virtually unarmed tribesmen.

It is a wise general who is conscious of his own limitations and Garibaldi showed his maturity of mind in sending at once for his old friend Anzani, whom he had met while both were fighting for the Rio Grande do Sol, to deal with the day to day provisioning and organization of the Italian Legion. Neither then, nor later, had Garibaldi any aptitude for administration but not a little of his success was due to the fact that he was not ashamed to acknowledge it. Anzani, from the province of Como, had been an exile since 1821 and had fought in Greece, Spain and Portugal for the republicans, and had received serious injuries in the latter war. He combined great personal courage on the battlefield with a talent for organization and so long as he lived, Garibaldi deferred to his opinion in most matters.

Having reorganized the Italian Legion, Garibaldi took every opportunity of engaging them in skirmishes with the enemy, most of which had little tactical or strategic purpose. His object was to give the Legion experience in warfare, a pride in achievement, and to win for them a reputation as warriors. One of Garibaldi's great attributes as a general was his conviction that morale made for victory and victory made for morale; it was something that was exemplified in the Uruguayan campaigns as much as later in his life.

For by now he was conscious that the defence of Montevideo was a drama being played out on a stage spot-lighted before a world audience, and capable of having repercussions on events in Italy. It was so, indeed; particularly as Mazzini from London, in a journal he had started called *L'Apostolato Republicano*, was lauding the exploits of the Italian Legion in a series of articles in which every Italian soldier appeared as a hero and every trifling engagement as a resounding victory; and Garibaldi himself was praised as the all-wise, all-conquering symbol of Italian virility. Surreptitiously at first, through Mazzini's underground network, in the *L'Apostolato* and in pamphlets, this story was spread throughout Italy; and when after 1847, a free Press was allowed in Tuscany and Piedmont, it was reproduced in all the liberal Press. Compounded, like all national propaganda, of as much falsehood as truth, it must be classed one of the most successful, if not the most successful, campaign of political warfare of all time. It inspired Italians of all classes with pride in national achievement, a sense of nationhood and a sympathy with the forces of reform. Mazzini may have created a myth about himself as well as about Garibaldi, as a recent Papist writer has suggested,[4] but what began in myth ended in reality and what was falsehood to start with soon became truth.

There were setbacks initially. One of the leaders of the Italian Legion deserted to the enemy with a handful of men; in December 1845 there was something like a mutiny in its ranks; but by February of the following year the opportunity that Garibaldi longed for occurred. On a foray up the River Uruguay, a section of the Legion under Garibaldi defeated a much stronger force of the enemy, in a confused and rather pointless fight at Salto Sant Antonio. It was big enough to be described as a battle, the enemy were sufficiently overwhelming in numbers for the victory to be applauded, and, as tokens of their courageous devotion, the Italians left thirty-six dead on the field and were wounded almost to a man; and Garibaldi's report of the affair to the Government and newspapers was so skilfully worded and in such terms of studied modesty, that he and the Italian Legion received universal praise. The Legion was given a position of honour in a victory parade in the capital; it was ordered that their banner should be inscribed in letters of gold with the battle honour, and that henceforth all legionaries should wear on their tunics a shield and crown bearing the word *Invincibili, combarrerono, February 8th 1846.* Garibaldi himself was offered promotion to the rank of general and refused in a characteristic letter. . . . *in the honourable position in which it pleased the Government of the Republic to place me, I have done nothing to merit the promotion to the rank of general. The sum awarded to me as chief of the Italian Legion I have distributed among the wounded and the families of the dead. Gifts and honours purchased with so much Italian blood would weigh my soul to the earth. I had no second thoughts in exciting the enthusiasm of my fellow-countrymen in favour of a people whom fate has placed in the power of a tyrant and now I would give the lie to myself were I to accept the distinction which the generosity of the Government wishes to confer on me. The Legion found me a colonel in the army . . . as such I shall leave the service when once the pledge to the republic is fulfilled.*[5] After his return to Europe two years later, he had not the same scruples about accepting the designation of 'General' Garibaldi even though, because of this refusal, that rank had never in fact been conferred on him.

By this time the safety of Montevideo was secure. The Great Powers, annoyed at the interruption of their trade with the River Plate, had intervened. Britain and France had both sent fleets and expeditionary forces. Rosas declined to accept the view that it was he who was fighting Uruguay and had referred the Powers to General Oribe; and failing to comply with their demands that he should cease hostilities, the Argentinian fleet had been seized by the British and French squadrons, who then proceeded to show Rosas what a siege was like by blockading his coastline. In the sacred name of intervention to ensure peace, they were in fact actively protecting Montevideo; which the politicians of that city immediately took as an invitation to break out into a fierce inter-necine quarrel which was little short of a civil war within a civil war.

Garibaldi had written to Cuneo on 27th February urging him to bring the rest of the Italian Legion from Montevideo to Salto: *You write to me of affairs in Italy. . . . Do pray keep together those few legionaries, otherwise all our labour is lost—our fatigues, privations and suffering will have been in vain. . . . I repeat to you that it is necessary to join me with the Legion, not precipitately, but in the way I will point out to you.* On the same day as he declined the promotion offered by the President of the republic, he repeated his exhortation to Cuneo; *I am still of the opinion that you ought to leave Montevideo with the Legion and join me. Every consideration convinces me of the necessity of collecting all together and remaining united.*[6] From that correspondence, it is clear that Garibaldi had already lost al interest in the affairs of Uruguay, probably in disgust at the antics of her politicians, and his mind was already turning to other fields, in which a seasoned and united force might be employed to better purpose.

III

The ill-tempered, illiberal and ill-loved Pope Gregory XVI died on the 2nd June 1846 at the age of eighty-one; and his successor was confidently expected by everyone to be the Secretary of State, Lambruschini, who was as pro-Austrian and as reactionary as his master. The liberals hoped for the election of Cardinal Gizzi, the only Italian prelate who had refused to allow the military commissions into his diocese to hunt out those suspected of liberal inclinations; but it was a vain hope. He did not receive a single vote. To the surprise of the whole world, on the third ballot, the virtually unknown Cardinal Bishop of Imola was elected. Lambruschini was so shocked that he collapsed.[7]

The election was received with indifference at first by the Italian people, but this turned to a wild enthusiasm for the new Pope, when one of his first acts was to release a thousand political prisoners, most of whom had been confined without trial since the start of his predecessor's reign, thirteen years before; when he appointed the popular Gizzi as his Secretary of State; and when it was discovered that he did not share the antipathy of his predecessor to railways or gas street lighting. It is some indication of the hysterical state of Italian opinion at the time that the trifling reforms of Pius IX should have been regarded as if they were the initiation of the millennium. As Garibaldi wrote: *Like many others, I believed that it was the dawn of an era of Italian liberty.* Such a delirium of excitement swept Italy that even the children in the streets were singing a song in praise of 'Pio Nono'; and soon there was no popular movement anywhere in Italy which did not claim him as a patron—without, of course, his knowledge or consent.

That the new Pope was a little more enlightened than his two predecessors was inevitable, but the real truth is that he was as fundamentally illiberal and opposed to any form of democracy as the old Pope. That can be seen from his correspondence as Bishop of Imola and his unhesitating condemnation of two documents which had been published calling for reforms in the Papal States. The first, the 'Manifesto of Rimini', was to him *that classic production . . . no Jesuits, no priests, no bishops, no Latin . . . no censorship*. Of the second, Massimo d'Azeglio's *Degli ultimi casi di Romagna,* the Bishop wrote that it contained *many abominable lies and defamations.* [The author] *is just worked up by the Italian delirium . . . if others think like him . . . there will be a good and bad end. The good will be that there will be no revolutions or seditions, which he condemns . . . the bad will be that we shall have a flood of writings . . . attacking the administration.*[8] Since both of these documents were carefully moderate in tone, essentially Catholic, and the reforms they called for were obvious and necessary, his misrepresentation and denunciation of them indicates how little in reality he was inclined towards any fundamental changes in the Papal system of despotism. But he had good cause to realize that the Popes were in their homeland the most hated and despised of rulers, and as a weak man he craved for popularity. His letters show that he recognized, too, that such was the ferment in opinion that there was nobody in any class of society who was loyal to the Papal authority and that revolution and sedition would certainly be his lot unless he eased the pressure somewhat. He was certainly not likely to forget that only three years before his elevation a plot had been discovered to kidnap him and two other bishops, or that there had been open revolution in Rimini the previous year.

What the new Pope hoped to do was to let his subjects blow off a little steam through safety valves. The thousand political prisoners who were released were fewer than one in twenty of those that remained incarcerated; it was, therefore, a gesture and no more than a gesture. There was a great deal of talk about building railways, but it was to take fifteen years before the first short stretch of line was opened. The Consultative Assembly he allowed had no powers at all and was to meet under the permanent presidency of a Cardinal. The press was freed; freed, that is, except for censorship by a board of five censors. In short the people were to be given the illusion of having some liberty, and some part in the administration of their own affairs, so long as the

State remained as before: a despotism with every real power firmly vested in clerical hands.

At the start the policy was successful; so much so, that early in 1847, the new Pope was able to tell a French pilgrim that a miracle had been wrought: 'Prejudice against the Holy See has given way to respect and love,' he said and confessed his amazement that God should have made use 'of a wretch like me to effect the change.'[9]

Even Mazzini was carried away by enthusiasm for the new Pope. From London, he wrote an open letter to him: *No man, in Italy or in Europe, is more powerful than you . . . You have accordingly, most Holy Father, heavy responsibilities. Europe is in a great crisis . . . faith is dead, Catholicism is lost in despotism, Protestantism in anarchy. But mankind cannot live without heaven . . . social ideals are the fruit of religious ideals. Sooner or later, therefore, we shall have both religion and heaven . . . but not from kings and the privileged classes . . . from the people. The spirit will then descend on as many as are gathered together in His name . . . The people have suffered on the cross for centuries . . . now God will bless them with faith . . . To fulfil the mission entrusted to you from God two things are necessary: you must believe and you must unify Italy.*[10]

And from Garibaldi and Anzani in Montevideo came another epistle to the Pope, dated 12th October 1847, addressed to the Papal Nuncio at Rio de Janeiro: *From the moment when we received the first news of the elevation of the Sovereign Pontiff Pius IX and of the amnesty he granted to the unhappy proscripts, we have . . . admired the footprints that the Supreme Head of the Church is leaving on the path of glory and liberty . . . at last, the womb of our country has brought forth a man who understands the needs of his century, wise enough to adapt himself to the times, yet still according precedence to our august religion, which is always new yet ever eternal. . . . We, who write to you . . . are men . . . who have taken up arms at Montevideo in defence of a cause that seemed just to us. We have gathered round us some hundreds of our fellow-countrymen. . . . In the five years which have passed . . . our Legion has been able to prove its distinction . . . on the field of honour it has surpassed all other corps. Now we offer the assistance of these men, who are not unaccustomed to bearing arms, to His Holiness. We shall consider ourselves happy if we can further the work of redemption of Pius IX . . . if needs be with the blood of all of us.*[11]

The Papal Nuncio in Rio de Janeiro, was a handsome Cardinal named Bedini, who reappeared later on the scene in Italy. He was

not to be outdone in eloquence of expression; in reply he wrote:
I feel it my duty to signify that the devotion and generosity towards our
Supreme Pontiff expressed in your letter is worthy of Italian hearts, and
deserves praise and gratitude. With the English mail that left yesterday,
I sent that letter to Rome, so that other hearts may be inspired with the
same sentiments. If the ocean dividing the two hemispheres should prevent
such magnanimous offers from being accepted, their merit cannot be
diminished, nor the satisfaction of receiving them lessened. May all those
enrolled under your orders remain ever worthy of the name that they have
honoured, and of the blood which runs in their veins![12]

The Pope himself did not reply to Garibaldi. By then he was
discovering that an even worse fate than believing one's own propaganda is having one's propaganda believed; for not only had he
succeeded in convincing his own subjects that he was in the van-
guard of liberty but the other Princes of Italy were equally convinced; and their subjects were demanding at least as many rights
as the Pope had conceded to his. Everywhere the bastions of royal
totalitarian rule began to collapse, undermined by the Pope's
apparent conversion to liberalism; the rulers of Piedmont,
Tuscany and Naples were all induced to grant reforms.

As these exciting items of news reached Montevideo, Garibaldi
more than ever determined to return to Europe.

In between his battles in Uruguay he had found time to pro-
create three more children beside Menotti, but one of these,
Rosita, had died while he had been up at Salto. He now decided
to send Anita on ahead of him to Italy, like a dove from the ark.
As early as July 1847, he was writing to Cuneo: *I have finally*
decided to send my family to Nice, and as we are utterly impecunious,
I shall be much obliged to you if you would help them to obtain a
passage.

It was six months later before Anita was able to sail and two
months more before the dove landed on dry soil, in Genoa. In
that city a royal welcome awaited her.[14] More than three thousand
people assembled under her window, shouting 'Long live Garibaldi! Long live the family of our Garibaldi!' She was presented
with a flag in the Italian tricolour and told to give it to her husband
so that he could be the first to plant it in Lombardy soil; she was
taken to the opera and the theatre and fêted everywhere; on
every mouth was talk of a united Italy and everybody hoped
Garibaldi himself would arrive on the next ship from Montevideo.

It was the 15th April 1848 before Garibaldi sailed from

Uruguay. All he carried away after twelve years in South America were crippling attacks of arthritis and the bones of Rosita, that he had secretly disinterred from the cemetery so that she might rest in the homeland she had never seen; the land where her father was still under sentence of death. More than half his life had gone. He had achieved nothing except a reputation.

VII

MAN OF THE PEOPLE

◆◆◆◆◆◆◆◆◆◆◆

THE VESSEL that carried Garibaldi to Europe left Montevideo
as the *Bilfronte*, flying the flag of Piedmont; she arrived in
the Mediterranean as the *La Speranza* under the flag of Uruguay;
Garibaldi was still uncertain what reception awaited him there
and he was taking no chances.

Of the 500 or 600 men of the Legion he had dreamed of taking
to Italy there were barely sixty on board, though they had two
cannons, 800 muskets and a good stock of powder. Even the
purpose of the voyage was obscure. Sometimes, Garibaldi spoke
of going to assist the Pope to drive the Austrians out of Italy,
sometimes of raising the standard of revolt in Tuscany; and he
had sent a young exile named Medici on ahead with instructions
to raise a body of men at Viareggio, then in the Duchy of Lucca.

Anzani who had received a bullet through his lungs while
fighting in Portugal, was on board, seriously ill. Off the coast of
Spain, they put into a little port near Alicante to buy provisions
for him. The captain came back to the ship big with news. All
Europe was in revolt. Early in the year, the people of Sicily had
risen and then those of Naples; the King of Naples, his throne
in peril, had granted a constitution; from there the revolution
had spread until nine-tenths of the peninsula had achieved the
constitutional reforms for which they longed. In France, Paris
had risen and expelled Louis Phillipe, and the Second Republic
was in being; and the best news of all was that there had been
rebellion throughout the Austro-Hungarian empire, in Vienna as
well as in Poland and Hungary; Metternich himself, for so long
the master of Europe, was in flight; and Charles Albert of
Piedmont had seized the opportunity thus presented to engage
in war to free Lombardy from the Austrian yoke.

At once a great shout went up on board, 'Make all sail!' Hastily, an improvised tricolour of red, white and green was hoisted to the mast; and instead of sailing for the coast of Tuscany, they made for the nearest Piedmont port. It was Nice.

More cautious counsels prevailed when they arrived off that port; the Uruguayan flag was hoisted again and some of the more timid souls on board were in favour of finding out exactly what the position was on shore before they landed; but Anita had hired a small boat to come out to them and the news she brought encouraged them to enter the port. No sooner had they dropped anchor than there was an enormous crowd on the quayside and in boats to welcome them and all quarantine regulations were brushed aside as the exiles rushed to plant their feet once more on their native soil.

The news they learned was exciting. Charles Albert had promulgated a Constitution on the 4th March. Venice had thrown out the Austrians without bloodshed and had been a republic under the guidance of Daniele Manin since the 22nd of the same month. Milan, after five days of heroic struggle behind barricades, had driven out the Austrians; and Charles Albert had led the Piedmontese Army into Lombardy in pursuit of them.

It almost looked as if Garibaldi and his men had arrived too late.

II

Just over a week later, Medici, coming straight from the death-bed of Anzani at Genoa, encountered Garibaldi strolling beneath the arcades in Turin. Although he was hurt that the General had apparently forgotten all about his mission to raise volunteers at Viareggio, Medici embraced him.

'What are we going to do?' they asked each other.

'Haven't you been to Roverbella and offered your sword to Charles Albert?' inquired Medici.

'These people,' replied Garibaldi scornfully, 'are not worthy of the submission of hearts like ours.'

It was some little time before Medici could get the story out of him. Garibaldi had attended at Roverbella where the King was with the headquarters of his army; he had been sent back to Turin to see the Minister of War, Ricci. Ricci, after keeping him hanging about waiting for an interview, had told him brusquely: 'You ought to go to Venice. There they will give you some small ship and you can ply your trade as a buccaneer. That's your place—there's none for you here.'[1]

In his earlier autobiographies, Garibaldi professed to have met the King personally, which account had grown by the time of the definitive editions to the plural: *the interviews I had with him*[2]; and the story of the encounter between the monarch and the man his courts had fourteen years before condemned to death is one of the immortal legends of the *Risorgimento*. There is even a plaque on the façade of the palazzo Benati in Roverbella to commemorate the historic occasion. But Garibaldi was throughout so evasive and inconsistent about what took place that it is most improbable that he ever in fact saw the King face to face.[3] What is much more likely is that he was shuffled about from official to official in the way that anybody who has ever had any business to do in Italy will be more than familiar. Nor is it very surprising. However important 'General' Garibaldi might have been amongst the 30,000 inhabitants of Montevideo, and whatever place he held in the esteem of that section of the populace who were extreme radicals, to the Piedmontese officials he was no more than an adventurer; an adventurer, moreover, who was tainted with Mazzinian republicanism and had been found guilty of treason and sedition. They might be prepared to overlook that latter fact; the King, in his generosity, might even be prepared to pay for the education of Garibaldi's children;[4] but there was no reason to believe that he and his handful of semi-brigands could make any significant contribution to the war. At that date, early in July, the Piedmontese army looked more than a match for the Austrians, for they were not up against the full might of that empire but faced only an isolated force which was cut off by revolution in its homeland from reinforcement and supplies. Moreover, Piedmont was supported by substantial numbers of regular troops from Tuscany and the Papal army (without the Pope's consent)[5] and a force of 9,000 volunteers from the Papal States; and the royal army had already, in May at Santa Lucia near Verona, won a battle against the Austrian army which was only prevented from being a decisive victory by the King's premature withdrawal of his forces from the field. There was good reason, therefore, why Ricci should suggest that Garibaldi's talents might be more profitably engaged in support of Venice; for amongst other things, Manin was a radical and was fighting to re-establish the independence and glory of the former Republic of Venice.

If Garibaldi were considering accepting the excellent advice tendered, however rudely, by Ricci, his mind was changed for him by Medici. For it was at the latter's suggestion that the two of them left the same night to offer their services to the committee of the revolution in Milan.

III

The two were welcomed by the revolutionary committee in Milan, by now overawed by the presence of Mazzini, who had hastened from London when the exciting news of the revolt arrived; and they were entrusted with the task of enrolling and training volunteers. Even so, there was some resistance in official quarters. When Medici applied to the Ministry of War for arms, an important little official told him: 'It would only be a waste of weapons. Garibaldi is only an *haut sabreur*[6] and nothing more'.

To that Medici replied, 'Very well—as to arms—we are all right. We will find our own. But we must have uniforms.'

'No uniforms,' replied the bespectacled official.

At length, he was persuaded to open the Austrian stores and supply the volunteers with white coats. This offer was at first indignantly rejected by the volunteers, who had no wishes to be attired in the garb of the enemy. *It was impossible to have some fighting in dress-suits and others in frock-coats; so we took the linen jackets of the Austrian soldiers and from them made a sort of a blouse. The result, however, was enough to make the spectator die of laughter,* wrote Medici. *We looked like a regiment of cooks.*[7]

Thus attired, the volunteers were dispatched to Bergamo. Hardly had they established themselves there, where they mustered some 3,700 men in all, than they received the order to return to Milan by forced marches. Charles Albert had engaged the Austrian forces again at Custoza and although his forces were, if anything, superior to theirs he had been defeated decisively in that he fled from the battle, though with his army intact. He had retreated on Milan in face of the enemy.

By the time Garibaldi's Legion had got to Monza on the 5th August, ominous news reached them that the King was engaging in negotiations for an armistice with the enemy and had surrendered Milan. At Monza they were joined by Mazzini who henceforth began to sign proclamations to the populace as 'Mazzini, a soldier of Garibaldi's Legion'. If, as is probable, this was the first time Garibaldi had seen Mazzini in the flesh for any length of time, he was little impressed with him. For though he might appear a mighty warrior on paper, he certainly had not the stamina Garibaldi expected from his men; and the seeds of dissension between them can be traced to the intolerance the General always showed for those who lacked his capacity for endurance. Weakness, inability to withstand long, forced marches or lack of rations, was always, to Garibaldi, proof of a craven spirit rather than anything else. Mazzini could do no more than struggle on until he was overcome by the fatigue of a life he was unaccustomed to and for which he was physically ill-equipped.

Panic seems to have swept through the ranks of the Legion in Monza and many deserted; but Garibaldi acted promptly on the news. Before his troops had even time to eat, having restored discipline at a quarter to four in the afternoon, he marched them off towards Como. The next day he sent a letter to his superior in Milan which was brief and to the point. *We have heard lately of the capitulation of Charles Albert, the evacuation of the city of Milan by Piedmontese troops and the other news. All that has nothing to do with us. The Italian war against Austria will continue . . .* From Camerlata outside Como, he led his troops to San Fermo; and there on the morning of the 7th, he marshalled them in the square and harangued them. He told them it was important to carry on the war by guerilla bands, that it was the most effective—and least dangerous—form of warfare. Medici, who was present, says that Garibaldi's address was spirited, picturesque and moving, but the thousand who heard him listened in unhappy silence; the next morning there were only 400 of them left in the ranks. Mazzini and a number of his friends had departed for Switzerland. Reluctantly, Garibaldi decided there was nothing for it but to retreat into Piedmont.

He passed through Varese, Sesto Calende and reached Castellelto on the Piedmontese side of the Ticino about the 11th. There he learned the humiliating terms of the armistice that Charles Albert had signed on the 9th; he sent Medici out to round up deserters and the latter was able to find and bring back another 300 or so men. Their ranks now numbered some 750; it was enough, he believed, to take the field again against the Austrians.

Sickened by what he regarded as the cowardice and duplicity of the Piedmontese King, on the 13th he issued a proclamation which was to become famous throughout Italy, and which won for him the leadership of those common people who longed for the unification of the peninsula. The Pope, by his Allocution of 29th April, had abandoned the mask of liberalism and renounced all pretence to leadership of the *Risorgimento,* which in that document he specifically denounced. He found that the miracle God had wrought through such an unworthy wretch had been replaced by another miracle of a less flattering nature; overnight the new Pope had become as hated as his predecessor. And now Charles Albert, by his hesitancy in the field and his capitulation, had similarly renounced all claim to leadership of the national movement.

It was a scathing document that Garibaldi signed. Headed significantly with the Mazzinian slogan of *God and the People,* it denounced the King as a traitor and contained the heroic phrase, *If the King of Sardinia has a crown which he preserves by force of arms and by villainy, I and my comrades do not wish to preserve our lives by equal infamy.* The war against Austria was to go on.

It was a futile hope, as Garibaldi well knew, that the 750 could drive out an army that was highly disciplined and efficient and which had inflicted ignominious defeats on three well-ordered Italian forces. Once again, he was playing the same game as in South America; hoping, by heroic resistance and some victories against overwhelming odds, to win a reputation for his forces and stir sympathy for the national cause. It was a policy that, pursued to the bitter end through 1848 and 1849, yielded its fruits in the harvest-time of 1859 and 1860.

During the night following his proclamation, Garibaldi led his men northward to Arona where he induced the Commune, by none too gentle means, to part with a large 'contribution' in money and bread and rice. There they seized two lake steamers and sailed up Lake Maggiore as far as Luino during the night. Here, during the afternoon, while he was marching towards Varese, Garibaldi, overcome with fatigue and with a high fever, sent for Medici.

'I really must have a couple of hours' rest,' he told the young man. 'Take my place and keep an eye on everything.' He retired to bed in an inn; neither had the slightest idea as to whether there were any Austrians in the vicinity. Half an hour later a scout came galloping back with a terrified shout: 'The Austrians!'

In the engagement that followed, a much larger force of Austrians were beaten off and fled in the direction of Varese in panic; and the next day Garibaldi and his force advanced in the same direction until they reached the heights overlooking that town. There three large columns of Austrians commenced an encircling movement designed to cut off his retreat into either Piedmont or Switzerland. Medici was detached with a company to engage one of the columns of some 5,000 Austrians; advancing from Como he took up a line in three villages on the slopes of the mountain of San Maffeo, with his left flank near the Swiss border. During the night, one of his sections deserted, but the rest resisted the attack at dawn for four hours until their last cartridge was spent. Then they retreated on a mountain path, led by a Swiss guide, into Switzerland. His sixty-eight men had held up the advance of 5,000 Austrians for four hours.

Meanwhile Garibaldi, after wandering about until August 26th, fortified himself in Morazzone, a small hill town south of Varese, and found himself cut off and surrounded, by one of the other Austrian columns. With 500 men he held out all day against a column of 5000 with eighteen guns and cavalry. When night fell, he formed his men into close columns, and under the shelter of darkness, passed through the enemy lines. Out in the open country, Garibaldi disbanded his troops and told them to make their own way into Switzerland.

Three days later Medici found Garibaldi in bed in an inn near Lugano, exhausted, bruised, barely able to speak.

'I have had a walk,' he told Medici, 'a long walk.' He had been on his feet sixteen hours across the mountains.

'Is your company ready?' he asked the other.

'Yes,' said Medici, who had preserved some sixty men intact in a body.

'Very well! Let's have one night's sleep. Tomorrow we'll rally the men and start afresh.'

Medici burst out laughing. Garibaldi's feet and legs were so swollen that it seemed that it would be impossible for him to move the next day.

The war in Lombardy of 1848 was over. If Luino and Morazzone barely rate as anything better than spirited defences, by the time the national propagandists had got to work they were regarded throughout Italy as resounding victories. Even some of the Royal officers were sufficiently impressed to meet Garibaldi, when shortly afterwards he returned to Piedmont. One of them was General La Marmora who wrote: *I have visited Garibaldi. He*

*has a good face, rough but open . . . in good hands he would be of use.
It was a great mistake not to employ him . . . Garibaldi is no ordinary
man.*[8] But by the time that general was in a sufficiently exalted
position to follow his own advice, he was not disposed to do so.

On the 10th September, a gentleman with a passport in the
name of Risso arrived in Nice and lodged himself with Anita
Garibaldi and the children at the Deideri's country cottage just
outside the town. A fortnight later, the same bearded Risso
travelled to San Remo, where he made a political speech from a
balcony to an enthusiastic crowd. From there, he took a ship to
Genoa with a Captain Pesante, with whom an eager cabin-boy
had once made his first voyage.

The King, after the issue of Garibaldi's proclamation of the
13th August, had given orders that the author should be arrested
and be brought to trial for treason. At the same time as his Council
of Ministers were debating whether Garibaldi should be re-
admitted to Piedmont, the people of Chiavari, whence his family
had originated, were busy electing him as a deputy to the
Constituent Assembly.

In his letter of thanks to the electors, Garibaldi wrote *Seeking a
man of the people to defend and enlarge your rights . . . You have chosen
me . . . I have only a sword and my conscience. Behold! I dedicate them
to that cause.*

But the 'man of the people' did not take his seat in the Parliament. He had other things to do.

IV

Other things to do; but what? Stories of continued resistance
to the Austrians in various parts of Lombardy continued to reach
him; they were almost without exception false, the produce of
the imagination of partisan newspaper editors, but he did not
know that. Venice was still holding out. In the south, King Ferdinand of Naples had revoked the Constitution he had granted and
was making war on the revolution in Sicily. So many battlefields
to choose from, that Garibaldi could scarcely make up his mind.
Two days after he had called for a renewal of the war in Lombardy, he sailed for Sicily. Emissaries from the island had succeeded in persuading him that he should go to their aid. He sailed
from Genoa on the 24th October with seventy-two followers on
the French vessel *Pharamond* bound for Palermo.

The next day the vessel put into Leghorn. There, a guard of honour awaited him on the quayside, and flags fluttered in the streets and piazze as soon as it was learned that he had arrived. The two governors of the city were so overcome by the enthusiasm of the crowd that they sent a telegram to the government of Tuscany in Florence: *Garibaldi, although intending to go to Sicily, would not be opposed to offering his services to the Tuscan government. Please advise. He will leave at four this afternoon if no news.*[9] At three o'clock the reply came from Florence: *Ministry not constituted yet ... if possible ask him delay departure.* Back wired Leghorn: *People of Leghorn want Garibaldi remain Tuscany, whatever terms. Have succeeded in delaying departure until seven. Must have reply at once. Population out of control.* There was no reply from Florence and the next telegram came from the general himself: *I want to know if you are putting Garibaldi in command of the forces of Tuscany to work against Bourbons. Yes or No?* There was a further flurry of telegrams, but no answer. The *Pharamond* sailed that evening for Sicily, but without Garibaldi and his men; they were all billeted on shore.

Still the Tuscan government showed no sign of welcoming them; telegrams flew backwards and forwards, until both sides began to show signs of irritability. *Leave us in peace for a bit*, begged Florence; *he is starting to grumble*, warned Leghorn. Four days after his arrival, Garibaldi went to the theatre with one of the local governors and received a tremendous ovation; while he was there a disturbance broke out in the town, and windows were smashed.

For their reluctance to accept his offer, the newly appointed liberal government of Florence has been roundly denounced as unpatriotic by both Garibaldi and his biographers; but their conduct is understandable. The Grand Duke of Tuscany has been persuaded, without great difficulty, to grant a Constitution; but the moderate ministers who took office were treading a delicate path amid the demands of the populace, stirred up by the more republican radicals, and the intrigues of the priests and reactionaries, who were determined to wreck the Constitution. Not unnaturally those ministers had not the slightest desire to have Garibaldi thrust on them by the populace as commander-in-chief of the ducal army; still less had they any desire to be embroiled in a war against the kingdom of Naples; and they would have been failing in their duty as ministers and men if they had accepted

his impertinent demands. Yet they had reason to fear the extent
to which 'the man of the people' could rouse the people, and the
consequences from the mob, if they rejected Garibaldi's offer out
of hand.

Luckily for them, a way out of their dilemma presented itself.
An emissary from Venice arrived to invite Garibaldi to go to the
aid of that republic. Forgetting all about Sicily, and his sound
strategic, but madly impracticable, plan to get the forces of Tuscany to intervene by striking southwards to attack Naples itself,
Garibaldi agreed to go. With happy alacrity, the Ministry in
Florence gave him leave to recruit for his Legion in Tuscany
and promised him any assistance he should need to get on his
way over the border, eastwards. In private correspondence, one
of the Ministers, himself a good liberal, made his views plain:
*They are like a plague of locusts . . . let us do all we can to get them away
quickly . . . so that they infest as few places as possible.*[10] It was not an
unfair description of the penniless general and his small band of
equally impecunious warriors. In spite of the enthusiasm of the
crowd Garibaldi found when he left Leghorn that his following
had been augmented by fewer than thirty men.

He passed to Florence where he was received by the people in
another delirium of excitement and rewarded the Ministers, who
had hitherto sheltered and fed his band, by a speech at a crowded
public meeting in the largest theatre of the city. 'The Tuscan
Ministry should not merely be pushed,' he declared. 'It should be
forced and whipped along. . . . Forced by demonstrations, I mean.
You must arouse the people . . . Italy can choose one of two ways
with her rulers. She can either overthrow them or drag them along
with her. There is no middle way. It is one thing or the other.'[7]
Thunderous applause greeted his speech. He issued, on the 5th
November, a proclamation calling for recruits for an Italian
Legion of Death under his command;[11] but not a single recruit
was forthcoming from Florence. In fact, the mood of the population of Florence was neatly hit off by the enthusiastic Mrs Browning, then in the city:

> *If we did not fight*
> *Exactly, we fired muskets in the air*
> *To show that victory was ours of right.*
>
> .   .   .
>
> *We proved that Austria was dislodged, or would,*
> *Or should be, and that Tuscany in arms,*

Should, would dislodge her, ending the old feud;
And yet, to leave our piazzas, shops and farms
For the simple sake of fighting, was not good.
We proved that also.[12]

In passing, it may be noted that neither Mrs Browning nor her husband showed any enthusiasm for leaving their comfortable lodgings either, *for the simple sake of fighting,* though both were ardent partisans of the Italian cause.

Garibaldi's inflammatory speech in the theatre did have results, however, if not in recruitment. The Minister of War withdrew the rations he had been issuing the Legion, so that Garibaldi had to borrow money from friends to feed them; and they were promptly hustled out of the town through the mountain passes to the frontier at Filigare.

Winter had arrived and up in the Apennines the snow was knee-deep on the roads. Most of the volunteers had only makeshift garments and many had no cloaks; a few were in rags. At the frontier, they found their path into Papal Romagna barred by a body of four hundred of the Pope's Swiss mercenaries sent up there for the express purpose of seeing that they did not enter the country; and for several days, the Legion were stranded at the top of the pass, unable to advance into Romagna or to return to Tuscany. They had little money and less food, and it was bitterly cold; all the officers had to turn out their pockets to reward a local innkeeper who did his best to relieve their distress.

At length, word came from Rome that they might be allowed to pass, though it needed demonstrations by the mob in Bologna before the local governor could be induced to let them in; even then, they were forced to relinquish their arms until they reached Ravenna and to agree not to enter Bologna.

But Garibaldi himself was permitted to enter the city and on his arrival the crowd took the horses from his carriage and dragged it through the streets. Bologna was a different place from Florence, and here he was able to link up with another body of volunteers, who augmented his forces; here, too, he met the Barnabite friar, Ugo Bassi, a saint of nationalism, with whom he was to develop a deep and affectionate friendship, severed only by death.

By the 10th November, Garibaldi, urged along by the Swiss Guard, arrived in Ravenna. There he showed a strange and inexplicable reluctance to take ship for Venice, much to the fury

D

of his reluctant hosts and the mystification of his men; it was
almost as if he were awaiting the call of destiny.

When it came, it was by the assassin's knife.

V

The *Consulta* that the Pope had granted his subjects failed to
satisfy their aspirations for self-government and in March 1848,
he had been forced to grant a Constitution with an Assembly
with some legislative powers. Even then, the new Constitution
had a very limited franchise, on a property basis, and its powers
were severely circumscribed. The Upper House was composed
entirely of clerics nominated by the Pope[13] and even if a decree
passed that, it was subject to veto by the Cardinals. It was a further
attempt to satisfy the public by giving the illusions of representative government without the reality thereof; even so, Pius IX
always took the view that, having been exacted from him by
'duress', he had not granted it. By his significant omission of all
reference to it in his recital of the acts of reform by the Papacy in
the first part of the Allocution of April 29th, he made it widely
known that it was to be regarded only as a temporary concession,
to be retracted when times were more favourable.

However, this Fundamental Statute did provide for a council
of ministers in which laymen were represented, and after what was
to him an unsatisfactory liberal ministry, the Pope thought he
had found in Count Pellegrino Rossi a strong layman who would
protect the position of the Papacy. Rossi, a haughty Roman
aristocrat, had been in his younger days something of a liberal,
but having spent years in the diplomatic service of France under
the influence of Guizot, he had lost all faith in representative
government. Like many a twentieth-century British colonial
governor, he thought good government was an adequate substi-
tute for self-government, and accordingly, he was firmly of
opinion that administrative and technical reforms were needed in
the Papal States. This was enough to make him detested by the
priests, and the Jesuits in particular. At the same time he alienated
the radicals by insistence on the preservation of the temporal
power, and by opposition to war against Austria for the liberation
of Lombardy. What raised their dislike of him to the fever point
of hatred, however, was his moral support for and assistance to
Ferdinand II, the King of Naples. That sovereign, in the early

days of September 1848, had reasserted his dominion over Sicily by the bombardment and massacre of the population of Messina; an act which earned for him the immortal title of 'King Bomba' and made him the *bête noir* of all civilized communities. It is irrelevant here to consider whether that monarch was in fact himself directly responsible for that dreadful event;[14] it is sufficient to observe that he was universally believed to be. When, therefore, Rossi chose to associate with, and support him, and more particularly had refugees from Naples and Sicily arrested and sent back to undoubted imprisonment and perhaps torture in their own country, the character of tyrant rubbed off on to him.

Men's passions were running high. On the 15th November 1848, as Rossi was about to enter the Council of Deputies in the Palazzo della Cancelleria, he was stabbed in the neck, and died on the steps of the palace.[15] It was an unmerited fate, but while it filled the weak Pius IX with abject terror, news of it was received all over Italy with rejoicing. Even a high-minded Boston intellectual then in Rome was constrained to write to her mother: *For me, I never thought to have heard of a violent death with satisfaction; but this act affected me as one of terrible justice.*[16]

To Garibaldi, up in Ravenna, harassed by the government of the Romagna and the Swiss Guard to depart for Venice, the assassination brought an immediate change. *From being proscribed wanderers, we acquired the rights of citizenship and found an asylum open to us on the continent . . . not a word more was heard on the subject of our departure;*[17] and not a word more either was heard from Garibaldi about going to the aid of besieged Venice. Henceforth his sights were fixed on Rome. It is difficult to understand why it should have been so, for Rome at that juncture was in no danger; in fact, to him, it looked almost as if she had risen to free herself.

Twenty years or more later, he was to shock his non-Italian friends and provide his Papist enemies with a stick to beat him (of which they have not failed to make use to this day)[18] by appearing to commend the murder of Rossi in his autobiography. What he then wrote was: *As a follower of Beccaria, I am opposed to capital punishment and therefore condemn the dagger of Brutus . . . Harmodios, Pelopidas, and Brutus, the men who freed their country from tyrants, have not been painted by ancient history in colours so dark as those in which our modern devourers of nations would like to exhibit any man who has touched the ribs of a Duke of Parma or a Neapolitan Bourbon. The ancient metropolis of the world, worthy once more of her former glory, freed herself on that day from the most formidable satellite of tyranny and bathed the marble steps of the Capitol with his blood. A young Roman had recovered the steel of Marcus Brutus.*[19]

It is difficult to understand the feelings this passage has aroused. Even if it were possible to draw a clear moral distinction between taking human life in war or by judicial execution and taking human life by political assassination (so that the attempt to kill Hitler, and Sartre's *Orestres* and the French Resistance he exemplified are all alike to be condemned) to criticize Garibaldi for this passage—or even to be sad about it, as was Trevelyan—is to lose all sense of period or occasion. Garibaldi knew less than nothing about the merits or demerits of Rossi; he believed *that the dagger stroke announced to all advocates of compromise with foreign powers that the people knew them and would not return to the slavery to which they sought, by falsehood and treachery, to entice them back;* and he lived in a country and in a period when a Cardinal Legate acting on behalf of God's Vicar on earth could employ a paid assassin to exterminate him[20]; and when Papal Courts thought nothing of executing radical sympathizers, after farcical trials in which they were not allowed to defend themselves.[21] Since Garibaldi specially condemned the dagger of Brutus and there is reason to believe[22] that when a proposition of political assassination was actually put to him, he rejected it in anger, he would appear to have been at least as noble as many who in self-righteousness have sought to condemn him.

Still, as Antigone said: 'Who knows if these thoughts be approved amongst the dead?'

VI

Nine days after the murder of Rossi, a white-faced Pope laid aside the robes of his office and put on those of an ordinary priest. He crept down a secret staircase out of the Quirinal and there was consternation when it was discovered that the key to the courtyard was missing. Trembling too much to stand on his own feet, he dropped to his knees to pray, and remained there until it could be found. A carriage bore him away out of Rome and as he turned his back on the Holy City, he turned his back for ever on his century. He fled to the most hated of Italian rulers, 'King Bomba', of Naples, the same who had, but three months before, so savagely massacred his subjects in Massina; and he took with him the most hated of prelates, Cardinal Antonelli, who, lecherous and corrupt as he was, was to dominate all the thoughts and actions of the weakling Pope until the Cardinal's death in 1875.

The Constitution, so Antonelli brusquely told a deputation of moderate politicians who visited him in the Royal Palace of Naples, was 'buried under the rock of Gaeta'; but the people of Rome determined otherwise. The Pope had left behind a note which did not contain anything of any consequence and made no provision for the government of his realms. But once safe in the arms of 'King Bomba', he sent back orders that the government was to be carried on by a Cardinal Castracana and a council which included the former Napoleonic adventurer Zucchi, who was to be cast in the role of the strong man of the counter-revolution. But the strong man was still in Bologna and none too sure of himself; the Carabinieri and the National Guard were on the side of the people; and on 29th December 1848, a Junta which had temporarily assumed power ordered the election of a Constituent Assembly for Rome on the basis of universal suffrage.

The Holy City had become the first in Italy to achieve democratic self-government. Even the State of Piedmont had an electoral role based on such a high property qualification that the vast majority of its subjects had no vote or voice in its affairs. The elections ordered in Rome were not to the liking of the Pope. In a furious document issued on the 1st January 1849, he denounced *the violence of the gang of lunatics who are tyrannizing Rome with barbaric despotism* . . . and described the elections as *a monstrous act of unconcealed treason and naked rebellion* and the invitation to the people to vote in them *a suggestion* . . . *so criminal and wicked*, as to arouse *holy indignation*. He absolutely prohibited that anybody should vote in the elections on the pain of the *Greater Excommunication*.[23] It is a document that should be meditated upon by those who like to portray Pius IX as a kindly old man with democratic leanings who was converted from his liberalism only by the extremes of the radicals.

In spite of the fact that the Pope's exhortation was read from the pulpits, and placarded on the walls by the priests, who also carried on a campaign of personal intimidation, nearly half the adult population of Rome risked eternal damnation by exercising their democratic rights. It is an astonishing figure for the year 1849, and one which conclusively refutes the suggestion of Papal historians that the people of Rome were not behind the republic.

In spite of the priests, and in spite of the resignation of many officials in obedience to the Pope's demands, the people went to the polls amidst scenes of joy and enthusiasm;[24] even a handful of priests voted. As soon as the Pope saw that his ruse had failed he issued an appeal to France, Spain, Austria and Naples to suppress the republic by force of arms; and he took other steps to restore his waning influence.

It is an interesting study to observe how each setback to the temporal power of the Pope resulted in his trying to boost his spiritual supremacy, either by inventing some new dogma or by conferring on himself greater authority, or both. Since Roman Catholic doctrine was by the middle of the nineteenth century well defined, the only scope for innovation lay up the wilder and more superstitious reaches of Mariolatry; so that many of those doctrines regarding the Virgin Mary, which the wiser and more intelligent of modern Catholics prefer not to discuss, but which they must believe for their Eternal Salvation, have their origin in manoeuvres for the sovereignty of a petty principality. Whether this course was adopted, as some believe,[25] in an effort to reclaim the allegiance of reluctant subjects or as a face-saving operation for the faithful elsewhere, who found it difficult to reconcile the defeats inflicted on the Pope on earth with his claim to be God's Vicar there, is difficult to say; perhaps both elements entered into it.

On the 2nd February 1849, Pius IX in exile in Gaeta enunciated the doctrine of the Immaculate Conception of the Blessed Virgin; a doctrine which has existed hitherto only as a medieval superstition and which was one, as St Thomas Aquinas had pointed out long before, that rested on no scriptural evidence whatever and was based on the heretical assumption that there was at least one human being who had no need of redemption; and the Pope did so, not in association with the Bishops, as all new doctrine had previously been annunciated, but on his authority alone as sovereign Pontiff. He also signed a Bull to establish a Roman Catholic hierachy in England which, discreetly, was kept secret for eighteen months; it was an act of particular impertinence since his adherents at that time were less than one in twenty of the English population; and it provoked a storm when it was eventually disclosed in 1850. Had it been revealed earlier, it might well have had a significant effect on the British Government's attitude to the Roman Republic, as it did indeed later to their attitude to the other events of the *Risorgimento*.

While these events were taking place in Rome, Garibaldi and his men had left Ravenna on the urging of the municipality who had grown a little tired of keeping them all, particularly since they had now grown in numbers to 528. From there, he moved from community to community through the Apennines towards Rome, welcomed by none but maintained by each;[26] the analogy of the plague of locusts was far from inappropriate and Garibaldi himself recognized that they were regarded as *importunate adventurers*.

When the news of the Pope's flight arrived they had reached Cesena, and Garibaldi went off to Rome in a diligence to offer his services to the provisional government. He was received with the usual wild enthusiasm by the crowd but after twelve days of argument with officials, he rejoined his men with only the rank of lieutenant-colonel in the Roman army and authority to maintain a force of not more than 500; and no stores, or even cloaks for those who were without. The Romans seemed no more eager than any other place to enjoy the pleasure of their company; the Legion was instructed to go to defend Porto S. Giorgio on the Adriatic coast, although exactly against whom nobody seemed to know. It was about the farthest place from Rome to which they could reasonably be sent and it involved another miserable trip through the mountains in the bitter cold. Garibaldi, taking the view that there was no object in their being sent to the coast except to remove them from Rome, interpreted his instructions very liberally and finding Macerata more congenial than the scruffy little port, established his headquarters there.

It was in that city at eleven o'clock on the Sunday morning of the 21st January, that the Legion proceeded to record their vote for the new Constituent Assembly. Garibaldi was himself a candidate for the multiple constituency of sixteen seats. *It was a striking sight,* he wrote, *that of the sons of Rome again called to the Comitia, after so many centuries of slavery and prostration under the shameful yoke of the empire or the still worse one of the Papal theocracy. Without tumult, without passions—unless patriotism and zeal for freedom are to be called by that name—without bribery, without prefects or police-agents to intimidate the voters, the sacred function of the plebiscite was performed.* What he omitted to record was that the men of his Legion were marched to the polls with their ballot papers already signed; and that, according to the new legislation, as employees of the government they were not entitled to a vote; and that, not one

of them being in fact a son of Rome, they were also disentitled
by reason of non-citizenship of the Roman states.

In spite of the 528 votes of the Legion, Garibaldi was placed
thirteenth only amongst the sixteen successful candidates; without them, he would not have been elected.

VII

The newly elected deputies assembled in Rome on the 5th
February and having first attended Mass, proceeded to their
deliberations. In the midst of the presentation of the credentials
of deputies, Garibaldi demanded the floor. He launched into a
tirade demanding at once the immediate proclamation of the
republic. His speech was greeted with some applause but also
with cries of dissent and the assembly proceeded with its business.
Three days later, they got round to considering the Fundamental
Statute. After a spate of oratory, which began at eight in the
morning and lasted until nine o'clock at night, the Chamber
eventually passed it. On that day, Garibaldi was so crippled by
rheumatism that he had to be carried into the Chamber for the
session. The Fundamental Statute had four Clauses.

*Article 1. The Papacy is deposed in fact and in law from the temporal
government of the Roman State.*
*Article 2. The Roman Pontiff will be granted all the guarantees neces-
sary for his independence in the exercise of his spiritual power.*
*Article 3. The form of government of the Roman State will be a com-
plete democracy and will take the glorious name of the Roman
Republic.*
*Article 4. The Roman Republic will have with the rest of Italy such
relationship as will lead to a common nationality.*[27]

So many hours of verbosity to produce what were, to him,
four platitudes; Garibaldi took himself back to his troops. But
before he left Rome he secured from the new Ministry of War
authority to move them to Rieti, only fifty miles from the capital
and to increase their numbers to 1,000. For the next two months
he was busy training them, and since they had not as yet been
supplied with muskets by the government, equipping them with
home-made lances and pikes. He entertained no doubt they
would be needed before long.

Early March brought Mazzini to Rome and he spoke in the

Assembly for the first time on 6th March, having previously been elected in his absence.

'I trust that . . . the stranger will never again be able to say . . . that this flame in Rome is merely an *ignis factuus,* a ghostly glimmer that flickers from tomb to tomb. No! The world shall see it as a star, eternal, brilliant, clear, such as those that shine in our Italian sky,' he said.

But he cherished no illusions.

'The foes are too many, too strong and too subtle,' he confessed in private two days later to a friend;[28] and it is some indication of his fearless generosity that he came to Rome believing that the republic was certain to fall to the forces ranged against it, and determined to save it if he could; but if the star was fated to be no more than a falling one, that none should fail to observe the brilliance of its passage through the heavens. *Since we were certain to fall, for the sake of the future, it was our duty to offer our* morituri te salutant *to Italy from Rome,* he wrote later.

On 14th March, the melancholy Charles Albert of Piedmont, egged on by his Parliament, after consulting his conscience and the visions of a nun, and after hours of prayer, denounced the armistice with the Austrians and led his troops in person across the Ticino to rescue Lombardy. Nine days later, the Piedmontese army was defeated and shattered at Novara. The same night a haggard, white-faced man in civilian clothes was admitted to the presence of an Austrian general in the kitchen of a peasant's cottage. He was, he said, a cavalry colonel of the Royal Piedmont Army who had resigned his commission after the battle and now wished to have a safe conduct so that he could return to his private estate near Nice. It was pouring with rain outside and bitterly cold. The Austrian general gave him a cup of coffee, signed a passport for him, and then gallantly accompanied him out into the rain to the door of the carriage.

'Good night, your Majesty,' said the general, 'I trust you have a good journey.'[32] There was no mistaking that moustache. Charles Albert had abdicated in favour of his son and was off to that Valhalla of ex-monarchs, Portugal.

His son, Victor Emmanuel, who succeeded him, was forced to make concessions to the Austrians, such as the withdrawal of his fleet from the Adriatic where it had been protecting Venice seawards. *But,* wrote Trevelyan[29], *there was one thing which he would not surrender and that was the Constitution granted by his father*

*to Piedmont. All the tempting offers made by Radetzky to induce him
'to modify' the great charter, which was destined to become the law of
the kingdom of united Italy, were met by his staunch refusal, now
celebrated in Italian popular art, which loves to depict the young and
spirited King turning away in indignation from the offers of the white-
haired enemy of freedom.* The picture of the young monarch so
devoted to his (partially) democratic constitution that he rejected
the temptations of the Austrians as if they were those of the Evil
One himself, must be revised somewhat since the publication in
recent years of his private correspondence with Pope Pius IX.
It is but another of the fictions of the *Risorgimento*; a fiction which
nevertheless sustained and nourished the cause of national unity.
In fact Victor Emmanuel, as he told the Papal Nuncio at Turin
'thought the constitutional system the worse possible' and
longed for 'the chance to bring about its collapse'.[30] Even making
all allowances for the Italian tendency to say that which is pleasing
to the hearer, there is ample evidence in this correspondence, and
in his subsequent acts and sayings, to show that the new King of
Piedmont would, if he could, have preferred to rule as a despot
without the restraint of a parliament. The only thing that kept
him from revoking the Constitution, reluctantly granted by his
father, was that he was warned on every side in Piedmont that
he would forfeit his crown if he did so, and he realized that the
warnings were right. In reality, Victor Emmanuel was a vulgar
little man, obscene in speech, and devoted in his private life to
nothing much except hunting (which meant shooting anything
from thrushes to goats) and fornication, and in his public life to
clinging to his throne at all costs and extending his domains
whenever possible; and he not infrequently allowed his two great
hobbies to predominate to the detriment of his public interests.
It was no heroic figure that Garibaldi, by heroic effort, placed
upon the throne of a United Italy.

VIII

With the defeat of Piedmont in March, it became apparent that
Rome would have to stand on her own feet. A triumvirate was
formed to head the executive and conduct the defence with
dictatorial powers; Mazzini was the dominant figure of the three.
Shortly after his election, he received a letter from one who had
had a few words to say about how he had vanished earlier in the
year at Como. It read:

Brother Mazzini,

This has no other object than to bring you greetings and I write it with my own hand. May Providence support you in your brilliant but arduous career and enable you to carry out all that is on your mind, to the benefit of our country. Remember that in Rieti are to be found your friends in the faith, and they are unchangeable.

Rieti, 3rd April   G. Garibaldi

The lieutenant-colonel, stuck out at Rieti with his thousand men, was obviously getting rather restive; there was a vacancy in Rome for a commander-in-chief.

Eventually, the Roman government remembered him; they delivered to him fifty muskets, the first he had received, and sent him off to the South to Anagni which was only forty-nine instead of fifty miles from Rome.

Something of his feelings may perhaps be gleaned in between the lines of a letter he wrote to Anita:

April 19, 1849

Most dear spouse,

I write to tell you that I am well and that I am proceeding with the column to Anagni, which probably I shall reach tomorrow but I cannot say how long we shall stay there. I hope I shall get muskets and the rest of the clothing for the men at Anagni.

I shan't be easy in my mind until I get a letter to assure me that you have arrived safely in Nice. Write to me at once. I must hear from you, dearest Anita. Tell me what you think of events in Genoa and Leghorn.

You, strong and generous woman, with what contempt you must look on this generation of hermaphrodites in Italy, on these countrymen of mine that I have so often tried to make noble, with such little result . . . I'm ashamed to belong to a family which has so many cowards. But I am not disheartened nor do I doubt my country's destiny.

Write to me, I say again. I must hear of you and my mother and our children. Don't worry about me. I'm stronger than ever and with my 1200 armed men, I feel invincible . . . I love you dearly and beg you not to fret. Kiss the children for me and my mother, to whose care I entrust you. Good-bye for now. G. Garibaldi.[31]

IX

The revolution of 1848 had brought a republican assembly to France, yet so strong was Catholic sentiment in that country that

General Cavaignac, as good a republican as any, as soon as he heard of Rossi's murder, ordered ships and troops to be ready to go to Civita Vecchia to protect the Pope. When that measure was debated in the Assembly, a sallow-faced deputy who bore an immortal name carefully abstained from voting.

He was quick to realize his mistake. Fumbling around for any cause which would commend him to the population, he made a speech championing the rights of the Pope. Never more than a cynical agnostic at heart, he realized that he discovered one step at least by which he could rise to power. When, the following month, he was elected President of the republic he was acutely aware that he owed his position, in part at least, to the support given him by the pious. Yet it was with no great alacrity that he responded to the Pope's appeal, and still less was it with any enthusiasm for restoring the Pope unconditionally to his throne; more than anything else it was the fear that if he did not, Austria would.

On 25th April, a French fleet anchored at Civita Vecchia and some 8,000 troops were landed.

Louis Napoleon, nephew of the great Emperor, President of the French Republic and soon to become Napoleon III, Emperor of the French (under the evergreen pretext for riveting the shackles of despotism on a people, that of saving them from the 'evils' of socialism) had stepped upon the stage. Pio Nono, Mazzini, Garibaldi, Victor Emmanuel and he; the cast were assembled for the first act of the greatest epic drama the modern world has seen. Only one star the spotlight had not yet fallen upon but he was already on stage in the shadows of the wings. Yet so great a role was his that it is difficult to realize that his part lasted only nine years; like Bohun, Q.C., although he only appears in one act, somehow it seems as if he were there all the time; but in 1849, Count Camillo Cavour was an ordinary deputy in the Piedmont parliament, more concerned about his private speculations than great affairs.

The day after the French had landed, Mazzini received a colonel of their staff, who made it clear that they had come to restore the Pope to Rome.

'And if the people of Rome do not wish to have the Pope restored?' asked Mazzini.

'He will be restored just the same,' said the colonel.[33]

VIII

THE FALLING STAR

❖❖❖❖❖❖❖❖❖❖

THERE WERE military bands playing, distant bugles sounding, everywhere flags and cockades, and Rome was full of soldiers in brilliant and varied uniforms, decorated with braid and flashes and gilt, clanking their swords against the cobbles; but on the afternoon of 27th April the attention of the crowds was attracted by a body of men who presented quite a different appearance as they marched in.

They were gaunt and untidy, with long, untrimmed hair and unkempt beards, tanned by the sun and covered with the dust of travel. Except for a few in red blouses, they wore ill-fitting navy blue tunics, held in at the waist by belts in which were tucked large daggers. On their heads they had black Calabrian hats with broad brims and high crowns, into which were stuck long black feathers. Most carried spikes but a few had muskets. In the midst of them rode their chief on horseback, dressed in a red tunic and a white cloak with a scarlet lining; on his head was a black felt hat, ornamented with long feathers, and round his neck a kerchief knotted loosely in front. His horse was white and as he rode he carried an unsheathed sabre. Behind him came a large negro in a blue cloak on a black horse, with a lasso dangling from his saddle. Not surprisingly, one foreign observer thought they looked like a gang of brigands; which was the name by which they were known amongst the clerical faction.

All down the Corso went the cry: 'He has come! Garibaldi has come!'; and the young women in the crowd were heard to exclaim 'Oh! Isn't he beautiful, beautiful!' A Dutch artist who saw him that day has left a detailed picture of what he looked like: broad-shouldered with massive chest, light chestnut hair falling over his shoulders, a big moustache and a light reddish beard which ended in two points. His face was red with the sun and covered with freckles; *the most striking feature of all,* wrote the observer, *was the nose with its broad base . . . which made one think of a lion; a similarity which, according to his soldiers, was even more noticeable in battle when his eyes flashed and his sable hair streamed from his forehead like a mane.*[1]

Although the government had sent for him three days before, when the news of the French landing had been received, no provision seems to have been made for billeting his men. When he discovered that, a furious Garibaldi rode up to the vast convent of San Silvestro and gave the nuns an hour to get out. As they carried their belongings out, the brigands started streaming in, and began to make themselves comfortable on bundles of straw on the floor. A few of them, less fatigued or more curious than the rest, started rooting in the drawers to see what the nuns had left behind, and were delighted to discover love letters, baby's attire and what an eyewitness[2] described as *all kinds of disgusting instruments for erotic use which modesty prevents me describing in detail.* The same modesty did not restrain the legionnaires; soon, they had made show-cases and were exhibiting to the gaping populace of Rome evidence of how members of the enclosed orders passed their time.

This ungentlemanly conduct was not restrained by their chief who, in fact, thereafter in all his campaigns took particular pleasure in billeting his men in nunneries and convents; partly because they were convenient places to house a large number of soldiers without inconvenience to the local population, and partly because, as he put it, he believed in making war on all his enemies; and, no doubt, also because it was always an entertainment for his soldiery to discover the erotic correspondence of those who were vowed to chastity and to be able to regale their comrades in the evenings with tit-bits read aloud amidst roars of laughter. The saintly Father Ugo Bassi, whose vast statue today stands in Bologna, had been sent as chaplain to the Legion while they were stationed at Rieti; it is not recorded what he thought of such pastimes, but there was one person to whom their antics did not appeal. Two days after their arrival in Rome, Mazzini had the Legion transferred out of the nunnery to billets in the Trastevere, the slum quarter of Rome; he was determined to keep the city, as one English observer found it to be, *a most respectable republic.*[3]

On the 30th April, the thunder of bells from the campanile of every one of Rome's hundreds of churches called the Legion to more serious things. A sentry from the walls of St Peter's had seen a column of French approaching the city.

II

As the French approached the city they found the countryside deserted; and on the walls they read notices in heavy black type which caustically bore the words of part of the French Constitution adopted only the previous year: *France respects other nationalities. Her might will never be used against the liberty of any people.* But the French heard the bells ringing and most believed what the Pope had been busy telling the world; that power in the Holy City had been usurped by a mere handful of men and it needed but their salvation to be at the gates for the citizens to repudiate them; and their spirits must have been raised when they heard from the walls bands playing the tune of the *Marseillaise*, and singing. It was the tune all right, but what they did not know was that the song that was being sung was a parody:

> *Allons enfants de sacristie*
> *Le jour de honte est arrivé*
> *Par vos mains de la tyrannie*
> *L'étendard sanglant est sauvé*
> *Entendez-vous dans la compagne*
> *Beugler ces féroces prélats?*
> *Ils viennent diriger vos bras*
> *Fier assassins de la Romagne!*
> *Aux arms, sacristains! Formez vos bataillons*
> *Marchons! Le pape est roi du droit de nos canons!*

But in any case, the French soldiers had been informed by their officers 'The Italians can't fight!'

They made straight for the Vatican and their plan was to divide into two columns in front of the former Porta Pertusa; one would go round to the north to Porta Angelica where, in accordance with a scheme concocted with priests in the city, the gate would be opened to them; the others would in the meanwhile distract attention by attacking the Porta Cavalleggieri.[4] But the whole scheme was disrupted by a storm of the grapeshot and musket-fire from the walls. In half an hour they suffered heavy casualties and were on the point of abandoning the attack.

This assault Garibaldi had watched from the terrace of the Villa Corsini on high ground outside his section of the wall and he decided that it was the moment to lead his troops stationed there, and in the Villa Pamfili a little farther out, to the attack. His intervention turned the defeat into a rout and after five hours' bitter fighting, the French fled with 900 killed or wounded and leaving nearly 400 prisoners in the hands of the exultant Romans.

That night all Rome was *en fête*. Lights blazed from a thousand casements, the cafés and piazzas were crowded and on every street the parody of the *Marseillaise* was being sung. The French prisoners were treated to drinks and given cigars and taken on a conducted tour of the sights of Rome.

Meanwhile Garibaldi was being visited by a surgeon to whom he had sent a brief note in his own handwriting from the battle-field: *Come to me after dark. I have been wounded but nobody must know*. He had been shot by a ball in the stomach, but had stayed in the midst of the battle to the end, even though his saddle became drenched with blood.

III

The generous treatment of the captured French was a policy initiated by Mazzini, in order that they might carry back favour-able reports to their comrades; and with that end in view they were released a few days later. Not unreasonably, Mazzini hoped that the French Assembly would intervene to prevent further attempts to conquer Rome; but he was, of course, in ignorance of the current political situation in Paris and still more of the true nature of Louis Napoleon. For him, the defeat made it a matter of *la gloire* and the war for Rome afforded him an opportunity of consolidating his position; within a few days he was writing to General Oudinot, the French Commander-in-Chief: *Our military honour is in peril. I will not allow it to be compromised. You can be certain of being reinforced.*[5]

Garibaldi, in spite of his wound, which was to pain him for the next two months, made a sortie out of the city in force at day-break the next morning. He was in favour of striking again at the French so that they should be scattered before they could regain their ships; but to this suggestion Mazzini was opposed on the ground that to inflict a crushing defeat on the French would make them mortal enemies and imperil any prospect of conciliation;

and when, that afternoon, a French surgeon was sent to Garibaldi to ask for a cease-fire and was passed on to the triumvirate, the order came for Garibaldi to retire back to Rome. He obeyed, but it went down as another mark in his account against Mazzini.

The cessation of hostilities with the French gave the republic the opportunity to turn their attention to another army that was marching against them on the Pope's behalf. From the South, 'King Bomba' of Naples had advanced with an army of 10,000, one-third the entire population of Rome. The main body had come as far as Velletri and columns had infiltrated into the plain between the Alban and Sabine Hill. On the 4th May, Garibaldi led a column of some 2,500 men against them and made for their right flank and stationed himself at Palestrina. A force of twice that number was sent out by the Neapolitan King to dislodge him and in a battle there on the 9th November, they were utterly routed and fled in disorder.

A vivid picture of Garibaldi in the field was given by a young Lombardy noble[6] who accompanied his troops. *By reason of his patriarchal simplicity, so great that it might almost be thought to be assumed,* he wrote, *Garibaldi is more like the chief of an Indian tribe than a General.* All his band looked after their own horses, the general included, and they would sleep under improvised tents made from their saddles, which were made to unroll, and a sword stuck in the ground. They would be provisioned by lassoing cattle and sheep, which they roasted by huge fires. *The hundred fires lighting the rocks and caverns made a bizarre and fantastic sight,* he recalled. Often, Garibaldi would himself go out disguised as a peasant to spy out the land.

Once more, he would have liked to pursue his defeated enemy but he was recalled to Rome, for there was thought to be a danger that the French might reopen their offensive; with his men, he covered twenty-eight miles in an overnight march and was back in Rome before the Neapolitans had realized he had gone. He was none too pleased to find that in his absence a General Roselli had been appointed commander-in-chief; it was in fact a political move to counter the papal propaganda that the defence of Rome was in the hands of foreigners, for Roselli's chief qualification was that he was a Roman. A few days after Garibaldi's return to the city a French diplomat arrived there to talk terms for an armistice. He was Ferdinand de Lesseps. He and Garibaldi had one thing in common. He, too, had met Emile Barrault. It was in Egypt towards the end of the same travels that the St Simonian apostles had commenced in *La Clorinda*. De Lesseps, too, was to be assured of his place in history by the influence of the same man; for from Barrault he had been inspired with enthusiasm for the St Simonians' scheme to cut a canal through the Suez isthmus. In all good faith, de Lesseps soon concluded an agreement for an armistice, subject to ratification by the French government, by which the French forces would station themselves outside Rome and would defend the republic from the Austrians, who by then were approaching from the North, and the Neapolitans; but it was silent on the most important point of all—what was to happen to the Pope.

In reliance on that agreement, a force of three brigades amounting in all to some 10,000 men, almost the whole military force at the disposal of the republic, was sent off to attack the Neapolitans. It was under the command of Roselli, with Garibaldi responsible for one of the brigades which constituted the central division of the advance. Three days after they had left Rome, Garibaldi who was out with the Van—for which he had no responsibility at all—committed them to an attack on the Neapolitans without waiting for the consent of his superior officers. At a critical point in the battle Garibaldi sent back to Roselli for reinforcements and received a curt message back that he was unable to supply them 'as the men had not yet had their soup.'

In the course of the fighting, a detachment of Roman cavalry fled from a similar enemy body. In a narrow defile Garibaldi turned his horse sidewards across their path and was ridden down and buried in a confused mêlée of horses and men. The Austrian cavalry charged over him. He was so bruised that he could not move and was only saved by a company of young boys of his Legion. As soon as he could, he leapt to his feet, placed his hat on the end of his sword and waved it to indicate to his men that he was still alive and unhurt.

That night he slept in the bed in Velletri that the King of Naples had occupied the previous night. The Neapolitans were in full flight.

Still suffering from his previous wound, and now covered with abrasions and bruises, he sent for the doctor, who wanted to bleed him. But Garibaldi would not hear of it. He went to soak himself in a hot bath and was in high spirits.

His servant in the next room heard him laughing uproariously.
'What's the matter, General?'
'My shirt's dropped in the bath and it's the only daughter of a
widowed mother!'
Since he was in the habit of sleeping in his shirt it was some-
thing of a problem.
None other could be found for him until the doctor produced a
garment he had 'liberated' from a monastery. That night Gari-
baldi slept in the bed of the King of Naples in the smock of an
Augustinian monk.[7]

IV

From the defeat at Velletri, the Neapolitan army retreated in
disorder back on Naples. Had Garibaldi been given his head, he
would have followed them but, once again, he was recalled on
Mazzini's orders. The Austrian army was outside Ancona and
already some 4,000 Roman troops had been dispatched to face
them. It was Mazzini's intention that Garibaldi, with his men,
should join them, in the hope that the General might inflict as
decisive a defeat on the Austrians as he had on the Neapolitans.

The final agreement between de Lesseps, on behalf of the
French Government, and the Roman Republic was signed on the
31st May; and the same day Garibaldi returned to Rome. He was
in an exhausted state from the fatigues of battle, the bruises and
abrasions which he had received when the cavalry had ridden over
him, and the still unhealed wound he had received on the 30th
April; on top of that, he could hardly move for rheumatism. His
doctors ordered him to bed, and he was confined there during
the next few crucial days.

Before sending further men against the Austrians, General
Roselli took it into his head to write a letter to General Oudinot:

31st May. Rome.
Citizen General,
*   It is my deepest conviction that one day the army of the Roman Republic will be fighting side by side with that of the French Republic to
uphold the most sacred rights of the people. This conviction leads me to
make the following proposals. It is known to me that a treaty has been
signed between the Roman Government and the Minister Plenipotentiary of France and that the treaty has not met with your approval. I do*

*not propose to enter into the mysterious realm of politics. I address you
simply in my capacity of Commander-in-Chief of the Roman Army.*

Roselli then went on to describe the position of the Austrian
army and their intention to link up with the Neapolitan one and
continued: *I cannot believe that you can remain indifferent to the
achievement of such plans . . . your ambiguous attitude paralyses our
efforts and may, in the end, ensure success to the enemy.*

*These reasons appear to me to be so strong that I feel entitled to ask
you to grant an armistice* sine die *and a fortnight's notice of any intention
to resume hostilities . . . Should the Austrian columns make their appearance at Civita Castellana, it is on the French army that will fall, in the
judgement of history, the responsibility of having forced us to divide our
forces at a time when they were so precious to us . . .*[8]

The reply of the French general to that letter filled the defenders
of Rome with consternation.

General,

*The orders of my Government are positive: they require me to enter
Rome as soon as possible. I have denounced to the Roman authorities the
oral armistice which, at the instance of M. de Lesseps, I consented to
grant for the moment. I have advised your outposts that one or other
army has the right to recommence hostilities. Only, to give time to those
of our nationals who wish to leave Rome and, at the request of M.
the Chancellor of the French Embassy, to give them the opportunity of
doing so with ease, I am deferring the attack upon the place until Monday
morning.*[9]

Mazzini sent a letter to Garibaldi to ask his advice: and received
a reply:

Mazzini,

*You ask me to choose what I want, to which I must say that I can only
exist for the good of the Republic in one of two ways: a dictator with
unlimited powers or a simple soldier. Choose.*

Always Yours,
Garibaldi[10]

It was a choice that did not appeal to Mazzini or his fellow
triumvirs and he wrote back a letter which virtually ignored this
offer and asked for Garibaldi's views about how the defence of
Rome should be conducted; no more. The reply was brief: the
republic should give to General Avezzano the command of the
forces. Although the letter did not say it in so many words, it

meant, and was understood to mean, that Garibaldi had no confidence whatever in his commander-in-chief, Roselli.

Three o'clock the next morning, Garibaldi was awakened by the sound of cannon. He sprang from his bed and leapt upon his horse. Everywhere was confusion. At midnight—the night of Saturday-Sunday—the French had resumed the attack upon the Roman outposts. One body had crossed the Tiber to the north of the city and driven the defenders back into the Porta del Popolo; another had seized the Villas Corsini and Pamfili, on the high ground outside the Porta San Pancrazio, and the Vascello villa at the very gate of the city. *Je diffère l'attaque de la place jusqu'à lundi matin*, Oudinot had written, and the defenders of Rome had interpreted this as meaning that no attack would take place anywhere until Monday morning. It is difficult to acquit the French general of having phrased his letter in words of such deliberate ambiguity that they would convey that impression, but his deceit does not excuse the neglect of the triumvirate and its staff. After the battle of the 30th April, it had been agreed between Avezzana and Garibaldi that the Villas Corsini and Pamfili were so important for the defence of the city that they should be fortified; nothing had been done in that respect and the troops holding them had, moreover, allowed themselves to be taken by surprise while they were all soundly asleep.

By the time Garibaldi arrived on the scene, the Vascello had been retaken and during all the arduous days that followed was to be defended by Medici and his legion with such skill and tenacity that it was never again lost. But the attempt to capture the Villa Corsini, which lasted until long after darkness had fallen, completely failed. The only approach to it was up a narrow lane commanded by French fire; in spite of that, the Villa was taken several times but could not be held. Garibaldi was subsequently criticized for launching frontal attacks with insufficient troops and for rashly sending men to their death in a senseless slaughter; certainly, he seems to have shown a lack of ordered planning both in the way he ordered attacks to be made and in his failure to ensure that reinforcements were available to repulse the counter-attacks, on the occasions when it was captured. In fact he demonstrated all the impulsive follies of desperation, for none knew better than he that upon the possession of the Villa rested the mastery of Rome.

I have seen some terrible fights, he wrote later,[11] *but never anything to equal the butchery of the Villa Corsini.* By the time the day was lost, more than one-quarter of his 4,000 men had been killed or wounded, amongst them the noblest and the bravest of his officers. It was only relieved from being an unmitigated disaster by the many individual acts of heroism, so that the 3rd June 1849 shines in Italian history in the peculiar light of sacrificial valour.

Mazzini and the others were for making an attempt to recapture the Villa Corsini the next day by a sally *en masse* of the whole of the Roman army and armed populace; but Garibaldi set his face against such a futile venture and dissuaded them from it. Thereafter, the battle for Rome settled down to a siege, with the French mounting artillery at the Corsini and running a series of trenches out from there towards the walls of the city.

Garibaldi established his headquarters in the Villa Savorelli, just inside the Porta Pancrazio which, although well within the range of French gun and musket fire, commanded a clear view of the country all around. There was a little wooden balcony on the upper floor, and there he was wont to take his breakfast *just by way of affording a little practice to the French artillerymen and snipers.* Avezzano, the Minister of War, paid a brief visit there and, the following day, Garibaldi found that, by his orders, the balcony had been protected with sandbags. Knowing that the Villa Savorelli was his headquarters, the French concentrated all their fire upon it.

v

In a shattered Villa Savorelli, Garibaldi sat down on the 21st June and wrote to his Anita at Nice:

Rome.

My dear Anita,

I know that you have been, and perhaps still are, ill. I want to see your signature and that of my mother, to calm me.

The Gallic friars of Cardinal Oudinot are content to bombard us; and we are so used to it by now that we don't care. Here, the women and children chase straight after the cannon-balls and struggle to possess them.

We are fighting on the Janiculum and these people are worthy of the grandeur of the past. They live, they die, they suffer amputation to the cry 'Viva la Republica!' One hour of our life in Rome is worth more than a century of ordinary living! Happy my mother to have given birth in a period so wonderful for Italy! ...

Get better quickly. Kiss Mama and the babies for me. Menotti has
given me the benefit of a second letter, for which I'm grateful. Love me
much.

Your,
Garibaldi

It was a letter which, although dispatched, she was destined
never to read.

During the night that followed, the French stormed the walls
and, before the defenders knew what had happened, had breached
and captured them. When day broke, they were firmly in possession of two of the bastions. Mazzini and other officials came and
demanded that Garibaldi should retake them; but he was adamant
in refusing to subject his men to a senseless massacre. *I consider*
Rome as fallen, wrote Mazzini that day.[12] But, even if the enemy
were within the walls, Garibaldi was not disposed to give up,
although it was apparent to all that the end was not far off. He
withdrew his troops some 200 yards behind the old Aurelian
Wall while, outside the Porta S. Pancrazio, Medici still hung on
grimly to the Vascello. During the night, the French had erected
cannons in their breaches on the main walls and the defenders
were now subjected, day after day, to direct bombardment from
them, as well as from the guns which had been harassing them
from the Villa Corsini. By the morning of the 27th June, the
Villa Savorelli was no more than a heap of rubble and Garibaldi
moved his headquarters to the Villa Spada, between the Aurelian
Wall and the Colle Pino in front of San Pietro-in-Montorio, on
which his own few guns were stationed. It was directly in the
target area and, before long, shells were exploding in the upper
floors, killing some of his staff.

He was eating some pieces of hard bread and cheese with his
officers, all of them in their shirt-sleeves, on the third floor of the
Villa Spada when he heard hurried footsteps outside. The door
opened. A woman entered the room. He ran to her and picked her
up in his arms.

'Gentlemen,' he said.[13] 'This is my Anita. We have another
soldier to fight for Rome.'

'Do you know, General,' asked the man who escorted her[14],
'how she has been amusing herself on the way here?'

'No.'

'In stopping all the way along San Pietro-in-Montorio to look at the French batteries. Just look how we are both covered with dust caused by their shells hitting the walls. And when I said to her, "Come along—do come along. It's no use getting killed here," she replied: "My dear, what do you think of the way the French, as good Catholics, arrange churches?"' (As a result of the bombardment, the roof of the S. Pietro-in-Montorio had fallen in.)

It was the third time Anita had joined him in recent months. He had sent her back from Leghorn to Nice when he set out to Ravenna with the intention of going to Venice; she had joined him again in late February at Rieta and been sent home by him from there on the 13th April, just before he moved to Anagni; now, pregnant and ill, she had come to him again.

According to his doctor,[15] *Garibaldi was sternly displeased but neither reproaches nor entreaties could induce her to leave his side.*

VI

Two days after Anita's arrival was the Feast of St Peter and St Paul, traditionally celebrated in Rome with bonfires and fireworks. That evening, all the city was illuminated—not only in celebration of the *festa* but as an act of final defiance to the French. Every window bore its lanterns in green, white and red, and the Colosseum and St Peter's blazed with the same colours. But thunder rolled across the dark sky, the heavens were split with lightning and the street bonfires were extinguished in a deluge of torrential rain. The bombarded arena outside the Aurelian Wall was turned into a sea of mud; and to the noise of the heavens was added the roars of the French cannon.

Outside the breaches in the walls, long columns of silent Frenchmen shivered in the rain, as they awaited the order to advance. By midnight, the thunder ceased, the rain died away, the lights were extinguished and the cannon silenced. For two long hours, a stillness shrouded the darkened city like a winding sheet; it was broken by three separate rounds of cannon fire. As they died away, from the breaches trumpets heralded the advance, and from behind the Aurelian Wall the defenders' trumpets sounded back the alarm.

At the first trumpet note Garibaldi, in the Villa Spada, leapt up, sword in hand, and sprang for the door.

'Come on—this is the final trial!' he cried.[16]

The French troops swarmed behind the Aurelian Wall, fighting only with the bayonet and giving quarter to none. In the midst of the confused mêlée, Garibaldi was seen, his sword drawn, shouting the Hymn of Italy. When day broke, the Italians had regained part of the Wall but, in the course of the morning, under artillery- and rifle-fire, and with bayonet charges, they were driven out again and the French were able to turn all their attention to reducing the Villa Spada, in which Garibaldi and a handful of his troops were surrounded. The doors were barricaded, and from every window the defenders poured out musket and carbine-fire; but the French cannon were trained upon it and through the gaping walls cannon-balls fell thickly, shattering masonry and spreading death amongst those within. The air was filled with the acrid odour of gunpowder, the floors were slippery with blood, the whole fabric tottered and swayed.

Finally, after two hours, when the defenders' ammunition was all but exhausted, Garibaldi led a final desperate sortie outside with the sword and bayonet. *There was nowhere to place one's feet, save upon the bodies of the dead or wounded,* wrote Vecchi,[17] who was in the charge. *Garibaldi was greater than I have ever seen him, greater than anybody has ever seen him. His sword was like lightning ... The blood of a fresh adversary washed away the blood of one who had just fallen.* But the French could not be driven back and it was the defenders who had to retreat to the Villa.

A truce was arranged so that each side could gather the dead and dying. Garibaldi received an urgent message to attend the Assembly on the Capitol and, with Vecchi, he galloped across Rome. On the way, he was saddened by the news that his faithful negro servant and friend, Aguyar, had been killed.

Covered with dirt and blood, his clothes pierced by shot and bayonet-thrusts, his sword so bent that it would only go halfway into its scabbard, he appeared at the door of the Assembly. All the members rose and cheered.

'To the tribune!' they cried.

Slowly he mounted the steps.

Mazzini, with his usual lucidity, had just told the members that three courses only lay before them. They could capitulate; they could fight from barricade to barricade in the city; or they could all, government and army, move out and take to the mountains; it was on these questions that Garibaldi's advice was sought.

'All further defence is impossible,' he told the Assembly.[18]

'Errors have been made, but it is not time for recriminations. Let us leave Rome with all the armed volunteers who are willing to accompany us. *Dovunque saremo, colà sarà Roma* (Wherever we shall be, there will be Rome).' It was Mazzini's proposal as well as his, but another senator, Cernuschi, followed him to the rostrum and, with tears in his eyes, declared:

'You all know that I am as ardent a defender of our country as any. I must tell you that there remains no weapon with which we can further oppose the French. Rome and her people must resign themselves'—and here his voice broke with grief—'to occupation.' It was the view that commended itself to the Assembly. With little further discussion, they resolved:

IN THE NAME OF GOD AND THE PEOPLE

The Roman Constituent Assembly
ceases from a defence which has become
impossible and remains at its post.

The Triumvirs resigned and the Assembly voted to vest in Garibaldi supreme plenary powers as commander-in-chief of the Roman army. It was an office that he liked to fancy he possessed in later years, which entitled him to try to re-establish the republic, notwithstanding the usurpation of the lawful government by His Holiness the Pope. In all that he did, he craved for some semblance of legitimacy.

VI

On the 2nd July, the American Vice-consul sent a note to Garibaldi inviting him to call on the Minister Plenipotentiary of the United States in Rome. Before he could do so, the Minister and he met in the street, and he was told that a corvette was at his disposal at Civita Vecchia to carry him and his comrades to safety.

It was an offer that Garibaldi declined for himself, though many of the other leaders were grateful for the services of the American and British diplomatic representatives who issued large numbers of passports to those who had most cause to fear the vengeance of the Papal authorities. He had other ideas.

The Piazza of St Peter, in the heart of the Vatican, was crowded with many thousands of Romans that afternoon. Amidst the swaying crowds appeared the black feathers of Garibaldi as, mounted on horseback, he made his way with difficulty to the

Egyptian obelisk in the centre of the Piazza. When he reached it, he had twice to call for silence before calm descended on the crowd.

'I am going out of Rome. Whoever wishes to continue the war against the stranger, let him come with me. I do not offer pay or quarters or provisions; I offer hunger, cold, forced marches, battles and death. He who has the name of Italy not only on his lips but in his heart let him follow me.'[19]

There were 4,000 men who met him at six o'clock that evening by the Lateran Gate. When they marched out some two hours later, Anita rode by Garibaldi's side, her hair cropped, and clad in a man's uniform.

In the twenty-seven days that followed, Garibaldi's force was hunted all over Central Italy by the three armies of the French, the Austrians and the Spanish, consisting of more than 60,000 troops. He had hoped to raise insurrection in the provinces or to make his way to Venice to join Manin, who was still holding out against the Austrian siege; but it soon became apparent that there was little support for him in the countryside. As the journey became prolonged it was obvious that they were no more than fugitives in inhospitable territory; and the majority of his men disappeared. Yet, owing to his brilliant feints and manoeuvres, never once did the pursuing forces catch him.

But, on the 30th July, the remnants of his band, numbering less than 1,500, came to the tiny independent Republic of San Marino and were surrounded on all sides by Austrian troops. The republic was reluctant to receive them, but early the next morning the Regent was persuaded to let them in, on condition that they laid down their arms.

And Garibaldi wrote his last order of the day:

S. Marino, 31st July, 1849.

We are in the land of refuge and owe the best possible behaviour to our generous hosts. In like manner, we too merit the consideration owed to persecuted misfortune.

Soldiers, I release you from your duty to follow me. Return to your homes, but remember that Italy remains in slavery and shame.

The Roman War for the independence of Italy has ended.

At midnight, with fewer than 200, he slipped out of the gateway of San Marino. Anita was amongst them, though he had begged her to remain under the protection of the republic.

VII

In the early hours of the 3rd August, the two moles where the river enters the sea at Magnavacca were crowded with more than a hundred Austrian and Papal soldiers and most of the inhabitants from the small fishing village. They were all straining their eyes seawards over the moonlit waters to where, from time to time, came the bright flashes and rolls of cannon-fire. All knew what was happening. The previous night, at Casenatico, Garibaldi and a hundred or so of his followers had seized a dozen fishing-boats and, while the Englishman, Colonel Forbes, in white top hat, and a few other men sealed the small town with barricades and prevented all exit or entrance, they had set sail into the teeth of a storm.

All day long, the Austrian fleet had searched for them and the sounds of battle indicated that they had been discovered.

As dawn broke over the waters, the watchers on the moles saw that some of the fishing-vessels had been captured, but that three of them had escaped from their pursuers and were heading shorewards a few miles north of Magnavacca, with other vessels following hard after. At the sight, a man detached himself from the crowd and ran to where his high-wheeled gig awaited him. Furiously, he drove off northward on the road that ran alongside the sea. He was Gioacchino Bonnet, one of the principal landowners of the district and a member of an ardently liberal family; two of his brothers had fought at Rome and one had died there. Gioacchino himself had met and helped Garibaldi while he was in Ravenna waiting to sail to Venice in the November of the previous year. Some three miles north of Magnavacca, he left his gig and sent his coachman on with it to a remote farm, while he left the highway on foot and plunged over the sand-dunes to the seashore. He was just in time to see the three fishing-boats beach about half a mile farther north and a group of men dash through the surf and disappear in all directions inland. The last three to come ashore moved slowly. One of them dragged a wounded foot behind him; the other stumbled through the waters with the still figure of a woman in his arms.

'It's he! It's he!' cried Bonnet to himself, and raced along the sand in desperation to reach them before they, too, could disappear into the marshes.

He came on them as Garibaldi was struggling up the first of the sand-dunes with his burden.

'Bonnet!' he cried in surprise. Before they had time to say
more, a ragged figure appeared from amid the dunes. Bonnet
recognized him. He was a beachcomber, Battista Barillari by name,
who maintained himself by begging and scouring the shores for
débris.

'Baramoro,' said Bonnet at once,[20] addressing the man by his
nickname, 'I need you to help take my friends to that cottage over
there, while I go to attend to some other business. The lady is very
ill. She must be carried. I will follow.'

The beachcomber and Garibaldi set off with Anita. Their companion limped along behind. He was Giovanni Culiolo, more
familiarly known by his *nom-de-guerre* of Leggero. A native of
Maddalena, he had served in the Piedmontese navy for seven years
and deserted in Montevideo in 1839, and had later joined the
Italian Legion there. He had been amongst the sixty who had
returned to Italy with Garibaldi in 1848 and had been wounded
fighting as a captain of artillery in Rome. When his leader left the
city, he was in hospital with a wound in his foot; he had only left
there on the 28th July, but had managed to find Garibaldi in time
to embark with him at Casenatico.

While the four of them were making their way to the cottage,
Bonnet ran back to the three fishing boats to try and rescue
various things, including arms and documents, left in them by the
fugitives. But by now the Austrian vessels had arrived off-shore
and they opened fire on him. He ran back to the cottage empty-
handed. Fortunately, the Austrians did not land but, by now, the
whole coastal region was swarming with their troops searching
for the Red Shirts.

By the time Bonnet reached the cottage, he found Garibaldi had
changed his soaked garments for ordinary peasant attire. Without
delay, they set off to carry Anita two miles to the farm where
Bonnet had sent his carriage; it took them two hours, for they had
to move slowly and under cover, across footpaths through the
marshes. At the farm, the Casa Zanetto, while Anita rested on a
bed, Bonnet took Garibaldi on one side and urged him to abandon
all idea of making for Venice, since every Austrian and Papal
soldier would be concentrated on seeking him in that direction;
and begged him, as his only chance of survival, to leave Anita in
their care while he made his flight across Italy to Tuscany. At
first, when the suggestion was put to Anita, she was disposed to
agree to it; but, when a boat arrived to carry him away, and the

moment of parting came, her condition had gravely deteriorated and she begged her José not to leave her.

'You cannot imagine the nature or extent of her sacrifices for me . . . or the nature or extent of the tenderness with which she cherishes me. I owe her an immense debt of gratitude and love. Let her stay with me,' cried Garibaldi.[21] The boat left without him.

As the church bells were ringing out across the lagoons to summon the faithful to celebrate the Feast of the Virgin Mary, Garibaldi, Anita, and Leggero were carried away from the Casa Zanetto in another vessel. The fishermen who ferried them had not been informed who the party of three were; and, by midnight, when the realization dawned on them, they abandoned their passengers in terror on a muddy island in the middle of a lagoon; the Austrians had threatened death to any who should aid them.

Bonnet, seeking a little sleep in his own house in Comacchio, was roused in the early hours by his sister-in-law hammering at the door.

'Guichi, get up!' she cried. 'The men who had charge of them have discovered the identity of Garibaldi and have refused to go on.'

By a miracle, Bonnet was able to find them another boat and boatmen, but not before the fugitives had spent five hours marooned on the tiny island. It was eight o'clock before they were able to move Anita off. Later, on the other side of the lagoon, they found a farm cart and lifted Anita on her mattress on to it. Five hours later, they came to a hut where there were two youths. Garibaldi begged a little broth for Anita.

'We have only fish soup.'

'Can't you find her some meat broth?'

They went to a neighbouring hut and killed a hen. When the broth was ready, Anita had a violent convulsion and was unable to drink any.

As they carried her on the cart further, Anita muttered: 'José— the children!' and closed her eyes. She was in agony and, before long, became unconscious.

About seven the next morning, they came to the dairy farm belonging to the Guiccioli family, near the hamlet of Mandriole some eleven miles from Comacchio. Outside it, Garibaldi saw a man.

'Are you the owner of this house?' he asked him.

The man, a peasant named Gaspare Baldini, told him that he was not.

'Help this poor, unhappy woman,' pleaded Garibaldi. Anita was lying on the cart, her eyes shut and foaming at the mouth. Garibaldi tenderly wiped her lips with a handkerchief.

Almost at the same moment as they arrived, Doctor Nannini appeared on the scene. Later, to the Papal police he professed, for good reason, to have been there only by accident to attend the sick wife of one of the farm managers, but in fact he had been summoned by Bonnet, and came knowing full well the risk he ran. The two farm managers, brothers named Giuseppe and Stefano Ravaglia, had undertaken to shelter Garibaldi and his party.

'For God's sake, try and save this woman,' said Garibaldi to the doctor.

'We must get her to bed.'

Garibaldi, Leggero, Stefano and the doctor helped carry her on the mattress upstairs to a room at the head of the stairs. Going up the stairs she had a short convulsion. *In laying her down on the bed,* wrote Garibaldi, later,[22] *I thought I saw the death look on her face. I felt her pulse—there was no pulse.* The doctor confirmed what he feared.

Garibaldi burst into tears and dropped on his knees by the bed-side.

'No! No! She is not dead!' he sobbed deliriously.[23] 'It is only another fit. She has suffered so much, my poor Anita. She will revive, she is strong . . . She is not dead, say she is not dead. It is impossible! Look at me, Anita, speak to me, speak to me.'

Behind him, Leggero too was sobbing.

'Oh! What have I lost! What have I lost!' cried Garibaldi. 'She was so dear to me. I am indebted to her for my life.'

He broke down and all the efforts of those present to console him were of no avail.

At length, they were able to persuade him that he must flee, for the Austrians were coming. As he left the house, he begged them to give her an honourable burial. Staggering, scarcely able to walk, he was guided to the house of a poor cobbler in San' Antonio.

VIII

Six days later, a girl of fourteen, tending some cattle on the scrubby pastures on the Guiccioli estate, saw a human hand

sticking out of a heap of sand. She told her father, who called the
police. They found the hand and part of the forearm of a woman
protruding from the sand, and partially eaten by some animal. From
the sand heap they disinterred a body, clothed in a blouse of white
cambric and a purple skirt with white flowers. It was in such an
advanced state of decomposition that the hair had parted from the
head and the natural colouring and features were unrecognizable.
A hasty post-mortem was held by a doctor who accompanied the
police and he found that the body contained a foetus some six
months old. The doctor also professed to find that the eyes pro-
truded, that the tongue was between the teeth, and that the
trachea was severed; which he took to be signs that the woman
had died by strangulation. *For reasons of public health,* ran the
police report[24] *it was re-interred.* The police also concluded that the
body was that *of the wife or woman who accompanied Garibaldi and
who was reported to have landed in this district.*

Three days after that report, the same senior police officer reported to the Governor that as the result of *inquiry by the police and
information obtained by secret agents* there was no doubt that the body
was that of the woman who accompanied Garibaldi. He had also
established that she had been brought in a cart to the cottage of
the brothers Ravaglia, that she was suffering from a malignant
fever and that Doctor Nannini had been present when she died.
In spite of that, the police arrested both Stefano and Giuseppe
Ravaglia and charged them with committing, or complicity in,
murder. The facts were investigated by the *giudice processante*
and, as the result of his report of the 31st August, and the deposi-
tions of the witnesses, the brothers Ravaglia were released on the
5th September. The doctor who had originally expressed the
view that death was by strangulation retracted his opinion and
accepted the view that the severance of the trachea could have
been caused post-mortem in the course of burial or as the result of
decomposition, and that death was due to natural causes.

That was the conclusion, too, of a further inquiry held by the
President of the Tribunal of Ravenna, at the request of the
Pontifical Ministry of Justice, as expressed in his reports of the 8th
October 1849, and the 6th November 1849.[25] The facts were also
accepted by the Chancellor to the Archbishop of Ravenna.[26].

But the venom of his enemies pursued Garibaldi's Anita beyond
the grave. The story was assiduously spread that, in his desperation to escape, Garibaldi had strangled the woman he loved; and

at least one Papal newspaper in the Romagna published it at the time as being the truth. In the light of the police report, the investigating magistrate's findings, and the further inquiry by the President of the Ravenna Tribunal—all of which have been available to students for many years and all of which have long been published—no doubt of any kind can remain as to exactly how and why Anita died. It could, therefore, be only inexcusable ignorance or mendacious malice which, in the year 1960, led a Roman Catholic writer[27] to state that *an autopsy was carried out by the pontifical authorities and it was established that the woman's death was caused by strangulation.*

IX

Three weeks later, Garibaldi and Leggero entered a small inn in the remote mountain village of St Lucia, on the borders of Tuscany. They had been passed from house to house and from one loyal conspirator to another, right across the Romagna in spite of the thousands of Austrian and Papal troops that were feverishly searching for them. Others of the party that had landed north of Magnavacca had not been so fortunate. The young priest, Ugo Bassi, and a companion had been arrested; so, too, had Garibaldi's saviour, Bonnet. He, while in prison in Ravenna had been shown a copy of the newspaper, *Monitore di Bologna*, by a visiting priest and must have been cheered to read: *Bonnet, Ugo Bassi and Livraghi are to be removed to Bologna to be shot.*[28] By a piece of incredible good luck he was to escape this fate, but the prophesy of the journal was true enough about the other two; they were put to death five days after their arrest.

As Garibaldi and his comrade were served in the inn at St Lucia by a beautiful girl of eighteen they were startled to hear her say[29]:

'The Austrian and Tuscan troops are looking everywhere for you.'

'You know me?'

'You are Garibaldi.'

'Where have you seen me?'

'Don't you remember that you came through here with your volunteers in November of last year?'

While they awaited their coffee, Garibaldi fell asleep on the long table with his head on his arms. He was awakened by

E

Leggero tugging his coat-sleeve. A party of Austrian soldiers had entered the inn and sat down at the same table.

The windowless little room was illuminated only by a lantern. Garibaldi took out a cigar. As he lit it from the lantern, he carefully adjusted the light so that his face was in the shadows. Smoking silently, he heard the Austrians tell the girl that they were the advance party of a troop of 3,000 Austrians who were coming to search the district for 'the infamous Garibaldi'.

When the Austrians had finished their wine and left the inn, their hostess hastily took them to hide in a mountain hut, whence they watched the arrival of the rest of their enemies.

From St Lucia, they fled across Tuscany, sheltered and guarded by the liberals of the Grand Duchy, until at length they reached the sea at Cala Martina, opposite Elba. At the sight of the waves, Garibaldi was seized with a frenzy of joy. Like a schoolboy, he tore off his shoes and stocking and dashed into the water. A fishing-boat awaited him. It was ten o'clock on the morning of the 2nd September.

Four days later, General La Marmora, Royal Commissioner at Genoa, sent a telegram to the Minister of the Interior at Turin: *Garibaldi has arrived at Chiavari. I intend to arrest him. What ought I to do? The best thing would be to send him to America.*[30] The same day, the reply came back: *Send him to America, if he will agree . . . If he doesn't, put him under arrest.* The next day, Garibaldi was arrested and taken to Genoa where he was detained in the ducal palace. Before long, a furious mob was storming the palace, demanding his release.

The Minister of the Interior found that he had put his hand in a hornet's nest. In spite of his protests that Garibaldi had 'not been arrested, only detained' and had forfeited all rights as a citizen of Piedmont by serving under the 'foreign flag' of the Roman Republic, the minister was howled down by the deputies. A resolution was moved that declared that 'the arrest of General Garibaldi and his threatened expulsion from Piedmont are violations of the rights guaranteed by statute and of the principles of nationality'. It was passed by an overwhelming majority. Only eleven deputies voted against it.

One of the eleven was Count Camillo di Cavour.

IX

THE CINCINNATUS OF OUR AGE

❖❖❖❖❖❖❖❖❖❖

WITH THE peace treaty after the defeat of Novara not concluded and the Austrians still occupying Alessandria, only
fifty miles from Turin, Garibaldi's presence in Piedmont was an
embarrassment to the government. As the result of the resolution
of the Chamber, he had to be released at once and he could not be
forcibly expelled. The government, headed by the thin, proud
aristocrat, Massimo d'Azeglio, was therefore forced to appeal to
his generosity to remove his disturbing personality from Piedmontese territory. No doubt because d'Azeglio thought that a
little inducement might not come amiss, rather than admiration
for his services to the Roman Republic, the government offered
him a pension. It was an offer that Garibaldi refused for himself
but accepted for his mother;[1] on the 11th September 1849, he
received 2,000 francs from the same General La Marmora who
had arrested him[2] and with it sailed to Nice.

He was carried by a Piedmontese warship, commanded by a
naval officer named Persano. It was not the first time they had met.
Persano was an officer in the *Des Geneys* at the time when a re-
bellious matelot had found it expedient to flee from his national
service; nor was it the last time they were to meet.

In the few hours Garibaldi was in Nice he saw his mother, now
in her eightieth year. His two boys, Menotti and Ricciotti, clung
to his legs and little Teresa greeted him with the words:
'Mamma will have told you in Rome how good I have been.
Where is Mamma?'[3]

Garibaldi turned pale and hugged his children silently to him.

From Nice, he was carried away into exile in Tunis; but the
Bey, fearful of the wrath of the French, refused to let him land.
So he was brought back to the island of Maddalena, off the coast

of Sardinia, and, for the first time in his life, saw the adjacent
barren isle of Caprera. In turn, Gibraltar and Spain refused hospitality to the wanderer but, by November, he had found a rest-
ing-place with Giovanni Battista Carpanetti, the Piedmontese
consul in Tangier.

II

On the 30th July 1850, the *New York Tribune* announced that
the world-famous Garibaldi had arrived in New York on board the
Waterloo. By now, his recurrent rheumatism had laid him so low
that he was carried off the ship *like a piece of baggage*.[4] Avezzana, the
Minister of War in the Roman Republic, had preceded him by a
short space of time and received the honour of entertainment and
a banquet at the Astor House Hotel. The same was offered to
Garibaldi, but he politely declined, and went to live for some
weeks in the house of a compatriot in Irving Place.[5] He then
moved to Staten Island, first to the Pavilion Hotel on Richmond
Terrace and, finally, into the house of one Antonio Meucci.

Meucci had organized a sausage factory to employ Italian refugees and, when that proved unsuccessful, turned it into a candle
factory. In his memoirs, Garibaldi claimed to have worked there
making candles, and the same news was conveyed in a contemporary letter to Cuneo;[6] but his employment must have been of
brief duration for, before long, he was off on a trip to California
to try to find a ship to buy; and on the 28th April 1851, he sailed
with his old friend, Francesco Carpaneto of Genoa, to South
America.

They arrived in Lima, Peru, on the 5th October and, within ten
days, Garibaldi had been placed in command of a vessel, the
Carmen, for a voyage to China.

On his saint's day, 19th March 1852, asleep in the midst of a
tempest at sea, he had a vision which convinced him that his mother
had died. *On that day and in that hour I was assuredly bereft of her who
gave me birth*, he wrote before he learned that she had, in fact,
died. Never far away when trouble was brewing, he was on the
Whampoa reach of the Canton river that year when another
schooner was raided by Chinese Red Sash pirates, and from
the vantage point of the cross-trees of the *Carmen* he was observed
watching the battle with a professional eye.[7]

Sailing via New Zealand and Australia, Garibaldi was back in

Lima by December of that year to engage in a fracas of his own which nearly landed him in prison. At a friend's house, a French-man engaged him in argument about the battle for Rome and tempers grew heated as the Frenchman declared:

'At least you will agree the French fought like heroes?'

'I don't know,' said Garibaldi,[8] 'I never saw more than their backsides.'

Enraged, the Frenchman published a violent and abusive article under a pen-name in the *Correo de Lima*[9] and was visited at his place of business by Garibaldi, who beat him up with his cane. Garibaldi received a blow over the head from the Frenchman's assistant, and emerged, covered in blood, but leaving both of them unconscious on the floor. *Some thousands of Italians . . . came in a body to the rescue and respectfully intimated to the Police Commissioner that he was not to arrest me*[10], is Garibaldi's description of how the affair ended.

III

The year 1853 he spent sailing in the *Carmen* in American waters but, on the 11th February the following year, the vessel *Commonwealth* passed Gravesend and docked in the West Indian Dock in London with Garibaldi aboard. In London, he met Mazzini again for the first time since the fall of Rome and the two of them, with refugees from France and Hungary, were enter-tained to dinner by the United States' Consul.

During his brief stay in London, he found time to become en-gaged to a wealthy English widow, Mrs Emma Roberts, who had a town house in fashionable Arlington Street and a country place in Yorkshire; but life in her mansion, where dinner took three hours and footmen waited on him at every turn, was little to his liking. He made known his intention of returning to Piedmont.

By now, Cavour had come to power as Prime Minister and, when the news was conveyed to him by his Ambassador in London that Garibaldi intended to return, he consented—though the exile was warned that his presence would not be tolerated for a moment if he engaged in any of Mazzini's revolutionary con-spiracies.

Garibaldi returned to his children in Nice and was put in com-mand of the coastal vessel the *Salvatore*, owned by the Orlando brothers, and sailing out of Nice on coastal voyages.

But, in November 1855, his brother, Angelo, died and, with
money he inherited from his estate, Garibaldi was able to buy half
the island of Caprera and take a share, with Mrs. Roberts, in a
42-ton ship the *Emma*. In May 1856, he entered into possession of
his new domain.

On the 8th January 1857, the *Emma* was wrecked off the coast
of Sardinia; it was the end of Garibaldi, *marinaio*; henceforth, he
was Garibaldi, *agricoltore*. It also seems to have been more or less
the end of his engagement to Mrs Roberts.

To keep house for him on the island, he carried off from Nice a
fisherman's daughter, Battistina Ravello.

IV

At that time, the only communication of Maddalena with the
Continent was the pacquet boat that sailed once a month from
Genoa and called at this island *en route* for Porto Torres and
again, a few days later, on the return journey. In October, 1857,
Garibaldi sailed across in his dinghy from Caprera when the
ancient paddle steamer, *Virgilio* was seen to arrive at Maddalena.
On board the vessel he found a merchant skipper, Captain
Dodero, whom he had last met in Constantinople, and from him
learned that there was a woman author on board who wished to
make his acquaintance.

He was presented to her in the ladies' saloon in the midst of
piles of cargo and baggage. Captain Dodero introduced her as
Marie Esperance von Schwartz, who wrote under the name of
'Elpis Melena';[11] she had come in the hope of obtaining the
manuscript of his autobiography for publication in Germany.
Although only thirty-six at the time, she had already been twice
married, once widowed, and, three years before, had divorced her
second husband. On the strength of having been born in London,
she professed to be, to quote her own words,[12] *a delicate fair-haired
daughter of England*; but her father was a wealthy German banker
and when she wrote it was in that language, although she had a
good command of at least four other languages. The only portrait
of her which is extant shows her with an over-prominent forehead, deep-set eyes, bulbous nose, and hair done in ringlets which
fell over her shoulders; in subsequent years, she was scathing in
her description of other women ambient to Garibaldi. Battistina
Ravello she found *small and ugly*.[13] Since they lacked her gift of

self-expression, there is unfortunately no way of knowing whether they found anything more pleasing about her appearance.

She claimed to have been in Rome during the siege and to have seen Garibaldi then; now, as she met him for the first time, she felt she understood fully *the operation of his powerful personality upon the people*.[14] He, for his part, seemed no less impressed.

'Where are you thinking of staying?' he asked.

'I'm told by my friend here that there is an inn.'

'We shall get a couple of rooms at Ruffo's,' interposed Captain Dodero, carefully.

'You can't possibly stay at that wretched place,' said the General. 'You had better come to my house. I'm sorry I can't offer hospitality worthy of you but whatever is mine, I offer with all my heart. If you'll step into my small boat, we shall be there before sundown.'

But she cautiously refused and promised only to visit him the next day. She spent a night of acute discomfort at the inn kept by the Fazio sisters, in a room where only a cloth curtain separated her from the other guests—one of whom talked in his sleep, another snored, and a third had an asthmatic cough—while a bitch suckled her litter in the corner, and *the smell of garlic was enough to make the whole English army retreat*.[15] The next day, the sky was heavy with cloud, dense rain turned the roads into mud and the wind whipped the sea into a storm; but Garibaldi himself came in his boat for her.

'I have plenty of leisure now,' he explained, 'for at the moment I am fighting nothing but rocks and stones. Look at the consequences: my hands are those of a complete labourer, aren't they?'

She spent the day inspecting his house and land. *There is a sublimity here,* she wrote, *as if Nature had predestined for the Cincinnatus of our age a solitude in harmony with his character. Lentisk, arbutus, myrtle, heather and a multitude of aromatic shrubs grow amongst the rocks and form clusters here and there in patches of greensward, ascending more or less precipitously from the sea to the . . . house.* She was introduced to Teresa, dressed up in honour of the occasion in a spencer of white piqué and a muslin petticoat; and she had occasion to observe that *Garibaldi's relationship with Battistina was not altogether straightforward.* For several hours he and she walked amid the rocks and then, after dinner, he sailed her through mountainous waves back to Maddalena and escorted her to her landlady's door.

What transpired between them on that one day they spent

together can only be surmised from the letter he wrote a month later, when the boat made its visit again to Maddalena. By then, she had returned to her lodgings in Rome, and had sent a parcel of clothes for Teresa.

My Speranza,

How can I possibly convey to you all the gratitude and affection you deserve? If ever I have wanted to lay all that I am and have at the foot of a woman, it is certainly now. It was only natural that I should love you before ever I knew you. You were already interested in me and, in my imagination, I cherished a precious vision of you. But the reality has transported me with delight and I am really happy and proud for one moment to occupy the thoughts of so dear, so tender, so noble a woman.

The promise I made you in front of your landlady's door was rash. I can't say more in a letter but, as soon as I have the joy of seeing you again, I will tell you what holds me back. In any event, when you want to start your journey, write to me. I shall be heartbroken if I can't come with you. In future, I am proud to be yours, completely and utterly, therefore, the more use you make of me, the happier I shall be.

Teresa is delighted with the beautiful clothes. All you sent were most gratefully received and our only regret is that we could not give you the welcome here that you deserve. Accept the thanks and love of all of us. Au revoir!

I kiss your hand and am always,

Your,[16]

While Garibaldi was thus occupied, digging his island and 'fighting nothing but rocks and stones', Cavour, in his own devious way, was cultivating a soil no less inhospitable and bedding out a few plants which, he hoped, would flower in their season.

X

PRELUDE TO WAR

✦✦✦✦✦✦✦✦✦✦✦

IN THE early days of January 1854, a sixteen-year-old bride of
rare beauty was brought from her home in La Spezia to a vast
canopied gold and purple marriage bed in a palace in Turin. The
first of her seven Christian names was Virginia and she was known
familiarly as 'Nicchia'. She came from an old but minor aristocratic
family in Tuscany, and in spite of her exceptional beauty, had it
not been that she was a cousin to Cavour, she would doubtless
have lived as obscurely as she died.

When but a child, Nicchia's fame as 'the pearl of Italian beauties'
had already drifted through the great houses of London; and it
was at a ball in one of them that the man who was to become her
husband first heard her praised in terms that sent him hastening
back to his own country to seek her out. He was a wealthy
widower of twenty-eight, owner not only of the palace in Turin
but also of an ancient crenellated castle in the country. He bore the
title of the Count di Costigliole di Castiglione d'Asti, a name not
unknown to the pages of history.

Within three weeks of their marriage the young couple were
quarrelling bitterly; in little more than a month they were talking
of a separation. After the warmth and laughter of her Mediterranean home, Nicchia loathed the chilly provincialism of Turin;
her husband she never loved; and for all her beauty and intelligence, she was petulant and haughty. He, for his part, shared her
aristocratic arrogance, was querulous and liable to sudden storms of
temper which were matched only by the depths of his misery and
contrition when they had passed. He loved her and went on loving
her long after she had done everything to forfeit his respect.

It was only a few months after the wedding that her secret
diary,[1] kept by her in bad French, spoke of a scene when she was

alone with one of her husband's friends, Ambrogio Doria. The entry ended with the obscure but significant words *malgré et quand même*. . . . (in spite of and even though. . . .) Thereafter, almost every day she entered the words *Soir, venu Doria* and before long they were accompanied by cryptic letters of a code that needs little deciphering, *f—quatre fois.*

Within a year of her marriage, the youth of Piedmont sailed away to the Crimea to take part with France and England in the war against Russia. It was a war in which their country had no possible interest save that of currying favour with the great powers which were her allies and of testing out the mettle of her army on a field of battle. Her lover, who was in the army, was posted away from Turin; she consoled herself with his brother; she gave birth to a son; her husband, with a post at the Royal Court, was frequently away on missions; and as the months of 1855 dragged on, she grew more and more bored with her life. She was eighteen. Day after day, the word *l'ennui* was entered in her diary.

It ceased to appear suddenly with an unexpected visit her uncle, an intimate friend of Victor Emmanuel, paid her one day in November 1855. He stayed until late at night, asking her innumerable questions about her relationship with her husband and with Doria. A few days later, on the 16th of that month, her husband was sent to Milan on a mission for the Court. Every door in her palace was locked that night at eight o'clock; every door, that is, except a small one in the garden. Behind that she stationed a trusted servant.

Shortly afterwards there was a knock and the door was quickly opened. A man sprinted through the rain across the garden and into the house.

It was her monarch, King Victor Emmanuel.

He left three hours later.

II

The participation of Piedmont in the Crimean War not only commended the country to her allies but also, as it drew to a successful conclusion for them, gave Victor Emmanuel an excuse for visiting France and England and cultivating the acquaintance of the rulers of both countries. Nine days after his visit to La Castiglione, he left Turin and in a few days was in Paris being entertained in style by the Emperor, Napoleon III.

There he did not commend himself to all Frenchmen. One

observer (admittedly an Orleanist) wrote: *The King of Piedmont is a proper sergeant-major . . . he has the bearing and manners of one . . . his conversation is less than polite; he glories in vulgar expressions . . . and speaks without restraint of his 'affaires'. All the important women in Turin he dismisses with the words ' She's been to bed with me.'* At one dinner-party, when the name of an important family in Piedmont was mentioned, the King burst out laughing and said 'I've slept with the mother and all the daughters.'

The British Ambassador to France, Lord Cowley, was a shocked observer of this conduct and retailed details to the Foreign Secretary, Lord Clarendon, in London. The King had scandalized a very proper Frenchwoman with 'It's a good job I've discovered Paris. The Paris women no longer wear knickers (*caleçons*). A new horizon opens before me.' The pious Walewski, the French Foreign Minister, he had shocked by saying: 'You want to shoot the priests. Shoot the bloody lot of them!' The account of the King's behaviour forwarded by Lord Cowley was received in London with joy. *Pray send more,* wrote the Foreign Secretary back to his Ambassador, *the roars of laughter in the Cabinet just now about the 'caleçons' might have been heard at Westminster Bridge.*[3]

If the 'curious Royal buffoon', as Lord Cowley termed him, made a very poor impression on polite Paris society, he and Napoleon III found they had other things in common besides an interest in the Crimean War. From the royal box during a gala performance at the Opéra, Victor Emmanuel noticed a dancer in the company who appealed to him.

'How much would she cost?' he asked his host.[4]

'I don't know,' laughed the Emperor. 'Ask my Great Chamberlain.' The Great Chamberlain was asked. It was not without cause that the Orleanist writer described the officials of the Imperial household as *the gilded pimps of the Tuileries*.

'For you, Sire—she will cost five thousand francs.'

'Damn it—it's too much,' exclaimed the gallant gentleman king.

'Put it on my account,' said the Emperor kindly. As the two monarchs compared notes of their adventures, a name was mentioned amid their lecherous chuckles. It was that of Victoria, Countess di Costigliole di Castiglione d'Asti.

Victor Emmanuel went on to England where he was entertained by the Royal Court at Windsor in a rather different fashion, and where he also behaved rather differently. *He looked like a bull*, wrote Lord Clarendon to his Ambassador in Paris, *but behaved like a lamb*. There was no looking down ladies' décolletés and passing observations on what he saw as he had done in Paris; so gallant was he that he impressed Her Majesty of England as *more like a Knight or a King of the Middle Ages than anything one knows now*.[5]

By the time Victor Emmanuel got back to Turin on the 10th December, Cavour had already arranged with Nicchia Castiglione that she would go to live in Paris; and under a tutor she was busy studying a secret code in which she was to communicate with him.

Her last day in Turin was December 17th. At eleven o'clock in the morning, her husband left for Genoa to prepare the way for her arrival later. Her diary shows that Doria visited her in the afternoon and made love to her on a settee in front of the fire, and later on the floor. In the evening His Royal Majesty the King of Piedmont also visited her. Against that entry in her diary are the familiar letters *f*. *At 11 o'clock, he left*, she noted—*I went with him into the garden where he gave me . . . francs*. Whatever was the sum she received for the royal favours, she seemed to have had some scruple about leaving it recorded even in her intimate diary, for at a later date she deleted it, so that it is now completely illegible.

Her husband and her child accompanied her to Paris, travelling first to Genoa, then by ship to Marseilles and thence by coach. They arrived in Paris on 7th January 1856.

Two days later, Nicchia met Napoleon III for the first time; it was on both sides a hopeful and premeditated encounter. It took place at the house of his cousin, Princess Mathilde, whom Nicchia had known in her childhood and who was an ardent partisan of Italian unity. The 'divine Countess' set herself out to make an impression. She wore her hair piled up high at the temples and spiked with rose-tinted feathers. *She seemed*, wrote an eyewitness of this meeting, *like a marquise of olden times*.[6] The pallid Emperor with his inexpressive eyes, the colour of muddy water, stood talking to her for a short time, twisting the ends of his vast moustache, and gave no indication of his thoughts. Niccha appeared so overcome with embarrassment that she could not find anything to say.

'She's beautiful all right,' the Emperor told a friend as he left the house, 'but she seems to lack spirit.'

He does not seem to have thought the same the next time they met, two weeks later. It was at a Ball given by his cousin Prince Jerome Napoleon, popularly known as 'Plon-Plon'. Although the occasion began at nine it was midnight before Niccha could be persuaded to go. As she descended from her carriage, the guard of honour suddenly sprang to attention and presented arms. The Emperor and the Empress were leaving.

As he passed her on the staircase, the Emperor said:

'Madam, you have arrived too late.'

'Nay, Sire, it is you who leaves too early,' replied the beauty without spirit. After that, the names of Count and Countess of Castiglione were inscribed on the Lord Chamberlain's list to receive both general and special invitations to Court functions. In the absence of the Emperor that night the Countess did not waste her time; her diary shows that she spent until 2.00 a.m. talking to the Duc de Morny, half-brother of the Emperor, organizer of the *coup d'état* of 1851 and, as befitted the grandson of Talleyrand, the most powerful man in France after the Emperor.

By this time the war with Russia was virtually over. The Tzar had acknowledged his defeat and accepted the conditions laid down by the allies. The reputation of Napoleon III was at its zenith; all France believed that he had expunged the memory of Waterloo and would, with the Congress of Paris which was to make the peace, obliterate that of the Treaty of Vienna. The statesmen of Europe assembled in the French capital. Walewski presided; from London came Lord Clarendon; from Russia a thin old man who wore gold and green; from Turkey a small fat man in a fez; and there came too the odd little Count di Cavour with his wire-rimmed spectacles.

On the 19th February 1856, Nicchia recorded in her diary: *talked to Cavour on behalf of Papa*. And on the 21st February *Cavour came: we talked for two hours about Papa and decided to send him to Russia as First Secretary and give him the Cross.*

The state of Italy was not on the agenda for the conference of Paris, but Cavour was in no way deterred. On the 22nd February he wrote to a fellow minister at Turin: "*If I don't succeed it won't be for lack of zeal. I make visits, I dine out, I go everywhere, I write minutes, I intrigue at the Palais-Royal, I do everything I can . . . I have even stirred up the patriotism of the beautiful Castiglione to get on with seducing the Emperor.* And on the day the Congress opened he penned a note to another friend: *I have to advise you that I have enrolled in the diplomatic ranks the beauteous Countess of X, and have*

urged her to flirt with and, if needs be, seduce the Emperor. She began
her mission most discreetly at the concert at the Tuileries yesterday.[7]

The crafty Cavour could not have chosen a more opportune
moment. The Empress was great with child, but all was not well
between her and her spouse. Napoleon III had not thought
when he married a lovely virgin of twenty-six that one explanation of her resistance to his advances before marriage might be
frigidity. His 'English chain' as Princess Mathilde termed the
blonde Miss Howard, to whom he owed so much, and to whom
he had, after his fashion, been loyal so long, were broken for ever.
There existed a vacuum in *the heart of the heart* of Europe; the
divine Countess set about her appointed task of filling it. Before
the Congress of Paris was over, the Countess was writing of *my
Napoleon*, and she was being spurred on by notes from Cavour.
One read: *Succeed, cousin of mine, succeed by any means you like,
only succeed.*

III

The immediate objective of Cavour was to persuade the Congress of Paris to debate the Italian question. It had, of course,
nothing to do with the Crimean War but before the statesmen had
dispersed, the Emperor, to the fury of the Austrian representative,
had persuaded them to discuss 'the problem of the bad government of certain Italian States'. Cavour went back to Turin, well
satisfied. 'Within three years we shall have war,' he exclaimed
gleefully, 'the *good* war.'

The task now was to persuade the Emperor to make war on
Austria for the benefit of the House of Savoy; it was a seemingly
impossible objective, for France had nothing to gain from such a
venture, and everything to lose. Yet Napoleon was haunted by
the shadow of his great sire who had liberated Italy from foreign
domination to subject it to his own. As a young man he had been
in touch with the Carbonari or some similar secret society, and in
1830 when the Italian patriots had risen in the Romagna against
the temporal power of the Pope, he and his elder brother disappeared. Their mother found only a note he had left for her:
*Your love will understand. We have undertaken obligations and cannot
go back on them. The name we bear compels us to go to the rescue of the
suffering people that call to us.*[8] The two young men were found in
command of the rebels attacking the Papal troops besieged in

Civita Castellana, and they had carried the town before the intrigues of diplomacy removed them from their command. In that venture Napoleon's elder brother had died, and he himself had barely escaped with his life.

The hands from the past reached out to pull him towards the cause of Italy; so too, did their voices, for he had fallen under the spell of a spiritualist medium through whom he was busy communicating with the spirit of his great ancestor and his dead brother. His preoccupation with the spirits caused more amusement to the English Ambassador. According to Lord Cowley, at one séance Napoleon III had asked the medium to raise for him the spirits of the first Napoleon and Louis Phillipe. He was told they were present in the room. He protested that he could not hear or feel them. 'Wait a little,' said the medium. 'Your Majesty will feel them present shortly.' *Soon after His Majesty experienced a violent kick on a certain part of his sacred person but never ascertained which of his predecessors applied it,* wrote Lord Cowley, to the delight of the British Cabinet.

With the voices of the dead, there was the even greater, more majestic, call of Destiny. While an exile in London, penniless and living on the charity of Miss Howard, he had declared: 'It is written that ere long I shall be the Emperor of France, avenge the defeat of Waterloo and drive the Austrians out of Italy.'[9] *This little man, four and a half feet high, ugly and vulgar with huge moustaches and pigs' eyes,* as one spectator[10] described him, had by 1856 fulfilled two-thirds of his destiny. He had not lost sight of the other part. As soon as he carried out his *coup d'état,* he had through his Foreign Secretary suggested to Marshal Radowitz of Prussia: 'Our first work is to re-establish the French Empire. When that is done we shall free Italy. While we are driving the Austrians out of Lombardy, why don't you seize the opportunity to drive them out of Germany?' In February 1853 he had assured the Piedmontese ambassador: 'Don't be impatient; the time is not far off when France and Piedmont will find themselves in arms for the noble cause of Italy.'[11]

Even more persuasive were the voices of the present. Cavour was spending a large part of the Piedmontese budget corrupting the French Press; in correspondence through his Ambassador he was busy pressing his views upon the Emperor; and La Castiglione was making progress with all her talents. By June 1856, Lord Cowley was complaining that he could never secure an interview with the Emperor because he was *so much engrossed and occupied with the beauteous Castiglione;* and he informed the Cabinet that *the latter is a decided liaison,* adding a comment of which only an Englishman would think: *It will do his nerves no good.*

At a great military parade while the Emperor was reviewing his troops she leant over to Saint-Beuve and uttered two words that left that gentleman gasping, and under no illusions about her status; the first was a possessive pronoun and the second was a crude term for a part of the male body which is never even mentioned by any name in polite society.

Amidst the gilt chandeliers and crimson velvet of the French palaces moved this statuesque beauty, never deigning to dance lest she should disturb her elaborate coiffure, basking in the admiration of the men, brushing aside the slights of the women, and all the time pressing the cause of Italy on the Emperor.

Her devoted husband poured out his fortune into the pockets of the new *grands couturiers* to provide startling creations for her; and that was not all he did for his country's cause. He gave the Emperor a rare drawing of Josephine he had come across; and he published a pamphlet extolling Cavour, justifying the Piedmontese dissolution of the monasteries, and flattering Napoleon III. The cuckold proclaimed: *We are led to believe that the Emperor, whose views are so wise, has interested himself particularly in the ideas formulated by Cavour.*[12]

But in 1857, as any other adolescent might have done, La Castiglione overplayed her hand. On 26th February of that year she appeared as the Queen of Hearts at a great ball given in the Ministry of Foreign Affairs in a diaphanous gown with a gold heart dangling from her belt in a place where it was liable to be confused with other organs. The import was not lost on the Empress: 'Her heart is rather low,' she remarked coldly, as she turned away.

In June the Countess suddenly went to London, where she was entertained by her old friends Lord and Lady Holland, captivated the town in a bonnet of rice straw tied up with a big bow of yellow taffeta, consorted with the exile Orleanist pretender to the French throne, and met a man who was to remain her close friend and intermittent lover for the rest of her life. She took a long time getting back to Paris.

And then, suddenly, her reign was over. She was sent scurrying back to live in an obscure house outside Turin. She was only twenty and she could not believe what had happened to her. 'My Napoleon grew afraid and I left him,' was her explanation, but it was an improbable one. It was long before she was convinced that it was all over, but by the time she was twenty-two, she was complaining 'I have barely flitted across life's stage and yet my role is played.' It was. In the Tuileries the Empress had the pleasure of removing her portrait from the Emperor's apartments where, she said, 'undoubtedly it must have been hung by mistake'.

Nicchia was left only with a giant emerald, 'the finest in the world', which the Emperor had bought for her for 100,000 francs; and her memories. They consoled her to the end of her life. 'I made Italy,' she would claim in her old age, when she wore a dirty dressing-gown all day, had nobody except two fat and smelly dogs to love her and only a serving woman to keep her warm in bed at night. When she died, in the last year of the century, her will expressed a wish to be buried in *the nightdress of Compiègne 1857, cambric and lace.*

It was not her presumption and arrogance which led to her fall. Another pair of bright eyes had bewitched his heart; those of the wife of Count Walewski, his Foreign Minister, he of *the empty mind and the abundant abdomen.*[13] There was a hint of destiny about the affaire that attracted him as well as her beauty. It was appointed for a Bonaparte always to seduce the wife of a Walewski; the Count himself was the fruit of one such union.

With the eclipse of La Castiglione, the cause of Italy also passed out of the sunshine of the Emperor's affections. For the new favourite, although Italian born, was a devoted daughter of the Pope and, with her husband and the Empress herself, formed a clique intent on seeing that, whatever happened, the Holy Father should not lose a square inch of his ill-governed territories. It looked for a time as if all Cavour's expensive intriguing had come to nothing. But the fortunes of Italy were to be revived in an unexpected fashion.

IV

On the 11th December 1857, a waiter from a Brussels restaurant crossed the frontier into France. He produced to the Customs Officers ten half spheres of cast iron, each with numerous protruding nipples. They were, he explained, parts of a new gas invention which he had been commissioned to deliver to an Englishman in Paris, along with a horse which was in a box on the train. The parts had been cast by a Birmingham manufacturer for 'a very reasonable price'. The French customs officers thought they were of so little value that they did not bother to charge duty on them.

The gas fittings and the horse were duly delivered at a small hotel in Paris to a stocky, bearded gentleman who said that his name was Alsop, a brewer's representative. He, curiously enough, had just arrived in Paris by the same route, having crossed from London to Ostend first, and then to Brussels. With him travelled a carpet bag containing a package, about two pounds in weight, carefully wrapped in linen and old newspapers; a package that he assiduously damped with water from time to time during his journey.

During the next month, in the privacy of lodgings he had rented in Rue Monthabor, he was busy spreading out grey powder from his packet to dry by exposing it to the air; and then, dissatisfied with that method, by warming it by the fire while he stood anxiously by with a watch in one hand and a thermometer in the other. When the powder had dried in this fashion to his satisfaction, he, with three friends who had also arrived from London, began packing it tightly into the 'gas fittings'.

By the 14th January, their work was finished; at six o'clock in the evening they regaled themselves with mulled claret and went into the gas-lit streets of Paris. Each of them carried in their pocket a sphere carefully, and appropriately, wrapped in black silk.

At half-past eight that evening, the Emperor of the French arrived in his coach at the Opéra. He was preceded by a carriage containing officials of his household, followed by an escort of twenty-four lancers of the Imperial Guard. With him travelled the Empress and General Roguet. The entrance to the Opéra was thick with soldiers and police agents and a small crowd had gathered on the pavement outside to watch his arrival.

As the Royal coach turned into the canopied approach, three spheres came lobbing in rapid succession over from behind the crowd. Three explosions followed. The first bomb exploded amongst the lancers, wounding all their horses and most of the riders. The second blew the horses of the Royal carriage to pieces; the third went off right under it and riddled it with shrapnel.

The windows of the theatre were broken. The gas-jets were blown out. The canopy was splintered. The ground was covered with the wounded and the dying. The pavements ran with blood. The air was filled with the screams of men and horses.

From the imperial coach stepped the Emperor. He was unscathed. So too was his Empress. General Roguet had escaped with a slight contusion by his right ear. But one hundred and forty-eight other persons were wounded, and eight were dead or dying. A few minutes later, to the Overture to *William Tell* and the cheers of the house, their Imperial Majesties took their seats in the royal box.

The vast machinery of Napoleon's police was at once put to work to discover the culprits. In the Restaurant Broggi a young man was observed in tears and a revolver was found under a cushion when he had left. One thing led to another, one person talked and then another, and in the early hours of the morning the police called on Mr Alsop, the brewer's representative. He was in bed. The passport in the name of Alsop was in order. It was a British one, signed by Lord Palmerston; but in those days there were no photographs for such documents and the British stubbornly refused to append even a description of the holder. But Mr Alsop, too, was induced to talk; he confessed that his passport was not his, that he was an Italian national and that his true name was Orsini.

When the news of the outrage and of Orsini's arrest reached London, the Librarian of the British Museum was spending his afternoon as usual in Brooke's club.

'Is this your pal?' his fellow members asked him, pointing to the name in the papers.

'Impossible,' declared Panizzi. 'The fellow of that name I know has an appointment tomorrow to see Lord Palmerston with me.'[14]

But it was.

Felice Orsini was well known in London as one of the most respectable of Italian political refugees. His book the *Austrian Dungeons in Italy* had been published by Routledge and told the story of his daring escape from prison. It was dedicated to *THOSE GENEROUS ENGLISH HEARTS who labour unremittingly for Italy's freedom*. The Generous English Hearts had applauded the work and it had been followed by a longer book, his *Memoirs and Adventures*,[15] which had been equally well received. He had been a

Minister in Rome in 1848 and had earned respect for the tactful but firm way he had suppressed disorder in Ancona.

In the first flush of fear at the attempt at assassination, Napoleon III sent a furious *démarche* to Victor Emmanuel. It was received by him in a truculent mood, and with his usual undiplomatic language.

'What's the bastard up to now?' he stormed. 'He's a parvenu of a monarch, an upstart amongst us. He forgets what he is and what I am—the head of the first and oldest house to reign in Europe.' His reply to the Emperor was couched in more polite language but breathed the same spirit. By the time it was read to him, Napoleon had quietened down; as his wife said, he was always calm and gentle 'even when in the wrong'.[16]

'That's what I call courage,' he said to the Ambassador, 'Your King's a good fellow—I like his letter.'

The Second Empire had a genius for drama. The trial of Orsini and his fellow conspirators was staged with a panache which would have done credit to any theatre. Three hours before the show opened the Palace of Justice was besieged as if for a first night. All the seats inside were numbered and the great, the learned, and the famous, contended for tickets for each performance. After the preliminaries, the Public Prosecutor opened with a flourish of rhetoric, lauding the Emperor 'on whose life all order and all the people in Europe depend', and casting a few jibes at England, where conspiracy flourished under 'the protection of laws which are opposed to our customs, our principles, and our instincts.' Orsini himself gave evidence and moved all hearts with his plea for his country; but the real success of the whole show was his advocate, M. Jules Favre, one of the handful of Republican deputies.

His speech was in the best tradition of French rhetoric.

'I come here not to glorify Orsini, not to justify him, not to save him—not even to defend him,' he declaimed. 'I come to explain his fatal aberration, to demonstrate to you that my unhappy client is not unworthy of some feelings of pity.' He began with Orsini's father who was 'one of the glorious phalanx who fought with France, marched under the same flag and mingled their blood with ours on the battlefield of Europe.' He went on to deal with the cause of Italian unity, the territorial dominions of the Pope and appealed to Napoleon 'Nephew of the great Emperor'. 'Prince, you boast of having come from the ranks of the people.

Well then, take courage . . . Do not allow Italy to be trampled underfoot by the children of the North.' He ended with a peroration which did not leave a dry eye in the house and which so paralysed the presiding judge with emotion that he was unable to speak for minutes. The only thing his speech did not do was anything for the accused; they were all condemned to death.

The orgy of emotion spread to the palace. Napoleon had sent to defending counsel a letter Orsini had supposedly written; it was used by that advocate in his speech and it was published in the official gazette. Now the Empress begged him to reprieve all the men for, she said, she hated bloodshed. He was strongly inclined to do so. *He has evidently been impressed by Orsini's letter read at the trial in which it was said that the fate of Italy was in his hands,* reported Lord Cowley to London, and added in his usual cynical strain: *There was never a man more easily caught by flattery of that kind.* Twice before the day fixed for the execution, the Emperor had the British Ambassador to the Palace to ask his advice as to whether he could reprieve Orsini. 'It would only be construed as weakness and would have the very worst effect,' Lord Cowley advised him.

On the 13th March, Orsini was up at six o'clock and taken to Mass to receive his last communion. In the Chambre de la Toilette the hair on the back of his neck was cut, he was put into a short jacket and a hood was placed over his head. An hour later he and his fellows were on the scaffold before Madame Guillotine. It was a bitterly cold morning. The old man reading the lengthy sentence of execution was trembling with emotion and stumbled over the words. The knife fell on the victims, and their heads dropped in the basket; within a few minutes the guillotine was dismantled and taken away, the troops dispersed, the spectators went silently off to their work and, before long, snow was falling on a deserted square.

A conspirator arrested in England was acquitted by an Old Bailey jury and Napoleon's wrath turned against the hereditary enemy of France. A long and complicated quarrel with England ensued, but all was well with Piedmont. At Napoleon's suggestion, Cavour published the whole of Orsini's last letter in the official gazette of Piedmont. *This publication,* he wrote joyfully to his Ambassador in Paris, *will infuriate Austria beyond measure. It is a provocation directed straight to their address, not only on our part but on that of the Emperor.*[17]

Orsini's head had not dropped in the basket in vain. He, being

dead, yet spoke; and those were unnecessarily cynical who believed that the Emperor's revival of interest in Italian unity was
due solely to his fear that, unless he did something to fulfil the
obligations of his youth, the next attempt on his life by mis-
guided Italian patriots would be successful. Two month's after
Orsini's execution a French general started on a journey as a
tourist, for the good of his health, through Northern Italy; the
good of his health necessitated a close inspection of Austrian
fortifications in Lombardy and Venezia.

v

In the sunshine of the afternoon of the 21st July 1858, two men
sat chatting in a light open carriage as their two horses trotted
through the leafy lanes of the Vosges valley, pausing now and
then while one of them peered short-sightedly through his dark
glasses at the view and exclaimed on its beauty. To any observer
they must have appeared like a couple of wealthy gentlemen
taking a pleasant little drive on their holidays.

The one with the fringe of beard and dark glasses, who looked
like a prosperous middle-aged attorney or banker (both of which
he was) had a Piedmont passport in the name of Giuseppe Benso.
It was near enough his true name, save that he was better known
in the Chanceries of Europe as the Count di Cavour. The other,
whose beard was greying, and whose eyes were barely visible for
the bags over and under them, was the Emperor of France. *This
great man, hope of the world of which his uncle was the terror,* according to the editorial writer of *The Times,* had *the same genius for
peace that the conqueror of Austerlitz had for war.*[18] He had been
demonstrating the nature of his genius that morning in a five-hour
conference. Cavour had arrived at eleven o'clock; before the two
of them had sat down to a meal they had arranged that France and
Italy should make war on Austria the following spring. They had
already settled what was to be done when they had won the war.
Piedmont was to take all Lombardy and Venezia and the Papal
States on the Adriatic. The Pope, without Austrian support, could
speedily be deprived of his other domains and these would be
merged with Tuscany to form a Central Italian State, though they
hadn't quite decided to whom that should be given; but since the
Pope was after all the Pope, he would be left with Rome. The
Kingdom of the Two Sicilies would be left as it was, except that

perhaps the Bourbons could be pushed out and Napoleon's kinsman, Murat, installed. All the new states would form a confederation of which the Pope would be invited to be titular head.

Two other deals were done on the side. France would be ceded Nice and the Savoy for her trouble; and Victor Emmanuel's young daughter would be given in marriage to Prince Jerome Napoleon, the Emperor's cousin. That she was fifteen, and he older than her father and notoriously brutal and lecherous, was of no importance. If Cavour could sacrifice a cousin on the altar of Italian unity, the King could surely sacrifice a daughter; after all, they were both patriots.

Ten weeks of elaborate correspondence in cipher, behind the backs of all the accredited diplomats and responsible ministers, had prepared the way for this meeting; the Emperor's doctor had made the final arrangements.

Now, as the two men drove in the phaeton only one thing remained to be decided. Napoleon had insisted on two essentials: the war they were about to undertake was not to be revolutionary in character; it must on no account bear the complexion of popular uprisings of the Italians; secondly, it must not appear to be a war of aggression. Austria must be provoked into striking the first blow so that there was lawful justification to satisfy public opinion. It was finding this pretext which was causing difficulty.

Cavour first proposed that a *casus belli* might be found in some pretended breach of the Austrian-Piedmontese customs union; but Napoleon quickly vetoed that suggestion as being too trivial. Cavour then suggested that the presence of Austrian troops in Bologna might serve; but this Napoleon would not accept either. If objection could be taken to Austrian troops occupying Bologna, it could equally well be taken to French troops in Rome. *My position was becoming embarrassing*, wrote Cavour to his monarch three days later, *for I had nothing else to suggest. However, the Emperor came to my rescue and we put our heads together and went through the whole map of Italy looking for a cause of war, which was so difficult to find.*[19]

With the horses reined in, and the open map spread between them on the rug over their knees, indifferent to the warm sunshine through the leaves and the river sliding quietly through wooded banks below them, they searched the whole of the Italian peninsula for some situation which could be exploited to start the war. At length they found found what they had sought, as

Cavour told his king, *with such fervour*. Massa was the place. There had already been two Mazzinian uprisings there; a third could readily be stirred up. That hot-head Garibaldi could be let loose to invade Modena with a handful of volunteers. The King of Piedmont would send a curt note to the Duke of Modena, demanding that he maintain order. The Duke, confident of Austrian support, would inevitably send an impertinent reply. Piedmont would then enter Modena to separate the belligerents and safeguard life. The Austrians would intervene; France would come to the rescue of little Piedmont; in the eyes of all Europe, like a hero coming to the rescue of the little man attacked by the big bully; the war would be on.

It all seemed too simple, especially as set out in writing by Cavour with brilliant clarity on one sheet of paper a little later in the year; so simple and attractive that it is not surprising that almost the same scenario was produced by two other equally honourable gentlemen meeting in similar circumstances, without advisers, in Paris ninety-eight years later.

The destiny of Italy decided, and the death and mutilation of thousands of men resolved upon, the two statesmen cheerfully folded their map and drove into Plombières to their dinner.

As they dismounted from the phaeton, Napoleon was given a telegram. He read it, laughed and handed it to Cavour.

'You see how well my ministers keep me informed.'

It was a message from Walewski, his Foreign Secretary, informing the Emperor that Cavour was believed to be somewhere in France *incognito*.

XI

STRANGERS BEGONE

❖❖❖❖❖❖❖❖❖

A WEEK AFTER Cavour had so nonchalantly agreed to give away Garibaldi's home town to the French, Speranza paid her second visit to Caprera.

Throughout the winter letters had come to her from the island, some couched in rather more prosaic terms than the earlier ones. *To tell you the truth,* Garibaldi wrote in January, *I suspect that my letters are opened and I am therefore forced to write less intimately than I would like to.*[1] He did not specify whether the suspected censorship was political or domestic.

Speranza wrote back to him:

Rome, 24th January 1858.

My dearest friend,

As soon as I received yours of the 26th December . . . I wrote you . . . and not having received as yet the longed-for lines from your dear hand, I began to fear that you had not received my letter. I am even more sad because that letter contained an explanation of certain expressions in my last but one which it seemed to me you had wrongly interpreted, since you do not appear to be sufficiently convinced of my boundless affection which I have and will always have for you, from near and from afar. When I told you that I could never be anything to you my only thought was how little worthy I am of your eloquent affection; because I lack all the qualities that you would like to find in a woman. But I hope that the future will prove the sincerity of all my protestations of affection, of admiration and, I can even say, the adoration I have for you. I beg you also not to deprive me of that dear name with which you made me so happy in your first letter; I beg you to continue to call me 'My Speranza, my Hope' because I am all that and want always to be that.

The idea that you could think me able to leave you without an answer torments me more than I can say . . .

I don't dare to say more about myself since I do not know what
project calls you to Genoa . . . but it is enough that you should know that
I am with you in spirit and with all my heart wherever you may find
yourself . . .

Only discretion stops me writing more to you. My heart, my head, my
mind, and my soul is full of you, because you are so much above every
other man . . .

Don't leave me without a word of consolation . . .

Farewell, my dearest friend. Don't forget me! Above all, don't forget
the living and profound affection, which the extinction of life itself will
never quell, from her, who is with her whole heart,

Your, Your, Your,

Speranza.

A voyage to South America together was discussed; a project
was in the air for Garibaldi to be given the command of a trader
for the voyage. There was some hope of a meeting in Genoa and
in May, he wrote to thank her for a present. *I have received the*
beautiful watch engraved with my initials. How can I ever thank you
for it? . . . Your lovely gift will always rest by my heart. My Queen!
But don't think of giving me further presents. What I already possess of
you is worth more than the whole world to me. When the time drew
near for her journey, he wrote: *When you arrive on the steamer at*
Maddalena, I shall be there with the dinghy. . . . He was, and carried
her across the straits to Caprera.

Speranza found that she had been given a little room on the
ground floor. The only furniture was a small table and a single bed,
so hard that it reminded her of the beds of orthopaedic centres;
there were no curtains to the window but, as the household went
to bed with the dusk and rose with the dawn, she did not find it so
embarrassing as she feared. The counterpane on the bed was in
yellow and white, and Garibaldi joked about the appropriate thing
to do on the pontifical colours. The counterpane came, he told
her, from Anita's house, so perhaps the joke was not a new one.

The family sat down to a meal. There was the labourer Fruscianti, and Garibaldi explained his presence by saying: 'He hoes
potatoes with me, why should he not eat them with me?' There
was Teresita, his daughter; and there was the unsmiling Battistina, obviously sour to have Speranza as a guest in the house.
Speranza was embarrassed to discover that when Garibaldi paid
her any special attention at the table, the housekeeper became

even sulkier and sat sullenly, like a spectre at the feast, refusing to eat, drink or speak, until Garibaldi himself fell equally silent and uneasy.

The next morning she noticed that Garibaldi had dressed himself with particular care, and he wore his poncho slung over one shoulder. It was a surprising garment to carry at the height of a Sardinian summer but perhaps it had its uses. He took her on a tour of the island, and on the way back to the house, he suddenly said:

'Go slowly, there is something I want to say to you while we are alone.'

They stopped in the shade of a fig tree, and clasping her hands, he said to her: 'Speranza—marry me. Join your fate to mine. Become a mother to my orphan children.'

In her memoirs, Speranza professes to have given an equivocal answer, saying only that she would give the matter serious consideration; but the letter Garibaldi sent her the very day her boat sailed away from Maddalena to carry her back to the mainland at the end of her stay seems to suggest a rather more affirmative answer was given—one that she did not care to recall twenty years later. Then, on the 29th August 1858, he wrote: *How can I express all my love and gratitude? How can I respond to the manifestations of your gentle soul? I can only say again that I am the happiest man in the world. This little room from which I write is dear to me since you shared it.*

Whatever the understanding they reached under the fig tree, they wandered happily back towards the house with their arms twined round one another. Suddenly, when they were in view of the house, Garibaldi withdrew his arm.

'The women in the house have the habit of spying on everything that happens on the island through a telescope.'

There was no other woman in the house besides Teresita, his daughter, except Battistina.

II

'Next year I shall be King of Italy or else plain Monsieur de Savoie,' declared Victor Emmanuel joyfully when he heard the satisfactory arrangements that Cavour had made at Plombières; but there was a great deal to be done before the war that would achieve that desired end could be started.

There was, for one thing, a little matter of finance. The Piedmontese finances, thanks in part to Cavour's lavish subsidies to the French Press, were in poor shape. And the Rothschilds, the traditional financiers of ambitious but impecunious monarchs, asked what Cavour considered were exorbitant rates when they were approached. An attempt was made later to raise two million pounds in the City of London but failed completely. In the end Cavour was forced to go back to the Rothschilds and to perfect the new device of a war loan by public subscription—an invention which was to be gratefully taken up by other rulers as a convenient means of persuading the people to finance their own destruction.

There was trouble too about the fifteen-year-old girl, Clothilde, whose hand was to be bestowed on Prince Jerome Napoleon. The Emperor regarded that as an essential term of the contract, partly because when he himself had sought a bride from amongst the old royalties he had been so rudely snubbed, partly because he had at the back of his mind conferred the proposed new throne of Central Italy on his cousin. If Prince Jerome could be planted there, linked by marriage to the enlarged Piedmont, and a Murat in Naples, with French troops still stationed in Rome, France would dominate the entire peninsula even more effectively than Austria had. And there was also the persuasive influence exercised by a letter in the possession of Prince Jerome. It was one from the first Napoleon and seemed to indicate clearly that the second Emperor of the French, whose sole stock-in-trade was his Bonapartism, was in fact not a Bonaparte at all and no more the son of the King of Holland than was the Duc de Morny. Prince Jerome was not a man to let an ugly name like blackmail come between him and his hopes of a Royal bride and a throne. So the Emperor made it plain to Piedmont: no bride, no war.

Cavour must have thought that this was one of the more difficult parts of the package deal, for of the fourteen pages of his report that he sent to his monarch after the conversation of Plombières no less than six dealt with Prince Jerome, and they were perhaps the finest mitigation for a scoundrel ever voiced.

As it happened, Victor Emmanuel was not deterred by the disparity in ages between his daughter and Prince Jerome, or the latter's legions of mistresses, or the stories of his beating them with horse-whips; but he was the gallant gentleman King, '*a member of a house which had carried its head high for 850 years, who followed the path of honour without reproach:*' to quote himself, and he would not actually force his daughter to marry anyone against her wishes.

The child proved stubbornly unpatriotic, and ungratefully resistant to every kind of inducement and pressure. From July until the middle of September the destiny of Italy hung on her decision, while the Royal palace was filled with her sobs; but at length her father was able to convey to Cavour a verbatim quotation from the lips of 'his dear little girl'. 'I have told papa to have Prince Jerome come here and if he is not actually repulsive to me, I will marry him.' Battle could commence. The Emperor had a conversation with his cousin on the sands of Biarritz and the same night the Prince set off for Russia for a quiet little chat with the Tzar and to offer him a revision of the Black Sea terms of the Treaty of Paris if he would mobilize his forces and station them on the frontier with Austria. The Tzar was quite willing to grant his acquiescence, for the price.

At the end of September, Garibaldi, unconscious of the role allotted to him in the play then being prepared, went off to Nice to attend to what he termed in a letter to Speranza *a somewhat advantageous family event;* his cousin had died leaving a modest fortune. On the 12th October, he wrote inviting her to join him there but the letter did not reach her until he had left a fortnight later to return to Caprera. On the 25th November, he wrote from the island to tell her that the voyage to South America would probably take place *and although I shall leave Italy with a sad heart your dear company that you have promised me makes me long for the journey. We will decide in our next letter whether Teresita should come with us.*

Three weeks after that letter was sent, a Piedmontese vessel called at Maddalena specially for him. He landed at Genoa on the 19th December and spent the evening in high excitement with Nino Bixio, and other democrats. So sure was he that the moment he longed for had come that when Mercantini, the author of several patriotic songs, called in, Garibaldi said to him:

'You must write a hymn for my volunteers . . .'

At six o'clock the next morning, spruced up in a frock coat and top hat, he had a secret interview with Cavour. It was an amiable conversation and it is clear from two letters that he wrote immediately afterwards to La Farina, Cavour's secret agent, that he was let into the minister's confidence to a considerable extent. Garibaldi would be familiar with the outline of agreement made at Plombières for Mazzini had already published quite an accurate account of it in his new *Pensiero ed Azione* on the 15th November and that journal, although it purported to be published in London (and perhaps, so far as that number was concerned, actually was) circulated widely and quickly in Piedmont. Although Cavour was busy denying it to the world and assuring anxious Ambassadors that it was a wicked fabrication, he did not deny the substance of it to Garibaldi. Moreover he apparently let him in on his new scheme to provoke Austria, which in Cavour's mind had been substituted for the original plan of raising insurrection in Massa. *The idea of the minister for enrolling men from Lombardy in the forthcoming levy will have stupendous effect* was what Garibaldi wrote to La Farina. They must also have discussed whether, in the event of war, the republicans and democrats would be content to follow the standard of Piedmont, for on his return to Genoa, Garibaldi was able to give an assurance *the revolutionary elements are all with us*.

Garibaldi returned to Genoa from Turin jubilant and alive with elation. He burst into the surgery of Dr Bertani in that city, his face radiant and his voice husky with emotion.

'This time we shall do it,' he cried as he embraced the doctor. 'I have an assurance from high places. I am authorized to tell my friends to be ready. We must all be united if we are to make Italy. I count on you and your help.'[3]

Dr Bertani was a close ally of Mazzini and inclined to his view that what was envisaged was only an enlarged Piedmont and French control over the rest of Italy.

'What about the French?' he asked sceptically.

'The more there are of us—the fewer of them will be needed'.

Repeatedly Garibaldi assured him: 'We must all be united and all armed if we mean to act for ourselves. When we are all soldiers some day or other we shall be able to fight for liberty— but meanwhile let us become soldiers.'

From there he sped on to tell Nino Bixio and Giacomo Medici to get on with the task of enrolling volunteers; and the next day he sailed back to Caprera there to await a further summons, overflowing with zeal for a movement which, as he wrote to Cuneo in South America, had a grandeur *not witnessed for twenty centuries*.[4] He had not abandoned his republican principles, he believed, but his attitude was that a republic being impossible just then and the opportunity presenting itself of uniting the peninsula by means of the combination of dynastic and national forces, he could give his wholehearted support.

The enthusiasm, almost intoxication, for the cause which breathes in almost every word of his letters at this time was strangely absent from those he wrote to Speranza. She had suffered some trouble with her eyes and on Christmas Day 1858—two days after he returned to Caprera from all the exhilaration on the continent—he wrote to her: *The time for our journey to South America draws near and you must get your eyes well since you have decided to give me the pleasure of your most dear company.* Even a month later when plans were much more advanced for quite another journey, he wrote to her *I am sad to know that you are ill . . . how I long to be there to take care of you. We shall have to postpone our trip. As soon as you let me know you are fit I will give you our departure date.* Of course, there were always the people who opened his letters (he never signed those sent to her in Rome), but it is difficult to believe it was only they who were being deliberately misled.

III

On the last day of 1858, a meeting of a large number of Garibaldi's followers and those of Mazzini took place in a villa in Genoa, somewhat to the consternation of the local police. Luigi Mercantini and his wife were present and as midnight drew near, the poet rose and declaimed the verses he had written as the new Battle Hymn for Garibaldi. As the strokes were chimed by the church clocks, his wife took her seat at the paino and they all sang for the first time words which brought tears to their eyes and which, before long, were to sweep like a prairie fire across the whole country. While the pious in the churches around them were on their knees, they ushered in the New Year to the strains of:

> 'Si scopron le tombe, si levano i morti,
> I martiri nostri son tutte risorti
> Le spade nel pugno, gli allori alle chiome
> La fiamma ed il nome d'Italia sul cor.
> Veniamo ! Veniamo ! Su, o giovani schiere
> Su al vento per tutto le nostre bandiere
> Su tutti col ferro, su tutti col foco
> Su tutti col foco d'Italia nel cor,
> Va fuora d'Italia, va fuora ch'è l'ora
> Va fuora d'Italia, va fuora o stranier.

They come from the tomb, they rise from the dead,
　Our martyrs break forth to ride at our head,
　With swords in their hands and wreaths on their brows,
　They come forth triumphant our nation to rouse,
Come follow! Come follow! Youth of our land,
　And let our flag flutter from every hand,
　Come all with bright steel and with fiery darts,
Come with Italia aflame in your hearts,
　Flee from Italia, flee from us now,
　Strangers begone, this our hour.

There were four verses to it and each time the refrain swelled louder, and at the end the company burst into wild cheers, while the church bells clashed in peals for the New Year; but there was a Judas amongst them, a police spy who copied down the words hastily and sent them off to Cavour, who found them not at all to his liking, and not only because they were doggerel.

Later the same day in the gilded palace in Paris, Napoleon III received the foreign Ambassadors of all the nations. To the Austrian one, he uttered an ambiguous solemnity that sent a chill through all his hearers. 'I regret that our relations with your government are not so good as in the past; but I beg you to assure the Emperor that my personal feelings for him have not changed.' There was a significant undertone in the words that recalled others used by the first Napoleon to the British Ambassador on a similar occasion fifty-six years before; and everybody knew the outcome of that. The Austrian Ambassador sat down and wrote a nervous and lengthy despatch to his monarch. In London, the *Morning Advertiser* was able to scoop *The Times* with its report, thanks to a young man named Julius Reuter, who had just started the first news agency; and as the electric telegraph chattered that sentence into every capital in Europe, stock markets slumped and diplomats held hasty and anxious conferences.

The tension was not relieved by a sentence uttered by the King of Piedmont in opening his Parliament on the 10th January; a sentence that Napoleon III, as it happened, had written for him. 'While we respect treaties, we are not insensible to the *grido di dolore*, the cry of pain, that comes to us from so many parts of Italy.' The diplomatic dovecotes of Europe were filled with the fluttering of frightened wings, and there were solemn assurances from Paris and Turin that *they* had no intention of making war;

and the Queen of England was assured by her Conservative Foreign Minister, Lord Malmesbury, that *no war is at present contemplated by the Emperor Napoleon.*[5]

To Odo Russell, a partisan of the cause of a united Italy who was passing through Turin, Cavour was more frank. When Russell warned him that if he declared war on Austria, all Europe would be against them, Cavour blandly replied:

'But I shall force Austria to declare war on us.'

'When?'

'About the first week in May.'[6]

The perspicacious Lord Cowley was writing from Paris on January 11th to Lord Malmesbury about Napoleon: *His Majesty finds himself on the verge of war without exactly knowing how he had been brought into that dilemma . . . The internal state of Italy is indeed deplorable but will war ameliorate it? I wish I could believe that Sardinia has as much the real good of Italy at heart as she certainly has her own aggrandisement.* To which Lord Malmesbury wrote back complaining about *the little conceited mischievous state now called Sardinia,* and adding: *That Europe should be deluged with blood for the personal ambition of an Italian attorney and a tambour major, like Cavour and his master, is intolerable.*

Prince Jerome visited Turin and, being found not utterly repulsive by the dear little girl, their engagement was announced. He was hissed in the streets of Turin but the wedding took place; even though only thirty people attended the ball Cavour gave in their honour; for there were many who feared that once the child was given the cradle might follow. Jerome took his young bride back to Paris, and Lord Cowley wrote: '*When one sees this child sacrificed, for it is nothing else, to the ambition of her father and Cavour what can one think of such men? It is positively horrible to see that poor frail creature by the side of that brute (I can call him nothing else) to whom she has been immolated.* All the influence that Britain could master was marshalled to prevent the war.

At six o'clock in the morning of the 2nd March, Cavour's valet came into his room to announce:

'There is a man asking to see M. le Comte.'

'What is his name?'

'He won't give it, but he has a big stick and a big hat and he says he has an appointment with M. le Comte.'

'Ah,' said Cavour eagerly, rising to his feet. 'I know who that is. Show him in.'[7]

F

Garibaldi brought with him a copy of a *Proclamation to all Italians* which he had signed the day before. It began with the words *On the commencement of hostilities between Piedmont and Austria, rise to the call of 'Long Live Italy and Victor Emmanuel!' Out with the Austrians!*

Later that day, Cavour took him to see Victor Emmanuel and for the first time the monarch came face to face with the rebel his father had condemned to death. They were attracted to one another at once and henceforth Garibaldi was unswerving in his loyalty to the King. Before he left, he was so bold as to give a word of advice to both of them about the alliance with France. 'Be careful what you are up to. The aid of foreign armies has always to be paid for some way or other. As for the man who has promised his help—I sincerely hope that he may redeem the evil he has done in France, by assisting in the resurrection of Italy.' Cavour wisely did not find it necessary to disclose to him that the price of the foreign assistance was already on the mantelpiece, in the shape of Nice and Savoy, waiting for Napoleon to pocket in due course. He must have known that had he mentioned it, there would be no help from Garibaldi or any of his followers. Nine days after that interview Garibaldi received a commission as Major General Commandant of the Corp of Hunters of the Alps in the Royal Army of Piedmont; and this time he did not return to Caprera.

There was still no war. England pressed for mediation; Russia proposed the holding of a European congress. Napoleon III wavered. Not only was he subjected to pressure from the great powers but in his own household he was now surrounded with pious clericals who feared that any intervention in Italy would endanger the Pope's temporal power. His Foreign Minister Walewski, was against him; his favourite mistress, the Foreign Minister's wife, was against him; the Empress wrote to a friend *the role of the redeemer is the role of a fool*[8] and she was the more determined than any to prevent the adventure. The Emperor weakened, and pressed Cavour for demobilization and a Congress.

Cavour was in despair. He returned from a trip to Paris and locked himself in his room, burnt numerous papers and was found about to commit suicide. He need not have worried. The young and arrogant Emperor of Austria was determined to play the part that, unknown to him, Cavour had assigned to him. Cavour's policy of enrolling in the Piedmont forces men who had escaped from Lombardy and from Austrian conscription there, had grossly provoked him, as it was intended to do. He was determined to teach the upstart nation a lesson.

On the 23rd April the Chamber of Deputies in Piedmont voted amid scenes of enthusiasm to give full legislative and executive powers to the King; and thereupon dissolved itself. Cavour declared with emotion: 'Today I leave the last assembly of the Parliament of Piedmont. When we reassemble it will be in the Parliament of Italy.'

As he was leaving the Chamber, he was met on the steps outside by two white-coated Austrian officers who saluted him and handed over a note from their Foreign Secretary. It demanded the complete demobilization of Piedmont, even though Austria was to remain fully mobilized, and it ended with the curt words: *If within three days the Emperor, my August Master, does not receive a satisfactory answer . . . His Majesty will, with great regret, be compelled to have recourse to arms in order to secure it.*

Cavour pulled out his watch.

'It is now 5.30 p.m.,' he said. 'Come back at precisely this time on the 26th April, and you shall have your answer.'

The Austrians saluted and disappeared. Cavour rubbed his hands together gleefully. 'We have made history. . . . now for our dinner.' His dinner party that night was a gay celebration.[9]

IV

On the 18th April, the faithful Speranza was in Rome enjoying a tête-a-tête dinner with an old friend, a German doctor, in her apartment in the Palazza Lovetti, when a letter from Garibaldi was delivered. It was dated a week before from Turin, and read: *My Speranza, If you're free, I'd desperately like to see you. I'm at Via San Lazzaro 31. Always yours.* Although there was an armchair by the fireside, and a pair of slippers waiting for her friend to have a quiet nap after the dinner, she managed to get rid of him as soon as the meal had ended. She rushed round to the police, obtained her passport with some difficulty, and within a couple of hours was on her way to the coast.

It was no easy task in those days to get from Rome to Turin. First she had to get to Civita Vecchia and catch the boat to Leghorn; there she had to wait fourteen hours for another boat to

carry her to Genoa. From there the train carried her in four hours
to Turin.

She arrived in the afternoon, three days after she had set off, and
rushed straight from the station in a carriage to the address in
Via S. Lazzaro. The house was defended by Garibaldi's friends as
if it were under siege. No doubt they had reasons of their own for
not letting her see the General. She was not allowed to alight
from her carriage, and they would not even accept her card to
take to him.

'The general is fully occupied from early morning until late at
night with the King, and other personages of importance,' they
told her. She went away and found a room in the Hotel Pension
Suisse.

A few hours later she was back again at the door. This time she
was luckier. Fruscianti, whom she had met on her visits to Caprera,
heard her voice raised in angry expostulation, recognized it, and
dashed out to speak to her. He accepted her card and promised to
give it to the General.

That evening Garibaldi came to her room in the Pension. He
was full of the affairs of State. He had, he said, just seen the King.
Victor Emmanuel, he said, had greeted him with 'the heartiness
of an old comrade-in-arms'.

'If Italy doesn't shake off the foreign yoke this time, she *deserves* to be Austria's slave. War's a disgrace but if anybody
breaks into my house, it's my duty to my family to throw him
out,' he told her.

He was disposed to go on at length in the same strain but
Speranza had other things on her mind; she hadn't spent three
arduous days of travel to be treated to a lecture on heroics.

'Did you bring me here to entrust Teresa to me?' she asked
him.

'Far from it,' he replied. 'It was only my desire to see you that
made me act so indiscreetly. Ah! if only I were ten years
younger. . . .'

'And Battistina?' broke in Speranza.

'She's provided for. I left her all the money I had—about five
hundred francs. She can keep all the household on that for a long
time. And I've asked a girl from Maddalena to keep her company
in case she's lonely while I'm away.'

He did not think it necessary to tell her that Battistina was about
to give birth to his child, no doubt realizing that a little womanly

calculation would quickly reveal to her that the child was probably conceived at the very time when she was staying on the island, and he was busy making love to her, with proposals of marriage.

He rose hastily.

'I can't stay any longer,' he said. 'Don't leave until I do. I'll come to have dinner with you tomorrow at midday.'

But the next day, a Sunday, brought only a brief note from the one who was so desperate to see her: *My Speranza, the painful condition of my knee makes it impossible for me to go up and down stairs today. It upsets me very much because it robs me of the pleasure of joining you for a meal. Forgive me, and command me always. . . .*

She spent a cold and miserable day in her room without going out once, staring in despair through windows at the rain which deluged unceasingly, and at the carts rolling over the cobbles. She was embarrassed to realize that news of her presence and her standing with the General must have been flashed around the town; she was visited by some English ladies who, restrained by conscientious scruples from travelling on the Sabbath Day, were nevertheless happy on that day to apply to the General's mistress for a copy of his autograph.

All day Monday she stayed in her room without going out, waiting for him to come to her. At nine o'clock in the evening there was a noise outside like an army on the march; and then there was a knock on the door.

'Am I allowed to visit a lady at this time of night?' his voice said softly. He was in an immensely good humour.

'You don't know what risks I've run to come and see you,' he said. 'I started off on foot but go so mobbed by the crowds that I had to take a hackney coach.'

He sat down.

'I'm sorry I haven't been earlier. Today, I've not even had time to wash my face and hands. Excuse me a moment.'

He disappeared into her lavatory. When he came back she took a bottle of eau-de-Cologne and sat beside him, gently bathing his big bronze hands with it.

'Ah!' he exclaimed. 'Even my troubled life has its precious moments.'

'Have you eaten?' she asked.

'Nothing all day.' She was about to ring the bell for the waiter, when he saw a tray with the remains of her tea.

'Don't do that—I want to drink out of your cup,' he said. He sat and ate the bread and butter and drank cold tea.

She noticed that the gold watch she had given him was attached only with a piece of ribbon and she went and got her gold chain. He would not take it at first and there was a struggle in his arms as she forced it on him. He asked her to write down something to his dictation, but they found other distractions and only a sentence or two was written.

When he left her that night, he promised to come and dine with her the next day.

The following morning she went out to the post and when she got back there was a note attached to her bedroom key. *My Speranza, At one o'clock I leave for Brusasco. I am depressed at not seeing you. Write to me there. Yours from the heart . . .*

It was just after noon. She started off in a carriage to the station, but the crowd was so dense and excited that she had to abandon it and fight her way on foot. The platform was crowded with soldiers and their women, and littered with the baggage of war; she stumbled her way through and found him at last in a group of his staff near the train. He was dressed in a uniform of a major-general of the Piedmontese Army, dark blue with bands of green and with the high collar and cuffs filigreed with silver.

He embraced her and she thrust into his hands a box of sweets. The station-master placed his private room at their disposal and the two of them retreated from the crowd to the sofa there. It was some time before their whisperings were interrupted, and they had to return to the platform.

The soldiers, many of them Bersaglieri with waving plumes and Crimean decorations, boarded the train. The bands struck up, the crowd cheered, the women dabbed their eyes with handkerchiefs. Speranza gave Garibaldi a final kiss and hug and he entered his carriage. The engine snorted; a cloud of steam rose up to the glass canopy; there were cheers and more cheers; and as the train puffed slowly out a song wafted back to the platform:

'They come from the tomb, they rise from the dead
Our martyrs break forth to ride at our head.'

It was the 25th April, and there was still more than twenty-eight hours to go before the Austrian ultimatum calling for an end to mobilization expired. The men in the train were going

precisely twenty-two miles; but they were going to war, a
glorious war.

'Come follow! come follow! Youth of our land', they sang,
and as the train drew away, the listeners on the platform joined
with them in the crescendo of the refrain:

> 'Flee from Italia, flee from us now,
> Strangers begone, this is *our* hour.'

I blush to write it, recalled Garibaldi, *but it must be confessed:
with France for our ally we went to war with a light heart;* so lightheartedly indeed that up to that date he had neglected to provide
himself with either a horse or even a saddle, and Speranza went
rushing round to find a saddler who would make one for him in a
hurry.

VI

The Austrians showed no signs of obeying the injunction of the
refrain. The two officers duly reappeared for an answer on the
26th April and were politely escorted back over the border. The
next day Austria declared war on Piedmont; Cavour's earlier
prognostication had come true a week sooner. On the 29th, a vast
army behind the standard of the black double-headed eagle ram-
pant on a field of gold crossed the Ticino, while the rain poured
unceasingly on their light uniforms of white, their brass helmets
and glittering scabbards, their swinging cloaks of blue or violet
or maroon and their plumes and feathers; and an official proclamation, already printed, denouncing the invasion of Piedmont by
the wicked Austrians had to have the date on it hastily amended
in manuscript; the Austrians were two days behind Cavour's new
schedule.[10] On May 3rd France declared war on Austria and the
narrow pass over the Mont Cenis was filled with regiments of
marching infantry and troops of clinking cavalry and into Genoa
were shipped the guns which for months past had been sent from
Paris for Algeria but which, mysteriously, had never got beyond
Marseilles.

On May 12th, the Emperor Napoleon landed at Genoa. 'It is a
quarter of a century to the day since my brother expired in my arms
for the cause of Italy,' he declared, with little regard for historical
accuracy. He was joined by King Victor Emmanuel; and the two
royal knights, who had shared the favours of the beauteous Castiglione, rode off together to share the delights of the battlefield.

XII

THE FIRST VICTORY

❖❖❖❖❖❖❖❖❖

IN HIS *Proclamation to All Italians* which Garibaldi had taken to
show Cavour on the morning of 2nd March, he had outlined
his conception of the task to be undertaken by the volunteers for
whom he called. They were to be a guerrilla force to operate behind the enemy lines, *disorganising the Austrian Army, disrupting
their lines of communications by blowing up bridges, cutting telegraph
wires and burning stores.* At their interview Cavour had approved
that declaration without dissent, but he had very different ideas
of the rôle Garibaldi and his men were to play in the war.

Cavour had not set out to enrol the national hero under the
Royal Standard out of respect for his military talents; still less did
he intend to let him achieve anything which would add to his
reputation. His motives are clear from a letter he wrote at the
time: *We are co-operating with Garibaldi . . . the Government feels
assured of victory but to achieve it we must inspire and maintain
public confidence.*[1] As an unscrupulous realist, Cavour recognized
that a war conducted by Victor Emmanuel and his regular forces
would arouse little popular enthusiasm, even though it professed
to be for the liberation of Lombardy and Venezia, if it were not
supported by the man who had become to the common people
the symbol of the struggle for national unity; and there would be
even less enthusiasm for the war if the Piedmontese monarch's
only comrade-in-arms were the French despot who had suppressed
liberty in his own country and who had, only ten years before,
been the executioner of the infant Roman Republic.

The support of Garibaldi and his followers was, therefore,
essential for propaganda purposes, but in determining to secure
it, Cavour was equally determined that they should not be
allowed to make any significant contribution to the war. If

victory came it was to be that of the regular forces of the Crown and their French allies; no glory was to be added to an already too bright halo. Indeed it is not impossible that even at this stage the idea had crossed Cavour's mind—as it certainly did the following year—that a dead martyr would be so much more convenient than a live hero. The treatment meted out to the General is scarcely explicable on any other basis.

His appointment as a major-general was not gazetted in the usual way and no notification of it was published in the official journal; but news of it flashed down the peninsula, spread as much by Cavour's agents as by the radicals; and it evoked tremendous enthusiasm. The volunteers came in response to Garibaldi's call: from Lombardy and Venezia, stealing away from under the enemy's nose; from the Central States; from far distant Calabria. They arrived in Turin, however, to find that few of them were to be allowed to serve under the one to whose call they had responded. Most were induced to enrol in the regular Piedmontese forces. Garibaldi was left with a body that amounted in all to little more than 3,000 men. As he wrote in his memoirs, with understandable bitterness: *In 1859, I was kept as a flag to attract recruits . . . to summon volunteers in large numbers, but to command only a small proportion of them and those the least fit to bear arms.*

The troops entrusted to him were christened by the War Office the *Cacciatori Delle Alpi*. The bulk of them came from the middle classes, the *dottorame*, and most had never in their lives walked a mile or shot at anything more dangerous than a partridge. Mingled with them were peasants who, through malnutrition or malformation, had been rejected for service in the regular army. One thing was common to all of them: none had any military training; they were as raw a collection of raw recruits as it was possible to find. It was a body that could succeed against the experienced and seasoned Austrian troops only by enthusiasm and continued successes; under defeat, without the discipline which can sustain the trained soldier by supplanting his own reasoning faculties by training, it would have been blown away like dandelion down.

Garibaldi was allowed to choose his own officers, but there was prolonged argument about what sort of commission they should carry. The military flatly refused to let them have the royal commission. La Marmora, the officer who arrested Garibaldi in 1849, was at that time the Minister of War; the *Cacciatori* were under the immediate command of General Cialdini, who had two years to wait before he could claim a similar distinction. At the time, however, the latter was reasonably sympathetic to Garibaldi and disposed to assist him, if he could, against the machinations of Cavour and La Marmora. In the end, the officers of Garibaldi's brigade had to make do with bits of paper signed by the President of the Council of Ministers; but not until these had first been issued, withdrawn, and re-issued. Even Garibaldi's own commission was not signed personally by the King, but by Cavour.

The officers chosen by Garibaldi had little need, however, of paper distinctions. They were the distinguished amateurs of war, and the list of their names read like the roll of honour of 'forty-eight and 'forty-nine. In command of the first of the three regiments into which the brigade was divided was Cosenz, famous as the defender of Venice. Medici, who had fought in the red shirt in South America, had been through Garibaldi's previous campaign in Lombardy, and had earned world-wide renown by his defence of the Vascello during the siege of Rome, commanded the second regiment. The third was under Nicolai Ardoino, who had fought through two Spanish civil wars and the campaigns of 1848 and 1849. His second-in-command was the impetuous Nino Bixio, veteran of the barricades of Paris in the 'thirties, of Mantua, of Venice and of Rome; whose name is perpetuated to this day in the street names and monuments of a hundred Italian towns.

With these there was Sacchi, Marchetti, Ripari and numerous others who had already fought for Italy with distinction; brave, zealous, determined men who had proved their worth in the encounters of an age before warfare became conducted by generals from safe châteaux remote from enemies' lines. Their presence with Garibaldi's forces did nothing to endear him to the professionals.

In addition to the three regiments of foot into which the *Cacciatori* had been divided, there was a body of mounted scouts, some fifty in number, led by Simonetti and including in their numbers the nineteen-year-old son of the general, Menotti Garibaldi. These had all provided their own horses. There was also a company of forty-four sharpshooters, mostly gentlemen from Genoa, who provided their own rifles. The last name on the list was Stefano Canzio, destined himself to become a general and the son-in-law of Garibaldi.

Without these two companies, the *Cacciatori* would have been completely ineffective, for the Army Command were reluctant to issue either arms or equipment to a body they despised, and which in any event they never intended to allow to become more than a token, propaganda force. Such small arms as were supplied to Garibaldi's infantry were museum pieces, old smooth-bore muskets (some of them the discarded relics of Napoleon's Grand Army) of limited range and of ponderous fire-power compared to the Austrian rifles. Insufficient blankets, tunics, cartridge belts, even boots were provided. There were no horses or litters for the ambulance unit; no instruments or knapsacks for the surgeons; not even stretchers.

Garibaldi asked for a company of engineers and was refused. He asked for a small battery of mountain artillery, and could even produce a wealthy patron who was prepared to supply the guns; but he was told that there were neither artillerymen nor mules to spare. He protested to Cavour, as did both Medici and Bertani. The wild Nino Bixio even went so far as to threaten the Minister with a revival of conspiracies if the volunteer forces were restrained or tricked.

Cavour received all their complaints with diplomatic serenity. It was all, he inferred, the fault of the military who were jealous of Garibaldi's reputation. He personally would see that it was all put right. He promised that the volunteers would get modern rifles, a field battery, everything they needed.

They never did, and the brigade marched away to face the highly-trained and well-equipped Austrians with makeshift weapons. Although the military blamed the politicos and politicos the military, the real truth is to be found in what Bertani wrote at the time to the interested observer in the British Museum in London. *The government is frightened to death of Garibaldi . . . of his name, his influence. They hate to hear him acclaimed . . . they are afraid his troops will increase on the march and that his volunteer corps will gain too much glory and too much sympathy and distract attention from, and diminish the importance of, the Piedmontese Army.*[2] For this reason when the main Piedmontese force moved to take up a line on the Po between Alessandria and Casale, the *Cacciatori* were left behind at Brusasco, twenty-five miles farther west and twenty-five miles farther from the enemy.

II

When the Austrians crossed the Ticino they did so in two columns, 170,000 strong in all. Against this force, the Piedmontese army could muster only 60,000 men, and inevitably, it was some time before the French could arrive to reinforce them. Had the whitecoats pressed their advance with vigour their two columns could have swept round Turin to the Alps and the coast and effectively blocked the routes from France into Italy. Instead, once having taken Novara and Mortara, their armies became bogged down in a morass of indecision which impeded their progress even more than the quagmire into which the roads were being churned under incessant rains. The Austrians did in fact cross the Seisa on the 2nd May, and the Po on the 4th, but these were merely reconnaissances with no more strategy behind them than that of a blind man fumbling his way along a wall. Indeed, the troops who had crossed those rivers retreated as soon as they met opposition and obligingly did the work of the defenders for them by blowing up the very bridges on which the Austrian army would have to depend to advance; and that at a time when, a few miles away, engineering units of the same army were trying to improvise bridges over the rivers.

While the Austrians lollopped about in this fashion, Victor Emmanuel sat in his headquarters at San Salvatore and waited for his salvation to come from over the mountains. It seemed a long time coming, for in 1859 there was no railway over the Alps and the main body of French troops had to march through rain and snow over the Mont Cenis pass to the railhead at Susa. In spite of all the months of preparation and planning, the French were as tardy and ill-prepared for war as they were on a later occasion when they boasted of being ready to the last button of the last gaiter.

For the reason, Garibaldi was ordered to move his troops up from Brusasco to Pontestura. No sooner had he arrived there, than he received a letter from General Cialdini, a letter as remarkable in its phraseology as for the inaccuracy of its information. *The Austrians have crossed the Po in force at Caresana. They are marching on us along the left bank. They will appear at any moment in front of my bridgehead at Casale. I have no orders to give you but shall be pleased to see you arrive with your Cacciatori . . . You should make haste. . . .*[3]

III

At what he construed to be the call to battle, Garibaldi rode forth at once in high spirits with his brigade. The rain was beating down and into his saddle-bag went his silver braided *Kepi*, not to be seen again until the war was at an end, and out came his old black slouch hat and his poncho. Hours later the brigade arrived at Casale, foot-sore and sodden, to find neither the enemy they sought nor the slightest sign of Piedmontese troops. They billeted themselves as best they could. One detachment crowded into a church to dry themselves out in front of large fires on the floor, to cook their tough ration meat in camp kettles, and roar ballads which had little in common with the sounds usually heard in such places.

For four days, Garibaldi and his columns ranged miles through the countryside around Casale. He received no further communication from the general who professed to have a bridgehead in that town, and saw in that time only two enemy hussars, who fled like scared cats as soon as one volunteer fired a premature shot. The war had been on for ten days by now. Two Austrians sighted, and one shot fired, was not Garibaldi's conception of the part his volunteers should play. Ignoring the chain of command, he rode off and saw the King at his headquarters. He came away from the interview with his monarch bearing a document, so comprehensive that it was difficult for any one to countermand it.

> *San Salvatore May 8th, 1859*
>
> *General Garibaldi, who is at present engaged in checking the enemy's advance on Turin, will in due course proceed to Biella by way of Ivrea, whence he will operate from Lake Maggiore on the Austrian right flank in any way he considers advisable. I, therefore order all military and civil authorities and all municipal bodies to give him every facility for provisioning and accommodating his troops.*
>
> *General Garibaldi is authorized to command all volunteers at present at Savigliano, Acqui and elsewhere and to enrol further volunteers wherever they may present themselves if he considers he can make use of them.*
>
> *Victor Emmanuel*[4]

According to Garibaldi, the King also said to him: 'Go where you like. Do what you like. I'm sorry I can't be with you.'

It was *carte blanche*, a triumph over La Marmora, over

Cavour, over the bureaucrats who wanted to tie his hands. By the next day, the *Cacciatori* were on their way out of Casale towards Biella, wading through roads knee-deep in mud, in which their waggons sank up to the axles; and their leader was to be seen in the mire putting his shoulder to the wheels until he was as mud-stained and soaked as any of them.

Garibaldi had secured the ace of trumps but Cavour had not yet played all his cards. As soon as news of the King's order reached him, he sent for Garibaldi to attend on him in Turin. The General obeyed, but before leaving his troops he instructed Medici to see that his men reached Chivasso the next day. Medici could see no particular reason for hastening them away from where the enemy lay and protested that they were all too worn out by their recent excursions to march so far in a day. The General did not enlighten him as to his reasons, but merely said: 'Very well—let all the officers march on foot as well . . . the men will make it.' No doubt he was concerned to harden his troops by pushing them to the limits of their endurance but a more pressing reason was that, in anticipation of his interview with Cavour the next day, he wanted to get them so far on their way from the Piedmontese lines as to make it not worth recalling them.

The interview with Cavour passed off without an order of re-call. In fact, Garibaldi was received with ingratiating suaveness by Cavour who promised him all he could wish for: a well-armed mountain battery, a squadron of cavalry, modern rifles and the command of the four battalions of another body of irregulars, the *Cacciatori degli Appennini*—another 10,000 men in all. No doubt, the Minister calculated that Garibaldi would be tempted to wait to receive them before carrying out the independent campaign the King now authorized him to undertake. If so, he was mistaken. Garibaldi was adamant about pressing on to Biella with all pos-sible speed with the resources then available to him.

Garibaldi rejoined his troops the same night in Chivasso, but before they could set out the next day, he was handed a message from Cavour.

Turin, 11th May 1859

General,
I request you to set out with your brigade for San Germano. There, you will place yourself under the command of General de Sonnaz, who has received instructions to drive the Austrians from Vercelli. When

*that town has been delivered, then you may act in accordance with the
instructions given you by His Majesty.*[5]

Obediently, Garibaldi took his troops up to San Germano, only
to find that the aged General de Sonnaz had not the slightest intention of taking on the massive Austrian forces holding Vercelli
with his small Army Corps and without artillery; and that he had
neither asked for, nor wanted, Garibaldi's volunteers. With his
connivance, and that of General Cialdini, the *Cacciatori* carried
out a reconnaissance around Vercelli and exchanged a few shots
with the enemy, to keep Cavour quiet. They then retired from the
scene. Cavour's intention that they should be left to shrivel on the
vine in front of that town was thus frustrated.

By the time Vercelli was relieved, Garibaldi and his men were
halfway to Venice. In spite of that diversion, Garibaldi was in
Biella by May 17th, dining with the Bishop (whom he nearly
persuaded to take up arms and enrol as a volunteer) and the
Cacciatori were receiving a welcome from the town's people that
justified all Cavour's worst fears.

It was only nine days since Garibaldi had returned with his
piece of paper from the King and he had won his first victory of
the war; a victory no less significant for being over his own compatriots.

XIII

LIVING IN A POEM

❖◆❖◆❖◆❖◆❖◆❖

FOUR DAYS later Garibaldi led his troops out of Borgomanero.
They had stayed but a few hours in that town, where they had
been ordered by him to abandon everything except their most
indispensable equipment. He had set the example by discarding all
his personal effects except a spare shirt and a change of underclothes which he carried with him, wrapped up in a piece of old
canvas. He rode at the head of the column, puffing away quietly
at a cheroot and chatting to his officers as if they were on the most
commonplace of route marches.

By seven o'clock that evening they breasted a hill and through
the trees saw below them Lake Maggiore shimmering like a trout
on grass. A great shout of elation went up from the troops, but it
was quickly suppressed and they were ordered to march in silence;
on the water of the lake was seen a steamer that could only be
Austrian. Half an hour later they reached the outskirts of Arona
and the column was halted while Garibaldi and a party of the
mounted scouts rode into the town.

They were gone nearly four hours and, in the absence of their
leader, as night fell the mood of the troops changed from one of
elation to sullen discontent. They had been acclaimed as heroes in
all other towns along their route and they now began to complain
to one another because the Municipio of Arona apparently had
not made similar preparation to receive them. Meanwhile, in the
town Garibaldi was busy ordering arrangements to be made for
the billeting and feeding of 3,000 men.

Just after eleven o'clock, Garibaldi rejoined his troops and they
were given the order to advance. To their surprise, they were led,
not as they expected northwards to a civic reception and supper
in Arona, but eastward towards Castelletto. They passed down

the long, shuttered street of that village, a silent muffled column, as the clock in the church tower struck midnight. At the end of the street, the column wound through the gates of a private estate and crept on quietly down a tree-lined avenue, as dark and sombre as a tomb. The shadowy outline of a large manor house stood up against the stars, and by a shrubbery a single candle guttered on the ground. The first company passed in single file through a gap in the hedge, and scrambling down a steep bank of rocks and bushes, suddenly saw a broad strip, bright as shining steel, glittering in front of them. It was the River Ticino, the dividing line between Piedmont and Austrian Lombardy; they knew then that they were destined to be the first to cross into enemy territory.

On the bank were two barges linked by ropes. No sooner were they filled by the volunteers than they swept across the swift waters and were carried away downstream to the opposite bank. An hour later the Austrian garrison of Sesto-Calende, all comfortably asleep in the barracks, were surprised and taken prisoners without a shot being fired. By daybreak the rest of the brigade was across the river, and from every house drifted the smell of fresh coffee as the inhabitants of the first town of Lombardy to be occupied by Piedmontese forces welcomed their liberators in a manner they were most likely to appreciate after their night's exertions.

The news of their arrival spread throughout the surrounding countryside. During the day, while the troops slept and rested, Garibaldi was occupied receiving messengers from all the neighbouring towns and villages, sitting in his shirt-sleeves on a bed in a room in the little inn which he had made his headquarters.

By five o'clock in the afternoon, the column was on the march again, refreshed and in high spirits. They wound along on footpaths in the evening sunshine, through a countryside green with hillocks and pastures, where haymakers in the fields ceased from their work to cheer them; through forests of chestnut trees which they made ring with their songs; beside rivers and lakes where, after the sun set over the hills, the meadows became alive with dancing fireflies, and the waters sparkled with the reflected stars. As they were beginning the long trudge up to Varese, black clouds formed, the sky was split with flashes, thunder rolled across the hills, and the rain teemed down in torrents, and the laughter and the songs died away. Tired and dispirited, they entered Varese about eleven o'clock to find the town alive with torches and banners, and bands out to greet them. A few hours before their arrival, the Sindaco of the town had summarily dismissed the few Austrian officials and had issued a proclamation calling on the citizens to receive Garibaldi's men with enthusiasm. They needed no urging. As the volunteers marched, bedraggled and soaked, through the street, young women fought to embrace them; from every balcony the tricolour fluttered; and cheers drowned the thunder, and dissipated their weariness.

Neither Cavour, nor the Austrians were inactive when they received news of Garibaldi's occupation of Varese. The Minister, who had placed every obstacle in the way of this independent venture, and who had hitherto opposed, by every stratagem his considerable ingenuity could devise, all plans to raise a revolution in Lombardy or elsewhere, now determined to further his own ends by fostering it. He sent a telegram to Garibaldi which said briefly: *Insurrection, General and Immediately*; and he dispatched post-haste a trusted aristocratic, Emilio Visconti Venosta, to act as the King's Commissioner in the administration of the territories newly occupied.

The Austrians reacted by a furious proclamation from their commander-in-chief, Field Marshal Gyulai, to the Lombards which threatened to put down vigorously any revolutionary movement and sought to command obedience by promising that: *any community which joins in the revolution or which hinders reinforcements reaching my army shall be punished with fire and the sword.* At the same time, he dispatched General Urban with a full brigade of infantry, a squadron of cavalry and a battery of guns to dislodge Garibaldi from Varese.

Arriving outside Varese in the early hours of the 26th May, Urban divided his force and sent a column of about 1,000 men round to the north of the city with instructions to attack from that direction. As the sun rose on a valley filled with mist, the rest of Urban's whitecoats advanced from the south-east across a small plain dotted with mulberry trees to find that a hastily erected barricade barred their entrance into the town. Behind it the second regiment of the *Cacciatori*, under Medici, confronted them. There was an engagement lasting some two hours, and then Medici's men charged from behind their barricade with fixed bayonets. The Austrians slowly withdrew across the plain and made a last stand some two miles down the road. As they were abandoning that position at about nine-thirty, Garibaldi rode up to his troops.

'Gentlemen,' he said 'I'm sorry you are kept without your breakfasts but you know it's not my fault . . . However, we must go on a little and see what has become of our friends. It would be ungentlemanly not to see them a little farther on their road after they came so far to visit us.'[1]

Fired with enthusiasm by their first taste of combat, the volunteers pursued farther but, after another brush with the Austrian rearguard, Garibaldi called off the pursuit and by one o'clock they made a triumphant re-entry into Varese, conscious that the applause this time was not unmerited.

II

The Austrian column detached to attack from the north had lost their way and failed to appear at all; Urban, withdrawing on to Como, was left to send a telegram to Gyulai explaining that he had been repulsed by a superior force of at least 7,000. That night two other brigades, consisting of some 6,000 men, were dispatched from Milan to his assistance.

The very promptitude with which these forces were dispatched added to his difficulties. He had considerable forces and stores in the town of Como, but the bulk of his troops were concentrated just south of that town, at Camerlata, for the sound reason that it was the railhead for the line from Milan, which did not in those days go on to Como. In the confusion of retreat, and the arrival of reinforcements, he had no time to station adequate forces on the hills around that city. Clearly he never contemplated for a moment any further advance by the *Cacciatori* that day. Had Garibaldi been a conventional general and had his troops been a conventional body, Urban would have been quite safe. As it was, in the midst of the detraining of the first brigade which had been sent to his support, his camp was thrown into a turmoil indistinguishable from panic by the news that the enemy had taken the offensive and were advancing along the *postale strada* on Camerlata. At daybreak, Garibaldi had led the whole of his *Cacciatori* out of Varese.

The illusion of an intended assault on Camerlata was maintained by one column of the volunteers under Cosenz who pressed on along the road through Olgiate; but, secretly, the rest of the brigade under Garibaldi struck off through unfrequented lanes towards a gap in the western range of hills surrounding

Como to the pass of San Fermo. Here, little more than two companies of whitecoats guarded the narrow defile. They were soon overcome, though not before the *Cacciatori* had suffered severe casualties, not a few of them caused unnecessarily by an intoxication that gave many of them an illusion of invulnerability.

Beyond the pass, through thickly wooded slopes, from tree to tree and from bush to bush, with sniping and with bayonet rushes, the brigade swept forward. *Sono nella poesia* was Bixio's description of his feelings as they cast themselves down upon the Austrians like a mountain stream. 'I am living on a poem'.

As dusk was gathering over the hills, the column reformed and Garibaldi rode to the front with his staff. Before them lay Como. Its squares were visible and filled with white-coated Austrians. Slowly, through the gathering darkness, in taut silence, they descended the road, expecting every minute to be met with a hail of bullets. It was completely dark by the time they reached the outskirts of the town, and it seemed as if they were deserted. The villas were shuttered, no light shone even through the crevices, the streets were empty. Suddenly, as the column approached, lights flared in the windows. *It was like the explosion of a mine,* wrote one observer, *in a flash the town lit up, windows became crowded with people, the streets blocked.*[2] Men with flaming torches met them at the gateway of the city; from every church tower the bells led the cheers; and amid shouts of 'Viva' Garibaldi rode into a city from which the Austrians had fled but an hour before.

So precipitous had been the Austrians' departure, that in the telegraph office their last messages were still on the tables. Garibaldi had great fun sending off telegrams to Varese and elsewhere calling on fictitious reinforcements, in the certain knowledge that they would be intercepted by the enemy and create the impression that he was but the van of a vast army.

The stratagem apparently worked. Urban, with three times as many men as Garibaldi, and an incomparable superiority in equipment, pulled out of Camerlata in such haste that he abandoned to the audacious victor an immense stock of arms, ammunition, foodstuffs and even money. For this, and for failing to garrison adequately the hills around Como he has been criticized by historians;[3] but unjustly. The geniuses of war have always been the quasi-amateurs like Caesar and Cromwell, partly because no man of intelligence willingly devotes the whole of his life to soldiering, but more because the amateurs are not blinded by the blinkers of training. Had Garibaldi stopped to make a 'correct' appreciation of the enemy position he would never have advanced that day without artillery or cavalry on Como. To the strictly professional mind of Urban it was inconceivable that his opponent should engage in such reckless folly, for none knew better than he that the successful defence of Varese was due mainly to the failure of the detached column to create the necessary diversion at the crucial moment. Even if he believed his own telegram about the strength of the forces opposite to him, he credited Garibaldi with the intelligence to recognize that it was a stroke of luck for the defenders that was unlikely to be repeated. In that he was right, for throughout the defence of Varese, Garibaldi had been greatly worried about the flying column. What Urban, as a professional, could not anticipate was that Garibaldi would react to this good fortune in the spirit of a gambler who, when the cards are playing his way, stakes his all on them. There is nothing about that in the textbooks on strategy.

III

Urban had gone, but he would return, Garibaldi knew. In one day he hastily reorganized the municipal authority of Como, enrolled a local guard, and leaving behind a small detachment, he set off with the weary but elated *Cacciatori* to return the way he had come. By the evening of the 29th May, he was back in Varese and writing a report to Cavour of their achievements. To his troops he announced that the purpose of their journey was to secure a battery of mountain guns which had been despatched from Turin, but the real purpose was to secure his lines of communication.

On Lake Maggiore, on a fortified hillock overlooking a sheltered bay lay the town of Laverno, still firmly in Austrian hands. So long as the Austrians held it they menaced his rear, for the bay sheltered two armed vessels which effectively controlled not only the waters of the lake but the upper reaches of the Ticino. From that position they could prevent the crossing of reinforcements to Lombardy. It was essential that Laverno be taken and the passage of the waters of the Maggiore and the Ticino be freed for Piedmontese forces.

Just before midnight on 30th May, Garibaldi appeared in front of the town. In spite of the object lesson provided by Urban's recent failure at Varese, Garibaldi adopted exactly the same tactics.

One party under Landi was detailed for a frontal assault on the fortress, while another column under Bronzetti was sent to out-flank it and create a diversion at the crucial moment. Although the town was held by only 580 Austrians and his forces greatly outnumbered them, Garibaldi's stratagem failed like Urban's; and for the same reason: the diversionary column lost their way in the dark and failed to arrive. The frontal assault on the fortress was bitter and bloody. The enemy artillery was silenced, but at great cost; some of the volunteers reached their objective by climbing up the loopholes on the walls only to topple over the castella-tions into the arms of death.

As day was breaking, Landi came to report to Garibaldi that they had been repulsed. The General was furious. 'It's not true,' he shouted,[4] 'Bronzetti must be in the fort. I bet my head Bron-zetti is master of the Castle. You blasted cowards.'

'General,' said Landi quietly, 'I am wounded.'

'Get out of my sight.'

With that he rode off.

A ragged and dispirited retreat of beaten men began walking towards Varese. Later that morning there was other news to de-press their spirits. Urban had appeared before Varese with three brigades; the inhabitants had fled to the mountains, and their de-serted homes were being subjected to an artillery bombardment in punishment for their rebellion.

As Garibaldi rode along in silence he saw the gravely wounded Landi, in convulsions, being carried on a cart.

'I was in the wrong this morning,' was all he could find to say to him.

To the west lay the guarded waters of Maggiore; to the south and east lay Urban with ten thousand men, straddling the road to Como and surrounding Varese; to the north were the mountains and Switzerland. The *Cacciatori* were trapped. So serious was the position that there were those on Garibaldi's staff who advocated flight over the mountains to internment in Switzerland. The alternative seemed certain annihilation. But Garibaldi told them: 'There are a hundred and one things to do before we think of fleeing Lombardy soil.'

The day and night they spent bivouacking out on the slopes of the mountain overlooking Varese, mingling with the despondent inhabitants of that town and sharing their misery as they watched the smoke from their burning homes.

It was against this background of gloom that Garibaldi was struck, as he put it, *as if by a vision*. He was on the high road near Robarello with his staff when there appeared coming from the east, a light carriage driven by a young girl. She was accompanied by a priest.

'The enemy have some charming spies,' remarked one of his staff, cynically. Garibaldi was no less impressed by her beauty. *At the first sight of this dear creature . . . her features were indelibly engraved upon my heart,*[5] he confessed in a fragment of autobiography apparently written before he had cause to realize that even the devil may appear as an angel of light.

The girl was no spy, she explained, but the seventeen-year-old daughter of a true Italian patriot, the Marchese Raimondi, who lived in a villa at Fino near Como. She had driven to Garibaldi through the Austrian lines with a message from Count Visconti Venosta begging Garibaldi to return to Como speedily, because the Austrians were surrounding the town and about to attack. The General was as impressed by her heroism as by her beauty.

He retired with her into a village inn beside the road and scribbled a note to Visconti. *I am in front of the enemy at Varese,* he wrote, *and intend to attack him this evening. Send those who are afraid out of the city and let the sturdy population sound the Tocsin . . . and resist to the uttermost.*[6]

The girl and the priest departed.

It is doubtful whether Garibaldi had ever any intention of taking on Urban's vastly superior forces with his own mauled and downcast companies. It may even be that he entertained some slight suspicion that the girl was not to be trusted.

There was no attack that night on Varese. When day dawned the *Cacciatori*, every one of them, had vanished from the mountains above the town. During the hours of darkness, in a single file so extended that all contact was lost between the head and the tail, the column, like a long grey snake, had wriggled its way along footpaths through the Austrian lines into Como.

IV

The Legion spent six days in Como. For the first time in a month, they were able to rest, to sit around in cafés drinking coffee, to write letters; some even found time to attend services in the cathedral.

Garibaldi established his headquarters in the lakeside inn known as L'Angelo. It was here that he was visited by a party of English who, confident that *English people and madmen might go anywhere,* drove over from Lugano on *a beautiful road, worthy of England,* to gratify their curiosity by inspecting the illustrious *guerrilla leader.* They found him *a man . . . of barely five feet seven or eight, broad shouldered and deep chested, with . . . the complexion of a healthy Englishman, beard and hair of chestnut brown, bordering on reddish blonde, cut short and slightly grizzled. He had the bearing of a real gentleman. He used little of the gestures of the Southerner and it was only when we were talking of the sympathy of the English people for Italy that his calmness, which is almost British, left him.* They observed that: *whilst he was telling the ladies the story of his travels in China and Australia, as complacently and amiably as if he had been in a London drawing-room . . . he could hear the Austrian reinforcements firing on his outposts by the railway line.*[7]

Satisfied that Garibaldi was as near an Englishman as any member of a lesser race dare aspire to be, they sent a satisfactory report of him to a London newspaper. It is sad that Garibaldi left unrecorded what it felt like to be patronized by these battlefield gapers, but it is more than likely that his mind was elsewhere while he talked to them. Not only were the Austrian reinforcements engaging his advance posts, there was also, to occupy his thoughts, the vision of charm that had surprised him on the road near Robarello.

The Marchesina had reappeared, bearing with her invitations from her father to visit their villa and to spend a night fishing on the lake; and thereafter she visited him frequently. On the fifth night, in the waterside garden of the inn, before a still lake gleaming like a pool of mercury, he had her to himself. Oblivious of his fifty-two years and his arthritis; oblivious of such claims as Battistina and her month-old baby, or the faithful Speranza might have on him, he went down on his knees before the girl of seventeen, kissed her hand and exclaimed: 'Oh! that I might belong to you in some way.'

These words seemed to me not to have achieved their purpose and I almost despaired of inspiring in her what I felt in my heart,[8] he confessed to paper.

V

In their six days in Como, the position of the *Cacciatori* was been transformed. No longer were they the hunted prey, pinned down in a corner of the copse, surrounded on three sides by enemy and with no way of escape save northward to humiliating internment.

On the 4th June, the French Emperor had stumbled on his enemy at Magenta. All through a sunlit day the battle had raged along the line of the railway embankment, unpleasantly close to the Imperial Person and with his generals fighting with swords in the village street like common infantry officers. When it was done and the battlefield left like a rag fair, covered in shakoes, knapsacks, muskets and cloaks, all scattered and soaked in blood; and the brave fools of each side had been carried off with their entrails dangling out, the Emperor was white-faced and shaken. But the Austrians, too, had had enough and began a retreat towards their impregnable redoubt, the Quadrilateral, formed by their fortress towns of Verona, Mantova, Pescheira and Legnago; so, a great victory for the French could be proclaimed throughout the world, to give its name to a newly discovered colour, and to inspire the ecstatic Mrs Browning to declaim verses that began: *Shout for France and Savoy*, and ended with the euphonious, but unprophetic, refrain: *Emperor, Evermore!*

As a result of Magenta, Field Marshal Lieutenant Count Urban received orders to withdraw from the pursuit of his elusive foe, who was not slow to realize the significance of the victory. On the 6th June, the brigade moved eastward, voyaging up Lake Como in two captured steamers to the cheers of excited peasantry on the banks, round the peninsula, and down the other arm of the Lake to Lecco.

By now the progress of the *Cacciatori* had become less like the advance of an army than the advent of a new prophet. As Garibaldi passed through the villages on the road to Bergamo, women brought their children to him to be blessed, and even baptized. Crowds thronged on him for the privilege of touching the hem of his cloak as he rode past. There were even those who claimed that miracles were wrought, that the blind saw, the lame walked. Time and again he was forced to stop and address the people. 'Come, follow!' was his call. 'I promise you weariness, hardship and suffering. We will conquer or die.'

In tears, womenfolk embraced their men and thrust them into the ranks. *You would not have said that he was a general but the head of a new religion . . . It was delirium*[9] recalled a Royal Commissioner, rather sourly. These phenomena were not unnoticed by the cynical gentry whose talents were usually devoted to making profits out of more conventional religious imagery; not long after Italy was flooded with pictures of Garibaldi as Christus, his hand raised in blessing; and his devotees could obtain their matches in boxes decorated with his Sacred Heart.

At the news of Garibaldi's approach, the Austrians in Bergamo hastily spiked their guns, abandoned them, and fled the city, leaving behind them all their stores and ammunition. His entry into Bergamo must have recalled to the pious another entry into a city; flowers were strewn on his path and showered from balconies as the townspeople, intoxicated with emotion, gave themselves over to welcoming the conqueror. While this was happening two and a half miles beyond the city at Seriate, the Austrians, pressed by an advance guard of the *Cacciatori*, had turned on their pursuers and cornered them in a wheatfield under the shell-fire of two batteries and in a ring of cavalry and infantry. Against a hail of grapeshot, the *Cacciatori*, using the bayonet and nothing but the bayonet, captured both batteries, defeated a cavalry charge, and advanced on the infantry. At a crucial point of the battle, when it seemed that they must retire, the *Cacciatori* saw a famous figure on horseback in their midst with upraised sword, crying as he charged with them: 'What, soldiers, is the regiment going to take flight?' They could not have been more inspired if he had come to them walking on the water. It was the Austrians who fled.

The same day, Garibaldi received instructions to attend on King Victor Emmanuel in Milan. The French Emperor had already made a triumphant entry into that city. Still chasing the shadows of the past, he had lodged himself in the Villa Bonaparte where the first Napoleon had stayed. King Victor Emmanuel had been permitted to accompany him into Milan.

Garibaldi was received by his King the next day and decorated with the Gold Medal for valour, the highest military decoration that Piedmont could offer. Various officers and men of the *Cacciatori* received other decorations, distributed without consultation with their leader and in a manner most calculated to cause the maximum discontent among his troops.

The date was the 9th June. His order of the day for the 10th is dated from Como.[10] It is difficult to know what occasion he had for visiting that city while the brigade were still in Bergamo. It was scarcely necessary to go that far north to avoid the Austrians; but perhaps he wanted to show a certain young lady a medal just received from the hand of a monarch.

VI

On the night of the 12th the *Cacciatori* moved out of Bergamo and struck south in the direction of Romano; from there they turned north again and the next day entered Brescia. The direct route between the two cities is some thirty-six miles but strong Austrian forces barred their way. In all the brigade must have marched nearer sixty miles, to appear at the Austrians' rear and to take a city that they, confident it was secure, had left ungarrisoned. It was on this march that there occurred an incident that received exaggerated praise, not least of all from Garibaldi himself. In the darkness he suddenly reined in his horse and listened. His staff not unnaturally thought he was alert for sounds of the enemy; but it was the song of a nightingale on the hillside that had entranced him. The incident was taken to indicate that under the soldier's tunic lurked a poet's heart.

Brescia received the brigade with the accustomed fervour, but here was delivered to him the first of the pills which had been carefully sugared in Milan. Garibaldi was deprived of independent command, and ordered in future to be subject to orders from Supreme Headquarters. The first of such instructions was to attack the enemy at Lonato, a task that he would never have dreamt of undertaking on his own initiative, since it represented a frontal assault on the main enemy army. He was promised artillery and cavalry support, which failed to materialize, and he was enraged by finding that in an engagement at Tre Ponti his men not only suffered heavy casualties in an encounter with an equivalent force of Austrians but that they fled from the battlefield in disorder. To the end of his days, he believed that the instructions had been given for no other purpose than to discredit and destroy his forces and his reputation; *the promise* (of reinforcements) *was deliberately broken to get rid of a man who had it in his power to become dangerous; it was a plot to compass the ruin of a handful of men,* he wrote. In that, he perhaps under-rated the stupidity of headquarters, and attributed to them not only malice, which no doubt existed, but also intelligence equal to his own.

The second pill was delivered. Garibaldi and the *Cacciatori* on June 20th were ordered to abandon their positions and occupy the Val Telline up to the foot of the Stelvio pass; so far as the war was concerned, they might just as well have been sent to Timbuctoo. Although various improbable reasons were subsequently advanced for this decision[11], the order cannot be ascribed to anything except the jealousy and hostility of the military, and the equally strong conviction of Cavour that Garibaldi had been far too successful. It arrived at a moment when Garibaldi, his forces enlarged to 12,000 men by volunteers, had taken Salo on Lake Garda and was planning to sail up those waters and launch a drive down from Riva towards Venice; a plan which if carried out with the daring and imagination of the rest of his campaign might have been a decisive factor in the war and might have won for Piedmont the whole of Venezia as well as Lombardy. He obeyed, but with sorrow and bitterness, and showed no interest in his subsequent movements up to the end of the war; nor has history. For him the war ended in Salo. It was even more galling because it was exactly what Mazzini had prophesied before ever it started. On 23rd January 1859, Mazzini had written to Garibaldi counselling him against participation and warning him: *You will be shut up in some corner of the Tyrol or the Val Telline, while the French Emperor does what he wants despotically without any possible intervention on your part.*

VII

It was a disappointed and disgruntled man that sailed from Como two days after his fifty-second birthday to rejoin his troops in the Val Trentino. The Marchese Raimondi and his beautiful daughter came to see him off at the quayside. *There was Giuseppina more bewitching than ever,* Garibaldi noted. *I looked furtively at her from the ship after I had said 'Goodbye' to them and decided that I must dismiss from my thoughts a woman who gave little or no sign of responding to the fire she had kindled in me . . . the boat drew away from the quay and I resolved that I must force myself to forget for ever the beautiful daughter of the Lake.*

It was, perhaps, to assist him in that resolution that the same day he wrote to Speranza the first letter since he had parted from her on the railway platform in Turin.

6th July 1859

My Speranza,

You are always good, always my dearest one. Your letters are the reflection of your angelic soul. And I am always slow and keep you waiting so long without writing. Love of my heart, take care of your health and when you are better, remember that I need to see and be near you, even if it is not possible at the moment . . . Write to me,

Always your,

G.G.

Battistina, nursing her six-week-old daughter in the lonely house on Caprera, does not appear to have been equally favoured.

VIII

The French Emperor continued to do what he wanted, despotically. On June 24th, his army had collided again with the Austrians at Solferino in a battle that lasted from four o'clock in the morning until eight o'clock at night. After it he telegraphed to Paris: *Grande Bataille, Grande Victoire*. Never did his official journal in Paris, the *Moniteur*, live up to its nickname of the *Menteur* more than on that occasion. According to that journal, casualties in the battle on the Allied side amounted to no more than 250. The truth was rather different. Hospitals in Brescia alone received 17,345 French wounded and 13,959 Italian, and nobody numbered the dead but they were something like 18,000.

The night after the battle, Napoleon III spent in the room occupied the night before by Franz Joseph and the Austrians had retreated nearer the Quadrilateral; but for all his *grande victoire* Napoleon was not happy. He had learned that martial glory, so wonderfully exhilarating in Paris, when drums were sounding and banners flying, and the horses trotted by obediently with plumes tossing in the wind, bore a different aspect on the battlefield; and that the bowels of an Emperor were no more immune than those of a common soldier from the bacteria which was sweeping through his troops. From Paris, the Empress and the pro-Papal Court were warning him of the danger of Prussia invading France while the French Army was in Italy: before him lay the redoubtable bastions of the Quadrilateral. On 3rd July, he learnt that the Diet of Frankfurt had accepted a Prussian proposal for a concentration of German troops along the Rhine. On the

7th he staggered the world with an announcement that *A suspension of arms had been decided on between the Austrian Emperor and myself.* The world's stock markets rose.

The two Emperors met in a house at Villafranca four days later and, while Napoleon III nervously plucked the petals from the roses in a vase on the table, peace was made. Lombardy was ceded to France, who graciously passed it over to Piedmont. Venezia was to remain Austrian. The rulers of the Central Italian states were to be restored. Italy could become a confederation of States under the presidency of the Pope.

The French Emperor left Milan the next day. He was escorted to the railhead at Susa by Victor Emmanuel, who had been informed, but not consulted, about the terms of the peace. They passed through Turin. The houses were shrouded in black crêpe and some rude shopkeepers were openly displaying portraits of Orsini. As the coaches of the French Emperor and his staff rolled out of the station at Susa towards the Mount Cenis pass, Victor Emmanuel muttered some very vulgar words in his peasant patois, which are best translated politely as 'Good riddance'.

Cavour was for continuing the war without French assistance but Victor Emmanuel would not hear of such folly. There was a furious interview between them, with each man hurling abuse at the other like a fish-wife. Count Cavour, *his face as red as a furnace*[12] was dismissed from office and the royal presence with the remark that he was 'no better than a guttersnipe'. There had never been much affection or respect between them and earlier in the year, Victor Emmanuel had written to his son-in-law (after various derogatory remarks about Cavour): *Luckily I am the master here. I am a king who governs in fact as well as in name.*

Garibaldi viewed the making of the peace more dispassionately than either of them. Having never held high hopes of the French alliance, he was not disappointed. Napoleon, he told his friends 'had a straw tail that anybody could set fire to'. He was disposed to be more generous to the French than some of his compatriots. *Let us not forget the gratitude we owe to Napoleon and the heroic French nation, so many of whose brave sons, for the cause of Italy, are now dead or lie gravely wounded on a bed of pain,* he wrote to his troops.

He could afford to be generous. Of all the principal characters in the struggle, he alone emerged with greatly enhanced reputation; a reputation no less effective for being greater than his achievements justified. Insignificant though his contributions had been to the war of 1859, without it there could have been no triumph in 1860.

Crippled with arthritis as the result of his exposure in the field, Garibaldi retired to his own bed of pain in Lovere, to read Caesar's Commentaries and to receive a shower of unpaid bills. Among them was a pressing one from his tailor, with a barely polite note demanding payment within seven days; the garment to which it related was the uniform of a general.

The newly liberated population of Lombardy found that they too had bills to pay for freedom in the form of higher prices as inflation, the inevitable camp follower of war, roared through the land; increased taxation; conscription; the imposition of an alien form of Italian language with letters in it unknown to them before; a swarm of Piedmontese officials in all the best jobs; and their aristocratic landlords returned from the overcrowded but safe comfort of the hotels of Lugano.

But such is the force of nationalist sentiment that the people of Lombardy were the envy of the rest of the peninsula.

XIV

A FOXY POLICY

◆◆◆◆◆◆◆◆◆◆

WHILE GARIBALDI was recuperating at Lovere, he received an invitation from Baron Bettino Ricasoli who was then in control in Tuscany.

During the preoccupations of the Austrians with the war in Lombardy, the populations of the Central Italian States had seized the opportunity of dispensing with their rulers, whose despotisms rested on nothing more substantial than Austrian bayonets. On the very outbreak of the war Tuscany had expelled, in a most gentlemanly manner, its own stupid old Grand Duke who was too closely related to and associated with the Austrian royal house to be tolerated longer, even though his own absolute rule was paternalistic and free from the grosser cruelties of Bomba or the Papacy. Baron Ricasoli had found himself charged by a Constituent Assembly with maintaining order until such a time as the ambitions of the inhabitants for union with Piedmont could be realized.

After the battle of Magenta, the Austrian troops had also withdrawn from Modena and with them fled Duke Francis, taking with him the public treasury and the valuable State collection of rare books and antique coins. He, apparently, had no doubt how he was regarded by his subjects and upon what foundations his throne rested. The Cardinal Legate in Bologna seemed to know also how he was regarded by the Pope's subjects, for he too fled with the Austrian Army. Uprisings in Umbria, the Marches and the Romagna followed his departure.

The rebellions in Umbria and the Marches had been suppressed by the Vicar of Jesus Christ with a barbarity worthy of the Goths. At Perugia on June 20th, the Swiss mercenaries of His Holiness had perpetrated a particularly bloody massacre after they had killed a man coming to parley under a white flag, and treacherous

friars had let them into a city through a secret door of a monastery.[1] But in spite of their efforts, the Papal army did not succeed
in the re-conquest of the Romagna and both there and in Modena,
as in Tuscany, Piedmontese commissioners had taken over power
at the behest of constituent assemblies, to await the day when those
provinces could be joined to Piedmont.

By the Treaty of Villafranca, however, Tuscany, Modena and
the Romagna were to be restored to their former rulers—a provision which had led Victor Emmanuel to sign the treaty with the
proviso, *pour ce qui me concerne*; a qualification which he considered
absolved him from any obligation to see this clause implemented.
He felt obliged, however, to remove from the three Piedmontese
commissioners their titles as such, although all three remained in
office. Wisely, the three newly independent states did not unite,
for fear that an empty throne in Central Italy might inspire
Napoleon with the ambition to plant Plon-Plon on it; an idea
that he had entertained as early as the conversations at Plombières. They had, however, formed a united army to defend their
independence if necessary.

It was command of this force that Garibaldi was now invited to
take.

It was unlikely that Austria would be in a position to enforce
these terms of the treaty of Villafranca, for, as the United States
Minister at Turin accurately observed to his government: *The
battles of last summer have prostrated Austria. All pride and spirit was
then taken from her. She rests an inert mass on the bank while the river
of Italian revolution runs a straight and now unresisted course.*[2] It was
equally unlikely that the other signatory, the Emperor Napoleon,
would seek to enforce them by force of arms, for he was weary of
war and could not quite so quickly reverse his role, although
there was strong pressure on him both from the Papacy and
Catholics at home to do so; all he could do was to refuse to let
Victor Emmanuel take over these territories.

The real danger threatening their independence was that the
Pope would succeed in stirring up some other Catholic power to
intervene or that he would enlarge his own army with volunteers
and invade the Romagna. Pio Nono was in fact planning by every
possible means *to restore to the Holy See what was unjustly taken from
it,* as he put it in a letter to Victor Emmanuel later in the year. To
that end he was actively canvassing all the Catholic monarchs. To
Queen Isabella, who five years earlier had demonstrated her

devotion by presenting him with a tiara of solid gold weighing a kilo and a half set with 18,000 diamonds, and who had written to commiserate with him on the loss of the Romagna, he wrote: *First of all let me say that, being Vicar of the Crucified God, it is a real comfort to me to be able to share, even in a small degree, in His glorious passion.*[3] How small a degree it was, may be judged from the facts that he himself suffered not the slightest inconvenience; and that the Romagna had been lost to him, not through the intervention of any other power, but through the determination of its inhabitants to be free of his odious rule. Belgium, Portugal and Bavaria were also invited by him to furnish an army to force the peoples of the Romagna to submit to his unwanted domination.

In the event, the intervention of any of these States was prevented by Palmerston, who had come to power again in Britain in June 1859, by his proclamation of the doctrine of non-intervention in Italian affairs; but at the time the call came to Garibaldi in July 1859, the threat to the liberty of the central States by an outside intervention from one of the Catholic powers was a real one.

Garibaldi characteristically welcomed with enthusiasm the call to serve, seeing in it not the prospect of defence but the opportunity of using the liberated central States as a springboard to carry the campaign of liberation farther into Papal territory. On the 1st August, therefore, he wrote to Victor Emmanuel a somewhat curt letter: *I have been called to the command of the troops of Central Italy, who intend to resist the re-installation of their former petty tyrants. I leave with pain the brave forces captained by Your Majesty.* His resignation was accepted by La Marmora with alacrity and after an interview on the 12th August with Victor Emmanuel, at which he appeared to the disgust of the Royal Court not in uniform but in a cotton jacket, he left for Florence. Four days later he was appointed a major general in the central Italian forces.

II

Garibaldi was received at Florence with ecstatic adulation by the crowd, and in every town *en route* to Modena, where he established his headquarters in the Duke's villa, used the Duke's furniture and ate off the Duke's plate. But he learned to his disgust that he was not to be in command of the army, as he had been led

to believe, but was to be second-in-command to General Fanti, a
Piedmontese officer; and that there was little or nothing for him
to do except exhibit himself to the crowds, make speeches, and be
applauded. Living in ducal state was not the sort of life he cared
for and the unwelcome inactivity probably turned his mind to
other things. On 23rd August, he wrote to Speranza:

*I would dearly love to have your beautiful presence here but at the
moment things are so precarious that I hesitate to tell you to come.
Deideri tells me that he is better and would like to make a trip for con-
valescence. Couldn't you join up with his family? I should be delighted
if you were all to arrive here together . . . Anyway, write and tell me
what your plans are and I will do everything in my power somehow or
other to see you.*

But before a reply could arrive from Speranza, he received a
letter from the beautiful Daughter of the Lake, Giuseppina Raimondi, and on the 3rd September wrote back to her:

*I love you . . . and would like to see anyone who would be able to
come near without doing so. I love you . . . and the love of a man could
not have come to rest on a more beautiful, a more charming, a more
attractive creature.*

*Once—Oh! God—pressing my lips to your beautiful hand, I said to
you 'Oh that I might belong to you, whatever the cost' . . . With the
audacity of a soldier, I threw at your feet a life which would have been
broken if not accepted. Oh! you with your angel face . . . Oh! you
with your spirit of a true Italian, you did not trample on the heart of
Garibaldi, who is devoted to you with the same fervour with which he
has been devoted to Italy throughout his life.*

*If only I might take it all back! Because when I told you that I might
belong to you, I committed perjury. I spoke blasphemy. I belonged to
another woman. Those very words 'Oh that I might belong to you in
some way or another' I pronounced on my knees when I was neither
physically nor spiritually free.*

*Now, you must write to me—Madonna!—and tell me that my
sweetheart still has a little friendship for me. I will content myself with
that as if it were the longed-for love . . . But—by God!—don't say to me
that it is a matter of indifference to you. I should be driven mad by that.*

To that passionate epistle, the Daughter of the Lake does not
appear to have replied and in the meantime, a letter had arrived
from Speranza, to whom Garibaldi wrote back on the 10th:

Never be afraid that you bore me—Your letters are true balm to my soul . . . whether you come alone or with the others, I shall be delighted to kiss your hand; if you don't want to come with them, come by yourself, I shall be just as happy. Anyway—Come.

Always your,
G.G.

Whatever you do—Come.

Speranza came. She travelled from Nice in some discomfort with the Diederis, and Garibaldi's fourteen-year-old daughter by Anita, Teresa.

They found the General at Ravenna on the 20th September, and as their carriage rolled under the archway into the Piazza del Palazzo, the news that the General's family had arrived to join him, sent the crowds into a frenzy of delight.

The General met them at the foot of the staircase. Speranza had a little present for him—a cap worked by her own hands in the Italian colours of red, white and green.

'See what a beautiful piece of work the signora has made for me,' Garibaldi said to his daughter. 'I wish she'd thought of bringing me some fruit from my native town—specially some bernissons.'

That evening while they were all at dinner in the Palace, the repeated shouts of the crowd induced Garibaldi to lead them out on to the balcony. As soon as he appeared, a silence settled over the square. There was no wind and the flags hung limply downwards as he spoke.

'When I find myself in the midst of the people of Ravenna,' he said 'I feel as if I were in the bosom of my family, because it is here that I find not only dear friends but my saviours. Ten years of resolving to thank you have already passed and I am happy to be able to couple the renewal of my vows, with the news that the independence of our country is already assured. . . .'[4]

Listening to his melodious voice, all those present must have recalled that it was indeed ten years since he fled like a hunted fox through the Romagna; and as Speranza joined in the fevered outburst of applause that greeted the end of his speech, she must have felt that she, too, was in the bosom of his family. When he had finished, Garibaldi went back to his dinner and left her and Teresa to enjoy the vicarious adulation of the crowd. The piazza was ablaze with light under a royal blue sky, gay with the multitude of stars. Long into the night there were torchlight processions, bands and cheers.

From Ravenna, the party drove out the next day, in three carriages and two light gigs, to visit the house where Anita had died, ten years before. There, in the room of death, they enjoyed a meal with eighteen people at the table and a host of curious spectators at the door. The health of Garibaldi was proposed; in his speech in reply, he did not mention Anita.

'For fourteen years, without pay or reward,' he said, 'I served the cause of liberty—in other lands; what, then, will I not do for the land of my birth? *This* time it must be accomplished. From the Alps to Sicily she must be free. Fifteen days is all that is wanted to make a brave Italian a brave soldier. . . .'

After they had left and were on their way home, there was a ceremony that was a little more congruous. They came to a small country church outside which stood a priest. Silently, he handed to each member of the party a circle of wild flowers and conducted them to a recess near the altar where, above all that remained of the body of poor Anita and her unborn child, they laid their garlands and shed their tears. Afterwards, Garibaldi was closeted with the priest for a time before rejoining the party.

The next day in Ravenna, Garibaldi received instructions to proceed to Bologna and the family party set out early the following morning. It was a triumphant procession. At every village, hands unshackled the horses and pulled the carriages through the streets and everywhere they were bidden into houses to take refreshments.

At Bagnacavallo, Garibaldi received numerous deputations in the *prefettura*. When he came to rejoin his party in the carriage, his face was white and he thrust a rosary into Speranza's hands.

'Keep this,' he said to her in a low voice stifled with sobs. 'It is a precious thing.'

It was the rosary of Ugo Bassi who, as he was led to his execution in Bologna ten years before, his hands streaming with blood (for the Papal followers of the sweet Lord Jesus had followed their usual practice when a priest was done to death of skinning the hands which had once held the sacraments) had entrusted it to a friend to be given to Garibaldi, and no one else.

III

From Bagnacavallo, the party eventually reached Lugo to find deputations from the guilds waiting them, all in costume. While Garibaldi was in one room listening to speeches, his party retired to another. There, Speranza sat down at a piano and played Garibaldi's hymn which had become a popular dance tune. The child Teresa, in the intoxication of the day, seized the squat plump Madame Deideri round the waist and tried to waltz with her. Madame Deideri freed herself and came over to Speranza.

'You ought to marry the General and become a mother to Teresa and her brothers,' she whispered. 'Think how you would save the family from disaster.'

Speranza stopped playing.

'What do you mean?'

'Surely you know that Battistina had a child by the General four months ago?'

'No!'

'He has promised to marry her as soon as he could get a certificate of his wife's death. He got that just after the requiem service the day before yesterday.'[5]

There flashed into Speranza's mind a strange request that Garibaldi had made to her the last time she saw him in Turin, just before the outbreak of the war, when he had asked her to go on one of her trips on horseback through the Romagna and to collect for him a certificate of Anita's death.

She was very quiet the rest of the journey into Bologna and there were constant quarrels about where they should all sit in the carriage. It was nearing midnight when they approached the city, for it had taken them seventeen hours to cover fifty miles, but an even more riotous welcome there awaited them. The city was illuminated in their honour, and they were greeted by the clamour of bells from every church tower, the thunder of cannon, the music of bands and the cheers of the crowd which lined every street. Under a rain of flowers and cigars tied with tricolour ribbons, the carriage was dragged by hand through the streets to the Hotel Brun. But Speranza was no longer in a mood to enjoy the applause of the public; she was beginning to find what others before and since her have done: that there is little sunshine in the shadow of the great.

Speranza found no joy in Bologna at the Hotel Brun. For one

thing, she now saw Garibaldi only at midday and during the evening meal and he never once visited her bedroom; for another, she was expected to pay her own bill—and the hotel was expensive. Garibaldi gave her two presents, a ring set with ruby, diamond and emerald—the national colours—which she suspected some other woman admirer had given to him; and a gold lizard on a gold chain—because, as he explained to her 'the lizard is a symbol of eternity'.

With Battistina in mind, she could not help wondering how much the symbol was worth; not once had he told her that his housekeeper had given birth to his child.

One incident that happened there she attached no importance to at the time, or for several months afterwards. As they were going in to dinner, Garibaldi showed two magnificent banners of the tricolour embroidered with the coat of arms of the House of Savoy.

'Can you imagine such workmanship coming from ladies' hands?' he asked. 'What do you value them at?'

Speranza was just telling him that they were as good as the work of the finest factory, and must be worth many thousands of francs, when the waiter came out to announce that the soup was already on the table.

Lowering his voice so that the waiter could not hear, he whispered: 'These banners are a present from and were worked by the two daughters of the Marchese Raimondi. He has repeatedly pressed me to spend some time with him at his villa near Como— *we* will go there as soon as I have more time.'

In spite of these occasional marks of favour, Speranza made up her mind to leave, and booked a seat on the diligence which left for Florence in the early hours of the morning. The night before she was due to go, all the family, except Garibaldi, had planned to visit the theatre. As the hour drew near for them to set out, Madame Deideri suddenly said to Teresa: 'Where's your father? Doesn't he know that the signora leaves tonight? Why doesn't he come and say good-bye to her?'

'Papa is well aware of it,' said the child tartly. 'But he's gone to bed.'

Speranza went up to his room and found him lying on the bed, engrossed in copies of the *Illustrated London News* describing his exploits.

Coldly, she offered him back the ring and the gold lizard.

'You must keep them as a symbol of my love,' he said.

She was about to say that they ought rather to be given to Battistina, when Deideri entered the room.

'Do you think I should have really let you go without saying "Good-bye"?' Garibaldi asked her. 'I was only waiting until all the others had gone to the theatre and then I should have paid you a visit—in my bare feet.'

Speranza chose to ignore the significance of that remark, and seeing that it had fallen on stony soil, he hastily added:

'I haven't got any slippers.'

'I'll embroider you a pair as soon as I get to Florence,' said Speranza.

He kissed her hand and they parted.

The hotel staff failed to call her in time for her departure and she was unable to rouse any of the party. No member of Garibaldi's family or his entourage came to see her off and she had to stumble out by herself through the unlighted corridors of the hotel, until she met a chambermaid, also departing in a similar fashion to catch the diligence.

The visit, which had begun with applause and held out for her such high hopes, ended with her creeping out from the impersonal doors of the hotel in the company of a chambermaid.

IV

Speranza had no sooner arrived in Florence than a telegram from Garibaldi caused her to postpone her departure for Rome.

A few days later the telegram was followed by the arrival of a messenger; not, to Speranza's surprise, a member of his usual entourage but a wild-looking female whom she had never seen before, and who seemed to have only the most hazy idea what it was all about. From her bosom, the mysterious messenger produced a letter which read:

Go to Messina, visit the English Consul, negotiate with the Committee there and establish relations between me and the Committee of Palermo. Take care!

There was also a Declaration which was to be delivered to the Committee for distribution to the people of Sicily.

Speranza set off for Sicily on the first available boat, accompanied by the messenger. The first night at sea, she was somewhat disconcerted to find that her beautiful companion apparently preferred to share a bunk with the captain of the vessel rather than the ladies' cabin with her; and when the ship put in to Naples, Speranza persuaded the other woman to depart to seek other prey.

In Sicily, Speranza found that the English Consul had no idea what it was all about and was no friend of the revolutionaries; and that there was no committee with which she could negotiate. The dramatic call to the people of Sicily was never delivered and the only result of her mission was that she found herself in prison, from which she only succeeded in extricating herself by bribing the jailer.

This fantastic expedition has the appearance of a fool's errand, and there have not been wanting those who concluded that the only purpose of it was to rid Garibaldi of a mistress whose devoted attentions were proving embarrassing, and who was complaining that she was being treated, as she put it, like the *concubine of a Cadi*.

Certainly, during her absence from Bologna, Garibaldi found another charmer to engage his attentions. He began visiting the luxurious Villa Letizia, home of Donna Carolina Pepoli Tattini, granddaughter of the Joachim Murat who had been placed by Napoleon on the throne of Naples and had reigned there until the restoration of the Bourbons. At the villa, Garibaldi met the sister of his hostess, a young widow, the Marchesa Paolina Zucchini, and under a tree in the grounds he proposed that she should become the mother of his motherless children. This time, the tree was a chestnut, and not a fig, and this time the invitation was unequivocally refused. In spite of that, some residual impression of the beautiful Paolina must have been retained in his impressionable mind. The next year when he had taken the Calabrian town of Pizzo, where Murat in 1815 had been shot in the castle (like 'an eagle trapped in a filthy cage and torn to pieces by vermin,' as Trevelyan aptly describes it), Garibaldi found in the castle one of the bullets which had ended her kinsman's life. He sent it, enshrined in flowers, to her with his respects to the memory of *the first soldier of Italian Independence*.

It is, however, no explanation of Speranza's mission to Sicily that Garibaldi wanted her out of the way. In fact Speranza's visit to Sicily might have well proved of great importance. Garibaldi was in closer touch with events and plans in that island than historians have commonly accepted; and the origins of the Sicilian campaign of the following year are to be sought earlier than the date of December 1859, usually given.

On the 7th July 1859, the Swiss mercenaries employed by the Bourbon government in Naples and Sicily mutinied, with the result that in the early part of August they were disbanded. The Bourbons depended so heavily on these troops, that the patriots believed that their time had come; and in August, a bespectacled traveller (who said he was from the Argentine) toured Sicily gaping at all the usual sights with other tourists. He was Francesco Crispi in disguise, a Sicilian patriot from London and at that time an associate of Mazzini. As the result of his efforts, plans were laid for a rebellion to take place in Palermo on October 4th. The conspirators wrote to Garibaldi seeking his assistance in this enterprise and he replied on 29th September: *The task of the redemption of Sicily is the task of our own redemption. We will fight for it with the same enthusiasm as we fought in Lombardy . . . If you can revolt with any prospect of success then do so . . . I will come to you with pleasure, indeed with joy. . . . But first, we need more intimate communication between yourself and myself: we need more reliable means of communication and we must find some way of effecting it.*[6] It was only two days after that was written that Speranza received the telegram, and it must surely be that Garibaldi had chosen her to be the trusted vehicle for communication with the insurrection in Sicily. It is most likely, therefore, that he knew the date planned for the rebellion, and expected that when she arrived there (about the 6th), she would find the revolution in full swing and revolutionary committees established in Messina and Palermo.

As it happened, when she arrived the plot had failed, as Crispi himself found when he returned on October 11th. There had been treachery and the Sicilian police had been advised of the plans. Crispi and his friends were firmly convinced that it was Cavour's agent the Sicilian, La Farina, who informed on them and this belief coloured their relations with him in the following year.

Speranza was back in Bologna in little more than a fortnight; only to find that Garibaldi had moved on to Rimini. When she found him there, he received her without enthusiasm, listened without much interest to her story and at the end of it, merely remarked: 'Well done! Now you have earned the right to wear the red shirt!' By then, of course, he already knew that the scheme had failed. Since she understood nothing of his purpose, she shared none of his disappointment, and was hurt by his apparent lack of appreciation. An even worse fate awaited her; historians have treated the story of her expedition with reserve, even scepticism, as if it was a meaningless piece of fiction; but a close attention to chronology reveals that it was no futile mission and had the revolt taken place as planned, it might well have been a very important one.

She did not, of course, know that, and at the time she felt that Garibaldi's words were an inadequate reward for the risks she had run and the trouble she had got herself into. So, she departed in a huff to Rome, there to find some consolation in translating English love letters for the handsome Cardinal Bedini, and received his lying assurances that, although he had been Cardinal Legate in Bologna in 1849 and Ugo Bassi had actually been condemned to death in his palace, he himself had no responsibility for the murder; and if the Prince of the Church retained any conscience at all, it must surely have been stirred when he held in his hands the bloodstained rosary of the martyred priest, which Garibaldi had allowed her to retain.

v

The project that now engaged Garibaldi's attention was the invasion of the Papal Marches from the Romagna. He had not come to Central Italy merely to carry out a defensive policy; his mind was, from the first, occupied with the prospect of carrying the revolution south to Rome. With him were most of the officers of the *Cacciatori* and many of his closest associates; his programme was, as one of them wrote at the time, *not local defence but war to make the nation.*

At first, this policy was accepted if not encouraged by General Fanti and Baron Ricasoli; and they agreed that if insurrection should occur anywhere in the Papal States, Garibaldi should not hesitate to cross the border between Romagna and the Marches and go to the aid of the rebels. But although Cavour was out of office he was not without influence. Through his machinations, Luigi Farini was appointed Governor of the newly formed State of Emilia (consisting of the Romagna with Palma and Modena) and the machine, which was creeping forward in low gear, was suddenly put into reverse. Fanti became as adamant as Farini that there should be no invasion of the Marches. There was already bad blood between Garibaldi and him over his refusal to accept the officers of the *Cacciatori* for the Army of Central Italy or enrol the volunteers which were still flocking to Garibaldi from many parts of Italy.

On the night of November 12, there was a stormy conference of the three men, and Fanti and Farini professed later to have extracted from Garibaldi a promise that he would not cross the Rubicon. The next day they learned by telegram that he was on the move to invade the Marches, in the belief that the revolution had already broken out there. As soon as they received the news, with no regard for his personal position or authority, they issued orders direct to his subordinates countermanding his instructions. The invasion did not take place.

As a result, Garibaldi wrote to General Fanti, a letter which expressed his resentment.

16th November, 1859

General,

The irregular proceedings and bad manners of your Excellency towards me, compels me to leave the military service. I therefore request my release from the Forces to which your Excellency was pleased to nominate me.

G. Garibaldi

He left Central Italy at once and more than a thousand officers and men of the *Cacciatori* followed him; many others from the army would have done the same had he not urged them to remain.

The next day he saw Victor Emmanuel in Turin. The monarch did his best to mollify the furious patriot by giving him his own shot-gun, and offering him back his office of general in the Piedmontese Army; but how little his temper was abated can be seen from a proclamation he issued to the Italian nation three days later in which he referred to '*the miserable foxy policy, that for a moment disrupts the majestic fulfilment of our cause*'.

In his desire to advance farther into the Papal States at that time Garibaldi was right and the policy of excessive caution, even though it has been most praised by some historians, was wrong. Less than two thousand Swiss mercenaries, many of whom cherished no zeal to be sacrificed in the cause of oppression, stood between Garibaldi and the conquest of all the Papal States, except Rome itself, which was still garrisoned by the French; and the population were keyed up to a fever of excitement, almost daily expecting their salvation from the north. The invasion might not have been looked upon with much favour by Napoleon III but by then the French Emperor had had more than his fill of war, and was not feeling well disposed towards the Pope. It was only six weeks after Garibaldi was restrained from invading the Marches that the pamphlet *Le Pape et le Congrès* was published in Paris, under Napoleon's inspiration if not his authorship; since such documents are not conceived or printed overnight, it must have represented the French Emperor's state of mind at the time when Garibaldi was poised to set out on his venture. Quite apart from any hesitation that Napoleon might have felt about intervening in face of England's declaration after Villafranca that the Italian people should be left to settle their own affairs, it is a misconception to think even that he wanted to prevent such a liberation. For *Le Pape et le Congrès* proposed that the Pope should be deprived of all his temporal domains except Rome itself.

It is more than likely therefore that the emancipation of the Papal States could have been achieved by Garibaldi in 1859, virtually without bloodshed and certainly without international intervention. By the following year, the Pope, unable to stir up the Catholic monarchs to make war on his behalf, was driven to praying for a general European conflict[7] and, as a last resort, to enrolling an army of volunteers. The muster of Belgians, Austrians, Poles, Spaniards, Orleanist French and faithful Irish— whose drunken and lascivious habits and lack of discipline nearly turned the whole enterprise into farce—began on the 1st January 1860. It produced a body that fought what they believed to be a holy crusade with zeal and courage. By the time Cavour had been forced to allow the Piedmontese forces to invade, the Papal States had to be bought with lives, and the manner in which the Piedmontese Army triumphed over their enemies did nothing to commend them to their future citizens.

It would have been very much better for all concerned if Garibaldi had been left to carry out his plans on the 12th November; that he was restrained, might have been due in part to the well founded fear that he would succeed in attaining his object, and that speedily; and that the credit for it would go to him and his irregular forces, rather than those of the Piedmontese crown.

It is not surprising that Garibaldi retired to Genoa, there to await the next boat to Caprera, a disgruntled man; or that, for the rest of his life, he cherished the greatest distrust of, and animosity towards Fanti and Farini who, in the year that followed, did even more to deserve it.

XV

THE DAUGHTER OF THE LAKE

❖❖❖❖❖❖❖❖❖

WHILE HE awaited the packet boat, due to sail from Genoa on the 28th November to Caprera, Garibaldi paid a visit to Nice, and caught up with his personal correspondence. He wrote to Speranza.

26th November 1859

My Speranza

I have received your letter, the box of sweets and all the things you have been so kind as to send to me and my friends.

I have retired from the service and as I want to spend my time writing, I would like you to send me the manuscript of my autobiography for me to finish. . . .

Write to him who is always,

Yours for life

and again, two days later, the day on which the boat was due to sail:

Genoa
28th November 1859

My Speranza,

If Mr L wants to see me here, where I shall be staying for a few more days, he can ask for me when he arrives.

If he can't find me here, someone or other will give him news of my whereabouts; and as soon as I can, I will do my best to have a talk with him, for I regard him as a dear friend of ours. I want to put every single thing aside, if I am able; while to you, most gratefully, I am yours for life.

It was the last letter Speranza was to receive for a long time.

II

The packet boat sailed for Caprera without Garibaldi. According to the definitive edition of his autobiography, it was because he received a call to go to Turin to see the King. *Going to Turin, I saw the King, with me always good. I saw also Rattazzi and I am sure that he inspired me with very little confidence.* But, not for the only time, we may wonder whether this account is not reticent to the point of untruthfulness. For it would appear that he could not have seen the King until 27th December at the earliest and in all probability it was not until the 4th January 1860; and there exists a letter written by him (and carefully filed later by the recipient in the State Archives of Mantova), which, if the date and place be correct, suggests that on the 28th November when he was writing to Speranza and telling her that he would be staying at Genoa *for a few more days,* and assuring her in the usually warm terms of his lifelong devotion, he already had his bags packed for another destination; and somebody else filled his thoughts.

This other letter is dated the 30th November and was written to the Marchesina Giuseppina Raimondi when Garibaldi was already lodged under her father's roof in the Villa Raimondi at Fino near Como. To get there by then he must have left Genoa the same day as his letter to Speranza was dispatched.

Fino, 30th November 1859

Adorable Giuseppina.

I am torn between two sentiments which trouble me in an inconceivable way: love and duty!

I love you with all my soul and yearn to give all that remains to me of this tortured life to be yours for a single moment. My duty forbids me to be yours . . . to make you mine, you the one I idolize.

This is the voice of duty: I have on the island a plebeian woman and by that woman I have a child—that would be only a minor obstacle because I have no more love for her and will never marry her!

If I were to marry you, most beautiful little girl (fanciulla) I would be renouncing the role of self-denial that partly explains a popularity which I prize and which may be valuable for the country, when the Italian cause once again calls me to lead her soldiers. It will be said of Garibaldi 'He has done himself well' . . . and has set himself apart from the people that he so often swore he would serve to death.

That I am poor, your warm and angelic heart has already pardoned; but that my age is disproportionate to yours and I am in none too certain health, is an insurmountable obstacle, which I cannot allow your kindness to overlook. . . .

Reply to me at once! I am in no state to be able to wait. Don't be angry, by God! with one who loves with a religious fervour! Let me go from you with your esteem, your friendship and conscious of having done my duty.

Yours for life—whatever may be.

With the date of that letter in mind, it is instructive to turn to an unpublished fragment of autobiography,[1] which from internal evidence it is clear was written sometime between the 6th and 23rd January 1860. *About the 3rd December 1859*, he wrote, *I received from the beautiful little girl* (fanciulla) *Giuseppina Raimondi a letter dated 28th November which opened a new phase in my life.* It is surprising that he should be so particular as to give two dates and even more surprising that, writing so soon after the events, both should be inaccurate. Perhaps as he wrote he could feel history peering over his shoulder and was at pains to prepare his defence against an accusation of deceit and faithlessness. Speranza, he knew, was a writer who was shrewdly conscious of the value of her reminiscences of him; one who kept a diary and carefully preserved his letters for posterity. What he could not know was that the eighteen-year-old girl would take similar steps to preserve a letter, which by its date and location, exposes the insincerity of his relations with both women. For a letter dated Como the 28th November, could not possibly have reached him in Genoa in time for him to have got there by the 30th; and it seems more likely that it was his impulse rather than her invitation which took him there to renew his suit to her; reading between the lines of the letter he sent to Speranza on the 28th November, it seems clear that he had by then already made up his mind to leave Genoa for Como.

From the 30th November until the 27th December, he was the guest of the Marchese Raimondi at Fino. *I abandoned myself entirely to happiness and gave myself without restraint to the woman of my heart and forgot all the miseries of my bizarre life,* was his own description of the period. But events called him elsewhere.

III

The persistent Sicilian, Crispi, had followed Garibaldi to the Central States and now he followed him north. He arrived in Turin and on December 15th saw Rattazzi, who had succeeded Cavour as Prime Minister of Piedmont. He laid before him the project of allowing Garibaldi and his volunteers to sail to Sicily to assist in the liberation there. Rattazzi welcomed the idea and had several interviews with Crispi, but when the plan was put to La Farina, as Secretary of the National Society, it was greeted with immediate hostility—a hostility which Crispi and Rattazzi ascribed, and ascribed correctly, to Cavour's influence over La Farina.

It was in these circumstances that Garibaldi left his retirement with his young love and rushed to Turin. The first thing he did on arrival there was to resign the presidency of the National Society. It is inconceivable that Garibaldi had not been informed by either Rattazzi or Crispi of the projected invasion of Sicily, and his resignation from the National Society is explicable only by his disgust at the discovery that La Farina would not support the project. There is no greater misreading of history than to believe that he was not yet thinking of invading Sicily; the thought had not been out of mind since he first considered it in September, though when the plot of October 4th failed, he was flexible enough to press forward with the revolution in another direction. In any event, the two projects were never regarded by him as mutually incompatible; rather he thought—and in the next year showed it by his deeds—that an invasion of volunteers from the north into the Papal States should be complementary to an invasion of Sicily.

His other reaction to discovering that La Farina (which meant Cavour) was impeding the plans for the invasion of Sicily, was to throw his whole support behind Rattazzi and Brofferio in an endeavour to keep them in office and Cavour out. They were for the plan, therefore they must be retained, if possible; Cavour and his associates were against it, therefore everything must be done to keep them from resuming office. As Cavour wrote quite accurately a little later, *Garibaldi permitted himself to be lured into association with my personal enemies, Brofferio & Co.* Since Garibaldi did not disclose his motives even to his close associates, this policy was a puzzlement and often a despair to some of them. '*Our poor*

Garibaldi . . . has allowed himself to be persuaded by discredited men to go to Turin, he comes with most noble intentions, but Garibaldi in alliance with Brofferio cannot succeed,[2] wrote Medici to Panizzi. With less than half the picture before him, Medici was disposed to patronise his leader in that letter written on the 8th January; but by the 19th, he had been enlightened about the projected invasion of Sicily and Bertani was writing to Panizzi, *Medici and I will set to work to persuade Garibaldi.* Apparently, he still did not know the full extent of Garibaldi's attachment to the Sicilian plan or of Cavour's opposition to it.

On the last day of the year, Garibaldi announced from Turin to the public his formation of a new organization to supplant the Society; it was to be called, 'The Nation in Arms', the *Nazione Armata.* Of it, Trevelyan wrote: *But the project failed to enlist support and was dissolved in ridicule;*[3] but there was no opportunity for the new society to measure the amount of support it would receive, still less for it to become ridiculous; it was dissolved for quite different reasons.

On the 4th January, Garibaldi was in the Hotel Trombella in Turin when a fat mulatto entered.[4]

'General,' he said. 'What's the time?'

'Eleven o'clock,' replied the General, astonished that anybody should enter his room just to inquire the time.

'What is the day of the month?' asked the unknown visitor.

'Wednesday, the 4th January.'

'Well, listen carefully, General. I predict that within a year from today, you will be the leader of all Italy.'

Slowly, recognition dawned on the General. 'You must be Alexandre Dumas,' he said. It was indeed, the most prolific of all authors and the greatest historical novelist the world has seen.

They embraced.

'Well,' said Garibaldi. 'I am happy to accept your prognostication, but we must not speak too loudly—especially today.'

'What has happened then?'

'Today we have a meeting of the *Nazione Armata*; of which I have been nominated President.'

They were in the middle of their conversation when an aide-de-camp in the uniform of the Piedmontese army presented himself.

'His Majesty Victor Emmanuel asks General Garibaldi to attend on him at the palace,' said the aide-de-camp. The General picked up his cap and left at once.

While he was away a dozen members of the Committee of the *Nazione Armata* arrived; amongst them was Brofferio.

'Well—what did I tell you?' said Garibaldi, when he returned from the palace.

'What's happened?'

'The Ambassadors of England, France and Austria are disturbed by our project of the *Nazione Armata*.'

He sat down and picked up a pen.

'Brofferio, publish this in your paper, the *Standardo*, and see the other Turin papers copy it.'

He wrote:

As the Nazione Armata is a conception that terrifies all that is disloyal, corrupt and despotic . . . the crowd of modern Jesuits has got together and cried 'Anathema':

The government of the Re Galantuomo has been beset by cowards and in order that it may not be compromised I have decided to relinquish the post with which I have been honoured. I therefore declare La Societa della Nazione Armata dissolved . . . and I invite every Italian who loves his country to join me in a subscription for the purchase of a million rifles. Let Italy arm herself and she will be free.

Dumas seized the copy as the author finished writing. He wanted it as a souvenir of the illustrious General Garibaldi, so he rewrote it in his own hand. But Brofferio wanted that copy as a souvenir of the illustrious Alexandre Dumas; so he seized that copy and transcribed it in his own hand. Nobody, it appears, wanted that copy as a souvenir of the illustrious Brofferio, so it was sent off to the printers.

That is Dumas's version and there is no reason to distrust it; the society which had been founded to replace the National Society was dissolved by Garibaldi at the personal request of the monarch, four days after it had been formed.

The next day Garibaldi returned to his young mistress at Fino. A fortnight later the Rattazzi ministry fell, and Cavour returned to office. The first thing he did was to expel Crispi, the author and begetter of the plan for Garibaldi to invade Sicily, from Piedmont.

But the Million Rifles Fund flourished, and the thousands of weapons they purchased were stored in Milan.

IV

It is given to few men at the age of fifty-two to conduct
successfully a war and four affaires more or less at the same time,
and it is not surprising that one of the matters that was currently
engaging his attention turned out disastrously.

On the 24th January 1860, with the full rites of the Church
from which he was excommunicated, he was married in the
chapel of her father's estate to Giuseppina Raimondi, natural
daughter of the Marchese Raimondi.

The engagement announcement had appeared in the *Corriere de
Lario* on the 6th January, if that is the right description for a brief
note that read: *We are in a position to give an assurance that the
family of General Garibaldi's fiancée have made all the arrangements for
the wedding to take place at once. The General is at Fino, with the
father of the bride.*

The wedding, however, did not take place at once because the
General, showing off his ability as a horseman to his future spouse,
was so unfortunate as to be unable to control his steed; and was
dashed into a wall, breaking his kneecap. For eighteen days, he
was confined to bed, finding, however, some consolation, as he
put it, *in the appearance of the dearly loved girl in my room, which
would not have been allowed if I had been in good health.*

By the 24th he was on his feet again and the wedding ceremony
was graced by the presence of the newly appointed prefect of
Como, his old friend Lorenzo Valerio. Present also were a
number of his other friends; his daughter, Teresa, was a brides-
maid.

As the party left the chapel and moved across to a terrace under
the trees, a man pushed his way through the crowd and thrust a
letter into Garibaldi's hand.

The General opened and read it. It was unsigned but as he read
it the colour drained from his face.

He took his bride, still in her wedding gown, on one side.

'Is this true?' he demanded, thrusting the letter before her.

She read it and did not reply.

'Answer me. . . .'

'Yes—but listen to me . . .'

'You whore!' he shouted. He picked up a chair and made as
if to strike her with it.

Something of her normal spirit returned to her.

'I thought I was sacrificing myself for a hero,' she said. 'You're nothing but a brutal soldier.'

He took his bride by the hand and led her back to her father. 'This is your daughter,' he said. 'She is not my wife.'

To her he said: 'See that you don't bear my name. I leave you for ever.'[5]

V

Who sent the anonymous letter and what did it contain? Neither Garibaldi nor the young Marchesina left their account of the affair, and his earliest biographers were united in their determination to throw no light on it, possibly because none of them had any to throw. The first of them, Guerzoni, declined to provide what he termed *any erotic anecdotes*; and Jessie White Mario, who wrote the valuable supplement to Garibaldi's own autobiography in English, passes the matter over with the remark that the reasons for the parting were best left to her and him.

Nobody was in a better position to hear Garibaldi's version of it than Lorenzo Valerio, who was not only his trusted confident and his *testimone* at the wedding (the equivalent of the 'best man' at an English marriage ceremony) but had also overheard the conversation between the newly married spouses. In a letter dated 4th February 1860[6]—which is about as contemporaneous an account as could be found—he specifically identifies the author of the letter as the bride's cousin, the Marchese Rovelli, who was present at the wedding ceremony. He, it seems, was a rejected suitor.

If this be right—and it seems more probable than other later speculations—both the motive for sending the note and the timing of it are explained. Overcome by jealous passion at the sight of the beautiful young girl he himself desired, being married to the old man, Rovelli had scribbled a note to the bridegroom.

As to the contents of the letter, it was probably much the same as Rovelli said nearly twenty years later when Garibaldi was seeking evidence for a dissolution of the marriage. Then he told a lawyer that from the age of eleven, Guiseppina had been accustomed to sexual intercourse with a large number of men, many of whom he named. They included himself. Her last regular lover was a young Army officer, Luigi Caroli, who was in the habit of coming up from Milan and spending the night with her in a little room on the ground floor of the tower of the Villa Raimondi.

Some confirmation of this is to be found in the only comment the beautiful Giuseppina made on these matters, some fifty years later. Then she said, 'It has been asserted that I ought to have maintained my refusal (of Garibaldi) to the bitter end; but even if in those times a young girl of eighteen was left quite free to go from Como to Varese in days far from peaceful, and was also allowed to choose her own lover, the choice of a husband was still guarded, and guarded jealously, by her parents. How could one ask so much courage from a young girl who had been abandoned by everybody? Even Caroli, who was sure of my affection, at the decisive moment left me on my own.'

The most persistent rakes often demand virtue in their brides, but it may be doubted whether Garibaldi entertained such ideas; and he had the best possible reason for knowing that his bride was no virgin. The fact that she had enjoyed other lovers before she met him is, therefore, no explanation of his outburst or of his decisive rejection of her.

Again, the clue is supplied by Valerio. According to him, the letter also contained the information that only two days before the wedding Guiseppina had bestowed her favours on a previous lover—and that the letter contained such precise and intimate details that it left no doubt that it was the author himself who had enjoyed them. Rovelli, having lost Giuseppina as a bride, had been consoled by her.

This seems the obvious explanation. Affairs of the past did not concern Garibaldi. Anita had been another man's wife; Speranza had been twice married; Battistina had had a previous lover before he took her off to Caprera; and the woman he was finally to marry came as a wet nurse to his daughter after giving birth to an illegitimate child. It was entirely foreign to his nature to be jealous of former lovers, however many. But treachery, disloyalty, on the eve of the marriage was a different matter; it humiliated his pride, and indicated above everything else that the girl in reality cared nothing for him.

Speranza at a later date professed to have learned from Madame Deideri that the real reason he left her was that Giuseppina was five months pregnant by Caroli when Garibaldi married her; but it is difficult to accept this. Had that been so, he would have had no difficulty subsequently in obtaining a decree of nullity of the marriage, for even Canon law has always recognized pregnancy by another as a ground for declaring the marriage void *ab initio*; and Garibaldi was sufficiently tolerant in sexual matters not to regard it as an unforgivable offence. It is true, however, that in the year 1860 Giuseppina gave birth to a child that was stillborn; but the person best qualified to know when that was, the midwife[7] who attended her, asserted that it was in either late August or in the first few days of September. If that be so, it was just likely to be Garibaldi's offspring as anybody else's, for on his own confession, his relations with Giuseppina were by no means platonic.

VI

Garibaldi stayed three days at the Villa Raimondi at Fino after the fiasco of his marriage; and he does not seem to have been entirely paralysed by the disaster. On the same day as the ceremony, he sat down and wrote to Bertani about the proposed invasion of Sicily, suggesting that the Million Rifles Fund might be used to provide arms for the venture and promising him that: *You can assure your friends in South Italy that I am always at their disposal when they are really willing to act.*[8]

After he had left, he was as good as his word. He never again saw the Marchesina Raimondi, even though the following year she made a special journey to Maddalena to see him. He returned to his spartan life on Caprera and was soon in furious correspondence with Mazzini, Bertani, and a Sicilian, Rosolino Pilo, about the projected invasion of that island.

He wrote on the 10th February to Speranza and made no mention of his marriage. That lady, who had passed her time *in her futile conjecture of the reason for his unwonted silence,* had read in the Rome papers of the ceremony. When she did so, the paper dropped from her lifeless hands.

On February 24th, Pilo wrote from Genoa offering to raise rebellion in Sicily if Garibaldi would promise to take over. On March 14th the General replied: *Arrange with Bertani and the Directors* (of the Million Rifles Fund) *at Milan to obtain the arms and necessities. Remember that the programme is always 'Italy and Victor Emmanuel'. I will not shrink from any project, however dangerous, when it is a question of fighting the enemies of our land. But at the moment, I do not think the time opportune . . . unless there is good promise of success.* Before he could receive further news from

Sicily, there were other events that raised his temperature to fever point and which engaged the whole of his attention.

On March 24th in accordance with the secret promises given to Napoleon III at Plombières, Cavour signed an agreement to give Nice and Savoy to France. 'Now,' he told the French Ambassador, 'Now, we are accomplices.' From his point of view it was a fair statement of the position. By the bargain with Napoleon, Piedmont had obtained Lombardy—and if nothing else was obtained, Nice and Savoy were a small price to pay. But Cavour had other gains in view. The transfer to France of these areas was to be subject to a plebiscite of the populations concerned. If the principle of a referendum was accepted by Napoleon as a valid justification for a territorial acquisition, he could hardly refuse it when it was applied to Tuscany and the other states of Central Italy. For the first time the self-determination of populations as expressed by plebiscite was accepted as a valid principle for determining natural frontiers; and, not for the last time, the plebiscite was to be manipulated according to the wishes of its authors. Looking back on these events of more than a century ago (and, as it happens, from the very territory which was then ceded) it is difficult to believe that the plebiscite as held did not substantially represent the true views of the peoples concerned, even if the results were falsified to show a greater preponderance than really was the case. For centuries, they had been subjects of the House of Savoy, but they had little love for their rulers, and the years between 1789 and 1814 when they had by force been incorporated in the French State had not been unhappy ones, and had left them with a predilection for things French. In Nice in particular there was great dissatisfaction with the rule of Piedmont. From the 16th century until that kingdom acquired Genoa in 1814, Nice had been not only the sole port for Piedmont but also the main port for Lombardy and parts of Switzerland. The incorporation of Genoa in Piedmont had diverted trade from Nice, and the privations brought about by a successful commercial competitor were aggravated by a decision of the government of Turin. From the earliest times Nice had been a free port, not subject to customs restrictions; in 1854, this was abolished and the Piedmontese customs officers moved in. Nothing did more to alienate the Nizzards from their country than the sudden consequent increase in the price of all imported goods. To Garibaldi, to whom such mundane considerations were as nothing, it was unbelievable that the inhabitants of his home town could even be induced to deny their country for commercial advantage; and he could never have believed, as a more shrewd observer did, that the Nizzards . . . would vote for France because they *have a keen eye to the value of building lots.*[9]

On the 25th March, Garibaldi was elected as deputy for Nice to serve in the Turin Parliament, for until the plebiscite could be held, the forms of legality were to be preserved. On the 1st April, he left Caprera to attend the Parliament in Turin and battle against 'the infamous sleight-of-hand', as he termed it, of Cavour. The new session of Parliament was inaugurated the next day and was a memorable one, for in the Chamber sat representatives from Lombardy and from the Central Italian States, not as yet annexed to Piedmont.

The sitting was purely a formal one and Garibaldi was unable to raise the matter with which he was so much concerned. He tried unsuccessfully when the House met again on the 6th, but it was not until the 12th that he was able to make his voice heard. The plebiscite was about to be held in Nice on the 15th. The most he could do then was to protest against the pressure being exerted on the people of Nice to vote in the manner desired by Napoleon and Cavour and to ask that the plebiscite should be postponed. His speech was reasoned and logical but there was an undertone of bitterness when he saw in the Chamber, and not supporting him, some of the newly released prisoners from the island of Nisida. 'When I was asked to liberate those galley slaves, did I hesitate?' he asked, pointing at them. 'Look at that deputy over there, pallid and grey faced—that is Poerio. He does not rise to demand that eight days' grace should be given us. But who can rely on gratitude?'

The Chamber escaped from the duty of deciding by voting 'Next Business', and Garibaldi left in a fury.

The same night he was present at two meetings. At the first, it was planned that he and 200 companions should sail into Nice on the day of the plebiscite, seize the ballot boxes and destroy the votes. By this plan, it was hoped that when the next vote was taken the effect of this little drama, together with intense campaigning in the meantime, would result in a quite different vote on the destiny of Nice. An Englishman who was present, Laurence Oliphant, was charged with the task of chartering a steamer for this exploit.

The second meeting was concerned with Sicily. On the evening of the 7th April, Crispi and Bixio had received news in Genoa that a revolution had broken out in Palermo on the 4th. At once they set off for Turin and broke the news to Garibaldi shortly before midnight while he was in bed. They called on him to honour his promise that as soon as there was a spontaneous and genuine revolt in the island, he would go to their assistance. Present at this second meeting in his lodgings on the night of April 12th were Bertani, Medici, and Finzi (President of the Million Rifles Fund). It was decided that Garibaldi should go to Sicily.

The next day, Garibaldi travelled in the same railway carriage as Oliphant,[10] but did not disclose to him that the invasion of Sicily had been resolved upon. At that stage, apparently, he thought it was possible to combine the foray to Nice with the Sicilian venture; so when the train reached Genoa, Oliphant set off to charter a boat. He returned to the quayside hotel that Garibaldi had indicated as his headquarters, to find the place in a flurry of excitement. Eventually, he was shown into a room where the General sat at supper with some twenty or thirty other men.

As soon as he saw him, Garibaldi made a place for Oliphant beside him.

'*Amico mio*,' said the General, 'I am very sorry but we must abandon all idea of carrying out our Nice programme. These gentlemen are from Sicily . . . I had hoped to be able to carry out this little Nice affair first . . . but the general opinion is that we shall lose all if we try for too much.'

VII

The next day,[11] Candido Augusto Vecchi, a wealthy lawyer who had fought with the Garibaldini in Rome in 1848 and had written one of the best histories of that campaign, was in his villa at Quarto, some four miles south of Genoa, when his coachman burst into his room.

'The General is coming!' cried the coachman. Vecchi got down to the door of the Villa in time to greet Garibaldi.

'Now that Nice no longer belongs to Italy,' said the General, 'I am like Jesus—I have nowhere to lay my head.'

'My house is yours, General,' said Vecchi.

'Good,' said Garibaldi. 'But Jesus is not alone.'

'The house is big enough for his twelve apostles,' smiled Vecchi.

'Happily—for the moment there are only five,' said the General. He did not think it necessary to remind his host at that moment that there were times when the apostles were followed by a multitude.

While Garibaldi was having a wash, his host picked up his purse and tossed it playfully in the air. It was very light.

'God, General, you must be rich.'

'Certainly,' said the General. 'I've enough to live on for a week.'

Vecchi emptied the purse into his hand. The man who was planning to set out to conquer a kingdom had four francs and thirty centimes.

XVI

BRANDY WITHOUT OFFER

❖❖❖❖❖❖❖❖❖

THE DAY after his arrival at Vecchi's Villa Spinola, Garibaldi received news that seemed to imperil the whole of the enterprise. While the Nice expedition was a live project, he had sent for 200 rifles from the Million Rifles Fund, intending to use them for the raid on his home town. Now he learned that the government of Piedmont refused to release them.

The Million Rifles Fund, in favour of which he had dissolved his movement the *Nazione Armate*, had been a success. It had not secured anything like the number of weapons suggested by its title, but funds had flowed in to the directors from all parts of the peninsula and from exiles as far away as New York. Some 12,000 modern rifles had been purchased and had been stored in the armoury of the society in Milan. The government of Piedmont had consented to the raising of funds for this purpose, on condition that the arms were stored under their surveillance; it was a condition to which the directors of the Fund, and Garibaldi, had willingly assented.

Since every receipt to the Fund bore the words *Subscription for One Million Rifles promised to General Garibaldi*,[1] he had assumed not unnaturally that he was at liberty to utilize them as he saw fit; but since the scheme had started there had been a change of government. *Brofferio and Co* had gone; Cavour was back in office.

The decision to refuse the rifles to Garibaldi was made by the governor of Milan, Massimo d'Azeglio, apparently on his own initiative; but it is hard to believe that he had not been instructed orally by Cavour what to do in such an eventuality. Having refused the release of the arms, d'Azeglio wrote to the Cabinet for directions. He received no reply; and he therefore concluded, quite correctly, that Cavour did not wish the weapons to get into the hands of Garibaldi, but was chary of taking the responsibility for issuing an order to that effect, since it might well be raised in Parliament and create a storm of protest outside that House as well as inside it.

In fact, Cavour was in a difficult and precarious position. Although recalled to office by Victor Emmanuel, he was aware that the monarch had done so reluctantly. Even in the Cabinet his position was far from secure. There had been far greater hostility to the cession of Nice and Savoy than he had antici-pated; and it came not only from the common people, who had no vote, but also from many notables. Inside the Cabinet, General Fanti was threatening to resign if the cession was effected and so, too, were other members; and, if they resigned, it would be the end of office for him. He would not be able to muster sufficient support in Parliament for a new Cabinet under his leadership.

He was opposed fundamentally to any intervention of any kind in Sicily. On the 30th March, he wrote to the Ambassador in Naples: *not to push the Neapolitan question to a crisis*;[2] he was firmly of the opinion that the existing state of affairs in the penisula should continue, at least for some considerable time. At heart, his belief was that Italy was best left as two kingdoms, one of the North under the King of Piedmont and one of the South, under a reformed monarchy of Naples; in that view, a century of Italian history has not proved him wrong. At the same time, he was conscious that events were moving fast and as he wrote to the Ambassador: *I think we may be forced to prepare plans for which I should have preferred to have had much more time.*

But about one thing he was adamant. If there were to be revolution in Sicily, and an intervention in support of it from outside, the intervention must not come from the radicals, the Mazzini republicans, or even Garibaldi. If the tree were to be shaken, he wanted to be sure of gathering the apples. To that end, as soon as he heard of the uprising in Sicily on the 4th April, he had Fanti write to General Ribotti, a Sicilian serving with the Piedmontese forces and then stationed at Rimini, to ask whether that general would resign his commission and go to the island to help the rebels. His reasons for this can be gathered from a letter he wrote to his closest confidant, Costantino Nigra, the Ambassador in Paris, on 1st August 1860, which was marked *Ultra-Confidential, To be destroyed after Being Read.* Although it dealt with a different situation, it accurately reflected his views, not only when he wrote it, but in the months preceding. If Garibaldi were to be allowed to succeed, he wrote: *King Victor Emmanuel will lose nearly all his prestige. He will probably keep his throne, but his crown will no longer shine in the lustre of the light that heroic adventure throws upon it. The King must not receive the Crown of Italy from the hand of Garibaldi. It would wobble too much on his head.*[3]

The day after Garibaldi received the news of the Sicilian outbreak, he had been to see the King and had asked leave to go to Sicily. He also asked to take with him the 46th regiment, the Bergamo brigade, which was composed almost entirely of his followers. The King was sympathetic to the project, but said he had to consult his Ministers. Two days later, on the 10th, Garibaldi had again seen the King who told him he could not possibly accede to either of his requests. Cavour had prevailed, as he had prevailed about the supply of arms from the Million Rifles Fund. Although he had won some initial success for his policy, that was not the end of Cavour's troubles.

News continued to reach him about the progress of Garibaldi's recruitment, and on 15th April, he authorized La Farina to supply a Sicilian named La Masa with weapons from the National Society's stock; his idea clearly was to forestall any expedition that Garibaldi might launch. But a week later, he was so alarmed by news from Genoa, that he abruptly abandoned a triumphant tour he was making in Tuscany with Victor Emmanuel and went to that city.

There he saw General Sirtori, who was considering joining the expedition.

As to what took place at that interview, there was subsequently great controversy. Dr Bertani asserted subsequently that Sirtori told him immediately afterwards that Cavour, gleefully, had said:

'I think they will all be captured.'

That version is confirmed, to some extent, by a contemporaneous entry in Crispi's diary: *Sirtori, while promising to assist our expedition, has great doubts of its ultimate success.*[4] At a later date, Sirtori denied Bertani's version and he wrote at the time that Cavour *led me to hope for help*,[5] but it is more than possible that he was acting throughout as Cavour's agent in the inner councils of the plotters. Certainly, somebody was, for Cavour always knew exactly what was being projected. A brave man and a true patriot,

Sirtori, who later became Garibaldi's Chief of Staff, was a monarchist to his backbone and would have seen nothing disloyal in informing the King's Minister of what was going on even while he was helping Garibaldi at the same time in his preparations for the invasion of Sicily.

Either Cavour alone was guilty of great duplicity or both Cavour and Sirtori were, for the former's subsequent actions indicate clearly that he had not the slightest intention of helping Garibaldi's expedition; and one thing is certain. Sirtori told Garibaldi, 'I think we shall all perish,' and as late as 2nd May, he was advising against the venture and trying to dissuade Garibaldi from it; and on the same day as the interview, Cavour wrote to Nigra: *the Government is making every effort to prevent Garibaldi going to Sicily.*[6] It was the truth, and not, as some have believed, mere shadow boxing to impress the French Emperor that the expedition was without Piedmontese sanction.

II

From Genoa, Cavour went straight back to Turin and called a Cabinet meeting. At that meeting it was decided to seize all the weapons at Milan belonging to the Million Rifles Fund, and to forbid public meetings in Genoa. The same day, Cavour wrote to Nigra: *I have given orders to watch and prevent if possible these desperate manœuvres in Genoa.* To that end he sent off a Colonel Frappoli to try to persuade Garibaldi to abandon the project.

As Cavour was taking these steps, the guns that he had allowed La Farina to give to La Masa from the stock of the National Society arrived at Genoa railway station. But La Masa had thrown in his lot with Garibaldi, and they were detained there.

Cavour's relations with the King had deteriorated further, and he was aware that Victor Emmanuel was contemplating replacing him. He wrote to Nigra on the 24th: *I have reason to believe that His Majesty, who for a long time had had a weakness for Garibaldi . . . is looking for some excuse to oust me.* For while Cavour was intriguing against Garibaldi, the latter's emissaries were busy pressing the King to consent to the Sicilian venture. So far, the King was standing by his Ministers and Farini was able to report to Cavour the same day: *The King told these gentlemen of the left bluntly that his own Ministers intended to keep a fast hold on policy, and were not prepared to have the initiative taken out of their hands by Garibaldi or anyone else.*[7] In spite of that, Cavour felt far from sure of his position, particularly as Farini had to warn him the next day: *that a crisis at this moment would inevitably bring the radicals to power.*

It was in those circumstances, that Cavour suddenly played what he thought was a strong card. He hastily called a General Election. He hoped partly to divert attention from what was going on in Genoa, which hitherto had been the cynosure of all Italian eyes; but even more than that, he hoped to be returned with such a majority that he could take a strong line with Garibaldi. But he miscalculated. He did not know that he had a majority in the election until May 7th, or the full extent of his victory until several days later; and he did not receive the vote of confidence of the newly elected House until May 28th; in that period of uncertainty many things happened that he was impotent to prevent by drastic measures.

His agent, Colonel Frappoli, arrived in Genoa to find preparations for the expedition in full swing. The Garibaldini had not managed to lay their hands on the guns from the National Society, which were still at the station, but they had a hundred of the new revolvers that a Colonel Colt of Texas had been so kind as to supply; and a parcel of new rifles from supporters in England. There were more than 1,000 volunteers in the town— more than half of them under twenty and most of these students; amongst the others, the *dottorame* were once again well represented. Money was as big a problem as arms, in spite of the long lists of subscriptions which were being published every day in the newspapers; and, of course, they had no ships.

Garibaldi was still undecided whether the expedition should set forth. In his view, everything depended on whether the rebellion had established itself in Sicily.

III

At 6.30 p.m. in the evening of the 28th April, Crispi, who professed to be in close touch with the revolutionaries in the island, produced a telegram purporting to have been dispatched at 3.15 a.m. on the morning of the 26th from Malta. It read: *Offer barrels 160 rum America pence 45 Sold 66 English 47. Expect Lire 114 barrels 147. Brandy without Offer. Reply immediately.* To this cryptic, apparently commercial, message, Crispi alone held the key. He decoded it as: *Complete failure in the provinces and in the city of Palermo. Many refugees received on British ships which have arrived at Malta.*

Consternation and dismay fell on the party at the Villa Spinola. Bixio went round muttering, 'Hell! Hell! Hell!' Garibaldi was nearly in tears. He shut himself up in his room with Crispi, La Masa and Bixio. 'It would be lunacy to go,' he told them.

The word passed round outside amongst the waiting crowd. 'We are not going.' Gradually and sadly, they dispersed, leaving only Vecchi's household. And that night in the strangely silent and deserted villa, Garibaldi sat down and wrote to reserve a place on the boat due to sail for Caprera at the end of the month; and Colonel Frappoli joyfully posted back to Turin to inform his master that the danger was all over.

The next morning, a party of young men, some eleven or twelve in all, appeared at the villa, led by a youth aged about seventeen. They were received by one of Garibaldi's officers, Giuseppe Bandi.[8]

'Who do you want?' he asked them.

'Garibaldi.'

'Garibaldi doesn't want to see anybody today.'

'He must see us—we are a deputation.'

'What do you want?'

'We want to tell him that we are determined to leave for Sicily. If he's afraid to come with us, we are going by ourselves!' Bandi went in to convey this information to the General.

'So, I'm afraid, am I?' said Garibaldi, his face as red as fire. 'Show them in.'

The General received them standing up, his arm crossed in front of his chest. No one spoke for several minutes, then the youngest began to talk in the Genoese *lingua* and the rest followed, until they were all talking and gesticulating together. Then Garibaldi talked to them. They grew pale, then red, then white as a sheet of paper, and their eyes filled with tears. So too did his, and he dismissed them with a wave of his hand, and went and leaned out of the window.

The debate continued all day in the villa and in various inns in the town. Crispi, La Masa and Bixio were for going; Medici, Vecchi, Sirtori and others advised against it. By the evening of that day, Crispi and Bixio had made an agreement about how they could get Garibaldi to start; and so confident were they of their prospects of success that they dropped a note to Fauché, the

H

manager of the Rubattino Steamship Company, saying: *We must see you, the news is good and we're back in business.*

Garibaldi was getting out of bed the next morning at his accustomed hour just before the dawn, somewhere about three o'clock, when his host came into his room. It is an entirely unusual event for Vecchi to be up and about at that hour.

'Heavens—What is it!' exclaimed the General in astonishment. 'Is the house on fire?'

'No—but today is the anniversary of the 30th April.'

When Garibaldi came downstairs, he found the house decorated with flowers and laurel leaves in celebration of the glorious day, eleven years before, when the French had been so decisively repulsed before the walls of Rome, and the Italian spirit been revived after the disgrace of Novara. To celebrate, instead of making his usual morning climb up the mountain behind the villa, Garibaldi went for a gentle stroll through the flower-filled gardens towards Nervi. At lunch, the party was in good spirits and while they were taking their coffee, Garibaldi filled Vecchi's cup with sugar. The historian swallowed it, nearly choked on an undissolved lump and was only revived by Garibaldi emptying a bottle of water over his head.

That night, at dinner, Bixio entered the villa to say that the newspapers carried the report that the Marchese d'Aste, in command of a Piedmontese frigate at Palermo, had confirmed in a dispatch to Turin that the revolt in the island was at an end.

There was an unhappy silence at the table.

Garibaldi rose, held his glass above his head and solemnly proposed the toast:

'To our dead, and to all those who are responsible for their death.'

Silently, each drank, replaced his glass on the table and left the room. The servants came in and put out the candles and the whole house was left as dark and silent as the tomb.[9]

IV

If that day was his Good Friday, the next was his Easter Sunday. Early in the morning Crispi and Bixio came to the villa with various telegrams and documents. Crispi professed to have received a further telegram from Fabrizi in reply to his request for a confirmation of the earlier one. He asserted that the message had been incorrectly transmitted, and should have read: *The insurrection has ceased in the City of Palermo but maintains itself in the provinces. This is the message received from refugees coming to Malta on English ships.* He had other dispatches, all of which purported to show that the insurrection, though it might have failed in the capital, was being most successful in the rest of the island. Vecchi, at the time, suspected that when events did not suit him Crispi 'made his own news;' and both Türr and Bandi[10] subsequently accused him of having forged all these mysterious messages. Nothing is more probable.

But Garibaldi received them as if from Mount Sinai; in a flash he was a transformed man: 'We will go!' he exclaimed.

They all streamed out of his room, shouting, 'Everybody get ready. We're going to Sicily! We're going to Sicily!'

No sooner had this decision been made, than Cavour in Turin was advised of it by one of his spies. He received the telegram and rushed down to the railway station and ordered a special train to be made up to take him to Bologna to see the King, who was due to arrive there that day by carriage from Florence. The railway staff thought it a somewhat peculiar request, for the line had only just been completed and had not yet been opened for traffic; however, they found an engine and carriage and sent him off.

Cavour was now in a panic. He wanted at all costs and by any means to stop the departure of the expedition. Yet he dare not do so by the obvious method. To arrest the nation's hero, in the middle of the General Election, was a certain way to procure his own defeat and probably his political eclipse for ever. He wanted to get the King to order Garibaldi to desist, as he had done the previous year when the guerrilla leader was poised to invade the Marches; and if that was not successful, he wanted the King to take on himself the odium of preventing the sailing of the expedition by force of arms.

What passed between the monarch and his minister nobody can say with certainty, save that Cavour completely failed to achieve his objectives. It is probable that Victor Emmanuel pointed out to him that he himself was not so secure on his throne that he could venture to defy public opinion in the fashion suggested; and that to do so, would be to play into the hands of the liberals and other radical elements who had only recently, and with great difficulty, been reconciled to the idea of an

Italy united under the house of Savoy; and that they had nothing to lose and everything to gain by letting Garibaldi go.

A French writer, two years after this interview, asserted that on being refused Cavour had exclaimed in fury: 'If nobody else dares, I will strangle him with my own hands.' It is quite possible that these words were derived from Cavour's own account of the interview, related subsequently to one of his intimates.[11]

Disappointed by this interview, Cavour returned to Turin and repeated the strict orders he had given earlier that every possible step should be taken by the police and port authorities in Genoa to prevent the embarkation of the volunteers. As a result, the port of Genoa and two neighbouring piers, which the authorities considered were the only places in the vicinity where men and materials could be shipped, were closely guarded.

If he dare not arrest Garibaldi, and the King dare not, Cavour could only rely on the threat of arrest to deter him. La Farina was dispatched to warn Garibaldi—in the friendliest possible way—that plans were already made to arrest him and imprison him at Alessandria. This message was duly conveyed to the General. Vecchi met La Farina as he was coming out of the dining-room after seeing the General. Although he was himself still hesitant and doubtful about his venture, Vecchi begged La Farina to get the government to think again; and what began with a courteous request ended in a brawling match.[12]

The same day, Bixio somehow managed to get a case containing 1,000 out of the 5,000 rifles which were at the station moved out to the Villa Spinola, in spite of the fact that the Governor of Genoa had ordered that they should be detained there.

The volunteers had a shock when they were unpacked. 'They're nothing but a collection of old iron!' declared Garibaldi, when he saw them. They were indeed. Almost without exception, they were rusty smooth-bore muskets, many of them converted from flint-locks, which had been condemned by the military and sold off as being of no further use to anybody. But in spite of their disappointment, the volunteers at the villa set to work to tie the muskets up in bundles of three so that they might be conveniently shipped.

The same day there arrived a gift that gave the General more pleasure. It was a South American saddle, sent by Cuneo from Montevideo. As soon as it was unpacked the General asked Vecchi for a horse on which to try it out, but there was none in the stables as the coachman had taken them all into Genoa to be shod. Impatient as a child with a new toy, Garibaldi repeatedly asked Vecchi if the horses had returned. At length, he could wait no longer. Colonel Türr returned from Genoa to find his General in the saddle astride the back of a couple of chairs.

V

The volunteers had been directed to report on the evening of the 5th May, and all through the evening small groups of men made their way out from Genoa silently along the coast. Inside the villa, there was a dinner-party with Garibaldi and most of his leaders. They were too tense and too exhausted after all the frantic preparations of the last few days for there to be much animated conversation, but after they had finished eating, Vecchi opened a bottle of fine old wine and they stood to toast:

'To the liberation of Sicily. *Viva l'Italia!*'

By the time they had finished their dinner, most of their men had already arrived on the seashore.[13]

At nine-thirty, Garibaldi emerged from his bedroom. Gone was the formal black suit he had worn since he arrived there; in their place he wore the familiar attire of a red shirt tucked in at the waist, grey trousers, and a silk square knotted loosely round his neck. His *poncho*, woven from a local Sardinian cloth, was slung across like a bandolier; on his shoulder he carried a heavy sword; and on his head he wore a shapeless black hat.

Surrounded by Crispi, Medici, and Bertani, he made his way through the lane in the grounds of the Villa Spinola down to the road near the shore, and from there on down a narrow footpath to the sea. An arm of rock gave a little shelter from the wind and there was the tiniest little cove, just sufficient for the bows of a fishing-boat to nose into.

Between ten and half-past, the volunteers were all embarked in small boats and set out about half a mile to sea. The plan was for steamers to appear to pick them up at eleven o'clock, and earlier Bixio had left the villa with a party of about thirty to seize two steamers in the port of Genoa. The two steamers, both paddle boats, were the property of the Rubattino company and were being taken with the connivance of the manager, Fauché. Eleven o'clock passed and there was no sign of the steamers; so did midnight, and by now there was a heavy swell running and a cold wind to chill the ardour of the volunteers. They strained their eyes for the expected signal and all they saw was the same grey distant horizon and the shadow of the clouds moving under the moon across the waters. One, two, three o'clock passed. Garibaldi grew impatient and his crew set out to row him to Genoa. About half-past three, just as day was beginning to break in the sky, across the waters came the flashing light in red, white and green that signalled the arrival of the steamers.

By the time they drew alongside, most of the gallant expedition, unused to small boats on such a sea, were prostrate on the floor-boards or lying retching over the sides; one of them was even so distressed that he threw himself overboard.

Bixio's party had successfully boarded and seized the vessels, but had experienced difficulties in raising steam and they had found that the engines in one of the boats, the *Lombardo*, were out of order. When they crept out of Genoa harbour, the other, the *Piemonte* had had to tow her.

VI

When the men were all on board and the steamers heading southward, Garibaldi turned to one of his officers.

'How many are we in all ?' he asked.

'With the sailors—more than a thousand.'

'What a lot of people!' exclaimed the General.

In fact there were 1089 on board, the youngest aged eleven and the oldest one who had fought under the first Napoleon; and one was a woman. There were, to his knowledge, more than 25,000 Neapolitan troops garrisoning on the island he was pro-posing to invade. Aboard his vessels there was no coal, no food and no water, and not even lubricating oil, a chart, a sextant or chronometer for the 600-mile voyage. And the General was somewhat disturbed to find that on his own vessel, the *Piemonte*, no muskets and ammunition had been shipped.

A call had to be made, just across the bay near the Cape of Portofino, for lubricating oil. While a man was ashore getting it, Garibaldi signalled the other vessel to come alongside.

'How many muskets have you on board ?' he shouted from the bridge of the *Piemonte* to Bixio on the bridge of the *Lombardo*.

'About a thousand.'

'How many revolvers ?'

'None.'

'How much ammunition?'

'None.'

The two boats laden with all the ammunition, and Colonel Colt's presents, had gone astray in the darkness.

'Let us go on all the same,' said Garibaldi.

They sailed on again southwards and he found on deck the prostrate form of Türr, the Hungarian.

'Türr,' he said, 'I've a job for you when we reach land.'

Türr half opened his eyes.

'When will that be?'

'Tomorrow morning.'

Türr groaned and rolled over. Before the day was out, most of the expedition were in a similar condition, unable to partake even of the brackish water and the hard biscuits which was all the refreshment that was to be found on board. It was more than twenty-four hours before the two ships came alongside the quay in a fishing village of Talamone on the coast of Tuscany, and they were able to find relief from their misery.

When Garibaldi appeared on deck that morning he was arrayed in the full uniform of a general of the Royal Piedmontese Army, silver braid, *kepi* and all; a uniform that he was certainly not then entitled to wear.

To Türr, he said: 'Well, are you ready to be shot?'

'I should certainly prefer that to going back to sea.'

'I want you to go to the Governor of the Royal Arsenal at Orbetello and get him to give us all the ammunition we need.'

Türr burst out laughing.

'Do you think he will give me as much as a cap?'

'Any rate, have a try.'

Garibaldi sat down and wrote out on a piece of paper: *Believe what my aide-de-camp, Türr, tells you and place at our disposal everything which will assist the expedition I am undertaking for the glory of Italy.* He was still making use of the notepaper provided the previous year and it was headed *Royal Piedmont Army*; he signed it as 'General'.

The Governor of the military fort at Orbetello was only a lieutenant-colonel, and he had no telegraph at his disposal to communicate with his superiors. He was most reluctant to part with any of his stores, but at length Türr was able to inveigle him into it. Waggon-loads of cartridges, loose gunpowder and even three old bronze cannons, were sent off to the two vessels. For this singular service to the expedition, the unfortunate Governor was subsequently arrested and court-martialled.

At Talamone, Garibaldi dispatched a party of sixty men to invade the Papal States. This was intended to be a diversion to attract attention away from Sicily and persuade the Naples government that the real objective of the expedition lay there and not in their dominions; but it was also intended to be the spearhead of a later expedition which Garibaldi planned should follow and which should be commanded by Medici. In the event, it was a disastrous failure and was forced to flee back to Piedmont territory; and for his services the leader was arrested on the orders of Cavour and kept by him illegally in prison for more than a year; any aggression that was not planned by Cavour was a crime.

At Talamone, too, a small party of diehard republicans walked off the ships when they discovered that Garibaldi's watchword was 'Italy and Victor Emmanuel'. That was not the only trouble he experienced in the port. The night of the 7th, most of the volunteers were so subdued by their experiences at sea that they slept on shore and were happy to bed down early and quietly. The next day the spirits of the hot-blooded young men revived under the influence of the excitement and the local wine. They were not content to admire the local girls in the evening *passeggata* but attempted to conquer them with such ardour that they did not stop to wait for consent.

Soon the whole town was in an uproar. What was worse than forcible seduction was that the men refused to obey the commands of their officers.

When this news was brought to Garibaldi he went ashore, as one eye-witness described it, *glaring like a wild boar*. 'Everybody back on board!' he roared. His rage was so frightening that the whole thousand filed back to their ships, as docile as lambs, and settled themselves down to sleep as best they could on the hard boards of the decks, which were so crowded that there was scarcely room for them all.

By the time he retired for the night, Garibaldi's anger had not abated. The officer he had sent off to obtain food had not returned and Garibaldi went to bed leaving word that when he did show up he was to be thrown overboard; fortunately for that officer, by the time he did return in the early hours of the next morning, with ample supplies, his leader's anger had evaporated.

The expedition was still without coal. So, they sailed across to Porte San Stefano where Bixio extracted supplies from a reluctant government officer by a strong arm persuasion.

By the time the sun was fully up on the morning of the 9th May, the two ships, thus provisioned and armed, by duplicity and robbery with violence, were heading out to sea; and Garibaldi could settle down to the important task of trying to write a heroic song for their expedition.

As the result of these diversions, he abandoned his original plan of putting into Cagliari in Sardinia before going on to Sicily. It was part of his usual fabulous luck; for in the coastal waters of Sardinia the Piedmontese fleet was cruising, and in the port itself, the Governor was awaiting him. Both had orders to arrest him, and to stop the expedition. Cavour had not been inactive.

XVII

PIECES OF THE ORANGE

❖❖❖❖❖❖❖❖❖❖

WHEN THE news of the departure of Garibaldi's expedition reached Turin, Cavour hastily called a Cabinet meeting for four o'clock that afternoon; and it was resolved to use force to stop them. No orders were, however, issued that day but the next day, the 7th May, when Cavour learned that he had secured a majority in the elections, orders went out to arrest Garibaldi and all his expedition, as soon as they put into a Sardinian port. Cavour was well posted on the movements of the expedition and knew that they planned to coast along that island and put into Cagliari. Admiral Persano, when he received his orders could hardly believe them, and wrote at once for confirmation. He asked that the Minister should wire the code word *Cagliari* if they were to be taken seriously. The reply was written in Cavour's own hand on the letter: *Le Ministère est decidé pour Cagliari.*[1] By the 11th, the orders from Turin showed signs of desperation: *All armed forces have orders to arrest Garibaldi and all expeditions are to be stopped AT ALL COSTS*; in the original, those last three words are underlined heavily.[2] The same day, receiving news of their adventures at Talamone and San Stefano, a man-o'-war was sent to arrest them, if they should still be found along the Tuscany coast. Cavour was now left to explain to the world and to his own supporters why he had failed to prevent the expedition sailing. To his confidant in Paris, once again he told the truth: *With the election on and dependent on the votes of every shade of moderate liberal opinion to defeat the opposition, and get the French Treaty through, I could not take strong steps to stop him. . . . I could not stop him going because force would have been necessary . . . The Ministry was in no position to face the tremendous odium which would have attached to it had Garibaldi been held back;*[3] and to Baron Ricasoli, much the same thing. *If Garibaldi had been kept back by force, he would have become very dangerous in internal politics.*[4]

In the great debate that took place in Parliament three years later, La Farina declared 'The party of Cavour helped the expedition in every possible way'; but it is the exact opposite of the truth. To the Italian people, Cavour was forced to appear as if he was in collusion with Garibaldi, and was only being restrained from more active assistance by diplomatic pressure from the Great Powers. It is a tribute to his powers of deception, that he succeeded in propagating that view, and even convinced the majority of historians of the truth of it. Garibaldi himself, for the best of reasons, was under no such illusion. His hostility to Cavour has been attributed by historians of the *Risorgimento*, and by highly competent and well-disposed biographers, to pique, unreasonable suspicion and a peasant's ignorance of the working of high diplomacy. But now that more of the documents are available, it is seen to be a theory that is completely untenable. A very different view must be taken of Cavour's part in these events; and, in consequence, of the soundness of Garibaldi's political judgement.

There were, however, good reasons for Cavour's hostility. Although the expedition had no strong political colour, there were some republicans with it; and in its preference for direct action rather than diplomatic manœuvring it took its lead from Mazzini. There was always the possibility that instead of a movement for Italian unity, it might turn into a movement for Sicilian autonomy; and there was always some danger that it might provoke a further French intervention in the peninsula, just at the moment when the French had announced that they were going to withdraw their troops from Rome.

But fundamentally the real reason for Cavour's strong objection to it lies in the nature of his character and the whole of his political beliefs. He was essentially a bourgeois capitalist who saw the highest good in order, and the security of private property; and he supported the monarchy as the bulwark of this. The unity of the north of Italy appealed to him, for it had a community of interest and was a viable commercial proposition; but for the *meridionale* of the south he had, as most north Italians have to this day, nothing but contempt. Rome for him had no mystic charm. He regarded it as an unhealthy and unpleasant place, full of brutish and unpleasant people. He was therefore quite content to see the peninsula divided into two States, with Rome preserved to the Pope, provided the Southern Kingdom granted sufficient constitutional reforms to prevent it being a source of disorders which might spread northward and disturb the security and order of Piedmont. The letter that Victor Emmanuel wrote on the 15th April to his brother monarch in Naples, on the inspiration of his minister, correctly expressed Cavour's views: *We have arrived at a period when Italy can be divided into two powerful States, one in the North, and one in the South. . . . but to realise this idea it is, I think, necessary that your Majesty should abandon the course you have taken hitherto . . . if you allow months to pass without accepting this friendly suggestion, Your Majesty will no doubt have cause to realize the terrible bitterness of the words—too late.*[5] It has usually been considered that the letter was written deceitfully and to cloak Cavour's real intention; but another letter from the minister himself, dated 13th March of the same year, shows that it was truly his policy: *We are hostile to the idea of creating embarrassments for the King of Naples. The Cabinet . . . wishes Francis II could succeed in reconciling the legitimate desires of his subjects with the conservative tendencies of his government.*[6] In short, if Naples would reform, and establish a constitutional monarchy of the same character as that of the northern kingdom, he would be happy to see a duality in the peninsula; and his view was that it would be the best solution. But if revolution in the south was inevitable, he was determined that what he regarded as the forces of law and order should reap the fruits of it, and not the revolutionaries themselves.

Even Cavour's much vaunted democratic ideas were strictly limited. Under him, less than two per cent of the population of Piedmont had a vote. The mere thought of universal suffrage was as abhorrent to him as it was to the conservative property-owning classes—and their sovereign—in England at that time. To him the highest good was the preservation of the existing forms of society, and the privileges of his class. These, he considered, were threatened by Garibaldi, and even more by Garibaldi's friends.

II

While messages about them raced along the world's telegraph wires, the two ships churned their way across the sea heading directly for Cape Bon on the north coast of Africa. Gradually, the *Lombardo* dropped behind, and was further delayed when the lunatic who had thrown himself in the water at Quarto went overboard again. By nightfall she was far astern of the *Piemonte*. In the middle of the night, Bixio in command of her, saw athwart their course a vessel he could not identify. Since she was lit, and he had agreed with Garibaldi that they should sail without lights, he concluded it was a Neapolitan warship. He prepared to ram and board her. With a boarding-party, he was lying in the bows as they charged towards the other vessel when he heard a well-known voice shouting: 'Bixio, are you trying to sink us?'

Garibaldi, having lost touch, had hove to, and had lit up in case Bixio should lose him. They had not, and could not, arrange any rendezvous since Garibaldi had not yet made up his mind where to land.

The following morning they sailed between the two islands of the Aegades, Marittimo and Favignana and turned westward towards Marsala. The good fortune which had been theirs in so abundant a measure since they set sail still favoured them. A Neapolitan garrison had been withdrawn from Marsala only two days before; and, barely a couple of hours before their arrival, a Neapolitan warship had sailed from the port. In fact her smoke was still smudging the horizon to the east. Had there not been the delay during the night, the two paddle steamers would have run straight into her.

The *Piemonte* made straight for the port and managed to anchor safely, but the *Lombardo* went aground near the mouth of the harbour. At once the invaders seized every small boat in the harbour to effect the disembarkation. A party went off immediately to the telegraph office. On the desk was a message that had just been sent to Trapani: *Two steamers have arrived in the harbour and are landing armed men.* One of the volunteers seized the key and sent a further message, *Sorry, I am mistaken, the two vessels are merchantmen from Girgenti with cargoes of sulphur.* The machine began to chatter again, and he hastily took down the message: *Imbecille!*[7]

Meanwhile, the Neapolitan vessel that had lately left port had returned, and fast behind it came two others. They did not open fire at once, partly because their commanders were uncertain of the attitude of two British men-o'-war that were in the vicinity; but the shelling began when most of the volunteers were assembled on the mole to march into the town. The sole casualty was a dog that had elected to join the invaders. Two days later there was issued an official communiqué from Naples, which was about as truthful as most similar documents: *Two Neapolitan frigates opened fire before Marsala and killed several buccaneers. Their vessel, the 'Lombardo' was sunk.*

The landing at Marsala was received by the townsfolk with patient resignation, but with a complete lack of the expected enthusiasm. The *municipio* was summoned, and they obediently proclaimed Garibaldi Dictator of the Island of Sicily. His reasons for requiring them to take this course were set forth in a similar, but more publicized decree, three days later: *I, Giuseppe Garibaldi, Commander-in-Chief of the National Forces, on the invitation of the chief citizens and after deliberation by the free municipalities of this island, considering that in time of war it is necessary for all powers, both civil and military, to be vested in the same person, hereby assume, in the name of Victor Emmanuel, King of Italy, the dictatorship of Sicily.*[8]

Marsala could supply the volunteers with bread, wine and blankets, but they could not furnish one essential which the expedition still lacked: a map of Sicily. When Garibaldi set out with his troops at four o'clock the next morning, he had only a plan of the immediate locality, 'borrowed' from the Marsala Land Registry.

The entry into the town of Salemi was more to the liking of the volunteers; they were received with the delirious emotion that those of them who had been through the '59 campaign had come to expect. This was partly due to La Masa being sent on ahead to whip up enthusiasm, but even more to the local priests; for the first time in his life, Garibaldi found himself being welcomed as a hero by the local representatives of the Church.

For two days, he remained in the town. Meanwhile, barring his way to Palermo, a strong force of Neapolitan troops began to muster at the strategic strong point of Calatafima. In all they numbered something like three thousand infantrymen, well armed with rifles, and with supporting cavalry and guns. Against these he could oppose only seven or eight hundred of his own men, armed only with antiquated weapons. Nobody in his force had the least idea what he intended to do.

III

The one-armed Bandi, who was attached to the staff in charge of the commissariat, was asleep in the next room to Garibaldi when he was awakened about three in the morning of the 15th May by the General's voice.[9]

'Is it raining?' he was asked.

He went to look through the window.

'It's been raining a lot,' he replied. 'But now it's a beautiful day.'

'That's a good sign.'

While he was getting the General a cup of coffee, he heard him singing snatches of opera:

> 'That gentle delight
> Quietens my spirit, as I see
> The vision serene
> Of time that shall be.'

'Good news, General?' asked Bandi, when he returned with his coffee.

'What do you think? When all goes well for our country, we are bound to be light-hearted.'

Two hours later, the ragged troops were on the march towards Calatafima.

At the peak of the midday sun, on opposite hillsides separated by a dry watercourse, amid vines and prickly pears and *agave*, the two armies met. The Neapolitans, seeing in front of them only a rabble in civilian clothes—for there had been only fifty red shirts to distribute amongst the volunteers—advanced first to the valley. When they were over the river-bed, Garibaldi's volunteers, without waiting for an order from him, flung themselves down the hillside upon them with fixed bayonets. The Neapolitans retreated back up their hillside. The volunteers followed.

All through the torrid heat of the afternoon, under a glaring sun, the fight went on as the volunteers stormed from terrace to terrace up the hillside. The enemy grew more numerous as the day advanced and reinforcements arrived, and the volunteers were thinned out by casualties and fatigue. Garibaldi, and all his officers, were in the forefront of the fight and twice at least he was within inches of death. Once he was saved by members of his bodyguard, and once by Sirtori, who had been so reluctant for the expedition to depart, but who now he was in it fought loyally and courageously.

Towards the end of the afternoon, even the mad Bixio was in favour of conceding that the battle was lost, and said what none else dare, as they crouched under a terrace near the summit of the hill.

'General, I'm afraid we ought to retreat.'

Garibaldi looked at him.

'Here we make Italy or die,' he said. It was no mere heroic expression but a plain statement of the truth; for had the volunteers retreated in the first encounter of the campaign, it would have been their end. The hills sloping around them were filled by peasants from the mountains who had come to join Garibaldi, but who prudently watched to see how the day went.

Suddenly, Garibaldi was struck on the shoulder by a heavy stone. He sprang to his feet.

'Come on. Their ammunition is finished. Charge!'

With his sword flashing, he led the rush which carried his small band over the crest. The enemy in fact had not exhausted their ammunition but the assault was so vigorous that after a bloody turmoil on the summit, they fled. Soon the plateau was covered with their thousands fleeing back to Calatafima. That night their commander sent a dispatch marked *Most Urgent* back to his superiors, which began: *Help, immediate help! The mass of the Sicilians, united with the Italian troops are in enormous numbers;* although it also contained the news: *We have killed the great captain of the Italians and captured their standard,* and gave the impression that the main loss of the Neapolitan forces was a gun which had inadvertently fallen off the back of a mule.[10] The dispatch fell into the hands of the volunteers, and was read aloud in Garibaldi's camp, to the hilarity of the hearers, not least of all the great captain who had been killed.

It was a decisive victory for the invaders, but their losses had been serious. Amongst the many fallen were three youths under sixteen, the youngest of whom had just celebrated his fourteenth birthday. Within a few days the news of the battle had spread across the island, and every hill-top was alight with beacon fires to celebrate it.

IV

Garibaldi's entry into the small town of Alcamo was accompanied by the spontaneous demonstration of fervour that had appeared in the campaigns of the previous year. As he passed through the streets, men and women fell on their knees before

him as if in religious awe; and here a new element entered the
campaign. The lower clergy of Sicily shared the thoughts, as
they shared the poverty, of the people more than their lickspittle
brethren in the rest of Italy. They afforded a welcome to the
invader as enthusiastic as any he received; and their sympathy
was returned. On Ascension Day, the volunteers attended solemn
Mass in the Cathedral celebrated by a Franciscan friar. On his
knees before the high altar, Garibaldi was blessed by the priest
and received from him a crusader's cross.

All the contemporary accounts describe the genuine mystical
elation with which Garibaldi received the blessing, and the
influence the ceremony exercised over him for long afterwards.[11]
Although he had long discarded the outward forms of religion,
and if his own beliefs at that time are analysed, they correspond
closely to the non-theistic Christianity which is the real religion
of most adults in the Western world in the twentieth century,
he was at heart a profoundly religious man. Not the least of the
sins of the Church into which he had been christened was that by
its devotion to materialism, its selfishness, its cruelty, and its lust
for power, it alienated one who had all the instincts of a saint.
When he found priests who were as devout, simple and devoted
to liberty as he believed all of them should be, he was constrained
to support them; for his hostility was not directed at religion, but
at those who used religion as the instrument of oppression. It
was not just policy that led him to kneel at the foot of the altar,
and he was happy to divert the religious fervour that attached to
his person into its accustomed channels; at the same time it was
also a wise policy, for it identified him more closely with the
people he sought to serve.

At Alcamo, he also showed his political wisdom in the organization of civil administration in the areas which were then, or in
the future might be, under his control. But there was still a
formidable enemy in front of him, and after only two days in
Alcamo, he set out again to press on towards the capital.

v

Outside the town of Partinico, which the retreating Neapolitans had pillaged, and where they had been set upon by the out-
raged peasants with a cruelty matching their own, Garibaldi led
his forces towards Monreale. By now he had been joined by

many of the peasants, and Rosolino Pilo had gone ahead with a
party of these in an attempt to surround the fortified town.
They were scattered, and Pilo killed, by an advance of Neapolitan
troops. As a result, Garibaldi was forced to take to the mountains.
In an overnight march in torrents of rain, through marshes and
over rocky trails, the expedition stumbled their way to Parco.
They were ragged, soaked, exhausted, and many were without
boots on their feet. Two days' respite was all they were granted
there, before the enemy caught up with them, and they were
forced to retreat farther into the hills towards Piana dei Greci.

On the afternoon of May 24th, Garibaldi sent his sick and
wounded and his cannon with fifty artillerymen, out on the high
road towards Corleone, fleeing farther from the advancing enemy.
After nightfall, the rest of his troops followed as if they were
taking the same road. Two miles outside the town, Garibaldi
swung the column round to retrace their steps on a route parallel
to the one they had taken. From there they dropped down into
Marineo and then pressed on to Misilmeri with only the briefest
rest. The pursuing column of the enemy, some four thousand in
all, continued chasing off towards Corleone, where three days
later they had the satisfaction of capturing two of the cannon
and a handful of the wounded. But by that time Garibaldi and
his men were fighting in the streets of Palermo; one of his
favourite ruses had succeeded again.

Outside Misilmeri, Garibaldi was visited by the local correspondent of the London *Times*, a man named Eber. It was one of
the curiosities of the campaign that while the Neapolitans were in
ignorance of his whereabouts, and were widely advertising that
he was in flight towards the south, a journalist should have had no
difficulty in locating him; but Eber was a Hungarian and his
compatriot, Türr, had probably communicated with him. Not
only did he find Garibaldi, but he rendered him the singular
service of providing him with the exact disposition of the
Neapolitan troops in and around Palermo;[12] and not content
with reporting news, he proceeded to make it, by joining up as a
combatant. He was probably the only representative of Printing
House Square to have taken part in a revolution of any kind.

He was able to inform Garibaldi that Neapolitan troops, to
the number of 20,000 and more, were concentrated on the hills
to the west of Palermo and in the western and northern parts of
the town itself. By this time Garibaldi's original forces were

down to about 700. With them he had gathered perhaps 3,000 peasants, most of them armed with nothing better than blunderbusses or scythes, and all of them unruly and of uncertain reliability. It was this motley crew that descended in the night of May 27th, not without confusion, down trails until they reached the outskirts on the south-east of the town. About four in the morning under fierce fire they crossed the bridge, burst through a barricade and broke into the city by the Porta Termini and through to the ancient market-place, the Fiera Vecchia; from there they swarmed to the Piazza Pretorio, near to the crossroads which are the centre of the city. By midday, almost the whole of the city except for the area around the Palace, was in their hands. The barricades went up and many of the citizens came to their aid, augmented the next day by the entire prison population, political prisoners and ordinary criminals alike.

The Neapolitans, who had ruled by terror, now sought to subdue the city by the same means. It was bombarded at random from the sea by their vessels and by their guns around the Palace and at the Castellamare; and their troops were licensed to loot and fire houses and churches. This reign of terror sealed their fate. Whatever doubts the inhabitants of Palermo may have entertained were resolved, particularly since Garibaldi's men who came as liberators, behaved for the most part like liberators, and even went so far as to pay for the food and provisions they received. Garibaldi was seen by an awed population, sitting in the sun unconcerned on the steps of the church in the Piazzo Pretorio, while the square was a special target for bombardment.

Street fighting continued in the city, and on the afternoon of the 29th while he was in the square, news reached him that the Neapolitans had broken out of their encirclement around the Palace and had launched a strong attack into the town. He got up.

'I must go myself,' he said.

There was a fierce and bloody battle around the Cathedral and along the Toledo. In the end, the Garibaldini succeeded in driving the enemy back into the Palace square, but not without many casualties and much expenditure of ammunition. By now the situation regarding ammunition was so desperate that during the night Garibaldi sent an emissary secretly across the harbour to beg powder from the Piedmontese Naval commander, the Marchese d'Aste. The Marchese, who was a devoted monarchist and a follower of Cavour, refused this aid to the man who was winning a new country for his sovereign; and Garibaldi was driven to despair, and to contemplate a withdrawal from the city.

But by half-past eight in the morning two Neapolitan officers presented themselves at his headquarters. They handed him a letter from the royal Governor. It was addressed *From General Lanza to His Excellency General Garibaldi*, and asked for a cease-fire so that a conference might be held between the contending forces on board the flagship of the British Admiral. To this, Garibaldi gladly consented and by ten o'clock the firing died away.

It was agreed that the formal armistice should come into effect at noon. Shortly after that hour, the Neapolitan column that had pursued the diversionary party down to Corleone, having returned, effected an entry into the city the same way as Garibaldi had done it, and penetrated as far as the Fiera Vecchia before they were stopped. They professed to be in ignorance of the existence o the armistice, but the timing of their attack suggests that it was an excuse to capture Garibaldi's headquarters in the Piazza Pretorio by a violation of the cease-fire; they halted, but refused to withdraw from their positions.

Garibaldi went to the quayside and was fired on by Neapolitan troops in Castellamare fort. He had dressed himself again on this occasion in the uniform of a general in the Piedmontese army, much to the disgust of the Marchese D'Aste, who also had been invited on board the British flagship, and the subsequent fury of Cavour when he learned of it. On board the ship, in spite of his grave situation, Garibaldi played a superb game of bluff with the two generals sent from Lanza to meet him. When they all left, a twenty-four-hour armistice had been signed.

VI

During the twenty-four-hour armistice, some powder was obtained from a Greek ship which had entered the port, fresh barricades were set up and the whole town set about preparing for a renewal of the battle; but a little before noon, two Neapolitan emissaries, General Letizia and Colonel Bonapane, presented themselves at Garibaldi's headquarters. They found the General stretched out in an armchair under his *poncho*, while between his legs was another chair covered with cigars, oranges, a sheath knife and paper.[13]

'Sit down, gentlemen,' he said. 'Have a cigar.'

He pulled out his watch.

'It's only a few minutes before the armistice ends.'

Before he could say more, Letizia interrupted him.

'That's why we are here, General, we have done what our duty demanded—and now . . .'

'And now,' said Garibaldi, 'you have come to bring to an end this fratricidal strife that is as distressing to us as it must be to you. For myself, I would think it well if the armistice were prolonged and prolonged indefinitely."

'If your conditions are honourable and wise, it will be possible to arrive at a truce,' said Letizia.

While the Neapolitan general talked, Garibaldi took the knife and peeled an orange.

'For you, General,' he said passing a piece over on the point of the knife.

Stabbing another piece, he passed it to Bonapane.

'For you, Colonel,' he said 'Good! Now let's hear your terms.'

The colonel, his mouth full of orange, began to read the terms of truce.

The terms were acceptable. Amongst other details, Garibaldi was to be allowed to take possession of the Royal Bank. When Crispi went there to take over, he found the equivalent of twenty-one and a half million lire; when the expedition left from Quarto they carried with them less than 30,000 lire.

It was the end of Neapolitan resistance in Palermo. On 7th June, the capitulation was signed and their army of 24,000 regular troops moved out of the city to a temporary camp to await repatriation. On that day their conquerors, who had sailed from Quarto 1,089 strong, and who had been sadly depleted in numbers during the campaign, had only 490 muskets left among them.

While these events had been taking place in Palermo, in Naples, the young King Francis II had been seized with such panic that he telegraphed five times in one day for the Pope's blessing.[14] Perhaps it was because Cardinal Antonelli sent the last three blessings without reference to His Holiness, that they proved to be so singularly ineffective.

XVIII

A WEB OF INTRIGUE

✦✦✦✦✦✦✦✦✦✦

ON THE 10th June 1860, Alexandre Dumas's yacht the *Emma*
sailed into Palermo harbour and dropped anchor under the
mouths of the tiered guns of a Neapolitan frigate. Dumas leaped
into a fruit boat and was rowed to the quayside.

He found the town full of men in red shirts galloping about on
horseback or rushing hither and thither on foot. The streets were
still barred by barricades made of paving stones, and there were
houses gutted by fire or shattered by shell-fire; but everywhere
there was excitement and happiness that left no doubt that the
conquest of Palermo by Garibaldi's men was indeed regarded as a
liberation.

At the Palace, Dumas found a young man in a red shirt who
had been wounded in the hand.[1] He asked him: 'Where can I
find General Garibaldi?'

'He has just gone to the Convent of La Gancia, which has been
pillaged and burnt by the Neapolitans.'

'Can I speak to his son, then?'

'I am his son.'

Dumas fell on Menotti Garibaldi and embraced him.

'My father has been expecting you,' Menotti told him.

'I'd like to see him as soon as possible. I've letters with me from
Bertani and Medici.'

They found the Dictator of Sicily near the Cathedral and Dumas
noticed that not only was his felt hat pierced by a bullet-hole
but that there was a ragged tear in his trousers just above the
boot.

'What's that?' asked Dumas.

'Oh! nothing,' replied Garibaldi lightheartedly, with a twink-
ling glance toward Menotti. 'Some clumsy fellow talking to me

let his revolver drop and it went off, burning my trousers and shooting off a piece of my boot.'

'You seem to have a charmed life.'

'I'm beginning to believe so myself,' smiled Garibaldi.

At the palace, Dumas shared the General's lunch of roast veal and sauerkraut.

'Where are you staying?' asked Garibaldi when they were having dessert.

'On board the yacht.'

'That might be very undesirable in certain circumstances.'

'Then show me where we can camp and I'll pitch tents.'

'I can do better than that for you,' said the General and he called a member of his staff.

'Give Dumas the Governor's rooms in the Palace,' he ordered and, to the novelist, he said:

'Make yourself as comfortable as possible. The King of Naples will be delighted when he learns you are his tenant.'

At that moment, several priests entered the room.

'Good God! What's this?' exclaimed Dumas.

'Not so fast,' said Garibaldi. 'They have done excellently. Each of them has marched, cross in hand, at the head of his flock.'

'Oh! Maybe you've been converted as well?' said the novelist satirically.

'Of course—and now I have a chaplain. I'll have to ask him to pay you a visit, my dear chap.'

Later that day, Dumas took possession of the Governor's suite of eighteen rooms in the Palace and installed his entourage there. Amongst them was an exotic figure, attired in a nautical style costume of violet velvet with sky blue and gilt lanyards, who was known to the rest of the party as 'the Admiral'. She was the nineteen-year old daughter of a bucket-maker and was pregnant by the novelist. There was also a Caucasian valet, resplendent in the gold and silver court uniform of a Georgian prince; a famous homosexual; and the best photographer in Paris. All this crew moved into their new lodgings, with a vast supply of champagne from the stores of the *Emma*.

Garibaldi also installed himself in the Palace, but it was in a small room in the gatehouse of the Porta Nuova. Although he had the vast funds of the Royal Mint at his disposal, he took only ten lire a day as salary; and, although he was immersed in military matters, he found time to organize boys' homes for neglected youths he found running about the streets, and a system of public relief for the distressed and destitute. But there were other things calling for his immediate attention. Although he was the master of the capital and most of the island, there were still some 20,000 Neapolitan troops unconquered in Messina, several thousand in Syracuse and smaller garrisons in Milazzo and Augusta.

II

When the victory in Palermo became known, Cavour discovered, to his surprise, that Garibaldi's expedition had *turned out to be the most poetic deed of the century . . . praised by almost the whole of Europe.*[2] He therefore resolved on two things. To regain some of the popularity he had lost at home over the cession of Nice and Savoy, he began to hold himself out as having been, if not the instigator of the whole Sicilian invasion, at least its active, though secret, collaborator from the moment of inception. Secondly, he determined to snatch the prize fish off Garibaldi's line into his own net before it could be landed.

He therefore began, for the first time, to give active assistance to the expedition. On 13th May, Garibaldi had written to Bertani giving orders that a further expedition, under the leadership of Medici, should be directed against the Papal States. The object of this was not merely to liberate the Italians living in them, but to launch an invasion from the north into the Kingdom of Naples to coincide with his movement from Sicily. For he knew that on the mainland the King of Naples had 100,000 regular troops, the best armed and best trained in the peninsula, and that the Neapolitan Navy was the largest and best equipped in Italian waters.

Cavour assisted the arming of Medici's expedition with the modern Enfield rifles of the Million Rifles Fund and he provided money out of the Piedmontese Exchequer for the purchase of ships. In return, he insisted that the expedition should sail for Sicily and not for the Papal States; and he managed to set up in Genoa an administration separate from Bertani's to supervise the departure of Medici's expedition, and a further expedition which sailed in July under Cosenz. His other objective, that of taking away from Garibaldi the control of affairs in Sicily, he sought to achieve in the first place by sending out there post-haste La Farina, with instructions to secure as soon as possible the annexation of the island to Piedmont and the supplanting of Garibaldi's administration by one that would be entirely subservient to the Turin government.

La Farina arrived in Sicily on the 6th June and carried with him a message to Admiral Persano from Cavour, in which he informed the Piedmontese naval commander that *La Farina enjoys my complete confidence, knows my plans, so you can pay attention to what he says.*[3] It has been commonly supposed that La Farina exceeded his instructions but, in the light of that letter, there is no reason to believe that anything he did was not in accordance with Cavour's intentions. It was nearly a fortnight before he found it convenient to call on Garibaldi; even so, he was received politely, if not enthusiastically, by the latter. By that time he had succeeded in placarding almost every wall and every door in Palermo with posters:

> *WE WANT ANNEXATION*
> *TO THE CONSTITUTIONAL MONARCHY*
> *OF VICTOR EMMANUEL*[4]

By 22nd June, he had stirred up the Civil Council of Palermo to present a demand to the General for immediate annexation to Piedmont. The answer Garibaldi gave ended La Farina's attempt to achieve his object through the Council: *I am the one who gave you the watchword 'Italy and Victor Emmanuel' . . . but . . . I came here to fight for the cause of Italy, not of Sicily alone. If we do not free and unite the whole of Italy, we shall never achieve liberty in any individual province.*

Shortly after taking the city, Garibaldi had appointed a Cabinet as representative of as many shades of political opinion as possible and including a number of Cavour's supporters. It was headed by Crispi, who had rendered such singular service in getting the expedition to start, and who was well qualified to lead the civil administration. He, in spite of his early addiction to Mazzini and republicanism, was reconciled to the annexation of the island to Piedmont and Victor Emmanuel. His only difference with Cavour on this was, as he himself put it, that he wanted Piedmont for Italy whereas Cavour wanted Italy for Piedmont; and he was not prepared for immediate annexation since it might prevent the liberation of the rest of Italy. By 27th June, La Farina had succeeded in bringing down that Cabinet by his agitation and by procuring the resignation of the Right Wing members. Crispi was excluded from the reconstructed Cabinet, and had to face a hostile mob screaming for his death. The attempt to under-mine Garibaldi's authority and to establish civil control firmly in the hands of Cavour's adherents appeared to have succeeded.

III

La Farina's triumph was short lived. On 7th July his house was surrounded by the police and he was taken on board the flagship of Admiral Persano. A notice of his expulsion from the island was published in the official gazette. The notice read: *By special order of the Dictator Messrs La Farina, Griscelli and Totti have been expelled from Sicily. The government, which has to maintain public order, cannot tolerate any longer these individuals with their evil intentions.*[5]

Griscelli and Totti were expelled for plotting to assassinate Garibaldi. It was a *malignant insult* to couple La Farina with the other two, Trevelyan wrote, *for he had no more to do with them than he had to do with the beggars on the steps of the Cathedral . . . the manner of his deportation was offensive, and leaves a stain on the chivalrous character of Garibaldi . . . a gross insult to the emissary of the Royal Government.*[6]

But a number of documents have come to light since those words were written and it is necessary to question whether those strictures on Garibaldi's conduct are justified.

Giacomo Griscelli had been employed the previous year by the Apostolic Legate, and a representative of the King of Naples, to assassinate Garibaldi while he was touring central Italy in the autumn. That fact had been discovered by Luigi Farini who, as has been seen, was responsible for administering Tuscany with Ricasoli and who was Cavour's instrument for frustrating Gari-baldi's attempt to invade the Marches in the November. Farini made a practice of intercepting all letters passing through the Central States and he did not hesitate to interfere with diplomatic correspondence. Documents from Cardinal Antonelli in the Vatican and from the French, Spanish and British diplomatic representatives were regularly obtained in transit and copied. In this fashion, Farini came into possession of a letter from Griscelli to his employers which proved conclusively that he was employed by those exalted personages to murder Garibaldi, by the knife or by poison;[7] and that he had shadowed the General for this purpose between August and November of 1859 but had never been able to find a suitable opportunity to achieve his object. The murder was to be, as Griscelli wrote, *for the service of God, the Church and Religion*; and, incidentally, for a very useful sum of money.

Instead of having the man arrested, Farini kept in touch with him as if, some day, the enterprise on which he was engaged was one to which other people might be happy to subscribe.[8] By May 1860, Farini was Minister of the Interior in Cavour's cabinet in Turin where he was responsible for a number of secret projects, including bribing the French Press. It is inconceivable that he did not disclose to his Prime Minister his discovery of Griscelli's letters and the fact that the Papacy and the Bourbons of Naples had engaged a hired assassin to murder Garibaldi. In fact, it could only have been Farini who brought Griscelli to Cavour's notice.

What construction can be placed on the fact that, with this knowledge, Cavour himself engaged the same Griscelli on the 31st May 1860;[9] that is, at the very time when the Prime Minister first learned of Garibaldi's victory in Palermo? And that he then paid him a substantial sum of money and sent him to Sicily?[10] What interpretation can anyone place on these facts? For what purpose does anyone engage a man who is known to be a hired assassin?

Subsequent events do nothing to rebut the obvious inference.

That Griscelli and his associate planned to murder Garibaldi in Sicily is beyond doubt, for he made and signed a confession. He and his assistant admitted being paid by the Neapolitans, but they also claimed they were being paid by Cavour for the same purpose. At first, nobody in Sicily would believe this latter claim, and they were about to be executed. But Admiral Persano, hastily enlightened by Cavour, intervened to save them. The letter that he wrote to Garibaldi on the 7th July[11] gave an explanation so improbable that it must have confirmed the suspicions aroused by his intervention. According to it, the men were being paid by Cavour to plot the murder of Garibaldi, so that the government of Naples should be blamed.

In the circumstances, therefore, it is not surprising that Garibaldi, and his close associates, believed on reasonable grounds that Cavour had sent Griscelli and his accomplice to assassinate him; and that, of necessity, La Farina, as Cavour's principal agent in the island, was in the conspiracy up to the neck. It is for this good reason, and not as a gratuitious insult, as Trevelyan believed, that the three men were expelled together and their names given together in the official notice of their expulsion.

If it be considered an altogether incredible belief that the respectable Prime Minister of Piedmont should stoop to such a dastardly scheme, it is first necessary to explain why Cavour, in the light of the knowledge he had, should have any truck at all with such a person as Griscelli, and send him on a mission to Sicily. If it be accepted as the truth, then a great many otherwise puzzling incidents fall into place. It would explain why Cavour adamantly refused to visit Naples later the same year when Victor Emmanuel took over, although he had previously always accompanied the King on similar occasions; and why he gave numerous conflicting and evasive explanations of his absence: amongst them, that he did not visit Naples with the King because the Garibaldini had some *ridiculous antipathy*[12] to him. The real truth is more likely to be that he could not face meeting the man he had paid to have murdered and who, he knew, was well aware of the fact. It would explain the bitterness of the exchanges between Garibaldi and Cavour when they did meet subsequently, in Parliament on the 18th April 1861. It would also explain why, when Garibaldi learned that Farini was to replace him as dictator of Naples, he determined to leave the city before he arrived; and why Farini found it necessary to write to Cavour that he had managed to take over from Garibaldi without having had to speak to him once or meet him face to face.[13] It all adds up to a formidable case against Cavour, particularly since he, when he received emissaries from the King of Naples on the 16th July, urged them 'not to wait always for Garibaldi to attack you, but go out and beat him, catch him and execute him'.[14] At that particular juncture, a fund for the removal of Garibaldi was one that would have been gladly subscribed to by Cavour as well as the Papacy and the Bourbons.

Nor was political assassination regarded as something so abhorrent that no statesman, king or prelate would ever stoop to it. The pious Francis II, who was so anxious to secure the Pope's blessing on his enterprises, sent a string of paid assassins to Sicily after the fall of Palermo. Pius IX, who was ten years later to declare himself infallible and for whom there is now a movement for beatification, later the same year promised absolution to anybody who would murder Napoleon III.[15] As Cavour himself said 'If we did for ourselves what we do for our country, we would be great scoundrels.'

There can be no doubt that Garibaldi and his friends believed, rightly or wrongly, but not without cause, that Cavour and his agents had conspired to bring about his death. His conduct in taking no other action than expelling La Farina, Griscelli and Totti was, therefore, not merely no stain on his chivalrous character but was, in the circumstances, an act of the greatest magnanimity.

Another man would have strung the lot of them up by the neck.

IV

Cavour reacted sharply to the news of La Farina's expulsion and to the failure of his plans.

One of the consequences of Garibaldi's victory in Sicily had been that Francis II, after consultation with the French Emperor, had declared himself on the 27th June a constitutional monarch, and brought into effect again the Constitution of 1848—which had never in law been abrogated. By that, he hoped to anticipate events and prevent Garibaldi carrying the revolution from Sicily to the mainland. Thereafter, he had been pestering Cavour for an alliance with Piedmont. At first Cavour had temporized but, as soon as he received the news of La Farini's deportation, he consented to receive the Neapolitan envoys, and began consultations with them directed to one end: how to frustrate Garibaldi and his declared intentions of invading the Kingdom of Naples. It has usually been assumed by historians that in these negotiations Cavour was playing his not unaccustomed game of duplicity, or at least was marking time to see how things developed. But that is far from the whole truth. Cavour was in earnest about an alliance with Naples, and on the 20th June, Farini was telling the Neapolitan envoy that a Bourbon victory over Garibaldi would be 'the salvation of Italy' and that they ought 'to throw Garibaldi and his army into the sea'.[16]

On the 8th July, Victor Emmanuel was persuaded to write to Garibaldi—telling him to agree to immediate annexation and on no account to invade Naples. On the 10th July, Cavour ordered that no more volunteer expeditions were to be allowed to sail from Genoa or anywhere in Piedmont. His assistance to the volunteers had therefore lasted for little more than a month.

Admiral Persano down in Sicily was deluged with a stream of letters.[17] On the 13th July, Cavour wrote to him instructing him to plant traitors in Garibaldi's handful of ships so that they could be seized when the need arose; the next day, he was told *at all costs to prevent Garibaldi from crossing to the continent;* on the 16th, he was urged to arrest Crispi and other leading Garibaldini as soon as the General himself was out of the way. Cavour was set on one thing above all else: to stop any further progress by Garibaldi.

V

The Medici expedition of 2500 men arrived in the gulf of Castellamare on the 19th June. The General went to greet them and was back in Palermo by ten o'clock the next morning. It was the day in which the last of the Neapolitan troops were evacuated, and the town was *en fête* and the streets packed with excited crowds. Garibaldi did not go out to see the conquered depart; he stayed in his porch room. The next day he sent off a column under Türr for Catania; five days later Bixio was sent off with another column to cross the south and then to join up with the others at Catania; another force under Medici was sent eastwards to Barcellona. The object of these operations was to sweep all the remaining Neapolitan troops up into the top of the island facing the continent.

On the 19th July, Garibaldi arrived in front of Milazzo. Soon after daybreak the following day, he moved to the attack with all available forces. There was an eight-hour battle in which a fifth of his men were either killed or wounded. Garibaldi was himself in the forefront of the battle and repeatedly exposed himself to fire. At one stage, he was closely surrounded and set on by a troop of enemy cavalry, from which he and a comrade extricated themselves by the use of the sabre and revolver. By the end of the day, the Neapolitans, although their losses had been much lighter than those of the attackers, retreated into the inner fort and the volunteers took the town. That night Alexandre Dumas, who had arrived in his yacht in the bay as the battle was ending, found Garibaldi lying in the porch of a church asleep on the pavement with a saddle for a pillow.[18]

Ten days after the battle for Milazzo, while the besieged Neapolitans in the castle still outnumbered the volunteers who had captured the town, four Neapolitan frigates appeared in the bay. These created consternation amongst Garibaldi's troops, for the volunteers were in no position to withstand a bombardment from the sea, nor had they the weapons with which to reply to it.

But the ships had appeared not to fight but to negotiate a capitulation. The Neapolitans in the castle, it appeared, had ample arms and ammunition but little food and water. Garibaldi's reputation left their commander in Messina paralysed with fear; and in Naples itself the newly appointed Ministers of the King who had so suddenly been converted to constitutionalism, were only too aware that they owed their positions to Garibaldi's victories and could contemplate the same fate as their predecessors of 1848 should his cause fail. The fort of Milazzo was surrendered to Garibaldi without further conflict, and the troops in it were allowed to depart with the honours of war. In spite of this agreement, the Neapolitan commander did not succeed in behaving honourably; a delayed fuse was left connected to the powder magazine.

VI

The news of Garibaldi's victory at Milazzo filled Cavour and Farini with fury, and galvanized them again into fresh activity to halt his enterprises. Cavour wrote again to his admiral in Sicily ordering him not to give the slightest help to Garibaldi in any shape or form; he wrote to his Ambassador in Naples[19] commanding that he should oppose any advance of the volunteers to the mainland, giving as his reason: *It is most important that the liberation of Naples should not be due to Garibaldi, for if that happens a revolutionary system will take the place of the monarchist national party.*

For the second time the King was requested to send a personal letter to Garibaldi commanding him not to invade the continent; and this Victor Emmanuel did on the afternoon of 22nd July. The bearer of his message to Garibaldi was a Count Litta and he arrived in Sicily with it on the 27th.

He found Garibaldi still at Milazzo Castle and delivered the letter from the King. As soon as Garibaldi read the letter, he went straight into an adjoining room where he found a number of his officers, talking and joking.

'Gentlemen, I have a letter to write,' he said. 'Please don't make such a row.'

He sat down and penned the following reply:[20]

Sire,
Your Majesty knows how much affection and respect I have for your person and how strong a desire I have to obey you. But Your Majesty can conceive in what embarrassment with the people of continental Naples

I would now be placed by a passive attitude if I were obliged to withhold my help at such a time from those to whom I have promised immediate relief. Italy cries out against passivity on my part, and I believe it would do immense damage.

At the end of my mission, I will lay at the feet of your Majesty the authority which circumstances have conferred on me and will be content to obey for the rest of my life.

Some historians have believed that, at the same time as Count Litta handed Garibaldi the letter from the King, he also gave him a second private letter inviting him to disregard the official one. There seems little doubt that Count Litta did carry such a letter from the King but, since it was discovered amongst his papers after his death with the seal unbroken, it is almost certain that it was never delivered; and that Garibaldi never knew of it. Probably it was only to be handed over if the General showed any inclination to follow the instructions which the King had sent on the advice of his Ministers; and to show that, whatever Cavour might have to say, the King secretly supported him.

But one thing is certain. The official letter, forbidding the invasion of Naples, was sent on the express instructions of Cavour and his Cabinet; and there is no evidence that Cavour ever knew of the second and secret letter. In fact, Cavour was doing everything he could to stop the General. His object, as he himself put it later, was *to fight the revolution with every means at my disposal.*[21]

Count Litta stayed to dine with Garibaldi before returning to Turin. He found that the first person at the table was a woman with an enormous sombrero hat decorated with velvet pompoms, dressed in a jacket and short skirt of Russian leather. She was another of the exotic adventuresses who floated in and out of the General's life, and called herself the Countess Maria Martini Della Torre. He had met her in London, apparently in May 1854, and she had joined him outside Milazzo just before the battle. She professed to have been in the Crimea with Florence Nightingale, and to have come to give succour to the troops; though it seems doubtful whether her interest in them extended far beyond their leader.

Meanwhile Cavour, working on the assumption that Garibaldi would disregard the King's letter of the 22nd July as he had disregarded that of the 8th June, laid his own little plot to take over Naples.

VII

He was not the only one concerned to prevent Garibaldi crossing the Straits. The King of Naples had already been in touch with Napoleon III and received from him what he believed to be a firm promise that the French fleet would intervene to prevent it. The British were hostile. The views of Lord John Russell, the British Foreign Secretary, had been expressed the previous year[22] *I dare say the dreamers wish to unite Naples and Sicily and make a Kingdom of the whole of Italy. But that is wild and foolish. It would make a despotism instead of a free government, an unwieldy power instead of a compact one;* and when Garibaldi had taken Sicily he had sent a message on the 23rd July to the British Ambassador, Elliott, in Naples to tell Garibaldi that: *he ought to be content with the whole of Sicily and not stir any further the fire of Italian insurrection.*[23]

The day after he had written that letter, Lord John Russell received the French Ambassador at his house at 37 Chesham Place. While he was closeted with him, discussing joint steps to be taken by the French and British navies to prevent the crossing of the Straits by Garibaldi, a nervous little man, snivelling with a bad cold, ran out of the rain up the steps outside, rang the bell, and stood shivering under the portico until the butler opened the door.

He was ushered into the large hall, elegant with its Georgian green walls and white figured frieze.

'Is Lord John at home?' he asked.

'He's engaged with the French Ambassador and I've strict instructions to let nobody in except the Minister for Naples,' replied the butler.

'Is Lady Russell at home, then?'

'Her Ladyship's ill in bed.'

The visitor was a former Naples lawyer named Lacaita, who had been Gladstone's guide on his visit to that city in 1850. On Boxing Day the same year, he had been arrested by the police, and on him had been found a card which read: *Will you come to tea and talk over the grand Republican days?* In vain, he had tried to explain that it was from an English titled lady and that 'the Republic' was no more than a party of tourists who had spent eight days together and jokingly adopted that title. The Neapolitan police did not appreciate the joke; on the strength of that

I

document he was indicted for sedition and conspiracy; and he had fled to London.

Puzzled now how to gain an interview with Lord John, Lacaita sent a card up to Lady Russell: *For the love you bear the memory of your father, please see me at once.* It was not entirely presumptuous, for Lady Russell's father had been a good friend of his. Soon he was by her bedside, and so convinced her of the urgency of his mission that she sent a message down to her husband: 'Come and see me at once.' The British Foreign Secretary raced up to his wife's bedroom to be confronted by the little Italian, who passionately poured out his arguments, interspersed with spasms of coughing. At length, Lord John patted him kindly on the shoulder.

'Go back to bed,' he said. 'And don't be so sure that I'm going to sign the agreement with France.'

The following afternoon, the British Cabinet resolved not only to reject the French proposal, but to oppose any outside intervention to stop Garibaldi crossing the Straits of Messina. In his official dispatch to the Ambassador in Paris, the Foreign Secretary wrote: *If France chose to interfere alone, we should merely disapprove her course and protest against it. In our opinion, the Neapolitans ought to be masters either to reject or to receive Garibaldi.*[24] But Napoleon III did not choose to interfere alone; and Garibaldi was left free to make his venture without interference by the great powers.

It was Cavour who had sent Lacaita to Lord John Russell and it has tempted some historians to believe that, in spite of all the evidence to the contrary, he was seeking to aid Garibaldi. The reason lies in what he told the British Minister in Turin at the time. Cavour was afraid of 'dangerous complications' if France and England were to intervene in the affairs of Italy; in other words, it was an open invitation to Austria to do the same, and might well lead to a European war; but, thereby, he rendered Garibaldi a singular service, if unwittingly.

VIII

By the end of July, it was obvious that Garibaldi had conquered the whole of Sicily and had freed the Straits of Messina for an advance to the continent. The 15,000 Neapolitan troops in Messina had yielded the town to Garibaldi without a fight, and on the 28th July signed an agreement with him whereby, in return for being allowed to remain in the citadel, they undertook not to engage in further acts of hostility. It must have seemed to Cavour when he heard that news that, if the Neapolitans could surrender so easily without a fight there, the prospects of a successful resistance in the mainland were remote. So, on the 31st July, he abandoned his attempts to make an alliance with Naples. Opinion in Piedmont was strongly with Garibaldi, but the opinion to which Cavour listened, that of the wealthy and influential conservatives, was pressing him strongly to do something to forestall another Garibaldi triumph.

His plan was to send Admiral Persano to Naples under the pretext of protecting the Princess of Syracuse; and have other ships laden with troops and arms ready in the harbour there. As he disclosed to his confidant, Nigra, on the 1st August, his plan was that his agents in Naples should: *provoke a movement which if successful will, without delay, invoke the protection of the King of Piedmont. The King accepts the proposal to send a division which will keep order and arrest Garibaldi.*[25] It was a plot which failed completely, in spite of the large amount of money Cavour lavished in bribes to effect it. Nobody was to be found in Naples resolute enough to carry out the proposed insurrection.

What Cavour most certainly did not know was that his monarch sent an oral message to Garibaldi four days later, urging him not only to invade the continent but, as soon as he had occupied Naples, to press on and take Umbria and the Marches from the Pope. Garibaldi needed no urging from his King. He had all his available men marshalled among the sand dunes on the seashore near the lighthouse on the tip of Sicily nearest the mainland, and a flotilla of small craft requisitioned to carry them across the Straits.

It was there that Alexandre Dumas found Garibaldi again on the 28th July. Dumas had been sent by him from Milazzo with a Letter of Credit addressed to the Municipio of Palermo with which he was to purchase arms; but Garibaldi had omitted to add under his signature the word 'Dictator'. As a result the Sindico of Palermo had refused to honour it, remarking that, if Garibaldi were killed, the municipality would have to stand the loss.

When Dumas told Garibaldi all this, tears streamed down the Dictator's face.

'When I get killed, it will not be for people like that,' he cried.

Fortunately, Dumas had been able to obtain the money from

another source and was about to leave to purchase arms in France.

'Be back as soon as you can,' Garibaldi told him.

'I can't undertake to be back sooner than a fortnight.'

'With the arms?'

'Yes.'

'I shall have to await your return before crossing to Calabria.'

Two miles only of waters separated Garibaldi and his forces from the mainland; but they were two miles that had already once that century defeated an invader.

XIX

THE APOGEE OF A LIFETIME

✦✦✦✦✦✦✦✦✦✦✦

DUMAS CAUGHT a French packet boat to Naples and, soon
after the boat had docked there, he was interviewed on
board by two police officers. As he had been sentenced *in absentia*
some years earlier to four years in the galleys, he naturally assumed
they had come to arrest him.[1]

He was quickly reassured.

'When do you think Garibaldi will be here?' asked one.

'Oh! In two or three weeks' time,' he asserted confidently.

'Excellent! Everybody here is impatient with waiting for him,'
exclaimed the police.

It was a strange expression to come from officers of a State with
which the rebel leader was engaged in undeclared war; but what
they said was true. The grant of the constitution by the king had
opened the gates to the expression of opinions that it had been
death to ventilate previously. Even most of the king's new ministers were waiting impatiently for Garibaldi's arrival. Liberal
newspapers were being published and, according to Dumas, no
less than five of them were featuring 'The Memoirs of Garibaldi'
—each claiming that it was their exclusive property and each
pirating the version that he himself had edited and published in
French.

In Marseilles, Dumas was able to purchase secretly the weapons
he required for Garibaldi. He observed that all the boats coming
from Naples were packed with titled refugees and those officials of
the Crown who had good cause to fear the vengeance of the
people; and that all the boats going to Naples were crowded with
liberal exiles returning. None of all these travellers seemed to
entertain any doubt about the shape of future events.

On the night of the 8th August, the volunteers, crowded on to the beaches near the lighthouse at Messina, thought the invasion hour had come. They were embarked in the small vessels and steamers. A party of 200 men was sent out in rowing-boats to cross the Straits, and Garibaldi departed with them out to sea. He was soon back. After hours of waiting, just as dawn was breaking, the order was given to the expedition to disembark. A landing-party had been sent in an attempt to capture a fort on the other side. But they were unsuccessful and had to take flight into the hills. In the days that followed, they kept up the spirits of their comrades in the island by beacon fires at night on the crests across the Straits.

Four days later, Garibaldi disappeared from Sicily and the island buzzed with rumours as to where he had gone. Dumas, landing a few days after his disappearance, was met by the captain of his yacht, who told him that the General had been sent for by Victor Emmanuel and was on his way to Turin. In fact, Bertani had come down from Genoa with the news that a further expedition of some 9,000 men, which he had raised, had been diverted from an attack on the Papal States by Cavour and was at the Gulf degli Aranci in Sardinia, nearly opposite Caprera. The General sailed away with him in the steamer *Washington*. It was Bertani's ambition to get him to lead this expedition on to attack Rome. He was furious when they arrived at the Gulf to find that Piedmontese warships had forced the bulk of the expedition to go on to Sicily; Cavour had been at work again. What was more, he had issued a further order that under no circumstances whatever were any more volunteers to be allowed to leave Piedmont to join Garibaldi's forces. Garibaldi consoled himself by going on to Caprera for a day to eat some of his own water melons.

On the morning of the 18th August, the General reappeared amongst his forces near the lighthouse and, after a few hours, disappeared as mysteriously as he had before, galloping off in a three-horse carriage.

He drove down the coast to south of Taormina, where he had made a secret rendezvous with Bixio and his force of some 3,000 men. Two steamers, the *Franklin* and the *Torino*, had been ordered to meet them. Garibaldi arrived at about two o'clock to find that the antiquated *Franklin*, a wooden-hulled paddle steamer, had sprung a leak when she had dropped her anchor and was taking water so badly that the pumps could not keep up with it. He at once ordered attempts to be made to find the leak.

Nobody seemed anxious to carry out his order, so he said:
'Very well—I'll dive myself.'

With that, the ship's crew came to life and, under his direction,
the hole was stopped up. When the expedition sailed that night,
he travelled in the vessel. The hole in the hull was patched with a
mixture of straw and cow dung. They landed safely near Melito,
save that Bixio drove the *Torino* on the rocks, where she had to be
abandoned.

Once again the General had taken his enemies by surprise. So
sure were they that he would cross the narrowest part of the
Straits from Messina, that all their considerable force of warships
was concentrated there; and they had no troops at all south of
Reggio. He had sailed thirty miles instead of two, but he had been
unopposed, and the next day every telegraph in Europe was
spluttering out the news that Garibaldi had crossed to the mainland.

Forty-eight hours later, he captured Reggio, after a brisk engagement; and the Neapolitan fleet chased off down there to
prevent reinforcements crossing from Sicily. That night, in their
absence, a swarm of small boats crossed from the island and landed
nearly two thousand men at Favazzina. The Neapolitan fleet got
back in time to bombard the empty boats returning to Sicily. The
invaders now had some five thousand men across the Straits and,
since the whole operation must have been organized in detail
before Garibaldi left on his trip to Sardinia, it showed strategic
planning of a very high order on his part.

His next move was to attack the forts guarding the narrow
passage of the Straits. He surrounded them and slowly closed in
during the night. When daylight came, they were surrounded by
a sea of Redshirts; at the sight, panic raced through the Neapolitan
troops. They surrendered without a shot being fired. Garibaldi
disarmed the troops and sent them off to their homes throughout
the country, to spread the news through the rest of the Neapolitan
army that if they surrendered they were free to return home.

II

Meanwhile, the good neutral Alexandre Dumas had sailed his
yacht into the harbour at Naples and anchored it so close to the
Royal Palace that from time to time he could see Francis II at the
window, scanning the horizon through a telescope. That monarch

had already stored his diamonds and treasure in an Austrian man-o'-war, as if he, too, had no doubts about the outcome of the war.

Under cover of darkness, a boat put off and came alongside the *Emma*. A party of two men and two women came aboard. One of the men was wrapped in a cloak and had a black hat pulled down over his face; he was none other than the Neapolitan Minister of Internal Affairs and Prefect of Police, Liborio Romano. He had been a party to Cavour's scheme to raise insurrection in Naples; now he had come to offer his services to Garibaldi. He professed he had taken office only to preserve his city from civil war and anarchy and, since he had in his younger days suffered for his liberal convictions, it may well have been true.

He told Dumas: 'I shall fight for the constitutional cause as long as I am able. When I can do so no longer, I will hand in my resignation and join Garibaldi.'

'You mean that?' asked Dumas.

'Yes—on my word of honour.'

Dumas therefore arranged with him to send word of this to Garibaldi; and when he had left, the novelist called on the British vessel *Hannibal* and obtained Admiral Mundy's promise that, if necessary, Romano would be received on board as a political refugee. The next morning, Romano sent Dumas his photograph, with a note: *If I fail to keep my promise given to you last night, write under this 'the portrait of a coward'.*

A few days later, Dumas received an order that he was to remove his yacht out of the harbour within half an hour or he would be fired on by cannon from the fort. The king had at last objected to what was going on under his window. For Dumas was busy distributing arms, had fourteen tailors working on the deck making red shirts, and at night treated the monarch to a display of fireworks in the provocative colours of Green, White and Red.

III

Dumas's messenger found Garibaldi in the mountain village of Soveria in Upper Calabria where, with a handful of redshirts and a crowd of local peasants, he had just taken the surrender of another 10,000 Neapolitan troops. The novelist's letter, in part, read: *Liborio Romano, the only popular Minister, is at your disposition, with at least two of his colleagues, at the first attempt at reaction on the king's part . . . At this first attempt, which will liberate him from his oath to the king, he offers to leave Naples to link up with you, to announce the disposition of the king and to acknowledge you as Dictator . . . You know that I will not ask you for anything for myself, except leave to shoot in the Capo-di-Monti and to continue the excavations at Pompeii . . .*

Garibaldi told the messenger to return to Naples and tell Liborio Romano to stay at his post and prevent the people doing anything until he arrived.

'Above all—no fighting in the streets of Naples. Palermo has suffered too much from that.'

As the messenger left, he repeated:

'Tell him to do all he can to get the king to leave, but no rising without me. It would be too dangerous.'

The advance to Naples now became a race, with Garibaldi travelling in a carriage out far ahead of his troops. In front of his party was a large Neapolitan army retreating on Naples, and whose intentions were uncertain. Garibaldi was persuaded to leave his carriage and take to the mountains on mules. 'Seven men on seven mules to conquer a Kingdom,' as Bertani described it. However fast Garibaldi travelled he did not manage to catch up with another party, composed mainly of mad Englishmen, which was in a carriage in front of him. One of them was a *Times* correspondent, one a commander in Her Brittanic Majesty's Royal Navy, and another was the bearded Peard who everywhere was mistaken for Garibaldi. *Within an hour of our arrival at Eboli, the town was brilliantly illuminated . . . brass bands banging away in every direction and the crowds roaring themselves hoarse and calling on the General to appear. Deputations arrived; first came the church headed by a bishop* wrote the Commander[2] of their arrival at Eboli, while the real Garibaldi was far behind. Peard sent a telegram to the Neapolitan general at Salerno to the effect that Garibaldi had arrived at Eboli with 5,000 troops, and that another brigade of the Neapolitan army had not merely surrendered but had deserted *en masse* to him. The message was passed on verbatim to Naples, and when it was received in the capital the king decided the time had come for him to leave. He instructed one of his ministers to prepare a royal proclamation to the people. On the evening of the 5th September, it was presented to him. He read it.

'You didn't write this,' he said. 'It's Romano. I recognize his style.

'Ah, well—when he likes, he writes very well,' he added, as

he signed it; what he did not know was that Romano had drafted it three days' before.

The next day, Francis II took leave of his ministers. To Romano he said, sinisterly: 'Look out for your head.' At four o'clock in the afternoon, the last of the Neapolitan Bourbons left his palace and boarded a ship for Gaeta; at almost exactly the same time, Garibaldi was driving into Salerno in an open carriage to the applause and wild cheers of thousands of the king's subjects.

IV

The following day, in the early hours of the morning, the Neapolitan ministers met to consider the next step. They decided to send a letter to Garibaldi, and the indefatigable Romano already had one drafted, which all present approved. It read:

General,

You have here a ministry placed in power by King Francis II. We took office at a difficult time as a sacrifice due to our country, when the ideal of unity of Italy under the sceptre of Victor Emmanuel . . . had become invincible, thanks to the might of your sword . . . We accepted power . . . in order to save the country from civil war and anarchy. All eyes are now turned to you; all our hopes are focused on you. We, the trustees of authority . . . surrender this into your hand, confident that you will use it worthily.

It was taken by messengers to Salerno, and at six-thirty that morning Garibaldi telegraphed his reply: *As soon as the Sindaco and the Commander of the National Guard of Naples, whom I am expecting, arrive I shall come.*

When the two Neapolitan officials arrived at Salerno, Garibaldi was surprised to learn that he was not expected to go to the city that day. Quite apart from the fact that the Cabinet wished to prepare a hero's triumph for him, there was still a substantial force of troops loyal to Francis II in the city, quartered in the four forts, with their artillery trained on the boulevards. His own staff tried to dissuade him from going until these had departed and he had some troops of his own to guard him; but he would not listen.

'Naples is in danger,' he said. 'We must go there today. We must go this very minute.'

The only railway line in Southern Italy at that time ran from Vietri sul Mare, two miles outside Salerno, through Naples to

Capua. At ten-thirty, Garibaldi and a small group of close companions took a special train from Vietri; everybody else, whoever they were, who could get on board crammed in. It took the train three hours to cover the twenty-seven miles to Naples, for, as it approached the city, the line was mobbed by peasants and fishermen in their thousands; and so, as he himself described it: *A son of the people, accompanied by a few of his friends... entered the splendid capital of the fiery mountain, acclaimed by its half-million inhabitants, whose fervent and irresistible will, paralysing a whole army, had driven them on to destroy a tyranny and assert their rights.*[3]

His first official act—less than one hour after he arrived in the city—was to hand over the Neapolitan navy which, unlike the army, had refused to follow Francis II to Gaeta, to representatives of Victor Emmanuel. There could have been no greater indication of his loyalty to that monarch; for, at the time, the Piedmontese navy consisted of no more than five frigates, whereas that of Naples consisted of twenty-seven steamships and more than sixty armed sailing vessels. It was no small gift to a king from the one Cavour was wont to sneer at as 'that cabin boy from Nice' and who sought nothing in return but that the vessels should be used to complete the work of unifying his country.

A week later, Alexandre Dumas arrived back in Naples and hastened to the Palazza d'Angri, a large private house which had been taken over for the volunteer's headquarters. He found Garibaldi installed in a room in the servants' quarters on the fourth floor.

'Well, here you are,' said the General. 'You've kept me waiting long enough. Now for the excavation at Pompeii and your permission to shoot.'

The novelist was given rooms in a small palace, and the post of Director—unpaid—of Museums and Excavations; much to the scandal of local office hunters who coveted the same post—paid.

There was great curiosity in Naples as to whether the miracle of Saint Januarius would be wrought. According to the priests, on the Saint's Day, the blood of the martyr changes from a state of coagulation to one of liquefaction—but only if he is satisfied with the administration of the city. Some hostile priests had spread the story about that, as the result of the expulsion of the Bourbons and the intrusion of an irreligious filibuster, the saint intended to show his displeasure by refusing to perform his annual miracle. Greatly to the discomfort of Garibaldi's detractors, the firing of salvos of artillery at nine in the morning announced to the delighted populace that the miracle had been performed. The saint must have been almost as enthusiastic for their new ruler as they, for the miracle took place three hours before the usual time.

Unhappily, the Pope was not impressed by the miracle, for he informed the British Representative in Rome a few days later that it would only be a short time before the Austrians arrived with a large army to destroy the Piedmontese forces, as well as those of Garibaldi; nor was Francis II, who had retreated north into the almost impregnable forts at Gaeta and Capua with 60,000, and at once began planning a campaign to retake Naples.

v

Cavour's plot to seize power in Naples before Garibaldi arrived there had failed, chiefly because the propertied classes on whom he relied were not willing to risk their necks to achieve what Garibaldi and his scalliwags would soon do for them at the risk of their own. If he were to achieve his object of *throwing all the Garibaldini into the sea*,[4] as he put it subsequently in a letter to Nigra, he had to think up another scheme quickly. He was quite prepared to make civil war on them but he knew public opinion in Piedmont would not stand for it, even though *the soldiers of Fanti and Cialdini want nothing better than to rid the country of the red shirts*, as he said in the same letter.

Cavour found his new scheme in one that had been canvassed earlier the same year by the army and some of his supporters in Turin, but which he had not then been willing to accept. It was nothing less than to steal the thunder of the radicals by himself invading the Papal States with the Piedmontese army. In short, doing exactly what he had stopped Garibaldi doing in November 1859, and Bertani in early August 1860. It was the 21st August before Cavour brought himself to accept this scheme, but he at once sent off Farini to obtain the permission of Napoleon III. That monarch's reply was: 'Do it, but do it quickly,' and, lest he should himself be involved, he took himself off on a sea cruise so that he could not be contacted.

Even with the French Emperor's acquiescence, it was a scheme that called for the maximum exertion of all Cavour's considerable powers of deception; it got it.

The day Garibaldi took over in Naples, the 7th September,

Cavour wrote to Persano to go and congratulate the General on his achievement and suggest to him that the Piedmontese Army and his volunteers should join forces for an expedition to invade Venice.[5] The very same day he saw the British Ambassador[6] and told him that he was *forced to resort to extreme measures to avoid the Venice difficulty.* 'Believe me,' said Cavour, 'Garibaldi shall not attack Venice . . . I have no intention of attacking Venice and Lord John may rely on me.' The same day he also sent an ultimatum to the Papacy, complaining of massacres by the Papal foreign mercenaries and demanding that they should be disbanded.[7] The next day, he went to see Victor Emmanuel to poison his mind against Garibaldi with a lying telegram which he had instigated Persano to send from Naples.

On the 11th September, the Piedmontese army moved into Umbria and the Marches and through a series of bloody battles at Perugia, Spoleto, Castelfidardo and Ancona they routed the Papal volunteers who, since the beginning of the year, had come from all the Catholic countries of Europe to fight for God and the Pope; and thereby achieved, with great bloodshed, what Garibaldi, the previous November, could have achieved without. Some of the bloodshed was caused by General Cialdini shooting peasants and priests in cold blood; crimes of which Garibaldi would never have been guilty.

On the 23rd September, Garibaldi's commander in charge of Abruzzi wired him asking what attitude to adopt if the Piedmontese troops appeared on the frontier. The General sent back his instructions: *If the Piedmontese troops enter our territory, receive them as brothers.*[8] At that moment, Cavour was paying some of the senior officers of the Neapolitan army he was fighting to maintain their resistance to the volunteers and to preserve their army intact for his own purposes.[9]

A week later, the Neapolitan army broke out of their fortress in an attempt to smash their way back to Naples through Garibaldi's redshirts. They had been inspired to attack by a minor defeat inflicted on the volunteers during a short absence from the front that Garibaldi had been obliged to make. He had been forced to go back to Sicily for three days to settle trouble caused by another Cavour-engineered conspiracy in the island.

It has been suggested that Cavour's motive in all these perfidious machinations was to prevent Garibaldi capturing Rome and thereby embroiling Piedmont in international complications.

Garibaldi's desire to press on to Rome has been denounced by practically every historian of note as an insane and dangerous idea, on the grounds that he was likely to bring Piedmont into conflict with France and, possibly, provoke Austria to intervene once more. But it may be doubted whether this view is correct. Austria could be counted out at once. In 1860, she was giving all the aid to the Pope she dared by sending 'volunteers' to fight in his army. She well knew that her whole cumbersome empire would collapse if she dared to wage war again; and that she invited further rebellions in Hungary and amongst every one of her subject nations if she attacked Garibaldi, who was as much a sacred hero to them as to the Italians. As for Napoleon III, he was perfectly happy to sink the Pope and all his works, provided that French Catholic opinion did not hold him responsible. That he might have attacked Piedmont is implausible; for she was the only friend he had left in Europe, and he had shed French blood the previous year to establish her as a strong buffer state between France and Austria. There was no reason at all, therefore, why Garibaldi's desired operation should not have succeeded without international complications. Cavour knew this as well as anybody, even though it suited his game to pretend otherwise from time to time.

Nor was Cavour's hostility to Garibaldi dictated by fear that the General was in danger of repudiating the monarchy, although he professed on occasion to fear republicanism in the ranks of the volunteers. Neither had he cause to doubt, nor did he doubt, the sincerity of Garibaldi's attachment to the person of Victor Emmanuel. In fact, one of his real complaints about the General was that he was too loyal to the King, and he deliberately set out to provoke a quarrel between them.

His fundamental fear of Garibaldi was not political but social. When he aimed at *preventing the revolution spreading to Piedmont*[9] his object was to oppose anything that endangered what he called *the principle of social conservation*.[10] What he really feared was economic reform and the spread of democracy. In fact, if Cavour were a liberal at all, he belonged to the type, still amongst us, who oppose as communistic any state interference with property rights, however illegitimately acquired or however harmful to society; and, like those of today, he never had enough foresight to see that social amelioration is the best barrier against communism.

The economic reforms that Garibaldi and his friends had

carried out in their advance up the peninsula did much to commend them to the peasants. For, in the preceding years, the large landowners had succeeded in robbing the peasants of their traditional common lands by enclosures, similar to those carried out nearly a century before in England; and, as in that country, starvation and misery became the lot of the peasants. *The labouring class in the South, numerous and without their daily bread,* was how a British consul[11] described them. But, whereas the enforced poverty of the British peasants had driven them into the new factories of the industrial revolution, there was no such alleviation for those of Calabria. There were no deposits of iron or coal there; Christ may have stopped at Eboli, but the industrial revolution stopped much further north.

Garibaldi had therefore sought to save them from their poverty by restoring common land in some districts where the enclosures had been very recent or not completed, and by removing taxes on food and lowering the price of salt; but these measures, both necessary and attractive to the peasants, struck terror into Cavour's heart, as he saw what he thought were the first signs of communism. In that, of course, he was not alone. The British Minister in Naples, Elliott, was busy writing to Lord John Russell of these mild reforms as evidence of the *Communist principles of the revolution*;[12] nothing, in fact, could have been further from the truth. The programme of the Roman Republic of 1848 may have been drafted by Mazzini, but it accurately represented Garibaldi's own views: *No class war . . . no wanton or unjustified interference with private property . . . but a steady bettering of the material conditions of the classes least favoured by fortune*;[13] and though he was wise enough to appreciate the necessity of a proper system of land reform in Naples and Sicily—such as is now only half-heartedly beginning —he had shown by his vigorous suppression of the unlawful seizure of land on the Brontë estates and elsewhere in Sicily that he would not tolerate irregular interference with property.

As much as Cavour disliked the social reforms of the revolution, he disliked its democracy more. That he managed to pose to his own generation as a parliamentary democrat, and to go down in history as such, is one of the most remarkable achievements of his deceit. For he never allowed Parliament to meet unless he was sure that they would do what he wanted. All through the war of 1859, he ruled without a parliament and, in 1860, after the first few months, parliament was not allowed to meet. He preferred to keep it as a reserve to fall back on in his struggles with the King, and he always manipulated elections through the Home Office and the police to see that only his own supporters were elected. At the same time, he was remarkably sensitive to public opinion—but by that he meant only the upper classes. He was resolute against any extension of the franchise to the lower classes, and he had no interest in what the common people thought or felt, provided their discontent could be kept short of rebellion against authority.

As has been seen, he really wanted a duality of powers in the Italian peninsula, but if that were impossible as the result of the fervour aroused by, and the actions of, Garibaldi and his party then he wanted, as Crispi put it: *Italy for Piedmont and not Piedmont for Italy*.[14] He was, therefore, neither a nationalist nor a patriot; it was part of his *conservation of social principles*. He was not even a true monarchist, for he supported the monarchy only as a means to that end. If the monarchy were to become linked to the principles of Garibaldi, he was hostile to it.

In short, the difference between Garibaldi and Cavour can be expressed in one sentence: the former had been made by the St Simonians into a man of the twentieth century, whereas the latter was very much a creature of his class and of his time. *The signor Count remains a Count in spite of his liberal mask*,[15] as a radical Genoa newspaper put it.

VI

On the last day of September, Speranza arrived in Naples and installed herself in the Hotel de Rome overlooking the bay. She set out at once seeking Garibaldi but, although the town was *glowing like a fiery furnace*[16] with redshirts, she did not find him. He was in the countryside outside Capua.

As he gazed, late at night, at the lines held by his enemy a vast flare of flames soared up into the sky.

'Gentlemen,' he said to his companions,[17] 'We must sleep lightly tonight.'

That night, under cover of a blanket of fog, the Bourbon troops stole out from their fortress and made their way along sunken roads, cut in olden times in the tufa of that area, through Garibaldi's lines. At daybreak, as he was driving in a carriage from Santa Maria to Sant' Angelo, he was caught in an ambush. His coachman and one of his staff were killed and his carriage riddled with bullets. He escaped in a brisk fight by use of his sword. During that day, there took place what is usually known as the battle of the Volturno, although it all took place just south of that river. The Bourbons, attacking from Capua, penetrated Garibaldi's front between Santa Maria and Sant' Angelo at the same time as other units attacked from the north down to Old Caserta and from the east, near Maddaloni, in a fight near a great viaduct known as the Arches of the Valley.

In Naples, Speranza was horrified to see train-loads of wounded Garibaldini arriving in the city and, as she drove out towards Maddaloni, houses filled to overflowing with the wounded, and carts bearing the volunteers bathed in blood from unstaunched wounds. She was so overcome by the sight that she returned to the city and consoled herself with two dozen oysters, a beefsteak and iced beer, and was surprised that during the night she was seized with stomach pains and diarrhœa. She was disgruntled when she found that no doctor would come to attend to her. They had a few other things to do than attend to a writer with the bellyache: in the course of the battle that day, 1,500 of Garibaldi's troops were wounded and some 300 killed.

As the result of audacious manœuvuring by the General, the Neapolitan assault, which had been determined and persistent, was driven off. For the first time in his life he had 30,000 troops under his command. They were pitted against a superior force of Bourbon troops but, by his constant presence on the battle-front and his coolness, the day was won. It was the only opportunity he had during his life to demonstrate that he could control a large body of troops with the same skill as his handful of fleet-footed guerrillas. By the end of the day, all the Bourbon troops were securely penned back in Capua, apart from one separated battalion, more than 2,000 of whom were captured the next day.

Speranza, unable to see the General, departed on the steamer for Sicily but with the rolling and pitching of the vessel was soon in trouble with her stomach again.

A week or so later, she was passing through Naples again *en route* back to Nice, when she met her old friend, Fruscianti.

'Why are you not with the General?' she asked him.

'I was wounded at the battle of Volturno,' he told her. 'Why are you not with him?'

'I've only this minute arrived from Sicily, and in an hour I go on by the same steamer.'

'Without seeing Garibaldi?' exclaimed Fruscianti. 'Impossible.'

Her steamer sailed without her and Fruscianti secured her a seat on the train to Caserta. There, she found the palace courtyard crowded with Redshirts, as were all the rooms inside. Hundreds were waiting to see Garibaldi and she sat for three hours, the only woman amongst the crowd of men. Eventually, Admiral Persano arrived and she persuaded him to take her in to see the General.

He was seated at a small table covered with papers, his *poncho* wrapped around his body and tied at the neck. He looked immeasurably older than when she had last seen him the previous year in Bologna.

As soon as he saw her, he got up and kissed both her hands.

'So you haven't run through Naples a second time without calling on me. May I order an apartment to be prepared for you?'

They could not talk privately, for every few minutes they were interrupted, and there were other people in the room all the time.

'See,' said Garibaldi in a low voice. 'Your present has never left me through all my troubles and dangers.' He pulled out the watch she had given him.

He talked about his daughter, Teresa.

'Don't you think it is time she was married?' he asked; but he said not a word to her about his own marriage earlier the same year.

A special train was ordered to take her back to Naples. She was repeatedly told it was ready, but still she lingered. In the end Medici came in with important dispatches before she could be persuaded to go.

A few years later, the Countess Maria Martini Della Torre offered to write her memoirs for a French newspaper but, unfortunately, her offer was not accepted; so there is no way of knowing what she was doing at that moment, save that she also was somewhere in, or around, the Palace of Caserta.

VII

After the victory of the Volturno, Garibaldi invited the Bourbon general to surrender Capua. He then set about raising batteries on the high ground near Sant' Angelo and along the railway embankment and threw bridges across the river, preparatory to taking the city. As he observed in a letter to the King: *The battle won on the Volturno and in the conflict of Caserta have rendered the soldiers of Francis II incapable, in my opinion, of further resistence.*[18] He therefore proposed to cross the river and reduce Capua. He received, however, express instructions from the King to desist from any further attack on the Bourbons.[19] The capture of Capua and Gaeta were to be reserved for the glory of the troops of Piedmont, not the Redshirts. He was also told by his monarch to take good care of the game in and around Caserta, and not to let his Redshirts poach the partridges.

VIII

On the 25th October, Garibaldi rode out from his headquarters on horseback with a handful of his staff. He took up his position on the roadside north of Capua, by a cottage near a few poplar trees. He was wearing his *poncho* and stained red shirt, and had bound a coloured kerchief round his hair under his hat. Before long, the first of the Piedmontese troops arrived. Regiment after regiment of them passed, silently and coldly, in front of the General, without saluting. Then there was the sound of a band and Victor Emmanuel arrived, prancing on a horse, his vast waxed moustache gleaming in the sun. He was immaculate in a uniform bedecked with medals he had done nothing to merit, as he came to claim a kingdom he had done nothing to earn. In his entourage were his mistress; Farini; and General Fanti, who had promised the Piedmontese troops that their mission was to see that *Italy did not remain subject to an audacious and lucky adventurer.*[20]

Garibaldi rode forward to meet him and swept his hat off his head.

'Greetings to the first King of Italy,' he said.[21]

The King shook him by the hand.

'How are you, *caro* Garibaldi?'

'Very well. How are you?'

'Excellent.'

There was little conversation. Garibaldi made some reference to the advance of his Redshirts against Gaeta and Capua. All the King said was:

'You have been fighting a long time. Your troops must be tired. Mine are fresh.'

They rode together for a few miles down the road and, as no invitation was given to Garibaldi to accompany the King further, they parted. Garibaldi and his friends turned off the road to a small village. There they had a midday meal of bread and cheese, and washed it down with a draught of water from a local well.

'Ugh!' he exclaimed, when he tasted the water. 'There must be a dead animal in that well.'

All that day it was observed that his face was full of sadness and he was strangely silent. He spent the night in the same village, sleeping on straw. The next day he said sadly to a friend:

'They have made us withdraw from the line.'

IX

However, it was found that the volunteers were still required to defend the Royal forces from their enemies, and Garibaldi consented that the orders of the King's staff should be transmitted to his men as if they had come from him. Meanwhile, worn out and tortured by his rheumatism, he retired to bed at Caserta. The only Royal general who deigned to visit him, found him propped up on pillows, wrapped in his *poncho*, with a little cap on his head, and a silk scarf around his neck, in a little room over the guardhouse of the Palace.

On the 2nd November, after a few rounds from the guns had been fired, the fort and the town of Capua capitulated, and the news could be splashed across the front pages of the newspapers of Turin, which had not yet found it necessary to mention Garibaldi's battle on the Volturno, as a triumph of the Royal armies.

Four days later, almost the whole of Garibaldi's force was assembled on the parade ground by the Palace at Caserta. The King had promised to review them. For two periods of six hours, in driving rain, 15,000 Redshirts stood with ordered arms on parade, awaiting the monarch for whom so many of their comrades had died. Then, as evening drew on, a messenger appeared to say that His Majesty would not be attending, with no further word of explanation or apology. After the parade, the troops crowded round Garibaldi shouting: 'To Rome! To Rome!' But he shook his head sadly, as he sat, pale and motionless, on his horse. 'Thank you, my old comrades,' he said. 'You have done much with little means in a short time. We have still more to do. Prepare for the early spring.'[22]

The King did not visit any of the Garibaldini who lay wounded in hospital but, the next day, he made a ceremonial entry into

Naples in a carriage with Garibaldi by his side. It was with great difficulty that the General had been persuaded to accompany the King, and, as they drove, neither spoke to the other. The following day, there was a formal audience in the Palace. Garibaldi and his men in their worn red shirts were on one side of the room, the officers of the Piedmontese army in their tailored uniforms and glittering decorations on the other, and, in the middle, the King occupied the throne so recently vacated by another monarch. Garibaldi was offered the decoration of the Collar of the Annunciation—which entitled him to be regarded as cousin to the King—the title of Prince of Calatafimi, a castle, a dowry for his daughter, and a steam yacht; all of which he politely refused.

Later that day, General Cialdini brought to Garibaldi a commission as full general of the Piedmontese army, signed by the King. Garibaldi screwed it up and threw it out of the window. The same evening, he sent a messenger to the British Admiral Mundy on the *Hannibal* to say that he proposed to leave early the next morning for Caprera and would like to pay his respects before departing. He spent the night in an hotel and, before dawn, was down at the port. There was nobody to notice him being rowed out across the still waters to the *Hannibal*.

It was before six o'clock and the British admiral was still in his bunk when he arrived, but soon they were sitting together looking out of the veranda windows in the stern of the great three-decker flagship to where, a cable length away, the *Washington* was blowing off steam.

Said Garibaldi in a melancholy voice:[23]

'There is the ship which is to carry me to my island home, but I could not depart, Admiral, without paying you a farewell visit . . . Your conduct to me since our first meeting in Palermo has been so kind, so generous, that it can never be erased from my memory.'

They talked of Caprera, of the Admiral's service in the Mediterranean, and Garibaldi's tone was of dejection and gloom, until the Admiral remarked that he did not expect to find him in Caprera in five months' time. He suddenly seemed to come alive with hope:

'Before five months have passed I shall again be in the field ! . . . I shall never rest satisfied till emancipation from foreign rule has been effected throughout the entirety of the Italian Kingdom.

Rome and Venice are not French or Austrian cities. They are Italian cities . . . They belong to Italy alone . . .'

Cavour was mentioned by him, but not by name, and he said that he could never offer his hand to an Italian Minister, however great, who had acquiesced in the degradation of his country.

During the whole of the interview, the name of King Victor Emmanuel was not once mentioned, in relation to his Majesty's entrance into the city, nor of the advance of the Sardinian army for the investment of Gaeta. It appeared to me that the dictator wished to avoid allusion to the subject . . . noted Admiral Mundy.

It was still early morning when Garibaldi was rowed across to the *Washington*. On her deck, he parted from a group of his close friends with the words: 'Till we meet in Rome.' As she sailed out of the harbour, there was only a handful on the quay to see her go. He left with a few hundred francs that his secretary had been able to borrow and a bag of seed corn, and a little coffee. All the newspapers in Naples were now in the pay of Cavour; none of them found it necessary to mention his departure.

The nearest he got to expressing his feelings was an observation[24] he made to Admiral Persano, a few days earlier, about the King and Cavour: 'They use men like they use oranges. They suck the juice out to the last drop and throw the peel away in the corner.'

IX

Cavour had given instructions to Farini as to how he was to conduct the administration in Naples and the south. They were contained in a letter dated the 2nd November, the day after the battle of the Volturno. It was a day on which Garibaldi had been disturbed during the early hours by the news that more than 3,000 Neapolitan troops from the north had attacked his headquarters at Caserta. It was a day he spent fighting against them. For four hours in the afternoon, he had sat nursing a dying boy of fifteen who had been mortally wounded fighting in the red shirt. When the child finally expired in his arms, he had burst into tears and cried: 'Can even liberty be worth *this*!'

Farini was, Cavour told him in that letter, *to take a whip and sweep them all into the sea* . . . *without mercy sweep away all the shit left in that stable.*[25] 'The shit' was the legislation Garibaldi and his friends had introduced into Naples. It included decrees for the establishment of twelve homes for children; the abolition of the national lottery and its replacement by savings banks; reduction in the price of salt; price controls on bread; the freedom of the Press; free education; a halt to all further enclosure of common land; preventing cruelty to animals; allowing the sale of the Scriptures to the people; freedom of religion; and the creation of railways. No doubt, as Trevelyan put it: *Neither Garibaldi nor Bertani had any conception of the proper limits to which a provisional government should confine its work, and many of their decrees made important changes in the principles of law, finance and State machinery, which should have been left to the mature decision of a future Italian Parliament.*

The people of Naples and Sicily quickly experienced under Farini and his successors exactly what Piedmontese administration meant, though Cavour waited no longer than did Garibaldi for the mature consideration of an Italian Parliament. The legislation of Garibaldi was repealed *en bloc*. Northerners took all the best jobs and ruled the south as if it were an occupied territory. Enclosures of common land received more official encouragement than under the Bourbons. The estates of the Church were sold off cheaply to wealthy profiteers. Taxation was increased. Conscription was introduced. Farini was told there was no reason why he should tolerate a free Press. Force was used at the slightest sign of unrest. Arrests, imprisonment, and executions without trial became a commonplace. Illegal deportations took place. Before long, the newly liberated south realized that it had only exchanged one slavery for another and there began what was virtually civil war, although it was officially termed 'Brigandage', which lasted at least five years; so that there were never less than sixty battalions holding the south down.

Worse still, the Piedmontese domination condemned the south to a century of neglect, poverty and misery which, even yet, has not been rectified.

In November, 1860, Panizzi was writing with reference to the civil adminstration in Naples under Garibaldi: *that he was surrounded by a set of scamps who made a fool of him, honest fellow;*[26] but in 1862, he spent five months' leave from the British Museum visiting Naples and the south and, while he was there, wrote: *The Italian Ministry has done everything in its power to create dissatisfaction by the pedantry of its regulations, the total disregard of the habits, feelings and prejudices of this ignorant population, and the incredible want of tact in its agents.*[27] He was asked why he did not go to Turin and make these facts known. He replied: 'The government knows of them as well as I do—and better.'

Just before he had left Naples, Garibaldi suggested to the King that he should act as his Viceroy in the south for a year until it settled down; and the suggestion has been universally derided by historians; but he, and his *set of scamps*, certainly could not have done worse than did the party of Cavour.

XX

THE WOUNDED LION

❖❖❖❖❖❖❖❖❖❖

THE COTTAGE on Caprera to which Garibaldi returned was as primitive and as sparsely furnished as that of any Calabrian peasant. Built of rough stone, it was square with four rooms in all including the kitchen. In his bedroom, the only furniture consisted of a chest-of-drawers and an iron bedstead draped with muslin to keep out the mosquitoes which then, and for nearly a century after, were the bane of life in Sardinia. Across the room was strung a cord on which the General always had a red shirt and underclothes drying.[1]

Worn out by fatigue and racked with arthritis, Garibaldi took to his bed and for several months hardly stirred out of the house. His condition could not have been helped much by the fact that his room was directly over the large cistern, so necessary on a barren island where no rain falls for months, and the uncovered flagstones were wet with condensation all the year round.

On Caprera, he was joined by Teresita, now a young woman of sixteen, and the Deideris who had brought her up since Anita's death; and the Deideris brought with them a few sticks of furniture. When the crew of the *Washington*, which had brought the General to the island, saw how the man who had conquered a kingdom for his sovereign lived, they clubbed together and bought him a set of chairs. Even with these gifts, the house was no palace.

His two sons, Menotti and Ricciotti, also came to join him, the elder from the battlefields of Naples, the younger from England where he had been the ward of his father's erstwhile fiancée, Mrs Roberts, who had had him educated at Manchester Grammar School. As a result, Ricciotti could speak little Italian and had acquired the air of superiority common to those who have been to public schools in England, which did not endear him greatly to the rest of the family.

With all these, and lodged in the hovels of outhouses, were a few of Garibaldi's retainers: Fruscianti, an ex-monk who had been with him since 1849 and whose sense of humour led him to nickname one of the donkeys after Pius IX as 'Pio Nono'; Basso, who had been with him ever since New York and who acted as his secretary; and Carpanetti, the former consul in Tangiers.

II

The electoral colleges that were responsible for nominating members to the Piedmontese House of Representatives were called for the 24th January. The people of Naples wrote to ask Garibaldi to return to them so that they could nominate him, and he wrote back: *No, I cannot come to Naples because my presence there would be the cause of fresh and more cruel persecutions against my friends and soldiers, on the part of those whose only aim is to cancel the memory of the good they have effected for Italy. Nor can I accept the candidature; my place is not upon parliamentary benches. Here I await the fresh call to arms.*[2] But as the months dragged on he roused himself from his bed of sickness to make a protest against the shameful way his Redshirts were being treated by the military authorities. He sent a telegram to Naples: *I accept the candidature of the first college at Naples, which I earlier refused.*[3]

He was duly elected and made the journey to Turin in great discomfort and pain, and was too ill when he arrived to attend immediately at the House. On the 28th April, cheered by crowds outside as he entered, he came in his red shirt and *poncho*, a touch of flamboyancy which irritated all the frock-coated gentry there assembled. He made a bitter attack on Cavour, accusing him of having tried to provoke a fratricidal war in Naples and of shamefully illtreating the volunteers and pampering their enemies of the Bourbon army who had been incorporated in the Piedmontese one retaining their ranks, while most of the volunteers, who had left their homes, sacrificed their careers and risked their lives to defeat them, had for the most part been dismissed without adequate compensation. Cavour, white-faced and furious, demanded the protection of the Chair; there was uproar. When it had subsided, Garibaldi said:[4] 'I believe I have obtained, by thirty years of service rendered to the country, the right to speak the truth to the representatives of the people.'

Cavour interrupted him again:

'He said we had provoked a fratricidal war—it's not true.'

'A fratricidal war,' repeated Garibaldi.

There were shouts from the Right of: 'Order! Order!' and from the Left: 'Let him speak!'

It is now known from Cavour's correspondence that the accusation was a true bill in that the Minister would have willingly made civil war on the volunteers if he had not been fearful of public opinion; but on the specific issue which so roused Garibaldi—the shabby treatment of his Redshirts—Cavour was the one member of the Cabinet who advocated more generous treatment but he was overruled by the King, General Fanti, the Minister for War, and the Army.

After the scene in Parliament, General Cialdini published an open letter in a newspaper accusing Garibaldi of having ordered the Piedmontese army to be received with bullets—a calumny which Cavour's papers in Turin had published and which had already been refuted by the production of the actual telegram containing the instructions Garibaldi had sent. The letter was considered by everybody to be a challenge to a duel; but one which Garibaldi answered only with a factual and conciliatory letter.

The King had Cavour and Garibaldi up to his palace and Cavour's newspapers afterwards proclaimed that there had been a reconciliation. But Garibaldi always protested that he had refused to shake the hand of the man who had made him a stranger in his own country and who had conspired, if not to do him to death, to compass his defeat at a crucial moment in his struggle for Italy. On the 2nd May, Garibaldi departed for the peace of his rural life.

Shortly afterwards, Cavour was taken seriously ill and before long he knew he was dying. In spite of his excommunication, a Turin priest administered the last rites to him—for which act of charity the Pope subsequently deprived him of his living. The King came to see Cavour and departed, it was said, in tears. On the 6th June, the Minister, who had so deceitfully but so loyally served the House of Savoy, asked:

'The doctors have given me up, haven't they?'

'No—not all of them.'

'Well—I've given them up.' They had bled him until not a drop more blood would come. The next morning he died.

When Sir James Hudson, the British Ambassador and sincere friend of Italy, heard the news, he sobbed like a child.[5]

III

Garibaldi's solitude on Caprera was disturbed not only by the guests who came to attend the marriage of Teresita on the 25th May—three months after her sixteenth birthday—to Canzio, one of the Genoese sharpshooters, but, three weeks later, by a gang of thugs who had been sent by the Vatican to assassinate him.

Even when that alarm was over, there was little peace on Caprera. There were so many people who wanted to visit him that, instead of a monthly service to Maddalena, the steamship company found it profitable to run a weekly one, and there was a boom in trade on Maddalena caused by the visitors.

Letters poured in to the island from all over the world. Many were from English and American women begging locks of his hair or other mementoes, or sending him poems, typical of which was one effusion from a Caroline Phillipson of London, which began:

7th May, 1861

> *Too high an honour—on my page*
> *To write thy Hero name,*
> *The greatest of this modern age,*
> *The purest known to fame.*
>
> *Deliv'rer from the Tyrant yoke,*
> *That bound thy glorious land;*
> *Thou hast the chains of slavedom broke*
> *With thy unflinching hand.*

and ended, ten stanzas later, with:

> *May'st thou attain the golden Crown*
> *Christ's holy warriors wear*
> *Amidst the blest sit calmly down*
> *Their endless joy to share.*

They were lines of which the author was so proud that she had them printed.

One letter was from a Frenchman who had invented a means whereby an army of two million could be exterminated; another from a priest who was convinced that the Pope was the representative of the Devil and should be exorcised with fire and the sword;

so many were unstamped that Garibaldi had to insert a notice in the Press declaring that he would not accept unfranked ones. Others were of more importance. One, dated the 8th June 1861, was from the United States Consul in Antwerp.[6]

The papers report that you are going to the United States to join the Army of the North in the conflict of my country . . . There are thousands of Italians and Hungarians who will rush to join your ranks and there are thousands and tens of thousands of Americans who will glory to be under the command of 'the Washington of Italy'.

In fact, the Consul wanted to resign his post and become one of them.

To him Garibaldi wrote back: *The news given in the journals is not correct. I have had and still have a great desire to go . . . I would go if I do not find myself occupied in the cause of my country. But first tell me: is this conflict over the emancipation of the negroes or not?*

The question he raised was one on which he might well entertain some doubt at that juncture. Better informed people than he —Lord John Russell and Gladstone, for example—at that time regarded the North American cause in the civil war as no more than a colonial war of aggression and took the view that the South was fighting for liberty. And without dissent, the North American Congress on the 11th February 1861, had adopted a resolution that the Constitution did not give Congress or any non-slave holding state the right to interfere with the institution of slavery.

The reply of the Antwerp consul did nothing to resolve Garibaldi's doubts: *I say this is not the intention of the Federal Government . . . but I would not be surprised if it results in the extinction of slavery in the United States.*

The defeat of the North in the disaster of Bull Ring on the 21st July provoked Abraham Lincoln's government to send out specific instructions to their Minister in Turin to secure Garibaldi's services. To a letter suggesting an interview, Garibaldi replied: *I would be very happy to serve a country for which I have so much affection . . . I am delegating Col. Trecchi to speak to the King.*

On the 6th September, the King—with alacrity one may suspect—indicated that Garibaldi might take himself off to America. As soon as they got the reply, the American emissaries chartered a steamer and set off. They found Garibaldi still an invalid but able to leave his room. After a long discussion, the whole matter resolved itself into two questions; the first was the status in which Garibaldi would serve; the second was the motive for the war. He was only prepared to go if there were a declaration for the abolition of slavery; without it, he said: 'it is only a civil war with which I have no sympathy.' The American Ambassador's dispatch could not have been read with pleasure by his superiors in Washington. *Garibaldi, he wrote, has never been ambitious of wielding power or winning laurels in a cause which did not commend itself to him as something more than a question of legal right and government interest and this the cause of the American Government and Union, as regards his point of view, have so far failed to do. I do not believe that he will take any part in the struggle unless he is convinced that the government and people of the North are united in determination to pursue a policy which shall necessarily result in the abolition of slavery.* The dispatch must have arrived at a particularly awkward time for the Union Government. Abraham Lincoln had just revoked General Fremont's order liberating slaves of those citizens in Missouri who had taken up arms against the Government.

The project lapsed into abeyance for the year; but it was not only the question of slavery that caused Garibaldi to lose interest. The first anniversary of his entrance into Naples had been celebrated in the city with wild enthusiasm and newspapers were calling to him:

Do not leave for America. The people have faith in you. You should have faith in them. Our national unity is not yet completed. You have laid its most solid foundation. You alone can complete the work. Let us wait . . . to march on Rome.

IV

The great and the not so great, English lords and Neapolitan peasants, gentlemen who wanted to study his phrenology and revolutionaries who wanted to enlist his support for revolts in half the countries of Europe, continued to flock to Caprera. On the 23rd September, Speranza set out from Nice to visit the island in the hope of obtaining a further instalment of Garibaldi's memoirs and, probably, an opportunity to reinstate herself in his affections. After a storm-tossed voyage on the *Sardegna, the worst boat in the world,*[7] she landed in Maddalena and returned to the room she had occupied the first night she ever set foot on that island. The next morning, she crossed to Caprera in a small boat and found Garibaldi on the quay.

His greeting could not be described as over enthusiastic.

'What fair wind brings you here?'

She told him she had come about his memoirs and he gave her the manuscript of what he had written since the last volume. She retired into Teresita's room, to the left of the entrance, to read it.

Half an hour later, the General's son-in-law, Canzio, opened the door.

'Do you want any dinner?' he demanded.

Since Garibaldi had hitherto always come himself to fetch her at meal times, *this cool proceeding made a bad impression* on her. The General was unaccustomedly silent at the dinner-table, and afterwards retired to play *boule* with twenty guests. Later, when she had read the manuscript, she asked leave to take it with her, but Garibaldi refused saying she might lose it. She gave him a box of cigars and some sweets. Ungraciously he said to her:

'You are always giving me presents and I do nothing to deserve them.'

Later on during the day she tried to get Canzio to persuade the General to part with his manuscript. He refused.

'The General is poor. When he dies, his children will find themselves out in the middle of the road,' he said almost angrily.

Having pumped Madame Deideri for her version of the fiasco of the General's marriage to the Marchesa Raimondi, she departed sorrowfully. *Oh! that the blue waves of the Tyrrhenian Sea, over which the Sardegna glides so smoothly this evening were a Lethe in which I could drown the remembrance of this tragic episode in the life of the Italian hero,* she confided to her diary.

V

With fishing and writing and gardening and receiving visitors, the days passed on Caprera. Garibaldi found time to aid in organizing girls' schools in Naples—a daring project for those days—and orphanages in Palermo, to try to persuade the government to allow Mazzini to return from exile, to sign a petition to abolish the death penalty, to help the development of friendly societies amongst the working classes, to formulate his thoughts about a United Europe where wars would cease so that *the vast sums now devoted to human destruction could be spent on developing industry,*

improving roads and bridges and canals and building schools. The
St Simonians would have been proud of their pupil.

But always his conversation turned to Venice, an Italian city
under the Austrians, and to Rome, an Italian city under the Pope.

He was beginning to despair of the Piedmontese Government.

'They will never attempt it, Fruscianti,' he said one day.[8]

'Only when they have obtained permission of their magnanimous ally, France.'

'To whom they must give a province in exchange.'

But in December, he was called to Turin and had a private talk
with the King, and early in 1862, an emissary from the Cabinet
came for a shooting holiday on Caprera.

VI

At the beginning of March, the paddle steamer once again
carried Garibaldi from his island retreat. He went to Turin at
the express invitation of the government. The new Prime
Minister, Rattazzi, promised him one million lire and Garibaldi
began a tour of North Italy, for which all his expenses were paid
by officials and which had every appearance of being sponsored by
the Cabinet, with the King's approval. Ministers and deputies
accompanied him in the initial stages. He was dined by the Royal
princes and entertained by the Governor of Milan and by senators.
Ostensibly, it was a tour to encourage the formation of rifle clubs
but it was quite apparent as the tour developed that it was, in
fact, a recruiting campaign. Agents everywhere were enrolling
volunteers, as they had in April, 1860; money and arms and
materials were being collected; and an attempt was being made
to raise a loan in England. But nothing was said publicly as to
what it was all about or what was the object of the expedition
that was being raised.

In every town he visited, Garibaldi was received with rapturous
applause rising, in some cases, to a delirium of ecstasy, although,
as the Governor was quick to observe, at the Opera in Milan the
gallery cheered him but the boxes were silent. At the end of
April, he retired to Trescorre near the Lago d'Iseo and it was
given out that he was taking the waters for his rheumatism. There,
on the 5th May 1862 met a full gathering of his faithful followers
to celebrate the anniversary of the sailing of the Thousand from
Quarto. Far from being a convivial occasion, there was a stormy

meeting in which epithets of various kinds were bandied about, although, once again, the public were not informed what was the subject of the controversy.

Ten days later, the public were shocked to learn that one of Garibaldi's principal lieutenants, the patriotic poet Colonel Nullo, had been arrested by the police at Sarnico together with a hundred volunteers; they were horrified when, shortly afterwards, some of the volunteers attempted to break out of prison and were fired on and a few were killed.

Garibaldi wrote to the Milan paper:[9] *I consider it my duty to declare that Colonel Nullo was acting strictly in accordance with my orders.* At the funeral of the victims, he made a speech and had the crowd alternatively weeping and howling for revenge against the unspecified enemies of Italy; and Garibaldi, clutching and unclutching his hat, was so overcome by emotion that he was unable to finish his speech.

There was a violent debate in Parliament but no information could be elicited from the government. Rattazzi declared that the million lire had been given to the General 'for the encouragement of immigration' though, not surprisingly, nobody believed a word of it. The opposition pressed for an official inquiry but Rattazzi used every parliamentary device to prevent it. When the dust of controversy had settled nobody was any the wiser as to what it was all about; and the mystery remained unsolved.

VII

What was the significance of these events? The historian will look in vain in Garibaldi's memoirs for an explanation; and none of the other participants ever provided a solution. From documents now available, it would seem that Cavour, early in 1861, was engaged in a grandiose but not entirely illusionary scheme for fomenting insurrection in various parts of the Austro-Hungarian Empire and was busy shipping arms to the Balkans to further his end. That Garibaldi was a party to the scheme is apparent from a letter Cavour wrote describing the reconciliation interview in the King's presence:[11] *My interview with Garibaldi was courteous though not friendly. I acquainted him with the line of conduct which the government intended to follow as regards Austria as well as France;* and from a passage in another letter of the same time:[12] *With all that, when the time comes, I will tuck Garibaldi's arm under*

K

mine and say 'Let us go and see what they are talking about inside Verona.' To Garibaldi he wrote[13] on the 10th May 1861 : *The news from Hungary has been serious for some days now, I hope they will not precipitate things, for many reasons but principally because no agreement yet exists between the Hungarians and the Croats. Attempts are being made to establish it. Klapka and Kossuth are to come to Turin shortly . . . you will be informed of our deliberations.* To this conspiracy it is more than probable that the French Emperor was a party, in the belief that revolution in Budapest meant revolution in Vienna and revolution in Vienna meant revolution in Berlin—and the opportunity for France to seize the Rhineland provinces from Prussia. Cavour, Victor Emmanuel and Napoleon III, all bitter enemies of radicalism in their own countries, were quite happy to promote red revolution amongst their enemies; none of them was adverse to burning down other people's houses to roast their potatoes.

The role allotted to Garibaldi in Cavour's scheme was an expedition from the Italian shores of the Adriatic, ostensibly to assist the rebels in Dalmatia, but in reality to make an attack from there through Venezia—Giulia on to Venice which, if the revolutionary fires were burning gaily in Budapest and elsewhere, would be co-ordinated with a frontal attack by the Italian Army on the Quadrilateral.[10]

Cavour died, and was succeeded by Baron Ricasoli, an honourable and upright man who set his face against underhand schemes of this kind. But the King pressed on with Cavour's master plan behind the back of his Prime Minister, in conjunction with Rattazzi.

On the same boat as that in which Speranza von Swartz travelled to Caprera in September 1861 were a number of Garibaldini—including Nullo. It is more than probable therefore that her chilly reception was due to the fact that she had, uninvited, broken in on a conference of the conspirators, rather than to any intentional discourtesy; and the unhappy silence at the dinner-tables that she noticed was the result of the twenty or so men present being unable to discuss what was on their minds so long as she was there. The visit of the German socialist, Ferdinand Lassalle, to Caprera on the 14th November 1861, was connected with the same scheme.

Mazzini was, as usual, well informed of what was going on, although he was no party to it. In a letter to Jessio Mario on the 12th February 1862—both of them were then in England—he set out the substance of it. *The scheme is between the King, Garibaldi and Rattazzi. Rattazzi went to Paris—I know it positively now—with an autograph letter of the King, to propose . . . moral co-operation for Venice and have in exchange an offensive and defensive alliance with Italy and our co-operation on the Rhine. Should Louis Napoleon have accepted, Ricasoli was doomed and Rattazzi was to replace him; but Louis Napoleon listened and did conclude nothing. Rattazzi still believes that action would lead him to accept. Hence the Garibaldi– Dalmatian scheme.*[10]

In the same belief as Rattazzi, that Napoleon III would consent or at least acquiesce once the scheme was under way, the king suddenly removed Ricasoli from office as Prime Minister on the ground of an unspecified 'lack of deference due to the throne'. Rattazzi took his place. Immediately, Garibaldi was called from Caprera.

The big controversy at the secret meeting on the 5th May can now be explained. Most of the Garibaldini were suspicious of the whole scheme, seeing in it, quite correctly, a Machiavellian design to exploit the cause of liberty for territorial aggrandisement; and as one which, without prior insurrection in Croatia and Hungary, was doomed to disaster. That the whole plot was then abandoned can be seen from a letter Garibaldi wrote to Speranza two days before Nullo was arrested.

Trescore, 12th May 1862

Speranza mia,

I want to speak to you: come to me as soon as possible. I shall be staying here seven or eight days longer. Afterwards, I go to Bergamo, Como, etc.

I kiss your hand affectionately.[7]

The arrest of Nullo and the other volunteers is explicable only on the basis that Napoleon III, as soon as he learned that the scheme was actually on foot, expressed his displeasure in no uncertain terms to Victor Emmanuel and Rattazzi; and they, to demonstrate an apparent readiness to comply with his wishes, had the arrests made; and it was done, perhaps, without prior knowledge that the plans had been abandoned by the volunteers. For the French Emperor, far from being interested in a scheme for raising general insurrection in the Austro-Hungarian Empire and in Prussia, was by now up to the neck in another conspiracy of a very different sort. Late on a summer's evening on holiday in

Biarritz in September 1861, he had been talked by an enthusiastic Mexican ex-diplomat[14] into a fantastic plot for overthrowing the liberal régime of Juarez, victor of the recent Mexican civil war, and establishing a monarchy in its place. The proposed monarch was none other than the Archduke Maximilian, brother of the Austrian Emperor, Franz-Joseph, and until 1859 Governor-General of Lombardy. It was an intrigue to which the Pope was party. Whatever Napoleon's motives—and it is probable that they were little more than mercenary[15]—the nature of the scheme required that he should be on reasonable terms with both the Austrians and the Papacy. It is an explanation that is substantiated by a speech Garibaldi made a little later.

The letter he wrote to Speranza on the 12th May did not reach her; but she saw him at the end of that month near Lake Maggiore. According to her, he had sent for her so urgently because he wanted her to accompany him on another expedition he had in mind. It was an invitation she hastily declined, saying that she had promised to address a meeting in London for the Society for the Protection of Animals.

On the 15th June, Garibaldi received an emissary from Victor Emmanuel and took him out rowing on Lake Maggiore at night. Only the still waters know what they talked about, but he returned promptly to Caprera.[16]

On the 27th June, he set sail with a band of his followers from there in a steamer.

'We are going towards the unknown,' he declared mysteriously.

VIII

The small steamer, the *Tortoli*, in which they sailed went to Palermo. There the reception afforded the returning dictator was all that he could have desired; the enthusiasm exceeded even that demonstrated earlier in Lombardy; and there, on Sunday the 6th July, to a vast assembly of the National Guard and people gathered in the Foro Italico, he launched into a violent diatribe against Napoleon III.[17]

'The master of France, the traitor of the 2nd December—he who spilt the blood of our brethren in Paris—occupies Rome under the pretext of guarding the person of the Pope and protecting the Catholic religion. Lies! Lies! He is motivated by lust, rape, by the thirst of evil imperialism. He is the main nourishment of brigandage. He is the chief of brigands, of assassins.

'People of Rome, People of 1860, Napoleon must leave Rome. If necessary, we must make a new Vespers.'

In other speeches his call was 'To Rome and Venice.' But at Marsala, which he entered through triumphal arches of flowers along a route lined by the National Guard, a fisherman raised the shout of 'Rome or Death!' It was a cry that was taken up by the crowd. In the packed Cathedral after mass, Garibaldi stood before the High Altar and raised his hand solemnly to swear 'Rome or Death!'; and a thousand hands were raised and a thousand voices behind him echoed the same oath.

On the 1st August, he raised his standard just outside Palermo and before long was joined by some 4,000 volunteers. Three days later, Victor Emmanuel issued a proclamation in which he declared that he alone must call for any attempt to complete the work of unifying Italy and denounced Garibaldi's present venture as *a call to rebellion, to civil war*. A few of his old friends took it seriously and begged him to abandon his project; but the majority considered it merely as a face-saving operation for the benefit of the Great Powers. Garibaldi had been entertained while in Sicily by the two sons of the monarch; the Royal troops in the island made no attempt to interfere with recruitment; a consignment of 3,000 rifles was unloaded at Catania without demur by the customs officers; anybody who questioned what he was doing was shown a document with a large red seal which was kept carefully in a tin box; and, as foreign observers noted, he was plentifully supplied with funds. It was hard to believe that he had no authority, especially when he marched on Catania on the 20th August, and the superior force of Royal troops obligingly shut themselves up in the citadel with their arms and equipment and left him for the next three days master of the city while he completed his arrangements.

In the harbour were two ships of the Royal Navy, the *Duca di Genova* and the *Maria Adelaide*; there were also two packet boats, the *General Abbatucci,* belonging to a French company, and the *Dispaccio,* owned by an Italian one.

On Sunday morning, the 24th August, the *Duca di Genova* left the harbour. As soon as she had gone, Garibaldi went to the packet boats and seized them. The French skipper was courteously escorted ashore and conducted to the French consulate where, it was explained to him, he could make his protest. Some hours later, at four in the afternoon, the *Maria Adelaide*, ignoring all that

was going on in the harbour, took up her anchor and sailed out.
At ten o'clock that night the expedition sailed, with the two
packet boats so crowded with volunteers that, as Garibaldi
wrote: *During my life at sea I have often seen vessels heavily laden,
but never so excessively as in this case . . . every man on board found it
impossible to move from his place or even to turn round.*[18]

Outside the harbour, the *Maria Adelaide* hailed them and then
moved off; by daybreak, they landed on the Calabrian coast on
almost the same spot as that on which Garibaldi had landed two
years before. He took the same road to Reggio as he had done
earlier but, as the volunteers marched up the coast road, they were
astounded to find that they were fired upon by a Piedmontese
cruiser. Outside Reggio, Garibaldi was interviewed by a deputation from the city who told him that it was garrisoned with some
4,000 Royal troops who were determined to resist, and begged
him to spare them an assault. Reluctant to commit his men to
warfare against their brother Italians, Garibaldi turned off up into
the mountains.

All day long they marched without food and at night were glad
to eat raw potatoes from a field; their guide had led them astray
and they had gone round in a circle; and, worse still, there was a
column of Piedmontese following them which had already had a
skirmish with the rearguard. The next day, they reached Aspromonte in the midst of the forest; and there, on the 29th, the
pursuing column caught up with them. Garibaldi stationed his
men in an impregnable position on the hillside, with his son,
Menotti, commanding the left wing, another officer commanding
the right, and himself in charge of the centre.

The *bersaglieri* advanced in open column, firing as they marched.
Before Garibaldi could give the word, some hotheads in Menotti's
section replied.

At once Garibaldi ordered the bugler to sound the 'Cease
Fire'.[19] He stood in front of his troops, repeatedly turning to them
and shouting: 'Don't fire!' His lines fell silent. Not a man spoke,
not a shot was fired.

'Don't fire!' he went on calling.

The *bersaglieri* continued to advance, firing.

Garibaldi was seen to clap his hand quickly to his thigh; he
took one or two paces and crumpled to the ground.

He was asked if he was wounded and replied: 'It's nothing.'
But he had been shot twice, once by a spent bullet and the other,

more seriously, in his right foot. There can be little doubt that deliberate aim had been taken at him. He was laid under the same tree as Menotti ,who had also been wounded. Five of his men were dead, as were seven soldiers of the Royal army.

His officers crowded round him.

He lit a cigar and said to them: 'Don't in any circumstances fight.'

The medical officer examined his foot.

'If an amputation is necessary, let it be done at once.' He was told it was not necessary.

There was a flourish of trumpets and an officer of the Royal army rode up to him and demanded his surrender. The wounded lion showed a flash of anger.

'I have seen thirty years—and more—of warfare!' he cried indignantly. 'Those who come to parley do not present themselves in this fashion.'

'Disarm him,' he ordered his officers.

A little later, in a manner more to his liking, a little stout officer with a bald head and waxed moustache rode up and intimated that the General must consider himself a prisoner. He was Colonel Pallavicini, commander of the column, soon afterwards to be promoted general by a grateful King for his services that day.

Garibaldi was taken on an improvised stretcher, in great pain, on the long journey down the mountain-side, and to the port of Scylla. There he was embarked on the *Duca di Genova*.

As he was carried on board, the lean, sardonic General Cialdini, with his small goatee beard, stood with his arms folded by the rails of another vessel. Garibaldi saluted his old comrade in arms. The General did not reply. He it was who had ordered Pallavicini to *pursue Garibaldi constantly without giving him a moment's rest; to attack him if he seeks to escape and to destroy him if he accepts battle . . . not to treat . . . and only to accept a surrender in the last resort.*[20]

The ship carried Garibaldi away to imprisonment in the fortress of Varignano.

IX

When Garibaldi learned that seven of his volunteers who had deserted from the Italian Army to serve with him had been executed, he was filled with rage and said to Jessie Mario:[21]

'Find me an English publisher and I will write the whole story.'

Some days later, she returned with the news that *the prince of English publishers* had agreed to publish anything Garibaldi cared to write; but by then his mood had changed.

'It is a sad, shameful page of family history written in blood—and more must be shed before Venice and Rome can be ours. No! Silence is best—at least till we are free.'

To this day, the explanation of the mysterious circumstances of Aspromonte must be based on conjecture. That Garibaldi had some sort of authority from the King and Rattazzi to raise volunteers in Sicily and to sail from there with them, must be accepted as incontrovertible. The passivity of the Piedmontese authorities and troops in the island during the two months Garibaldi was openly making preparations; and, above all, that of the Royal Navy, at the time when he set sail, can bear no other construction. It is more than probable also that he was being financed by the government, for the lavish funds with which he was supplied could have come from no other source; and the 3,000 rifles for his volunteers which the customs admitted without question could not have been found, or admitted to the island, without the connivance of the government.

Moreover, when the question arose in the Council of Ministers afterwards as to what was to be done with him, Massimo d'Azeglio suggested:

'He ought to be tried like any other citizen and after being sentenced, be reprieved at once by the King.[22]

But he was told by Rattazzi that it was most inexpedient for Garibaldi to be put on trial publicly because the Redshirts possessed 'a certain piece of paper . . .'; better that he should be granted an amnesty and freed.

Yet it is inconceivable that Victor Emmanuel had authorized an attack on Rome. For one thing, his correspondence with the Pope and his whole conduct before and up to 1870 shows that he was most reluctant to interfere with the Pope's sovereignty over the Holy City. Moreover, it was the most inopportune moment to choose for such an assault, for there were gathered in Rome, by invitation of Pius IX, 323 prelates of the Church, most from outside Italy and France, and thousands of foreign pilgrims, who had come to celebrate the canonization of twenty-six martyrs. Nothing could be more calculated to involve the new kingdom in difficulties with the great powers than to embroil these dignatories and the faithful in the operations of war.

The real explanation can only be that Victor Emmanuel and Rattazzi, balked by Napoleon III of Garibaldi's venture against Venice from Dalmatia, had authorized him to try again from Sicily in circumstances for which they could more easily disown all responsibility. This was a favourite project of the monarch, which he revived once again in 1866, only to be overruled by his War Council; and no doubt they reckoned that if it were successful they could get away with it even against the express orders of Napoleon III. For the Mexican scheme was going badly; on the 5th May, 1862, the French army had been ignominiously defeated in an attack on Puebla and the Emperor's great pre-occupation now was to reverse that defeat at all costs. To that end an Army Corps of 30,000 of his troops was on its way to Mexico. It was no moment for him to be entangled in a conflict with his former ally, even if he were so inclined. When Garibaldi sailed, therefore, in spite of his protestations of 'Rome or Death!', the government may well have thought that, in fact, he was making for the Dalmatian coast; and the King was furious when it was discovered that his objective really was Rome. As Giacomo Durando, Minister for Foreign Affairs, noted in his diary at the time:[23] *The King is in a very bad temper. He says that Garibaldi has caused him great trouble and annoyance, and has already cheated him two or three times.*

This theory would also explain why the determined attempt was made by the Royal troops to kill Garibaldi; he was a man who knew too much and who could, if he chose, gravely compromise his monarch. It was one which was held at the time by Sir James Hudson, who was close to the ministers in Turin, and by Jessie Mario, who was an intimate of Garibaldi; and it is the only one which adequately explains all the facts.

x

It was as well for the security of Victor Emmanuel's throne that Garibaldi had not been killed, for there was such a scream of protest from the whole country that, in the end, Rattazzi's ministry was forced to resign. Had he been killed, nothing would have stopped the Redshirts publishing all they knew and the chasm between the republicans and the monarchy would have been unbridgeable. As it was, Garibaldi acted as a restraining influence on his followers and kept many who at heart preferred an Italian republic loyal to his programme of 'Italy and Victor Emmanuel'.

Garibaldi's wounds provided the sacrificial element hitherto lacking in his cult amongst the superstitious elements of the populace. A typical print of the period shows him hanging on a cross, upon which an angel crowns him, and at the foot Cialdini and La Marmora dice for his garments and Pallavicini hurries away with the ladder; at the side Napoleon III and Pius IX dance a *pas-de-deux* of joy.

To his bedside flocked a host of female devotees from all over the world. Jessie Mario was there to nurse him; the faithful Speranza arrived to cook for him and was distressed to find that his followers excluded her from his room; even his lawful wife, the Marchesa Giuseppina Raimondi wrote to Vecchi to find out whether she might be permitted to console him in his hour of pain. Dozens of others, of all nationalities, whose names are unrecorded came to beg a lock of hair or a nail paring from the suffering saint. Letters, cigars, presents poured in from all over the world.

No fewer than twenty-three surgeons, from France, from Russia, from England, and from all parts of Italy, assembled by his bedside to debate how to extract the ball which was still lodged in his foot. Lady Palmerston sent a special iron bed contraption and her husband subscribed to the fund which was raised in England to send a famous surgeon, a Mr Partridge, to Italy.

The wave of sympathy proved irresistible. Even Napoleon III spontaneously sent a telegram to the Italian monarch urging that Garibaldi should be granted an amnesty, though it may be suspected that the cynic of the Tuilleries was moved more by the probable consequences of a public trial and sentence than by compassion. On the 5th October, Garibaldi and his volunteers were pardoned by a general amnesty.

It was some time before he could be moved from his prison but eventually he was transferred to a hotel in Spezia and, later, to the Hotel della tre Donzelle in Pisa, with the ball still embedded in his foot. In that hotel, on Sunday the 23rd November, eighty-seven days after the wound, the surgeon Zanetti proceeded to operate to extract it.

At the foot of the bed stood three other doctors and a nurse. Garibaldi gripped a handkerchief between his teeth and clutched the hand of Jessie Mario.[24]

As Zanetti probed the wound, he cried:

'By God! That's it.'

A second later the bullet was in the tweezers of the surgeon. The General kissed him and everybody else in the room. The news spread through the hotel. The Marchesa Pallavicino, wife of the Governor of Sicily, Menotti Garibaldi and Jessie Mario's husband, Alberto, were the first to arrive.

And they all, doctors and friends alike, scrambled for pieces of the bandages stained by the sacred blood of the hero.

XXI

PLUM PUDDING AND TURTLE SOUP

❖❖❖❖❖❖❖❖❖❖❖

IT WAS drizzling with rain when the P. and O. liner, the *Ripon*, entered Southampton Water on the 3rd April 1864. A tug steamed out to greet her in the Solent, carrying on board the Duke of Sutherland, Charles Seely, who was the Member of Parliament for Lincoln, and a deputation of Italians resident in London.

The gentle rain turned to a torrent as the *Ripon* came alongside a pier to berth, but it did nothing to quench the enthusiasm of the enormous crowds waiting on the quays. At the sight of a solitary figure perched on the paddle box, wrapped in a grey *poncho*, a tremendous cheer went up.

Garibaldi was paying his fourth visit to England, though exactly why he had come remains to this day something of a mystery. Later, to his intimates[1] he claimed to have sought to interest the British Government in the cause of little Denmark, then struggling against the German nation for Schleswig-Holstein; but to Lord Shaftesbury, who bluntly asked him whether he had any political motive, he professed to have none.

For many months after his wound at Aspromonte, he was confined to his bed and when Speranza came to visit him again at Caprera in the autumn of 1863 he was hobbling about on crutches. During that period, there were a great many mysterious comings and goings from the island. The Duke of Sutherland had visited him by yacht, and on the vessel on which Speranza arrived was the rich and beautiful Sarah Nathan, Mazzini's current mistress, who, according to Speranza, had come to enlist Garibaldi's support in a plot to assassinate Napoleon III. It was a suggestion which he indignantly rejected, according to her, and she wrote: *I shall never forget the expression on his face, inflamed as it was with noble rage and almost as red as his jacket, when he looked up proudly and said in a voice of thunder 'Italy shall be united . . . but not by the dagger of a traitor.'*[2]

It is an account which was denied by Menotti Garibaldi when it was published[3] and, although it is true that Sarah Nathan travelled on the same vessel and more than probable that, at some time or other, Garibaldi expressed those sentiments, Speranza, for all her intelligence, was often confused in political matters and was never at any time admitted to Garibaldi's confidence about them. Certainly the conclusion of her account of the affair: *From that hour, he broke completely with this conspirator* (Mazzini) had not, as will be seen, the slightest foundation.

As the *Ripon* docked at Southampton on that wintry spring day, the Mayor of the city launched into a panegyric of his visitor which his hearers thought, if not too fulsome, much too long considering the weather. When it was over, Garibaldi was driven in the Mayor's coach, drawn by four greys, through cheering excited crowds (*though it was Sunday and raining to boot,* as one newspaper observed) to the Mayor's house.

Next day there was a reception in the Town Hall and, afterwards, Garibaldi was conveyed through streets decked with the Union Jack and Italian tricolour to sail from the Royal Pier to spend some days in the Isle of Wight as the guest of Charles Seely at Brook House. He had scribbled a note for publication:

My dear friends,
    I do not desire to receive political demonstrations.
                                    G. Garibaldi
PS. Especially, I beg you, not to create disturbances.

But a meeting of working men in Southampton, finding their hero a prisoner of the gentry, passed a resolution: 'Garibaldi is being worked upon by sinister influences to isolate himself as much as possible from the working classes'.

II

He passed seven days as the guest of Mr and Mrs Charles Seely at Brook House and there was visited by a succession of notables.

The great Lord Shaftesbury, the recognized leader of the Evangelicals—at that time a much more important section of the community than they are today, when the Anglican church has been captured by the medievalists—came to call on him. Not a little of the welcome that was to be afforded him in London was due to the conviction that he was secretly a Protestant, as witnessed by his gift of land for an English church while he was Dictator of Naples. And Garibaldi, who, when he chose to exercise it, possessed to the full the art of pleasing his hearers, did nothing to disillusion them. To a deputation of the Evangelical Continental Society, he said: 'I do not say that I am a Protestant for, if I did, the priests would raise the cry of heretic against me and my influence would be gone. We are sons of the same God.'

Lord Tennyson also came to call and later recorded his impressions: *What a noble human being! . . . I expected to see a hero and was not disappointed . . . He is more majestic than meek and his manners have a certain divine simplicity in them such as I have never witnessed in a native of these islands, among the men at least.*[4]

A few days later, Garibaldi was driven over to the poet's house and there planted a tree, which the poet subsequently described, in what was scarcely the finest example of his verse, as:

> *. . . the waving pine which here*
> *The warrior of Caprera set,*
> *A name that earth will not forget*
> *Till earth has roll'd her latest year.*

But there were other visitors to Brook House to see him besides the gentry and the aristocracy. Deputations arrived from all over the industrial north to beg him to visit their cities. The Russian revolutionary, Alexander Herzen, came to intercede with him on behalf of Mazzini. As it happened, Mazzini was under a cloud. There had been an abortive attempt to assassinate Napoleon III in Paris in January of the same year, led by a man named Greco, and Mazzini, who collected death sentences like other men collect medals, had been sentenced in France in his absence as being the instigator of the plot. He denied any complicity in it and his friend and protector, James Stansfield, a junior minister in the government, had resigned his office so as to be free to defend him. When Garibaldi learned all this, he exclaimed: 'One of my first visits will be to Stansfield!' and he sent a telegram inviting Mazzini to visit him at Brook House.

The day before Garibaldi visited Tennyson, Mazzini arrived and the two had a long and friendly conversation in their incomprehensible Genoese dialect.

III

There was a special train provided to take Garibaldi to London on Monday, the 11th April, and he walked to it at Southampton station through an avenue of women clothed for the most part in scarlet. The dressmakers had been busy; Garibaldi hats and Garibaldi blouses had suddenly become the fashion; and a biscuit maker, introducing a new line to the public, had seized upon the prevailing craze to christen his product after the General.

The journey to London took a long time. At Winchester, the Mayor insisted on haranguing the General at the door of his compartment and the band that struck up 'The Conquering Hero' was drowned by the roars of applause. As the train approached Vauxhall, the line was encumbered by hundreds of thousands of spectators crowded on railway waggons and locomotives, and on the roofs of houses, who howled their heads off as it passed. At its destination at Nine Elms Station, a large portrait of the hero decorated the platform and there was a vast concourse. There were innumerable speeches of welcome and it was long before the General could escape to the Duke of Sutherland's carriage which awaited him.

But the reception was nothing to what followed as the carriage, with its four horses, struggled along the Wandsworth Road towards the West End. It was estimated that more than half a million people packed the streets. Every working men's society was out with banners and bands, but they were swept aside by the exhilarated crowds, climbing on the carriage, all seeking to shake the hand of the General, all shouting and cheering and waving emblems.

It took so long to reach Westminster Bridge that the sun was setting as the cortège passed over with bells clanging and cheers resounding and when, at last, the carriage reached the quiet square outside Stafford House, there were scenes never before witnessed by that almost regal precinct. When the carriage was eventually taken into the stables it fell to pieces. That night, the Duke's lackeys were busy selling bottles of soapsuds alleged to have come from Garibaldi's washbasin.

The next day it was midday before Garibaldi appeared to the
waiting crowds and he was then driven off to lunch with the
Prime Minister, Lord Palmerston. What passed between them is
not known but it was thought by some that Garibaldi emerged
with a rather red face, as if there had been some acrimonious
dispute; at any rate, in the afternoon when he visited the Dowager
Duchess of Sutherland at her house in Chiswick, and met a host
of titled aristocrats, there was no such atmosphere, although the
Earl of Malmesbury was shocked to see him commit the un-
pardonable sin of lighting up a cigar in the Duchess's drawing-
room. But the Duchess does not seem to have been offended, for
in the next few days he was seen with her so often on his arm at
receptions that it was widely rumoured that the fifty-seven-
year-old sailor's son was going to marry the fifty-eight-year-old
Duchess.

That week he was fêted by all the town as if he were royalty.
Receptions were crowded for him; there were scenes of ecstasy at
the opera; he was taken to Bedford to inspect the railworks; he
dined with Gladstone, the Chancellor of the Exchequer, and with
Lord John Russell, the Foreign Secretary; he was taken, of course,
to see Barclays and Perkins brewery at Southwark and received
a very different reception from that afforded an Austrian dignitary
a few years earlier; at a great gala at the Crystal Palace he was
presented with a sword of honour, all the Garibaldi hymns were
sung and the whole house rose to its feet as Arditi's *La Garibaldina*
was reached with its refrain:

> O Garibaldi, nostro salvator,
> Te seguiremo al campo del'onor,
> Risorga Italia,
> Il sol di liberta,
> All'armi, all'armi, andiamo.
>
> *Garibaldi, oh! our saviour,*
> *Thee we'll follow to the field of honour,*
> *To raise Italy,*
> *Sun of liberty,*
> *To arms! To arms! Let us go!*

He dined at Panizzi's house in a small circle of influential men,
and Gladstone again sat next to him and they had an intimate
conversation.[5] He was escorted to Eton by the Duchess of Suther-

land and received there with greater enthusiasm than if he had been royalty. And on the 25th April, there was conferred on him the honour of the freedom of the City of London. The banquet given to him the next day by the Fishmongers' Company was marred only by the fact that Menotti and Ricciotti—with their father—were under the impression that it was to be an assembly of tradesmen who dealt in fish; whereas, of course, that august body's closest acquaintance with the commodity was the *truites de Spey à l'Italienne* which appeared on the menu in honour of their guest. Consequently, they did not attend in evening-dress and were excluded. Their father, in his red shirt and grey trousers, led a glittering assembly in to dinner with the Dowager Duchess of Sutherland on his arm.

The applause for the hero was almost universal, but there were some dissenters. Across the Channel, a satirical journalist proclaimed in the *Courier du Dimanche* that Garibaldi had come to England to get the budget surplus of the Chancellor of the Exchequer for his million rifles' fund and prophesied that *he will get plenty of plum pudding and turtle soup but no money for muskets*; and Napoleon III was sending such angry protests about the reception of this pardoned rebel that Lord Clarendon had to be sent specially to Paris to placate him. From Italy, the British Minister was writing of the *extreme irritation and annoyance* there which he found it *hopeless to try to appease*; and was attributing radical victories in by-elections to Garibaldi's reception in England.

The future Cardinal Manning, leader of the Roman Catholics, was furious that the Archbishop of Canterbury should have attended a reception in honour of the leader of what he termed, with the aptitude for inaccuracy invariably displayed by dignitaries of that Church to their opponents, the *socialist revolution* which was *licentious, unjust and without moral necessity*; and *associated with public and private immorality*.[6] The discreet Mr Disraeli, almost alone amongst his party, found it inopportune to meet such a character. Karl Marx, on the other hand, *flatly refused* and described it all as a *miserable spectacle of imbecility*.[7]

The views of Queen Victoria were identical with those of Karl Marx; she was, she wrote, *half-ashamed of being the head of a nation capable of such follies*;[8] but her heir, the future Edward VII, came up to London specially to meet Garibaldi and took care not to receive Her Majesty's telegram forbidding him to do so until after the interview had taken place.

IV

Amidst all the plum pudding and turtle soup, Garibaldi found time to keep his promise to call on Stansfield, and to be present at an informal meal in the house of the Russian revolutionary, Hertzen. There were a number of Garibaldini leaders present, including Mordini and Guerzoni, together with Polish and Russian revolutionaries—and Mazzini.

At the end of the meal, Garibaldi rose to his feet with a glass of Marsala in his hand and said :[9]

'Today I want to fulfil a duty which I ought to have performed long ago. There is among us a man who has rendered the greatest service to my native land and to liberty in general. When I was still young and had only vague aspirations, I sought for a man who would be able to guide me, and be the counsellor of my youth. I sought for him as he who is dying of thirst seeks for water. I found him. He alone kept watch while all around slept. He became my friend and has remained so ever since. In him the sacred flame of love of country and of liberty has never flickered or died. That man is Giuseppe Mazzini. I toast him, my friend, my master !'

He spoke in a low, solemn, sincere voice and when the toast had been drunk Mazzini, greatly overcome with emotion, rose to his feet, clasped Garibaldi's hand and uttered two words only in reply:

'È troppo.'

'It is too much.'

Shortly afterwards, the suspicions of Lord Palmerston having been aroused, Garibaldi was taken to task for his association with such revolutionaries and he passed it off by saying that had he found Mazzini in prosperity he would have been able to avoid all misunderstandings by not seeing him, but finding him in adversity he could not throw him aside. It was a very noble sentiment but it was very much less than the truth. For the day after the meeting in Herzen's house, the Italian embassy sent a telegram to an aide-de-camp to Victor Emmanuel (as it happened none other than the Count di Castiglione, Virginia's estranged husband) which informed His Majesty that at that meeting a united plan for action had been agreed.

For not only had three more of Garibaldi's chief officers arrived in London for some unexplained reason, but two high ranking

Piedmontese officers also arrived, one of them a Colonel Porcelli, with messages from Victor Emmanuel to Garibaldi; and, incredible as it may seem, there was also present in the British capital a gentleman who was busy acting as intermediary between Mazzini and the Italian monarch.

V

Garibaldi had been invited by more than fifty provincial towns and cities, mostly in the North of England, to visit them; and he had accepted. The country was therefore astounded to learn, shortly after the Sunday meeting of revolutionaries and in the middle of his London programme, that he would be leaving England and returning to Caprera. It was announced that the strain of his tour was proving too much for his health, which only served to excite public curiosity as to the real reason for the abrupt termination of his visit; especially since another assembly of many thousands, this time of working men, at the Crystal Palace had the opportunity of observing for themselves that he showed no signs of strain. Speculation was increased when the Mr Partridge who had been so handsomely paid for two brief visits to the prisoner of Varignano wrote to *The Times* to say that his former patient was doing well; and when, the next day, the personal physician of Mr Charles Seely, at whose town house in Princes Gate the General was then staying, wrote to the same journal to the effect that the General was exhausted by his tour and needed rest; an opinion that the General's own Italian physician promptly repudiated in the same day's edition of the *Evening Sun*.

The report was published in some papers that Gladstone had been deputed by Lord Palmerston to express to the General the view that his visit was proving embarrassing to the Government in their relations with the French Emperor and that the Chancellor of the Exchequer, at a loss for the correct Italian word to describe his presence had fallen back on the Latin one, *impedimentum*; and with that the General had taken offence. It was a report which was probably substantially correct, in that a request had been made.

However that may be, the General packed his bags and left London on the 22nd April, leaving behind him a letter of thanks for his reception which contained a sting which confirmed the suspicions that he had been forced to depart: *I shall be happy to return among you under more favourable circumstances . . . For the moment I am obliged to leave England.* A meeting at Highgate called to plant an oak tree to the memory of Shakespeare, passed an angry resolution protesting against 'those domineering upper classes who are sending our guest away so soon'; and was dispersed by the police amidst scenes of some disorder.

It may well be that Mr Charles Seely, whose personal physician had been so vocal in asserting that Garibaldi must retire to Caprera for rest, had his own reasons for wishing his guest to depart. For, hardly had the General left their house, than Mrs Seely sat down to write a letter[10] to him, which began:

> *26 Princes Gate,*
> *23rd April '64*

Beloved General,
*   When, Alas! you had left me yesterday, and my heart was heavy with grief, I went to your little bed—full of emotion—and sorrow, that your dear and revered head would not rest there again for long. I stood, so sad . . .*

and in the months that followed there were numerous letters from her to Garibaldi in terms which certainly would not have pleased her husband had he read them.

Garibaldi left London for Cornwall where he called on his old comrade-in-arms, Colonel Peard, now at last settled down to a respectable life as a country squire and justice of the peace. On the 28th April, on a day of cold and drizzling rain, such as that on which he had arrived, the Duke of Sutherland's yacht, the *Ondine*, sailed into grey skies and sea from Fowey with the warrior. The eclipse was already over his sun the day he departed from British shores, never to return. Neither great achievements nor great renown lay ahead of him and his popularity with the British nation steadily declined as it was discovered that he entertained political ideas which were unacceptable to a country where no new thought is ever welcome. At the same time as he was receiving the tumultuous applause, an unknown man travelling on the top of a London horse omnibus was struck by an idea about the nature of matter, which less than a century later was to expose, finally and for ever, the fatuous absurdity of Garibaldi's basic thesis that personal courage could always triumph over advantage in numbers or weapons. As he was jogged along, Kekule suddenly saw how frequently two atoms united to form a pair; how a large

one embraced two smaller; how still larger ones kept hold of
three or four smaller; how the whole kept whirling in a giddy
dance—the dance of the atoms which, interrupted, has provided
for all future mankind a dance of death in which the noblest and
the bravest of men are rendered no more than particles of dust in
a mushroom-shaped cloud.

It was his hosts' intention to take him for a long cruise to the
Greek islands, but his mind was set on other things. At Gibraltar
he found time to drop a note to Speranza, on a piece of paper
emblazoned with the arms of the Duchess of Sutherland:

3rd May, 1864.

My most dear Speranza,
    *I don't know if I owe you a letter but I know that I ought to send you
cordial greetings, I shall be happy to see your dear handwriting when I
arrive at Caprera, where I hope to be in a few days.*

Always yours,

His persistent hosts managed to get him as far as Malta
before he could persuade them to take him to Caprera and he
could write to Benedetto Cairoli: *I am home once again, in spite of
the plans made for me by others for a longer cruise.*[11]

The ducal yacht, the *Ondine*, still hovered off Caprera after it
had delivered the General, and on the 17th June it carried him to
the island of Ischia, so that, purportedly, he could take the mud
baths there for his rheumatism. The real reason for his visit,
however, was a council of war with his followers. He had been
visited at Caprera shortly after his arrival by Victor Emmanuel's
mysterious emissary, the Colonel Porcello, and there was a
scheme, mooted by the monarch, which was under active consideration. It was the same as that put before the revolutionaries
in London at Herzen's house. The King was set on enlisting their
aid to raise revolution in Polish Galicia and attack Vienna from
there, so that if it were successful, he could launch an attack on the
Quadrilateral to secure Venice.

Most of Garibaldi's followers were opposed to the scheme,
seeing in it no more than a move by the King to lure them to their
destruction or, at best, an attempt to provide a throne outside
Italy for one of his sons. Mazzini also wrote from London advising
against it. The great debate continued for nearly a month but
it ended abruptly when one of the conspirators, fearing that
Garibaldi was likely to accept, leaked the whole of the plot to

a newspaper. The next day, Colonel Porcelli arrived with a letter from the King calling everything off.

Guerzoni, Garibaldi's secretary and subsequently his biographer, was blamed for the inspired report. He was dismissed and Garibaldi sailed, furious, home for Caprera.

The hour of the liberation of Venice drew near, but it was destined to be achieved as an incidental to conduct as foolish and as bloody as any of Victor Emmanuel's madcap schemes.

It is to be feared that Garibaldi was unappreciative of the services Guerzoni had rendered him. That wise patriot was left behind in Ischia to fight a duel with Colonel Porcelli.

XXII

I OBEY

✦✦✦✦✦✦✦✦✦✦

I N THE late summer of 1864, Speranza paid a further visit to
Caprera. To her, Garibaldi confided that Victor Emmanuel
was continuing to make approaches to him for some project or
other; but he seems to have been under no illusion about the
nature of them.

'The King wishes that we should be on good terms with each
other,' he told her.[1] 'On the one hand he makes advances, but on
the other he guards himself from danger. If the undertaking
succeeds, his will be the merit; if it falls to the ground, we shall
hear of proclamations . . . and sentences and imprisonments will
follow.'

The object of Speranza's journey this time was to try and
persuade Garibaldi to entrust to her custody his five-year-old
daughter, Anita, then with her mother, Battistina, in Nice. As
her hopes of capturing the lion had diminished, Speranza was
now intent on having one of his cubs.

When she left the island, she carried with her a letter from the
General to the child's mother.

20th September 1864.

Dear Battistina,
   *Madame de Schwartz, the bearer of these lines, has been good enough
to offer to undertake the charge of Anita. Discuss the matter with her,
and I will approve any measure which has your joint agreement.*

But the mother proved strangely reluctant to relinquish her
child, which Speranza could only attribute to the fact that *she
considered her as so much capital on which her own future depended;*[2] a
conclusion she arrived at as the result of the fact that Garibaldi
was making Battistina a monthly allowance. When the poor

illiterate mother dared to say that she doubted whether Garibaldi could really have written such a letter, Speranza was indignant with the presumption of it, and broke off negotiations. Before the news of that reached him, Garibaldi had written to her *of the happiness of seeing you more frequently at my house together with Anita, when we can talk about the time when you will come and live at Caprera*; and when news of the refusal of Battistina to part with her only child reached him, he wrote again:

22nd November 1864.

Most dear Speranza,

As long as I live I shall feel love and gratitude towards you. You have behaved nobly in this matter. The wicked nature of that woman is only too well known to me.

Write to me about yourself, and love me for ever.

A year later, the determined Speranza tried again to obtain Anita from Battistina; and, failing, she turned her attention to an attempt to capture another cub. The forty-four-year-old, twice-wed, authoress proposed marriage, by letter, to Menotti Garibaldi, then aged twenty-five; a proposal he declined gracefully, giving as his only reasons *his erratic life and the perils of war* to which he was exposed. Fortunately, an outbreak of cholera in the coastal ports of Italy prevented her coming to Caprera to pursue her project in person.

The year passed quietly for Garibaldi on Caprera, playing with a steam yacht presented to him by English admirers (though he had difficulty in finding the funds to maintain her), fishing, and digging his barren soil, though the effect of his wounds and his crippling rheumatism continued to hamper his movements. Since the King appeared to be so anxious to utilize his services, he wrote to suggest that he should be sent as viceroy to govern Naples and the South. *The government is now more hated there than the Bourbons,* he wrote, quite accurately, *and the day war breaks out against Austria there will be a cataclysmic rebellion against us in the South.*[3]

He could scent the powder in the air again and, for once, seems to have been ready to accept a more passive role than hitherto; but it was an offer that Victor Emmanuel was in no danger of accepting, though it would have been greatly in his interests to have done so.

II

In the early part of 1866, there arrived a new inhabitant for the island of Caprera. Teresita had returned home from Genoa, where she was living with her husband, Canzio, for a short time to show her father her latest baby and with her had brought, as wet nurse, a young peasant girl from Lombardy. Francesca Armosino, who had had the misfortune to give birth to a child by an unknown soldier shortly before, was rather small, with a broad nose and a large mouth, but she had a smooth white skin and her lips pouted prettily with a certain petulant charm. Soon, if Speranza can be believed[4] Teresita wished for good reason to send her away; but Garibaldi insisted on her staying and it was Teresita who departed in high dudgeon.

But Francesca did not enjoy the pleasures of her master's bed for long before he was obliged to leave her. On the 8th April, Italy had made a secret alliance with Prussia to attack Austria and in early May the General learned from an emissary of the King that his services would shortly be required on the field of battle. He sailed from Caprera on the 10th June and the vessel that bore him away was the old *Piedmonte* that he had commandeered in 1860 for the expedition to Sicily. By the time he left, Francesca was already pregnant again, this time by no private soldier.

Garibaldi was put in charge of an army of volunteers who, unlike 1859, were allowed to wear the red shirt, principally, no doubt, because the army thought it a convenient way of getting them to provide their own uniform without the trouble and expense of having to clothe them from official sources. La Marmora and Cialdini were the commanders-in-chief of the Royal forces and, though each was jealous of the other, both were jealous of Garibaldi. For that reason, they combined to resist the King's original plan for the volunteers which he had communicated to Garibaldi in May. It was Victor Emmanuel's long-cherished scheme to dispatch the Redshirts from the Adriatic coast of Italy for an invasion of Dalmatia, *to throw the firebrand of insurrection*,[5] as their leader aptly described it, amongst the subject nationalities of the Austro-Hungarian Empire. It was a scheme which now had Bismarck's blessing, and would have fitted in with Prussian strategic requirements, since it meant that the Austrians would have to detach a sizable army from the other fronts to combat the danger at their rear.[6] But it also meant, inevitably, that Garibaldi would have to be given an independent command and a free hand to pursue the campaign as he saw fit; which, undoubtedly, would have been with revolutionary fervour. Moreover, the army suspected that, once again, he would prove all too successful and detract from the glory of the regular forces. At that prospect, La Marmora and Cialdini combined with the conservative politicians to veto the plan.

When the danger of being engaged in war with both Prussia and Italy became apparent, Austria immediately offered to cede Venezia if Italy would stay out of the war. It was an offer that was refused, partly because Italy wished to acquire Trieste and the southern Tyrol and drive her frontier up to the natural barrier of the mountains, but more because the Royal army lusted for some glory of its own in the making of a united Italy. Lombardy had come through the grace of Napoleon III, Tuscany and central Italy through the insistence of the radicals there for union, Sicily and the whole of the Neapolitan kingdom through 'the cabin boy of Nice' and their record was only of defeat, apart from trifling victories over the insignificant Papal troops. Now, outnumbering the Austrians in Venezia by three to two, as they also outnumbered them in vessels of war in the Adriatic, the Royal Italian forces were confident that their moment to shine had come.

For that reason, Garibaldi was sent off to make his way, with his volunteers, to Salo on Lago di Garda and to advance up the western side of that lake on to Trento and the Tyrol. As before, they were supplied with nothing but old muskets, inadequate medical resources and supplies and left to fend for themselves by feeding off the country; but this time they were supplied with some artillery support, although more than half of those who had enrolled under Garibaldi's standard were left behind, stationed in the toe of Italy.

The rest of the volunteers assembled in Como and sailed from there under a shower of roses to Lecco, and then made their way through Bergamo and Brescia amid the usual scenes of enthusiasm. They were even more motley a crew than before. Veterans of 1860 mingled with youths, there were even more bad characters than usual, those who came along only in the hope of pillage; and a large number of foreign nationalities was represented, including a sizable English contingent. The energetic wife of Colonel Chambers travelled behind Garibaldi with a patent silver cooking apparatus to ensure that he, at least, received proper nourishment;

and Jessie Mario was there to do what she could for the sick and wounded. All this horde, to the number of 10,000 or more, descended on the small town of Salo where they were hard put to find accommodation and, even more, anything to eat.

Scarcely had they arrived there, than the news came of the defeat by the Austrians of one of the two armies, into which the regular forces had been divided, at Custoza on the 24th June.[7] Without being pursued, it retreated in disorder thirty miles behind the river Oglio. The other army, that of the Po, took the opportunity of retreating as well, although it had not yet been engaged by the enemy. Garibaldi was ordered to abandon the plans for an advance and cover the flank from Brescia to Salo. He withdrew his forces to Lonato.

Within a short time, however, he was back in Salo and commencing a drive with his volunteers up into the Trentino, towards Trento. Through a countryside of deep valleys, high mountains, gorges and crags, the volunteers progressed through a number of small engagements. In the first of these, Garibaldi was wounded and a day afterwards wrote to his daughter:

14th July, 1866.

My dear Teresa,
  I am wounded with just such a wound as Anzani gets when playing. So don't heed any rumour you may hear. A kiss to our children and remembrances to all our friends.

It is to be doubted, though, whether Teresa's son ever received, while playing, a penetrating wound by a bullet in his upper left thigh. It incapacitated the General for several days and thereafter for the rest of the campaign he was obliged to conduct operations from a carriage.

Between the volunteers and their objective lay a miniature Quadrilateral of Austrian forts in commanding positions. Garibaldi's tactics throughout the campaign were to command the crests of the mountains, *acting the eagle*, as he called it, before advancing up the valleys, and his volunteers had some tough uphill battles to gain the heights. Eventually, after prolonged bombardment, the fort of Ampola capitulated, and the way was freed to Riva. The first column of the volunteers advanced cheerfully into a small hamlet outside Bezzecca with their band playing at their head only to find themselves set on by a large body of Austrians. They panicked and fled and it was Garibaldi's sons, Menotti and

Ricciotti, and son-in-law, Canzio, with the old General urging them on from his carriage, while the buglers sounded unheeded orders to advance, that stemmed the rush. A body of regular *Bersaglieri* remained steady and at length the Redshirts were persuaded to resume the attack; after a battle of twelve hours against some 8,000 Austrians the rout was turned into victory and Bezzecca taken.

It was a decisive, if minor, victory. In Riva, the Austrians threw their cannon in the lake and smashed their mortars and began a hasty retreat; and Garibaldi was joined by his old friend, Medici, now a general in the royal forces, and his troops, while on the eastern shores of the Lago di Garda his other old comrade, Cosenz, was advancing towards Trento with substantial bodies of regulars.

The Austrian general, handicapped by the decisive victories by the Prussians over his nation at Sadowa and Königgratz, decided on a withdrawal into the Austrian Tyrol. The way to Trento and the whole of the southern Tyrol lay open.

News arrived of another defeat of Victor Emmanuel's forces. In a naval battle off the island of Lissa, Admiral Persano had disgracefully lost an encounter between twelve of his ironclads and seven of the Austrians'.

The Prussians had gained all they desired out of the war. Hostilities were suspended, and as Garibaldi prepared to advance further, he received a telegram from La Marmora: *Political considerations require imperatively conclusion of an armistice for which it is necessary for all our forces to be withdrawn from the Tyrol. By order of the King . . . the troops under your command are to retire beyond the frontier of the Tyrol by 4 a.m. on the 11th August next.*

There were those amongst his number who urged Garibaldi to ignore it and carry on up into the Tyrol; there were others who suggested he should proclaim an Italian Republic and invade the capital. Perhaps if Medici had not been there he might have been tempted to yield to one or other of these propositions. Instead he sent a famous reply by telegram in one word more eloquent than any of his wordy proclamations: *Obbedisco.* I obey.

III

Of all wars, that of Italy against Austria in 1866 was the most futile and unrewarding. For all the blood shed and treasure squandered, Italy gained just what she could have achieved without war, and that in the most humiliating way possible. Disdaining to surrender Venice to an enemy whose superior forces she had decisively defeated, Austria handed it over to Napoleon III, who graciously made a present of it to Victor Emmanuel.

In his island home, Garibaldi was left to fulminate against the folly and cowardice of his country's politicians and generals, but there was little he could do. For most of the rest of 1866 he was confined to bed because his Aspromonte wound had reopened and he was, as he put it, *nailed to the island by appalling rheumatism.*[8]

In the spring of the following year, Speranza met him in the Hotel de Rome, in Florence, by then the capital of Italy. 'See how thin I am,' he said to her and gave her his arm to feel. He looked tired and nervous. They talked of many things: of her horses and dogs; of Crete, where she was then living; of course, of Rome. To her pleasure, he appeared to be reconciled to the difficulty of taking the Eternal City.

With a mischievous smile, he said:

'Now that I've reached my sixtieth year, it is high time I became more reasonable. The Papacy has more friends and supporters than one fancies and it will be very difficult to get rid of them.'

Amid all the topics discussed, he did not, apparently, find occasion to mention that his sixtieth year had been commemorated by the birth to him of another child, his sixth, every one of whom had been born out of wedlock. Francesca had given birth to a daughter, Clelia, on the 16th February.

At his suggestion, Speranza and he slipped away to spend a few days together in a small village outside Florence. When they parted he did not, as he had told her he would, return to Caprera but began an electioneering tour all over the north of Italy in which reasonableness about Rome was conspicuously absent. At Venice, he had the crowds shouting: 'Death to the Priests!' though he quietly chided them with: 'Death to No One!' It was perhaps the messianic rapture with which the mobs greeted him that converted him from his reasonableness. At Verona, the multitude brought him a child to baptize, whom he christened Chiassi, after one of his faithful warriors who had fallen in the war of the previous year, 'In the name of God and the lawgiver, Jesus'. The results of the election should have warned him that the applause of the voteless populace were not of great consequence in Italy of that day. Although he himself was elected, not one of the sixty candidates he sponsored was; and Rattazzi, the man of Aspromonte, returned to power as Prime Minister.

Even his most faithful followers were opposed to any attempt to dislodge the Pope. He wrote to Mario, Jessie's husband:

9th July 1864.

My dear Mario,

I have already written that I wished to see you. If it disturbs you to come to Vinci, where I am going tomorrow, set all the ladies to work on red shirts. Prepare yourself in any event for Rome.

Mario came to see him at Vinci with another Garibaldini, General Acerbi. As they travelled, they made notes of what they would say to dissuade the General from his course.

For, among other reasons, there was a new factor in the struggle to acquire Rome for Italy. On the 14th September 1864, Italy had entered into a treaty with France whereby she undertook to recognize and protect the sovereignty of the Pope over Rome and oppose any attack upon it by regular or irregular forces. On the faith of that undertaking the French troops had withdrawn. If, therefore, Garibaldi were to attack Rome there could be no ambiguity about the duty of any Italian government. Moreover, there was every danger that, if they neglected their obligations under the convention, France would intervene.

When the two men saw Garibaldi, his first words were:⁹ 'General Acerbi, you will command the volunteers. Viterbo is to be our meeting-place. Treat with Rattazzi, and tell our friends in Parliament that I give them yet a month to prepare.' Without a word of protest, Acerbi accepted the commission; but Mario was more inclined to resist. When he had advanced all his arguments, Garibaldi said:

'All this we can think about in Rome. Meanwhile—march!'

Before long, all Italy was in tumult. Under the eyes of the government the volunteers were arming themselves, preparing red shirts, raising funds under thinly cloaked pretexts. The prefects were ordered to suppress the movement by arrests, but one wrote back in despair: *Arrests are useless. How can we arrest an entire population?*

In the midst of these warlike preparations, Garibaldi suddenly disappeared from Italy. He went to Geneva to attend a conference of the International Society for Peace and Liberty. It was a gathering of pacifists, democrats, socialists, anarchists and political theorists of every shade of radical opinion. He was elected honorary president of the convention and stayed long enough to make a speech containing eight points. Some of them were far-sighted and sensible proposals for international arbitration to end wars and pleas for brotherhood amongst the nations. The others set the conference squabbling as only idealist theoreticians can squabble. The Catholics amongst them objected to his declaration that 'The Papacy, being the most obnoxious of the sects, is declared fallen'; the Protestants resented his advocacy of a non-theistic new religion based simply on the brotherhood of man; the pacifists disliked his proclamation that it was a duty to make war on tyranny. Leaving them all to their battle of words, he returned to Italy where the volunteers were already assembling in their thousands on the Roman frontiers for a more bloody conflict.

Ten days after his return, he was arrested at Sinalunga, near the Roman frontier and was conveyed to imprisonment at Alessandria. From his prison he managed to have smuggled out a piece of paper on which he had scribbled: *The Romans have the right of slaves to rebel against their tyrants, the priests. Italians have a duty to help them . . . in spite of the imprisonment of fifty Garibaldis.* It was published and there were unseemly scenes outside his prison and two regiments of the Royal army there mutinied to cries of 'To Rome with Garibaldi!' Soon after, the prisoner was released through a guard of honour and escorted down to Genoa and taken to Caprera.

There was a scheme to enable Garibaldi to escape by steamer from the island, to which the Prime Minister, Rattazzi, was a party;[10] and behind the scenes the government was busy supply-ing money and arms to the volunteers. There can be little doubt that the Cabinet wished to aid the venture in every way possible, so long as it was not apparent that they were doing so. The big stumbling-block was the King. In spite of his irregular life, he was a superstitious Papist and was fearful of depriving the Pope of his remaining temporal power, though he hoped that, at some distant time, the House of Savoy would be allowed to rule over Rome with Papal consent.

The scheme for an escape by special steamer came to nothing, so Garibaldi calmly took the packet boat to Genoa, but it was stopped by a Royal warship and he was escorted back to Caprera.

Nine warships of the navy were now stationed off Caprera,

and the adjacent island of Maddalena was garrisoned with troops, all charged by Royal command with the important task of preventing one crippled old man leaving his island sanctuary.

Meanwhile, three columns of volunteers, one of them under Menotti Garibaldi, and innumerable bands swarmed across the Papal borders without him. Not only Rattazzi, but some of Garibaldi's most loyal friends, counselled him to remain on Caprera so that the Italian government might not be compromised in the eyes of the world while the Pope was being pushed off his throne.

IV

Dark clouds covered the heights of Caprera and a febrile sirocco was whistling through the shrubs and undergrowth and dashing waves violently against its pink granite shores, when three men left the house on the evening of the 14th October. They made their way to the loose stone wall that divided the cultivated parts from the wilderness of the rest of the island and, one after another, they clambered over.

'It's still too light,' said Garibaldi, whose familiar russet beard was dyed black. 'Let us wait awhile and smoke half a cigar.'[11]

The three crouched down out of the wind under the shelter of the wall and puffed away, until night fell and a vague brightness was distinguishable behind the mountains.

'In three quarters of an hour, the moon will rise behind the mountains—we must not wait any longer.'

At the tiny beach, they found the Sardinian boatman who had preceded them. He had bailed out the old punt that was used for duck shooting. When Garibaldi was on board and concealed at the bottom, the fisherman took another boat and rowed out towards the warships which lay at anchor farther out. He was quickly hailed and, while the attention of those on the warships was diverted, Garibaldi slid the punt out and along the shore. Paddled vigorously and driven along by the wind, the punt crossed the seas to a tiny islet just off the coast of Maddalena. From there, Garibaldi waded across the shallow waters between it and the island and, after a difficult scramble amongst the bushes and boulders, he rapped cautiously with his stick on a window at the home of the English widow, Mrs Collins, whose husband had once owned half of Caprera.

She was expecting him and there he passed the night with the widow and a beautiful black-haired Maltese girl, *the subject of the most loving and delicate attentions,* as he described it. The next night, with Basso, he was able to cross to the mainland of Sardinia where they spent the rest of the night and most of the following day in a cave. Two days later, having travelled through the rocky wilderness of Gallura, he reached the point on the coast where Canzio was waiting for him with a fishing-vessel. It took them fifty-two hours in heavy rain and a gale to make the mainland of Italy; on the 25th he drove into Florence in a carriage.

He spent two days openly in the Italian capital, addressing the populace from balconies, and no move was made by the Italian authorities to arrest him. The Prime Minister, refusing to comply with Victor Emmanuel's demands that he should denounce the invasion of Papal territories, had resigned; and the King was finding it difficult to replace him. La Marmora was offered the post and refused it; Cialdini was offered it and came to discuss the matter with Garibaldi. According to Crispi, at whose house the meeting took place, Cialdini told Garibaldi that, if it were not for the state of disorganization in the Royal army, he would order them to march on Rome with the volunteers. After the discussion, he declined the King's offer on the ground that no government which failed to come to terms with Garibaldi could survive in view of public opinion; and the King was obliged to find as a Prime Minister who would be subservient to his wishes another soldier, Menabrea. But by then Garibaldi had left Florence, travelling in a special train for the Papal frontier.

The volunteers had an initial success when Garibaldi defeated a strong Papal force at Monterotondo, but by now, alerted by the long preparations and dissatisfied with the Italian government's failure to stop them, Napoleon III had moved. As Garibaldi's train was steaming towards the Terni, unknown to him a French frigate was sailing for Civita Vecchia. On the 3rd November, at Mentano, the volunteers were faced by a superior force of Papal and French troops, the latter armed with the latest weapon of destruction, the *chassepot*. Although it was not, perhaps, so wonderful a weapon as the French liked to pretend, it could fire twelve times a minute and inflicted terrible casualties on the Redshirts who were armed mainly with ancient muskets, some of them relics of the Napoleonic wars. The Garibaldini had no prior knowledge of the arrival of the French until they found themselves in combat with them, armed with these terrifying new rifles and,

L

as a result, they were thoroughly demoralized. Many fled from the field of battle and, although there were individual acts of heroism, defeat was in the air and nothing the General could do could dispel it. The Redshirts retired in disorder leaving 150 dead, 240 wounded, and 1,600 prisoners; the total casualties amongst the enemy were 32 dead and 11 wounded—and only two of the dead were French soldiers. It was the first battle of a new kind of war, and the General, versed only in personal conflicts at close quarters and steeped in the conviction that bravery could overcome all odds, was, in his old age, ill-equipped to meet it. But whatever he or his men had done that day nothing could have saved them from the fate that inevitably awaited them.

The invasion of the Papal States was no act of senile folly, as some have represented it to be. If it had not been for the French, Garibaldi would have certainly carried Rome. The only error was one of timing, for far too long had been taken in noising the project abroad, so that Napoleon III had the chance to prepare counter measures. Had it been carried out with the swiftness of the 1860 moves, and had proved victorious and been supported by the Italian government, it is improbable that Napoleon III would have cared, in spite of pressure on him at home, to launch a major war to restore Rome to the Pope. The delay was due to the obduracy of Victor Emmanuel and the temporizations of his Ministers. It was the latter who urged Garibaldi, as he put it,[13] 'Do but fire a few musket-shots, even in the air, and the Italian army will be with you'; and it was their subterfuges and machinations which caused the delay and led to his defeat.

After Mentana, what remained of the volunteers fled over the border. At the frontier a train was put at Garibaldi's disposal to carry him to Florence; when it reached the station at Figlino a lieutenant-colonel of the *carabinieri* announced that he had orders to arrest him. Garibaldi protested his immunity as a deputy in vain; in vain he told the *carabinieri* officer that Rattazzi had told him: 'Go on—with the first shots the army will follow'. After he had taken a bowl of soup in the waiting-room, he continued the journey under escort to his former prison at Varignano.

But, once again, too many important people were implicated for him to be brought to trial on any charge. On the 25th November, he was put at liberty and returned to Caprera to continue work on the novel he had begun to write before he became involved in these events.

V

By December 1867, he had finished his first venture in fiction and, as he wrote to Speranza: *I need all your kind endeavours and those of Jessie Mario to make this book presentable to the public . . . Moreover, for the love they bear me, my literary co-operators must tone down certain expressions which might offend feminine susceptibilities and think of me only as a brother who loves them very much and has great need of money.* He also referred to it as *my poor work.*

When Speranza read the manuscript, she decided it was necessary for her to go to Caprera to try and dissuade the author from publishing it if that were possible; and she wrote to tell him that she would be coming. He replied:

Caprera, 8th June 1868.

Most dear Speranza,

On my crutches I hobbled down to the harbour yesterday to meet you because I was told you had arrived on the steamer.

And do you know whom I met? Battistina and Anita. Your presence here might possibly persuade the mother to entrust the child to you, but I'm afraid you wouldn't succeed even now. B. wants money and is very cunning. Come, and don't stop at Maddalena . . . come straight to the house.

Speranza came. For the first time she met Francesca, now established as the permanent mistress of the house, whom she found *a rough-looking woman*; and baby Clelia, *pale and not at all pretty*, was decked out as an angel, with wings, in honour of her coming. Battistina and her child, Anita, were still there. While this trinity of women, who had only one thing in common, were in the small house, it would be interesting to have known what sort of atmosphere prevailed; and how Garibaldi passed his time.

A few days after her arrival, he gave Speranza a letter of authority entrusting her with *the education and endowment* of his daughter, Anita. He had not as yet said a word to Battistina. That was one battle from which he shrank without an ally.

Speranza's description of the battle merits reproduction in full:

The love of money, which is so strong a characteristic amongst Italians, was exemplified on this occasion in a most striking manner; for it was only when the General told Battistina that, as in future she would not have upon her the charge of Anita, her allowance would be reduced by one half—it was only then that her anger burst forth. Beside herself with rage, she rushed sobbing from the room in which, with closed doors and windows, and candles lit, sentence had been passed upon her. Going straightaway to bed, she refused all food, affirmed that she was ill and rejected all attempts to cheer and console her.

But by various means, including a promise to make up the allowance, Speranza persuaded Battistina to depart from Caprera for Genoa the next morning. When Anita, who in her nine years had never previously been parted from her mother, saw her go she threw herself on the ground and rolled, sobbing, about on the sand.

When Speranza left the island a few days later with Anita and was on the deck of the steamer, the child, *publicly and without a sense of shame or modesty renewed the same scenes.* And, later, in a carriageful of people, she even had the effrontery to strike her new guardian.

Persuaded by this that her ungrateful ward was in dire need of discipline, Speranza dumped her in a boarding-school in Switzerland under a stern teutonic headmistress and cleared off to Germany; and was disgusted when Garabaldi wrote a kindly and affectionate letter to Anita, which she could only attribute to his *extreme weakness about his children.*

XXIII

A THUNDERBOLT FROM A
CLOUDLESS SKY

❖❖❖❖❖❖❖❖❖

THE NOVEL, which Garibaldi laboriously wrote by a hand so
gnarled by rheumatism that for days he could not hold a
pen, was called, in the Italian version, *Clelia*. The kindest thing
that can be said about it is that it was no worse than a multitude of
other novels of half a century earlier. An octave of improbable
lovers, all of them excelling in purity of character, even though
their relationships were more in accordance with Garibaldi's own
than with those approved by the Church, have a series of incredible adventures until they all expire nobly on the battlefield of
Mentana, struggling to liberate Rome. The author's *need of
drawing an honest profit from his labours,* to which Garibaldi, with
typical naïve honesty, referred in his preface, was fulfilled by the
publication of it in 1870 simultaneously in Italian, English and
German versions—the two latter as *Rule of the Monk*, which lurid
title was not an entirely inaccurate description of the theme. In it
every crime known to the calendar is ascribed to the clergy, including the savage rape of one of the heroines by a Cardinal.
The book, wrote the 'Saturday Review', *is like the first attempt of an
enthusiastic and clever lad . . . the politics are those of innocent young
ladies, who believe everybody who differs from them to be a black-
hearted traitor. Such simplicity makes the book almost more pitiable
than absurd, but it is not inconsistent with the possession of certain great
qualities which in times of disturbance may convert a tenth-rate novelist
into a formidable enemy. This strange mixture of absolute childishness
with genuine heroism would make Garibaldi a far better hero, than
author, of a romance.*
Within a few days of its publication, from the same Italian

publishers there appeared a second novel written by Garibaldi, *Cantoni il Volontario*, in part based on his experiences during the Roman Republic. This and a later effort, *I Mille*, based on his Sicilian expedition, would have merited more consideration by the reviewers, but the English publishers had had enough. Neither has been translated into English though both contain a good deal of interesting autobiographical material, laced with priestly transgressions. In the latter work, for example, a high dignitary of the Church rapes a young woman who is, unknown to him at the time, his own illegitimate daughter.

Meanwhile, Garibaldi had been as industrious in procreation as in creation. In July 1869, Francesca gave birth to another daughter, named Rosa, in memory of Garibaldi's mother and his first little girl who had died in South America.

II

On the 13th July 1870, Pius IX, in face of substantial opposition, including two-thirds of the American bishops, many of the English and all of the Hungarian bishops, induced a General Council of the Roman Church to resolve what the devout Catholic, Lord Acton, termed at the time *the worse excess*.[1] The Council voted that the Pope *is possessed of that infallibility with which the divine Redeemer ordained his Church to be endowed . . . and therefore definitions of the Roman Pontiff are irreversible . . . and not made by the consent of the Church*. His triumph was due to the large numbers of Italian bishops in the Council; the political manœuvring and packing of committees, worthy of Tammany Hall, by Archbishop (as he then was) Manning; and the letters of vitriolic abuse in which Pio Nono had denounced those who opposed it.[2] At the time when the resolution was handed to the Pope and he knew he was victorious, a great thunderstorm was at its height and so darkened the chancel of St Peter's that a large candle had to be brought to his side so that he could read it. Some thought it very appropriate; it was at any event a symbolic precursor of storms that were to come.

The discussion in the Council had been abruptly terminated by the use of 'the guillotine,' for it was apparent that before long France and Prussia would be at war. The day that Antonelli had envisaged ever since Mentana, the day when France would be so preoccupied with other matters that there would be no *chassepots* to defend the Pope's temporal authority, drew near. The Pope's spiritual authority had been bolstered up just in time: the day after Pius IX formally signed the resolution of the Council, the 18th July, France declared war on Prussia.

Although Napoleon III had declared that he would never remove his troops from Rome, by the 4th August the French situation was so desperate that most of them were on their way to Civita Vecchia. On the 2nd September, France was defeated at Sedan and, two days later, Napoleon III was no longer Emperor of the French. It was an event for which he was not entirely unprepared; ever since 1859 he had been secreting money in England and had a house, Camden Place, bought in the name of his solicitor and decorated even with the great gates which once graced the Paris Exhibition.

Pius IX, whose only endearing quality was the habit of making bad puns, when he heard that, in consequence of Sedan, the French protection of the Holy See would have to be withdrawn, perpetrated one of his better efforts. It was, he said, an act to which he could do nothing but consent, seeing that 'La France a perdu ses dents'. The inevitable sequel followed. Shortly, an emissary from the Italian King presented himself to His Holiness bearing a letter in which that monarch, *with the love of a son, the faith of a Catholic and the spirit of an Italian,* wrote *that only to save at one and the same time the Papal tiara and the Royal crown from the international revolution now menacing both* . . . he *assumed the responsibility of entering Rome in order to maintain and occupy such positions as were indispensable for the preservation of order in the peninsula and the security of the Holy See.*

The Pope had one of his outbursts of violent rages when the letter was read to him and told the bearer that his master was 'a whitened sepulchre and a viper' and ended by assuring him that 'I am neither a prophet nor the son of a prophet but I say you will not get possession of Rome. *Non possumus.*'

But in that he was less than infallible. On the 3rd November the Italian army blew a breach in the Porta Pia, from which the Papal and French troops had emerged three years before to defeat Garibaldi, and occupied the city. Rome, by almost unanimous plebiscite of the people, voted to be united to Italy. Popes became the 'Prisoner of the Vatican', as they were to remain for many years until one found a politician (named Mussolini) to his liking with whom he could do business.

The man who by his inspiration and efforts had done more than any to bring about the union of Rome to Italy was not there on that day when the Italian army entered the city in triumph. Great care had been taken that he should not be. On his island, he was guarded by warships and soldiers and watched night and day; as he wrote to his son-in-law: *this shoddy article that calls itself the Italian government keeps me a prisoner on Caprera.*

The glory, that of triumphing over a few thousand Papal troops and a resistance that was no more than token, was reserved for the Italian army and the King. He, reluctantly, took the step of entering Rome, knowing that the temper of the Italian people was such that if he did not he would lose his throne; and that if *he* did not, Garibaldi certainly would.

III

The outbreak of the war between France and Prussia and the course of it was viewed with dismay by Victor Emmanuel and the right-wing politicians; the radicals rejoiced in it and in the humiliation of Napoleon III. Shortly after its commencement, the Prussian Ambassador to the Holy See paid a swift visit to Caprera; neither he nor the General left an account of what transpired, but it may safely be surmised that some project of an invasion of France by Garibaldi volunteers was mooted.

To Speranza, on the 15th August 1870, Garibaldi wrote: *The enthusiasm of your noble nation delights us and Napoleon, the lying emperor, will now doubtless be rewarded for all his villainies;* and later: *I deplore bloodshed but I rejoice in Napoleon's defeat. I hope the comedy of blood and lies is at an end.*

When Napoleon was replaced by a French republic, the attitude of the Italian radicals, even those of them who were republicans, did not change; none forgot that it was a French republic that had destroyed the Roman one. And when the Prussians offered the French an ignominious peace, they rejoiced to see their ancient enemy trampled underfoot.

Four days after the rejection of the Prussian terms, Garibaldi offered *what remains of me*, as he put it, to the French Republic. As Jessie Mario wrote:[3] *A thunderbolt falling from a cloudless sky could not have produced a greater sensation. The Garibaldian chiefs were beside themselves with vexation.*

His motives are best recorded in his own words, gleaned from several letters of the period. *If I desired the triumph of Prussian armies, it was that they should destroy the most execrable tyrant of modern times;* and when that was done and the Germans persisted in their war he wrote: *Now I in turn become the enemy of Germany because she abuses her victories and tramples on a generous nation which has done so much for human progress . . . Individual liberty, the liberty of the nation, the France of 1789, is in peril . . . It is Italy's duty to fly to the assistance of France now that Napoleon no longer dishonours her.*

It was a month before he had any reply and even that does not seem to have come from the French government, but early in October, General Bordone, who had fought with Garibaldi in 1860 and seems to have been the instigator of the scheme to call on his assistance, arrived for him with a steamer at Caprera. On the 7th, he landed in Marseilles to the applaud of crowds as enthusiastic as any who had greeted him in Italy; the same sentiment was not entertained in Tours, where the new ministry was struggling with the chaos and problems inevitably consequent on defeat: 'My God—we needed only *that*!' exclaimed Cremieux, the Minister for Defence, when he learned the news.

But now Garibaldi had arrived, the Government would be reproached if they failed to utilize his services, so after a vain attempt to persuade him to take command of a handful of men, he was assigned to Dole in some ambiguous role which he promptly turned into an effective one. To his standard flocked his faithful from Italy, some of them newly released after years of incarceration in the Papal dungeons; and with them came Poles and Greeks and Spaniards. Even Jessie Mario, the most Mazzinian of all Mazzinians, came to look after the wounded and to report the events for the *New York Tribune*. She found him in a hut which was his headquarters at Arnay-le-Duc and shared his supper of bread and cheese and dried fruit. Not having seen him since Mentana she was shocked to find him looking older than the three years warranted and before the campaign was over a French newspaper was describing how he appeared with *white beard and pale face . . .* so ill that *his wounds will not let him walk* and he had to be *carried in a litter* or in *a carriage into which he had to be helped.*[5]

Notwithstanding these disabilities, and the fact that by the end of November the countryside of the Côte d'Or was submerged by the heaviest snowstorm known for years and, thereafter, was in the grip of ice and snow, Garibaldi considered his French campaign to have been the finest achievement of his life. In spite of his detractors who, when the war was over, were anxious to blame everybody but themselves, there can be little doubt that in that view he was correct. As an effort at morale building it was an incredible achievement, for he not only inspired the dispirited and defeated French under his command with the will to win but, a no less difficult task, he excited the Italians, who had no rational reason apart from loyalty to his person, to fight and die with bravery greater perhaps than they had ever shown under his command before.

The first engagement of the forces under his command came when his son, Ricciotti, with 400 men, engaged in battle at Châtillon with more than 1,000 Prussians, and decisively defeated them and took 167 prisoners. Ricciotti, foppish and petulant as a youth, was now a man of twenty-five and he lived to serve in the French army once again in the war of 1914–18. Five days later, the Garibaldini fell on an enemy column advancing from Dijon and routed it at Lantenay; the enemy replied by sending out a superior force, before which Garibaldi withdrew into Autun, where he successfully repulsed a surprise enemy attack on the 1st December.

The purpose of these operations was to check the enemy advance southward, until the large French Army of the Loire under Bourbaki could move eastward to take up their positions in front of it, and to prevent the enemy seizing the armament works at Le Creusot; in that they were highly successful.

As the Army of the Loire moved eastward, the Prussians evacuated Dijon, which Garibaldi promptly advanced to occupy; but the French army was in poor shape and demoralized. Its leader, Bourbaki, attempted to commit suicide and it disintegrated and many units fled to the safety of Switzerland. On the day that Garibaldi occupied Dijon the enemy regrouped three Army Corps to make a vast Army of the South under General Manteuffel comprising some 150,000 men. On the 21st January, they mounted a major attack on Dijon and in a battle that raged three days, Garibaldi successfully repulsed them. Ricciotti had the honour of presenting to his father the colours of the crack 61st Prussian regiment. Never content with a defensive action, Garibaldi, to prevent himself being encircled, began to sweep the countryside round about and was outside Dole, which the Prussians had occupied, when news was received of an armistice signed by Favre with Bismarck.

He was left in ignorance by his superiors of the fact that the terms expressly provided for the continuation of operations on his front and, while he had ceased action, the Prussians advanced and occupied all the strategic positions around Dijon. When the terms became known, he had no option but to withdraw out of the trap laid for him, which he did skilfully and successfully with the whole of his forces, to take up a position at Chagny.

By now the war was all over, bar the recriminations. There were those who accused Garibaldi of having, by his operations impeded the movements of the Army of the Loire and also having withdrawn from Dijon, which he had been instructed to hold. Such criticisms were the cantankerous self-justification of the defeated and those far removed from the field of operations; and were inspired by jealousy of one who, as Victor Hugo told the French Assembly amid howls of disapproval, was the only French general never to be defeated in the war. Gambetta's views were expressed in a letter he wrote to the General on the 5th February: *Dear and Illustrious Friend, How much I thank you for all you have done for our Republic . . . When will the days come when my country shall be able to express all the gratitude which it reserves for you?* The Prussian commander, Manteuffel, who was perhaps best qualified of all to judge, wrote that his tactics were characterized by the great rapidity of his movements, by wise disposition given under fire during the combat, and by energy and intensity in attack . . . *the successes of Garibaldi were partial successes and were not followed up, but if General Bourbaki had acted on his advice the campaign of the Vosges would have been the most fortunate of the war of 1870–71.*

While Garibaldi was away, his baby daughter, Rosa, died on the 1st January 1871, just as his first Rosa had died while he was campaigning in South America. When the news of her death reached the Mayor of Maddalena, he crossed to Caprera to demand her body for lawful burial in consecrated ground since there was none on that island. Francesca barricaded herself in the house and refused to yield the body. The Mayor found himself facing a rifle-barrel poked from a window on the first floor.

'Garibaldi is not here,' shouted Francesca.[6] 'But his gun is. Clear off!' The Mayor beat a hasty retreat. Nobody could complain that any of Garibaldi's women lacked spirit.

After Garibaldi's return to Caprera, Rosa was buried under a juniper tree by the roadside, in ground that was consecrated only by her father's labours.

IV

Garibaldi paid a brief visit to the Bordeaux Assembly, to which he had been elected, in the hope of persuading the delegates to continue the war, but the majority were in favour of peace and would not allow him to take his seat or be heard. He left for Marseilles to return to Caprera and, in that city while he was waiting for the boat, talked to Jessie Mario, to beg her to go and look after his wounded on the Côte d'Or.

He spoke of the novel he was then writing (*I Mille*) and said to her:

'To do something to please you, I won't print what I've written about Mazzini.'

It was a promise which he seems to have forgotten for, when it was published, it contained severe criticisms of Mazzini and his friends.

In the chaos and impotence to which France had been reduced, there were Italians who thought it an ideal opportunity for their country to seize Nice; and Jessie had been charged by some of them to inquire as to the General's intentions.

'Are we to get Nice back or not, my General?' she asked point-blank.

His face clouded over.

'Nice is my birthplace, but the bitter days of France have just begun. Germany will be unmerciful. France will be rent in twain by civil war.

'How can I add to the troubles of this unhappy people? Besides—how can I, who came to help them voluntarily—ask for a recompense on leaving? No! It seems to me that we must be silent about Nice for the time being. What do you say?'

Jessie, disappointed, kept silent. Then, changing his tone, as if to justify his own renunciation, he said sternly:

'Tell them that 229 representatives of the Italian people voted for the sale of Nice; and that vote has never been rescinded nor the cession cancelled by any succeeding Italian parliament.'

The renunciation was due in part, no doubt, to his habitual generosity of mind, that even in the anguish of battle made him treat captured enemy as his sons and led him to guard with his own person from the wrath of his own troops at Monterotonde, priests who had been caught firing on his wounded. But even more, it was because his mind was once again preoccupied with what he termed, when the St Simonians had attracted his attention so long ago, *the great questions of the human race*. After a lifetime of living in the conviction that he had but to drive out the enemy and liberate his fellow-countrymen to initiate for them an era of liberty and prosperity, he had reached the conclusion that perhaps things were not quite so simple as he had thought. He had been shaken during the 1866 war to find that the peasants of the Trentino were in no way inclined to the view that bad government by their fellow-countryman, Victor Emmanuel, and corruption in Parliament, was preferable to moderately good government by the Austrians.

As always, his essentially simple mind searched for simple formulae. In the midst of the war in France, Jessie Mario had found him reading a book and he looked up from it to ask her, with reference to Cromwell's régime:

'Why did your republic fall to pieces so soon?'

'Oh! We don't like dictators—couldn't have put up with poor Dick at all.'

'Nonsense! A dictatorship must never be hereditary. One man for a short, fixed season. That is what France needs now.'

The talk turned to the constitutional monarchy of England and he observed:

'Singular—is it not?'

'Yes—but it answers.'

'There, yes. But it won't answer in France. I wonder if it will in Italy?'

'Not if you go on as you have done. Our ministers are not the King's servants but men whom Parliament chooses.'

It was a singularly unperceptive analysis of the source of power in the British Constitution, but it served to satisfy the General, though the real tenor of his mind was revealed by a later observation he made:

'The Americans are republicans and they elect dictators . . . and they are wise.'

That sentence shows that, despite the word Garibaldi used to express his conception of the form of government he preferred, all he meant by it was the necessity for strong executive power in

a nation to lead it; a recognition that democracy is not self-exe-
cuting. His conception of a dictator was, in character, the same as
that of the St Simonians: that the leader should rule *con amore*;
and of his powers, those of a President of the United States.
For all his naïveté, there was a profound wisdom in his thoughts.
As the history of every newly emancipated nation in the twentieth
century, of Britain in time of war, and of other nations such as
France and Germany in time of crisis, shows, such leadership as
Garibaldi believed in is in no way incompatible with democracy;
rather, it is essential for its preservation.

Now as he returned to Caprera and took up again his simple
life, handicapped by his infirmities, his mind was active with
schemes for the amelioration of the condition of men. He supported the First Socialist International, though he had reserva-
tions about it. *The International,* he wrote, *wishes all men to be
brothers, the abolition of priests and privileges, hence I sympathize
with it . . . I hope to see the International reject the 'doctrinaires' who
urge it on to exaggeration . . . the agents of monarchy and of the clergy
are the instigators of those exaggerations, in order to terrify the wealthy
classes, who are always conjuring up the terrible spectre of agrarian
laws. These classes will do well to remember that not legions of 'sergents
de ville' and numerous permanent armies, but only a government
founded on justice for all, constitutes the safety of the State and of
individual property.* They were words of profound truth, ignored
by Italy's rulers to this day.

Advocacy, by personal correspondence and by letters to the
Press of the world, of an International Court of Justice and of a
United States of Europe, of free education, of labour unions, of
extension of the franchise, poured from his pen. In all this, he was
very much more enlightened than the men of his day and even
than Mazzini, who though an internationalist of sorts, thought
that political measures alone were the solution of all mankind's
ills. Indeed, one of the last acts of Mazzini was to write a pamphlet
which, though it did not name Garibaldi specifically, was aimed
at the social ideas he was propagating.

On the 19th March 1872, Garibaldi at Caprera learnt by telegram that Mazzini had died. Generous as always to those who
opposed him, he wired back to Genoa: *Let the flag of the Thousand
fly over the bier of The Great Italian.* There was no greater tribute
he could offer.

V

Garibaldi was not content with theorizing and propaganda for his message. In 1875, he left Caprera for Rome to attend the National Assembly. Since it was the first time he had visited the city since he had left it at the head of his column in 1849, his arrival was regarded with some apprehension by the government. But it turned out that he had come to advocate a scheme for canalizing the Tiber. Every year the river flooded parts of the city and, from time to time, there were serious floods that inundated all except the highest parts; moreover, as he pointed out, the swamps which abounded caused malaria. By a simple diversion of part of the course of the Tiber, the floods would be averted and the channel made navigable for quite large vessels so that Rome could become a seaport. For nearly eighteen months he was active, taking soundings in the river, and trying to raise the necessary finance to carry through the project. He received little help from the government, for their minds were set on a fatuous scheme to fortify Rome and all the funds they could raise were to be devoted to that end.

He took the opportunity, while speaking to the King to beg him to annul the marriage with the Marchesa Raimondi so that he could marry Francesca who, with the birth of a son, Manlio, in April, 1873, when the General was sixty-six, had two living children. Apparently he thought that the King had only to say the word and it could be done. But His Majesty did not find it that easy.

'If I could legitimate your bastards,' the monarch told Garibaldi,' 'I would first do my own.'

XXIV

WITHOUT AN EPITAPH

❖❖❖❖❖❖❖❖❖

ONE DAY, while Garibaldi was still on the continent wrestling with the intractable problems of the Tiber, a girl with long, dark hair and beauty, who moved with the tenseness of a frightened cat, was left locked up alone in the shuttered stillness of a room in Crete. Outside was sunshine, below the bustle of the cafés and narrow streets, but up there she was as solitary as a star. It was her birthday, her sixteenth. In her loneliness and misery she wept.[1]

Through her tears, she wrote a letter to her father. She did not know his address and the envelope which she slipped through the shutters and which fluttered to the courtyard below, bore only his surname: *Garibaldi*. The carpenter who picked it up posted it in the same condition as he found it. Within three days, it was delivered to Anita's father in Rome, and from there he wrote to Speranza:

Rome, 7th May 1875.

Most dear Speranza,
    ... As regards Anita, tell me if Menotti can come and fetch her about June or any other time that is more convenient to you. Let me know how you are and believe me, I am yours for life.
        G. Garibaldi
Francesca and all the family send you greetings.

Menotti was not allowed by Speranza to come to Crete, so the girl was sent in the custody of a servant to the island of Syria, where he collected her. Soon, she was united with the father she had not seen since she was nine and with a half-sister and brother of whose existence she had never learned.

When Speranza published the letter quoted above, she added:[2]

This was not the last letter I received from Garibaldi but I stop here . . .
I prefer to throw a veil over the treatment with which father and daughter
requited me for all I had done for them. It was not the last letter, but it
was the penultimate one, and there was, perhaps, good reason why
she chose not to reproduce the last:[3]

Frescati, 24th June 1875.

Most dear Speranza,
Anita arrived with Menotti today, well, and already a woman; but
with a load of lice more than I have ever seen on any human creature. . . .
Francesca has begun combing her and hopes that a month of daily clean-
ing will free the girl from her unwelcome guests.
From Anita I have learned that you are well and it makes me happy.
Write to me always; command me and hold me for life, with gratitude,
always yours,

G. Garibaldi

P. S. Everybody here sends you greetings.

It was a letter to which, apparently, Speranza did not care to
reply, and there was no further communication between them.
She died in a room of the Hotel Adler at Ermatingen, Switzerland, on the 20th August 1899.

Poor little Anita did not live so long. One morning she was
happily playing with Clelia on the seashore, paddling and searching the rocks for crabs. In the afternoon she was stricken with the
fever of meningitis; less than two months after she had been re-
united with her father, she was dead.

II

It was perhaps her death which turned Garibaldi's mind to the
hour of his own departure from this world; for before long he
was busy giving instructions about what was to happen to his
body. On Maddalena lived the Captain Roberts who had assisted
when Shelley's body had been burned on a funeral pyre by the seashore; from him Garibaldi gleaned the details. He wished to be
cremated in a similar fashion, in a little hollow bounded by a wall
north of his house, on a pyre of acacia, myrtle and linden on which
his body, dressed in his red shirt, should lie with his face upturned
towards the sun. Afterwards, his ashes should be put in a pot—
any old pot will do', he told a friend—and placed in the little
sepulchre with the remains of Anita and the first Rosa.

But meanwhile the living must live. In 1875 the Italian Assembly had voted him a gift of a million lire and an annual pension of fifty thousand. He told Menotti to refuse it, saying:[4] 'I should lose sleep, I should feel the cold of the handcuffs, see on my hands the stains of blood, and each time I heard of government depredations and public misery, I would cover my face with shame.'

But by the following year, he was in acute financial difficulties. He had become security for a loan from the Bank of Naples for Menotti who was engaged in a building venture in Rome, which had proved unsuccessful; and he had spent a great deal of his own money on plans for the fruitless project to divert the Tiber and drain the *Campagna*. When the time came for the repayment of the loan, he was unable to meet it. Faced with the possible disgrace of allowing the hero of their country to become bankrupt, the government exerted pressure on him to accept the gift voted by Parliament; it was a new liberal government, headed by Depretis who had been Pro-Dictator under him in Sicily in 1860, and one in which he had at first some faith. In spite of that, there was, according to Jessie Mario, *a terrible struggle*[5] before he could be induced to consent. Visiting him just after the ministers had left, she found him pale and agitated, looking twenty years older than the day before. To her, he exclaimed in anguish:

'I never thought I should be reduced to the state of a pensioner!'

With the capital he paid off the Bank loan, settled portions on Francesca and his children and was left with a substantial sum over. Learning that the great shipbuilding firm of Orlando and Co. were insolvent as the result of the bankruptcy of another firm and were almost certain to follow them into liquidation, he insisted on lending the money to them. It seemed so improbable that it could ever be repaid, that Luigi Orlando refused it.

'Luigi,' the General said to him. 'Obey me. It is no question of you or of your interest, but of the hundreds of working men who will be reduced to starvation if your dockyard is closed.'

The loan was accepted, and in due course repaid, and the vast enterprise, the pride of Italy, survived as a result.

III

Gradually, the great protagonists began to disappear from the scene. Cardinal Antonelli had died on the 6th November 1867, leaving a vast fortune and enormous collection of diamonds and precious stones to his relatives; the service of God had not been unrewarding for the peasant boy from Naples who was never ordained priest. On the 7th January 1878, Victor Emmanuel died; to be followed exactly a month later by Pio Nono. He was so unpopular with the Roman populace that none dare remove his body from the Vatican to the Church of *San Lorenzo Fuori le Mure* as had been planned. Three years later, it was done at dead of night but the news got out, there were demonstrations, and mud was flung at his coffin.

For Garibaldi there yet remained a few years of happiness. On the 26th January 1880, all his family gathered together in the stone house on Caprera. There was Menotti with his wife, Italia; Teresa with her husband, Stefano Canzio, and one of her sons; three of Francesca's brothers and one of her sisters; Fruscianti and several others of the General's followers. The Mayor of Maddalena was there with two colleagues.

Garibaldi sat in his wheel-chair wrapped in a snow-white *poncho* and a tartan rug, with a scarlet kerchief knotted round his neck, and on his head one of the little hand-embroidered caps that Speranza used to give him year after year. Francesca was in a gown of white with an orange blossom headdress; after twelve years cohabitation and three children she was a bride. Clelia, now a big girl of thirteen with hair to her waist, was in attendance on her mother and Manlio had a new suit for the occasion with a big watch-chain. Twelve days earlier, the Civil Court of Appeal in Rome had granted an annulment of his marriage of 1860 to the Marchesa Raimondi. She, no less than he, was grateful for her liberty; she remarried and lived until 1919.

When the Mayor had performed the marriage ceremony there was a feast at which Garibaldi, his face alive with joy, sang some of his favourite songs; and all day long telegrams of congratulations, including one from the new King, Umberto, poured in.

He left his island only twice after that; once to go to Milan for the erection of a monument to the fallen of Mentana; once, the following year, to be present at the celebration in Sicily of the sexcentenary of the Vespers, when the Sicilians had risen to drive out their Norman overlords.

By the 1st June 1882, his breathing had become so difficult that a doctor was sent for. The next evening, while the children were down at the landing-stage awaiting the doctor's arrival, Garibaldi got Francesca to prop him up so that he could look out on the roseate hues of evening spreading over the bare pink rocks and cobalt sea. Two little finches came and landed on the window-sill.

'Let them stay, Francesca,' he said. 'Perhaps they are the spirits of my two little children come to bear me away.' A few minutes later, he was dead.

His wish to be cremated in an aromatic pyre was disregarded. He was buried near the house in the presence of dignitaries of the Crown and government under a solid block of granite bearing the single word: *Garibaldi*. Without an epitaph, one might well have been supplied by the words uttered by Victor Hugo of him, two decades earlier: 'His compatriot, Virgil, would have termed him *Vir*.'

And there he rests, guarded perpetually by a soldier of the Italian Army, as if successive Governments shared the superstition current amongst the credulous of his day, and were fearful that he might yet roll away the stone and rise to rouse the nation against them.

NOTES AND BIBLIOGRAPHY

CHAPTER I

THE PERSECUTED APOSTLES

1. The extensive archives of the St Simonians are preserved in the *Bibliothèque de l'Arsenal,* rue de Sully, Paris 7. The description of the embarkation of the Companions of the Woman is based on:
Letter by Hoart to Père Enfantin, 30 April 1833, Arsenal, 1734.
Le Sémaphore of Marseilles, 23.3.1833, 24–25.3.1833, the only copies of which are in the library of the *Chambre du Commerce de Marseille.*
La Garde Nationale, 23.3.1833, in the *Bibliothèque Municipale* of Marseilles.
Mémoires d'un Piano, Paris, 1876, Anonymous, but by Rogé who was co-director with Félicien David of *le service musical* of the St Simonian establishment at Ménilmontant and who witnessed the embarkation.
The Song of the Woman was written by Barrault; music by David.
2. A water-coloured drawing of the costume of the Companions of the Woman, by Machereau (one of them) 1833, is in the Arsenal, and is reproduced in *Les Saint-Simoniens,* by D'Allemagne, 1930.
3. T. Carlyle to J. S. Mill, 13.6.1833, pub. *New Quarterly,* April 1909.
4. *Procès des St Simoniens en La Cour d'Assises de la Seine,* Paris, 1832.
5. *Mémoires d'un Piano,* op. cit.
6. Words by A. Rousseau, music by David.
7. *Mémoires de Garibaldi,* edited by Alexandre Dumas, Brussels 1860. This edition of Garibaldi's autobiography, although it has some extraordinary errors in dates, names and places, has a good deal of information which is not contained in the *Life of General Garibaldi written by himself,* translated by Dwight, New York, A. S. Barnes and Burr 1859, the *Denkwürdigkeiten,* translated by Elpis Melena, Hamburg, 1861, or subsequent editions of his autobiography; and which is verifiably authentic. The circumstances in which Dumas acquired the MS of the Autobiography, and further information, is given in MSS discovered and translated by R. S. Garnett and published in his *The Memoirs of Garibaldi, Edited by Alexandre Dumas,* London 1929 and in *The Cruise of Emma,* London 1931. The latter contains a text of Dumas's *Les Garibaldiens: Révolution de Sicile et de Naples,* 1861, and additional material; it is a first-hand and contemporaneous account of events from June 1860, and apart from the usual minor errors (due no doubt to the incredible speed with which Dumas worked) is substantially accurate, wherever it can be tested by the primary documents.
If there is some romancing in the *Mémoires* (as it will be seen there is) it seems to have come from Garibaldi and not Dumas.

CHAPTER II

THE COURSE TO MARSEILLES

Much of the information in this chapter is based on original research into the archives of Nice. I am deeply indebted to Mlle A. Royer, Conservateur des Archives de la Ville de Nice, M. Georges Mathiot, Mlle Josiane Clairac and Princess Jeanne Tckegodaieff, all of whom have assisted me in these researches.

1. Dwight's *Life* contains no date. Dumas's *Mémoires* give the incorrect date of 22nd July 1807, although Melena's *Denkwürdigkeiten*, based on the same MS, gives the correct one as shown by *Les actes d'état-civil de naissance* and the record of his baptism in the church of St Martin on 19.7.1807.

2. Sacerdote: *La Vita di Guiseppe Garibaldi*, 1933, says that he was born 'in a house on quai Lunel today quai Cassini', but this is a combination of errors. There was no *quai Lunel* in 1807 and the west side of the port was not given that name until 1830 when the quay was built and named after the Piedmontese general who was then Governor of Nice; *quai Cassini*, once the north side of the port, was never *quai Lunel*; and even *quai Cassini* disappeared after 1889 when that quay was excavated to enlarge the basin, and the new north side of the port then became *place Cassini*. In copying Sacerdote's statement verbatim, de Polnay: *Garibaldi*, London 1960, adds a further error. There has been no *place Cassini* in Nice since December 1945 when it was changed to *place Île de Beauté*. But that is not surprising since there is hardly a page without a factual error in that book.

3. Dumas: *Mémoires* op. cit. The tradition is that Massena was born on the outskirts of Nice not far from Grand Hotel and the convent of the Augustins (Hildesheimer: *Exposition de Levens*, 1958), on the other side of the town from the harbour, and he was certainly baptized in the Cathedral, the parish of which covered this area and not in St Martin, as might be expected had he been born near the port.

4. Previous biographers have apparently been unaware that the first child of the marriage was a girl, Marie-Elisabeth, born on 28.8.1797, who died on 24.11.1799; entries related to both events are contained in *Les actes d'état-civil*. In all the couple had six children, although only four survived infancy; Ange (usually called Angelo) born 25.7.1804; Joseph Marie (Giuseppe); Michel born 6.6.1810; Felix born 10.1.1813; all at Port de Lympia; and Thérèse born at Maison Abudaram on 5.5.1817, who died there 17.1.1820.

5. The story, propagated at one time by Elpis Melena and Jessie White Mario, that the Garibaldi family were descended from the Dukes of Bavaria of the same surname is, however, quite unfounded, as also is the assertion of Karl Blind, the German revolutionary, that the family were of noble Prussian origin. The name Garibaldi was, and is, common around Genoa in one form or another amongst peasants and fishermen.

6. Jessie White Mario's *Supplement* to Werner's translation of *Autobiography of G.G.*, London, 1889.

7. On the 16th April 1864 Garibaldi was the guest of honour at a private dinner-party at the London house of Sir Anthony Panizzi, Principal Librarian

of the British Museum, who played a minor but by no means insignificant part in the task of Italian liberation. Gladstone was seated next to the guest of honour and later recalled that Garibaldi had said to him 'When I was a boy I was at school in Genoa. It was at the end of the wars of the French Revolution. Genoa was a great military post. There was a large garrison always in the town, constant parades, and military displays with bands and flags that were beyond everything attractive to schoolboys. All my schoolfellows used to run here and there all over the town to see if they could get a sight of one of these military parades and exhibitions. I never went to one.'

Admittedly, it was twenty years before Gladstone publicly recalled this conversation (*The Times* 4.6.1883) but it seems impossible that he could have mistaken Nice for Genoa, since the whole world knew through the quarrel with Cavour over the cession of Nice, that Garibaldi was a native of that town. The description of military garrisons fits Genoa but not Nice. Garibaldi assiduously gave the impression that he never went to any regular school and had gone to sea at an early age. He was certainly not a pupil in Nice at either the *école primaire* or *le Collège National*, which was the successor to the *Lycée Imperial*.

In fact, as can be seen from the text of this chapter, he did not go to sea until he was sixteen and a half and it is difficult to believe that he was left hanging about at home until that age, without even being signed on as crew on the *Santa Reparata*, as he was for the voyage of 26th March 1825 to Rome.

If in fact he went to school in Genoa, why was he at pains to conceal the fact? A possible explanation is that he was sent at an early age (perhaps in 1815 in the unsettled conditions in Nice following Napoleon's return from Elba), to a religious seminary in Genoa and was unwilling later in life to acknowledge that he had received his education at the hands of those he termed the *degenerate, bastard, crooked successors of the Apostles*. It would be consistent with the known wishes of his mother than her second son should become a priest and the fact that his father *offered as much opposition as he could* to his desire to become a sailor. *The wish of that admirable man was that I should follow some peaceful calling such as priest, a lawyer or a doctor.* (Dumas: *Mémoires*).

The fact that none of his schoolmates came forward in his own lifetime to state this fact is matched by the absence of known friends of his boyhood days in Nice apart from Deideri (who lived in the same house) and is perhaps explained by the fact that the identity of individuals, especially those with common surnames, was not so easily established as it is in these days when there are rapid communications, photographs and newspaper reproductions of photographs.

8. Garibaldi: *Cantoni il Voluntario*, Milan, 1870.

9. Similar passages of ecstatic prose about Rome are to be found in his novels *Clelia* and *I Mille*.

10. Schmidlin: *Histoire des Papes*, Vol I Part 2, and Farini: *Lo Stato Romano dal' anno 1815 al 1850*; of which there is an English translation by W. E. Gladstone, London 1851-4.

11. There is, however, no entry of his service in this vessel in the Registry of *Mousses* or of the voyage from Genoa to Cagliari. The account of a shipwreck he witnessed while on board her appears in all editions of his autobiography and there seems to be no reason to doubt it.

12. Dumas: *Mémoires*, A similar passage appears in Melena so it cannot be attributed to the fertile imagination of Dumas. It does not appear in subsequent editions, but Garibaldi repeated it in a letter to *Cassell's Magazine* in 1870, where he attributed it to a voyage in *Il Cortese*, adding the picturesque detail that after the first raid he was left even without shoes and was given a pair by an Englishman.

13. *La Marina Italiana*, for September 1927; and documents quoted therein.

14. *Archives del Museo del Risorgimento*, Milano, *collezione Curatulo*.

15. Recounted to the present author by Clelia Garibaldi, his last surviving child, in her old age. She recalled her father telling the family when he married her mother 26.1.1880 that his first love had been a Francesca and his last; and these details. Clelia was nearly thirteen at the time and as she no doubt heard the story repeated in the two years before her father's death I have no hesitation in accepting it, especially since Francesca Roux's marriage in 1830 and birth of a child in 1831 are recorded in *Les actes-civiles* in Nice. Clelia Garibaldi was mentally alert and extraordinarily well preserved physically (she had shoulders and chest as supple and white as a young girl) in her eighties during the seven years I knew her and her recollection should not be judged by the book *Mio Padre*, Florence, 1948, which was ghosted for her by a journalist, and which infuriated her by its errors.

16. Jessie White Mario: *Supplement*, op. cit.

17. The voyage to Taganrog and back to Nice lasted from 24.2.1832 to 1.9.1832 and it must have been during this period that he met the young Genoese patriot *who was the first to inform me of the progress of our cause* (Werner) Dumas's *Mémoires* places this unnamed person as being actually on the voyage and this seems probable since Mazzini made a point of specially recruiting young sailors for 'Young Italy'. J. M. White's *Supplement* and others have it that he was C. B. Cuneo but he was Garibaldi's first biographer and it is incredible that if it were so neither he nor Garibaldi should mention the fact. There is other evidence to suggest that the two first met in South America in 1836. But, on the other hand, there is a significant phrase in the letter I have quoted on page 48.

CHAPTER III

A STRANGE LIGHT

1. Dumas: *Mémoires*, op. cit. All quotations in this and subsequent chapters are from this unless otherwise specified.

2. Files of the *Producteur* are in the Arsenal library in Paris. Most of the quotations that follow are from its pages, from the proclamations of Enfantin, or *Les Doctrines des Saint-Simoniens*. In the present work it has not been thought necessary to annotate them separately. D'Allemagne: *Les Saint Simoniens 1827–37*, op. cit. has a useful chapter on Les Théories du 'Producteur'.

3. von Pastor: *History of the Popes*, Vol 38, English translation, 1951.

4. Schmidlin: *Papstgeschichte der neuesten Zeit*, French translation, 1938, Part I *Pie VII*.

5. Interview with Pius IX by Odo Russell, British Diplomatic representative to the Papacy on 12.7.1860. Public Records Office F.O. 17/330, Rome.

6. Letter dated Fino 30.11.1859 to Giuseppina Raimondi in Archives of Mantova. For full text see p. 191.

<h2 style="text-align:center">CHAPTER IV</h2>

<h1 style="text-align:center">THE GOD OF GOOD MEN</h1>

1. Melena: *Denwürdigkeiten*.

2. Consalvi: *Mémoires, 1866*, Introduction. He professed to have found a sympathetic listener in the Prince Regent.

3. The Brief, *Dominus ac Redemptor Noster*; see Pastor op. cit. Vol. 38.

4. Codignola: *I Fratelli Ruffini*, Genoa, 1925.

5. Ruffini: *Lorenzo Benoni*, Edinburgh, 1853.

6. Accursi's dispatches to Gregory XVI were published in *Il Risorgimento Italiano*, 1923–8, from Vatican sources by Rinieri under the title *La conspirazione mazziniane nel carteggio di un transfuga*.

7. *Scritti editi ed inediti di Guiseppe Mazzini*, Imola 1905–12 and Appendices, in which the extracts which follow are published.

8. Letter to Bianco, 8.7.1833.

9. Letter to Melegari, 9.7.1833.

10. Letter to Melegari, 28.7.1833.

11. Dumas: *Mémoires*, op. cit. but substantially the same account appears in the earlier Dwight, and Melena: *Denwürdigkeiten*.

12. White: *Supplement*, op. cit.

13. See dates of all letters in *Scritti*, op. cit. The only exception appears to be a letter dated 29th June, Marseilles, but there is another letter dated 28th June from Geneva and the month should properly be May since from its contents it is obviously earlier than another one about the *Veri Italiani*, dated 1st June.

14. Even the careful and critical Mack Smith in his small book *Garibaldi*, 1957.

15. Mazzini in his Autobiographical Notes appears to accept that he enrolled Garibaldi, but he gives no date and says: 'His name in the association was Borel' which suggests that he only became aware of his existence at a later date (see note 24). In any event these Autobiographical Notes were not compiled until 1860–65 and by then he would certainly have read Garibaldi's autobiography either in the Dumas version or in the numerous newspaper features that were plagiarized from it. It seems unlikely that he would remember one of a number of sailors he enrolled, who at that time had no special distinction. I have considered the possibility that they met before March 1833, although that makes nonsense of Garibaldi's narrative, but the record of his voyages and Mazzini's movements in fact exclude that possibility.

The flight to Geneva was due to the fact that the Piedmontese police had communicated with those of France, and Mazzini had been rooted out from his secret hiding place in the house of Démosthène Ollivier in Marseilles as Emile Ollivier (the latter's son) says in *L'Empire Liberal*; his child was left behind with Démosthène.

16. Elia Benza, Federico Campanella, Napoleone Ferrari.

17. General Mitre who knew him in South America and who wrote in *La Patria* 19.6.1904 that '*His blue eyes alone revealed his emotions, by taking on a dark colour like that of the sea*' must have been wrong, although a surprising number of other people seem to have thought that his eyes were blue. But his daughter, Clelia, said 'His eyes were the same colour as mine', and of hers chestnut would be a good description.

18. On his return to Nice after the events narrated in this chapter, he says that his own aunt did not at first recognize him.

19. From the evidence given when he was subsequently tried *in absentia*, as narrated by Sacerdote: *La Vita*, op. cit. on information provided by Professor Eugenio Pasamonti from study of the records of the proceedings.

20. These barracks still exist at the moment of writing, but are unoccupied and dilapidated.

21. The records of the *Des Geneys* seems to show that Mutru was arrested on board on the 5.2.1834 and was detained there until he was lodged in prison on 13.2.1834.

22. Copies, but not the originals, are in the *Bibliotèca Universitaria di Genova* of the letters dated 23.9.1866, and 28.12.1866 to Teresa Forzano (Schenone).

23. Joseph Pane seems to have been a real person who befriended Garibaldi when he arrived, destitute, in Marseilles and who apparently allowed him to assume his identity for the purpose of seeking employment. Garibaldi used the same name in 1851 when he obtained a French passport to go to England and again in 1867 on his escape from Caprera.

24. In this I have followed the authorities who have assumed that Garibaldi adopted the name of Borel when he joined 'Young Italy'. However, I entertain some doubts as to whether he was ever known by this pseudonym until after he reached South America. Giovanni Borel was in fact the name of one of those executed (February 1834) for taking part in the Savoy invasion and it may well be that Garibaldi assumed that name as an act of piety. The first written reference to him as such seems to appear in a letter of Rossetti to Mazzini dated 19.1.1836.

CHAPTER V

RECOURSE TO EXTREMES

1. The Pact of Young Europe was signed by revolutionaries representing Young Germany, Young Poland and Young Italy under Mazzini's inspiration in Berne on 15th April 1834, as *an association of men believing in a future of liberty, equality and fraternity for all mankind.* Young France, Young Switzerland, and Young Austria associated later.

2. Luzio: *I primi passi di Garibaldi in America*: in *Garibaldi, Cavour, Verdi*, Turin, 1924.

3. Luzio, op. cit. No copy of this newspaper appears to exist.

4. Published by J. W. Mario: *Garibaldi e i suoi tempi*, 1884, her translation from the *Supplement*, op. cit. The actual text has the abbreviation of 'P⁰' for Pippo; 'the higher things' sentence is a rather pretentious translation of *Sii certo che siamo destinati a cose maggiori*, which might be rendered more happily as *Be sure that we are destined for something better*, but the rest of the passage is so good that a change for the sake of one expression would not be justified.

5. Mario, op. cit.

6. *The Jornal do Commercio* of Rio for 14.6.1837, which carried a report of the incident attributes it to the 17th May (Varzea: *Garibaldi in America*, Rio de Janeiro, 1902), but this may be an error in transmission, as Garibaldi in all his accounts makes it clear that it happened the same day as the *Mazzini* sailed; and the same journal on 8.5.1837 carried the report of that vessel sailing the previous day.

7. In the early versions of his autobiography he gave the number as sixteen.

8. Dumas: *Mémoires*, op. cit. The source af any conversations not annotated separately.

9. Werner: *Autobiography*, op. cit.

10. Dumas: *Mémoires*, op. cit.

11. Werner: *Autobiography*, op. cit.

12. The vessel engaged with the *Farropilha* was the *Maria* of Montevideo; and the date 15.6.1837, as can be seen from the reports to the Commandant of the Port published by Pereda: *Garibaldi en el Uruguay*, Montevideo, 1914–16.

13. Mario, op. cit.

14. Mario: *Supplement* omits these words in quoting the letter.

15. Cuneo: *Biografia di Giuseppe Garibaldi*, Genoa, 1850.

16. The letters of marque, for some reason, were dated 14th November 1836, perhaps because on that date the republic had some semblance of existence.

17. He was released on 2.12.1839 on condition that he returned to Europe.

18. The date as would appear from Garibaldi's report (as 'Commandant of the Fleet of the Republic') published by Varzea, op. cit. was 17.4.1839.

19. Garibaldi in his autobiography gives the name of his vessel as the *Rio Pardo* and on one occasion as the *Rio Grande* (Werner, op. cit.) but it would appear from the documents cited by Varzea, op. cit. that it was in fact another *Farropilha*. That is the name he mentions in a letter dated 28.7.1839 to Donna Anna da Costa Santos; Ciampoli: *Scritti politici e militari di G. Garibaldi*. The date of the shipwreck was 4.7.1839.

20. Werner: *Autobiography*, op. cit.

21. Dumas: *Mémoires* adds the detail that she was engaged in domestic duties which has led some to surmise that she was washing clothes.

22. The words he used were *Tu devi esser mia*, of which Werner's translation is 'Thou oughtest to be mine'. Apart from not being English, this completely lacks the forcefulness of the original expression.

23. Dwight: *Life*, the sin was *removing her from her peaceful native retirement to scenes of danger, toil and suffering*. According to Guerzoni, op. cit. it was her father who was the aggrieved man; according to J. W. Mario, *Supplement*; *That he would have married her then and there if he could have obtained the consent of her family is quite certain but her father, a proud, severe man, accustomed to implicit obedience, had betrothed his daughter to a very wealthy and very old man*; which is the explanation accepted by Trevelyan: *Defence of Roman Republic*, 1907, after talking to Ricciotti Garibaldi (who had no more authentic information than anyone else, since Garibaldi always refused to discuss his mother's origins with him; see Castelloni: *Legioni rosi* and Sacerdote: *Vita*, op. cit.).

24. Varzea: *Garibaldi in America*, op. cit; Anita Garabaldi (Ricciotti's daughter and therefore the grand-daughter of the first Anita) *Garibaldi en America*, Buenos Aires, 1930.

Her marriage to Manuel Duarte de Aguiar took place on 30.8.1835 in the parish church of Sant' Antonio, Laguna, according to the record discovered by Dr José Boileux and published in *Corriere della Serra* of 18.6.1932. From the entry, it would appear that her father was dead in 1835.

25. In Dumas: *Mémoires*, alone, Garibaldi alleged: *Anita . . . insisted on embarking with me.*

26. In *Museo del Risorgimento*, Milan.

27. By Girolamo Induno, reproduced in Ximenes' *Anita Garibaldi*.

28. As may be deduced from the fact that he believed it to be the day on which Menotti was conceived. Dumas: *Mémoires*.

29. Other reasons which led me to conclude that it was not a valid marriage include the facts that (*a*) he never mentioned it in any edition of his autobiography; (*b*) it was widely asserted later by his enemies, which could not have escaped Garibaldi's notice, that he was not married to Anita. He never produced the marriage certificate in his own lifetime although it was found after his death amongst his papers (Curatulo: *Garibaldi, Vittorio Emmanuele e Cavour nei fasti della Patria*, 1911 and *Anita Garibaldi*, 1932) (*c*) even close friends such as the Marios were kept in ignorance of the existence of the ceremony. (*d*) there is a persistent tradition that his pious mother would not allow Anita and he to cohabit under her roof when he returned to Nice in 1848 because she knew they were not validly married. In fact the records show that Garibaldi joined Anita in the Deideris' house at Magnan after he returned to his home city on 21.6.1848. The same thing occurred when he returned at the end of the war in Lombardy, when he was at St Laurent du Var on 8.9.1848 and Magnan again on 10.9.1848 and back in San Remo on 26.9.1848. Since Anita and the children had resided with his mother for three months before his arrival, it looks as if there may be some foundation for the story; and Signora Garibaldi was such a pious Papist that as soon as the parents were out of the way, in defiance of their known wishes, she had the children educated by the Jesuits.

It is also said that during this latter period, Garibaldi's mother persuaded them to go through a ceremony of marriage (T. Bent, *Garibaldi* 1882; no authority is quoted for the statement but the story is widespread). There is no record of it in the Registers of the likely parishes, the Port, Ste Hélène, la Madeleine, or St Pierre d'Arène. See also Appendix, page 346.

30. Melena: *Denkwürdigkeiten*.

CHAPTER VI

▓▓

THE RED SHIRT

1. The story of the South American struggle and its background will be found in Dawson: *South American Republics*, New York, 1904; Fletcher and Kidder: *Brazil and the Brazilians*, London 1863; Sarmiento: *Life in the Argentine Republic*, New York, 1868; Robertson: *Letters on Paraguay*, London 1838 and *Letters on South America* 1843; Anita Garibaldi: *Garibaldi en South America*, Buenos Aires, 1931; Pereda: *Garibaldi en el Uruguay*, op. cit; De Maria: *Anales de la Defensa de Montevideo*, Montevideo, 1883–87.

2. Mario: *Supplement*, op. cit., who relies chiefly on Cuneo's diaries.

3. Winnington-Ingram: *Hearts of Oak*, London, 1889.

4. E. E. Y. Hales: *Mazzini, The Making of the Myth*, London, 1956.

5. Mario: *Supplement*, op. cit. Her translation. The date of the letter is not given there but was 10.3.1846.

6. Mario: *Supplement*, op. cit.

7. The generally accepted story is that it was the new Pope who fainted, but Chisalberti: *Nuove ricerche sugli inizi del Pontificato di Pio IX*, Rome 1939, gives a very different account (based on that of Cardinal Feschi) which is much more convincing.

8. Letters published for the first time in Serafini: *Pio Nono*, Vatican, 1958, an enormous work covering the early years of Pius IX's life, prepared to assist the cause of his beatification. While it reveals that he was by no means blind to the evils and cruelties of the Papal government, it makes clear that his mind was far from sympathizing with reform, and destroys the theory held previously by most historians that he was a liberal sympathizer when his reign began.

9. O'Meara: *Frederic Ozanam*, London, 1878.

10. Mazzini: *Scritti editi ed inediti*, op. cit. Vol. 36.

11. Ciampoli: *Scritti*, op. cit. but there are several variants. The letter is very much longer and verbose and flowery; to prevent its being quite unbearable in English, it is here condensed and paraphrased.

12. Mario: *Supplement*, op. cit. Her translation. The original text (dated 14.11.1847) was published by Luzio in the *Corriere della Sera* 15.4.1932 and is reproduced by Sacerdote, op. cit.

13. Mario: *Supplement*, op. cit.

14. See Anita's letter to Stefano Antonini, quoted Mario: *Supplement*, op. cit.

CHAPTER VII

MAN OF THE PEOPLE

1. Dumas: *Mémoires*, op. cit, includes a memorandum by Medici giving his account of the war in Lombardy. According to Mario: *Supplement,* this was written in 1850. Source of any conversations in this chapter not separately annotated.

2. Werner: *Autobiography*, op. cit.

3. I had reached the conclusion before I found that Sacerdote: *La Vita*, op. cit. entertained similar views about this alleged interview.

4. Menotti, then eight, had been offered a free place in the Royal College of Raccongi by the Intendante-General in the name of the King: Luzio: *Garibaldi, Cavour, Verdi*, op. cit. publishes Anita's letter in reply to the offer, in which she (tactfully) refers to Menotti not by that name (by which he was always known) but by his first Christian name of Domenico. It may be doubted whether this (and many other letters) bearing her signature were composed by her; the only letter extant in her own handwriting in Italian is short and full of grammatical errors.

5. The Papal army had been sent north with instructions to defend the borders of the Papal States (Farini: *Roman State*, op. cit.; Minghetti: *Miei Ricordi*, Turin, 1888) but the commander was a Piedmontese officer, Durando,

who intended to use it in any event against the Austrians in conjunction with Piedmont. The Pope denounced this use, *inter alia*, in his Allocution of 29th April, but Durando engaged the army with the Austrians in defence of Vicenza on 10th June (and was defeated).

6. Dumas: *Mémoires*. A *haut sabreur* is a cavalryman whose dashing appearance is matched only by military uselessness; the word used by the Italian authorities in giving Medici's account is *sciabolatore*, which has a slightly different meaning: one who is a brave soldier and a good swordsman but a poor general.

7. Dumas: *Mémoires*, op. cit.

8. Sforza: *Garibaldi in Toscana nel 1848*, 1890.

9. Sforza, op. cit.

10. Guerrazzi, quoted by Sforza, op. cit.

11. The document in the *Museo del Risorgimento, Milano, Raccolta Curatolo,* is endorsed by him *Firenze 5 8bre,* but I have assumed that this is an error for 5 9bre, i.e. 5.11.1848; even so, there is some unexplained mystery about it, for the chaplain to the brigade is named as P. Alexandro Gavazzi, and it seems unlikely that he had any contact with Father Gavazzi until he arrived in Bologna later the same month.

12. Elizabeth Barrett Browning: *Casa Guidi Windows.*

13. Farini: *The Roman State*, op. cit.

14. All that can legitimately be said in favour of King 'Bomba', and more, will be found in Acton: *The Last Bourbons of Naples,* London, 1961.

15. One opinion is that the assassin was Luigi Brunetti, see Trevelyan: *Garibaldi's Defence of Rome*, London, 1907. If it were so, Brunetti met retribution when he, his father, and his twelve-year-old brother were shot in cold blood the following year by the Austrians in the market-place of San Nicolo. But as late as 7.6.1851, the son of Rossi called Carlo Bonaparte, Prince Canino, the murderer of his father and provoked a duel. Mario: *Supplement,* op. cit. says: *Pietro Leopardi, at one time Neapolitan Ambassador to the Court of Piedmont, attributed the act to the Jesuits and made out his case pretty clearly.* Another man was tried, convicted and sentenced, and executed by the Papal Courts for the crime; the one thing everybody seems agreed about is that he did not do it. Whatever Garibaldi's views might have been about the matter, Rossi's son was not ashamed to serve under him subsequently.

16. Margaret Fuller (Ossoli): *Memoirs.*

17. Werner: *Autobiography*, op. cit.

18. See, for example, de Polnay: *Garibaldi,* op. cit. and E. E. Y. Hales: *Pio Nono*, London, 1954. Both omit the significant words: *I . . . therefore condemn the dagger of Brutus.*

19. Werner: *Autobiography*, op. cit.

20. See page 234 *et seq.*

21. For example, the abortive attempt to kidnap Pius IX in 1843, when he was Bishop of Imola led to seven executions and fifty condemnations to the galleys for life.

22. Melena: *Garibaldi, Recollections of his Public and Private Life,* London, 1887.

23. The full text is published in Farini: *The Roman State,* op. cit.

24. Gatta: *Le elezioni del 1849* in *Archivio della Societa romana di Storia patria,* Rome, 1949. The persistent clerical accusation that the Republic of Rome and

its defence was carried on by outsiders against the will of the inhabitants of the city is considered by Ghisalberti in *Mazzini e la repúbblica di Romani* in *Il Risorgimento* of February 1952; and by Morelli in *Archivio della Societa romana di Storia patria,* Rome, 1949; and conclusively refuted.

25. Woodward: *Three Studies in European Conservatism,* London, 1929.

26. See Loevinson: *Garibaldi e la sua Legione,* Rome, 1902 for the best account of the adventures of the Legion en route to Rome. Where no separate annotation is made in this chapter Loevinson is the source.

27. A copy of the proclamation, printed at 1 a.m. the following morning, can be seen in the *Museo del Risorgimento,* Rome.

28. Margaret Fuller: *Memoirs* op. cit. He said much the same to Arthur Clough a few weeks later, *Prose Remains,* London 1888.

29. Trevelyan: *Garibaldi and the Roman Republic,* op. cit.

30. Pirri, *Pio IX and Vittorio Emanuele II Dal Loro Carteggio Privato,* Rome Vol. I, 1944; Vol. II, 1951.

31. Curatulo: *Anita Garibaldi,* 1932 and Guerzoni: *Garibaldi,* op. cit.; both of whom have incorrectly transcribed the number of his troops as 200. The reference to Genoa is to the suppression of a republican revolt there by Victor Emmanuel and to Leghorn to the lack of resistance to the restoration of the Grand Duke (who had fled) by the Austrians.

32. Gründorf, Ritter von Zebegeny: *Memoiren eines österreichischen General-stäblers,* 1832–66, Stuttgart, 1913.

33. Vaillant: *Le Siège de Rome en 1849,* Paris, 1851.

CHAPTER VIII

THE FALLING STAR

1. Koelman: *In Rome 1846–51,* Arnheim, 1869.

2. Koelman, op. cit.

3. Clough: *Prose Remains,* London, 1888.

4. Trevelyan, in his *Garibaldi's Defence of the Roman Republic,* London, 1907, took the view that the French possessed only old maps and directed their attack against the Porta Pertusa in the belief that this entrance to the city still existed; but after consideration of the authorities named below, the present author considers that this theory is untenable and that which he has suggested is more probable. Der Portes: *Expédition Française de Rome,* Paris, 1849; *Le Moniteur of 1849* for Oudinot's dispatches; Vaillant: *Le siège de Rome en 1849,* Paris, 1851; Vecchi: *La Italia: Storia di due anni,* 1848–9, Turin, 1856.

5. Clermont and Bourgeois: *Rome et Napoleon III,* Paris, 1907.

6. Dandolo: *I Volontarii ed i Bersaglieri Lombardi,* Turin, 1849; English translation, London, 1851.

7. Guerrazzi: *L'Assedio de Roma,* Milan, 1870.

8. Vaillant, op. cit.

9. Loevinson: *Giuseppe Garibaldi e la sua legione nello stato Romano,* 1848–9, Rome, 1902–7, Vol. III, 1907.

10. Garibaldi: *Scritti,* op. cit.

11. Werner: *Autobiography,* op. cit.

12. Mazzini: *Scritti editi ed inediti*, Imola, 1905–54.

13. Loevinson, op. cit.

14. Vecchi: *La Italia*, op. cit.

15. Mario: *Supplement*, op. cit.

16. Vecchi: *La Italia*, op. cit.

17. Vecchi: *La Italia*, op. cit.

18. Vecchi: *La Italia*, op. cit. and Loevinson: *Garibaldi e la sua Legione*, op. cit.

19. Koelman, op. cit. Of the various versions of this speech the present author regards that accepted by Bellozzi: *La Ritirata*, 1899, as a later and less accurate version, including the first sentence, 'Fortune, which betrays us today, will smile on us tomorrow.'

20. Bonnet: *Lo Sbarco di Garibaldi a Magnavacca*, Bologna, 1887.

21. Bonnet, op. cit.

22. Werner: *Autobiography*, op. cit.

23. The version of the events of Anita's death is a collation of Bonnet's account with the evidence of eye-witnesses collected and reported upon in the following official reports:

Report of A. Lovatelli, Delegate of the *Direzione generale di Polizia* in Ravenna 12.8.1849 and 15.8.1849 (published by Guerzoni, op. cit. and Ximenes, op. cit and many others).

Report of *Giudice processante* Giuseppe Francesconi, Ravenna, 31.8.1849 (published in Beseghi, *Il Maggiore 'Leggero' e La Verita sulla Morte di Anita* and Curatulo: *Anita Garibaldi*, 1932.

Reports of Giov. Guaccimanni, President of the *Tribunale di Ravenna* 8.10.1849 and 6.11.1849 (MS in *Musèo Civico* of Bologna; text from a copy retained by author published by Beseghi, op. cit.) Garibaldi, in his novel *Clelia*, gives an account of Anita's death; but as that is professedly a work of fiction, the present author has not relied upon it.

24. Lovatelli's report, *supra*.

25. Guaccimanni's report, *supra*.

26. Luzio in *Corriere della Sera*, 25.3.1932.

27. de Polnay: *Garibaldi*, London, 1960.

28. Bonnet, op. cit.

29. Stocchi: *Un paragrafo inedito della vita di G. Garibaldi* in *La Rassegna Nazionale*, June, 1892, with Teresa Baldini's statement.

30. MS *Archivio di Stato*, Turin.

CHAPTER IX

THE CINCINNATUS OF OUR AGE

1. MS Letter d'Azeglio to Panizzi. Panizzi MSS, British Museum.

2. MS Receipt in *Archivio di Stato di Torino*.

3. Mario: *Supplement*, op. cit.

4. Werner: *Autobiography*, op. cit.

5. Gay: *Il secondo esilio di Garibaldi* in *Nuova Antologia*, 1910.

6. Quoted by Mario: *Supplement*, op. cit. from the Cuneo archives in her possession.

7. Morison: *An Old China Hand*, London, 1889.

8. Mario: *Supplement*, op. cit.

9. Garibaldi, Werner: *Autobiography*, op. cit. The date of the article in the periodical was 4.12.1851.

10. Werner: *Autobiography*, op. cit.

11. A literal translation in Greek of her real name; at that date she appears to have written one travel romance, which had been a minor success.

12. Preface to the English version of her *Blick auf Calabrien und die Liparischen Inseln im Jahre 1860*, Hambourg, 1861.

13. Melena: *Recollections*, op cit.

14. Melena: *Recollections*, op. cit.

15. Melena: *Recollections*, op. cit.

16. Curatulo: *Garibaldi e le donne*, Rome, 1923.

CHAPTER X

PRELUDE TO WAR

1. After the death of the Countess di Castiglione in Paris in 1899, a young attaché at the Italian Embassy seized all her papers (as being of State importance) and destroyed most of them. For long it was believed that her archives were lost, but in 1952 four cases of her papers, which had been left in Italy, were discovered in that country. These included her private diary and many letters. The diary is now the property of the present author, who has in preparation a book based upon it. The quotations and information in this chapter are from this hitherto unpublished diary.

2. Le Comte Horace de Viel-Castel: *Mémoires*, Paris, 1883–4.

3. Cowley: *The Paris Embassy during the Second Empire*, London, 1928.

4. La Comtesse de Damrément to Thouvenez, quoted Loliée: *Les Femmes du Second Empire*, Paris, 1927.

5. Queen Victoria: *Letters*, London, 1907.

6. de Reiset, *Mes Souvenirs*, n.d.

7. Chiala, op. cit.

8. Ollivier: *L'Empire libéral*.

9. Quoted, Leslie: *The Letters of Mrs. Fitzherbert*, London, 1914.

10. Alexis de Valon to his mother. Quoted Parturier: *Correspondence générale de Prosper Mérimée*, Paris and Toulouse, 1941–55.

11. La Gorce: *Histoire du Second Empire*, Paris, 1894–1905.

12. François Versasis: *Italie*, Paris, 1857.

13. Cowley, op. cit.

14. Fagan: *Panizzi*, London, 1880.

15. Orsini: *Memoirs and Adventures*, London, 1855.

16. Loliée: *La Vie d'une Impératrice*.

17. Cavour: *Carteggi: Cavour–Nigra*.

18. *The Times*, 3.6.1858.

19. Chiala, op. cit.

CHAPTER X

STRANGERS BEGONE

1. Melena: *Recollections*, op. cit. (which is also the source of all conversations quoted in this chapter at which she was present); Letters quoted by Curatulo: *G e le donne*, op. cit.
2. Della Rocca: *Autobiografica di un veterano*, 1897.
3. Mario: *Agostino Bertani e i suoi temp*, 1888.
4. Quoted Mario: *Supplement*, op. cit.
5. Malmesbury: *Memoirs of an ex-Minister*, London, 1884.
6. *Quarterly Review*, July, 1879.
7. De la Rive: *Le Comte de Cavour, récits et souvenirs*, 1862.
8. Loliée: *La Vie d'une Impératrice*.
9. De la Rive, op. cit.
10. The *Proclama Della Guerra* in the *Casa Mazzini*, Genoa, has the printed date 27.4.1859 which has been amended in manuscript to 29.4.1859.

CHAPTER XII

THE FIRST VICTORY

1. *Il Carteggio Cavour–Nigra*.
2. MS Letter Bertani to Panizzi. Panizzi MSS, British Museum.
3. Quoted Sacerdote, op. cit.
4. Quoted Sacerdote, op. cit.
5. Quoted Dumas: *Mémoires*, op. cit.

CHAPTER XIII

LIVING IN A POEM

1. Peard: *War-journals of Garibaldi's Englishman*, ed. G. M. Trevelyan, *Cornhill Magazine*, London, January 1908, and June 1908. Trevelyan's *Garibaldi and the Thousand*, London, 1909, contains a chapter which is a useful, brief summary of the campaign and strictly accurate, save that he makes the volunteers leave Sesto Calende at 5 a.m. whereas Peard and others say it was 5 o'clock in the afternoon. Carano: *Cacciatori delle Alpi*, 1860, is the best authority, as he was on Garibaldi's staff during the campaign. Cf. Gaiani: *I Cacciatori delle Alpi*, Citta de Castello, 1909, and the study of General Rocca; *La campagna del 1859* in *Garibaldi il Condottiero*, 1929, and Bertani: *I Cacciatori delle Alpi* in *Politecnico*, Milan, 1860.
2. Peard, op. cit.
3. e.g. Trevelyan: *G. and the Thousand*, op. cit.
4. Carano, op. cit.
5. MS fragment of autobiography by Garibaldi written at Fino in January 1860; recovered by Curaluto and published first in the 1932 (Italian) edition of the Autobiography.

6. Ciampoli: *Scritti*, op. cit.

7. *The Times*, London, 26.7.1859.

8. As (5) *supra*.

9. Venosta: *Ricordi di Gioventù*, Milan, 1904.

10. Ciampoli: *Scritti*, op. cit.

11. See Trevelyan's interview with Venosta quoted Trevelyan: *G. and the Thousand*, op. cit.

12. Bianchi: *Storia Documentata della diplomazia Europea in Italia*, 1814–62, and Chiala: *Politica segreta di Nap. III e di Cavour*, 1895.

CHAPTER XIV

A FOXY POLICY

1. The facts were disputed at the time and subsequently but a review of the contemporary accounts confirms that substantially this is what happened though it lost nothing in the telling. For summary of the evidence see Bolton King: *History of Italian Unity*, London, 1899.

2. Daniel to Cass, 4.6.1860. (Copy in *Museo del Risorgimento*, Rome.)

3. Pirri: *Pio IX e Vittorio Emanuele II Dal Loro Carteggio Privato*, Vol. II, Rome, 1951.

4. Ciampoli: *Scritti*, op. cit.

5. Melena: *Recollections*, op. cit. The source of subsequent conversations at which she was present narrated in this chapter.

6. Ciampoli: *Scritti*, op. cit.

7. MS Odo Russell, F.O., London.

CHAPTER XV

THE DAUGHTER OF THE LAKE

1. See note 5 to Chapter XIII.

2. Panizzi MSS, British Museum.

3. Trevelyan: *G. and the Thousand*, op. cit.

4. Dumas: *Les Garibaldiens*, 1861, and Dumas: *Causeries*, 1885.

5. The account of these incidents is based on Valerio's description given to Finali: *Le Marche*, Ancona, 1897; Monti: *Garibaldi e la marchesa Raimondi* in *Secolo XX*, 1923; and the Crispi and Mancini MS file in the *Curatulo* collection, *Museo del Risorgimento*, Milan; Luzio: *Garibaldi, Cavour and Verdi*, Turin, 1924; Curatulo: *G. e le donne*, op. cit.

6. MS letter Valerio to Risso, *Casa Mazzini*, Genoa.

7. MS *Archivo Curatulo*.

8. Ciampoli: *Scritti*, op. cit.

9. Sir James Hudson to Lady John Russell, 6.4.1860, published Trevelyan: *G. and the Thousand*, op. cit.

10. Oliphant: *Episodes in a Life of Adventure*, 1887.

11. The account which follows is based on Dumas: *Les Garibaldiens*, 1861, op. cit. Dumas followed hard on Garibaldi's heels to Genoa and interviewed Vecchi shortly after these events, so that in essence this is Vecchi's own account.

CHAPTER XVI

BRANDY WITHOUT OFFER

1. See Receipt in *Casa Mazzini*, Genoa. Trevelyan G. *& the Thousand* believed that the Million Rifles Fund was formed only on 4th January, 1860 and that, is the impression one might gain from Garibaldi's declaration of that date. But there are receipts extant, as this one, dating back to 1856.

2. Cavour: *Carteggi: La liberazione del Mezzogiorno.*

3. Cavour: *Carteggi: Cavour–Nigra.* Trevelyan, without the text of this letter, came to an entirely erroneous conclusion about its contents: *G. and the Making of Italy*, 1911. It was first published by Colombo in *Il Risorgimento Italiano*, 1912.

4. Crispi: *La Spedizione dei Mille*, his diary for 1859 in *Scritti e Discorsi Politici*, 1890. Cf. *Diario dei Mille* in *Rivista de Roma*, 12.1.1905.

5. Letter to Guilini, 3.5.1860, published by Guerzoni, op. cit.

6. Cavour: *Carteggi: Cavour–Nigra.*

7. MS *Carte* Farini; *Biblioteca Classense*, Ravenna.

8. Bandi: *I Mille*, 1906.

9. Dumas: *Les Garibaldiens*, op. cit. This departs from the chronology adopted by Trevelyan but is confirmed indirectly by *Resoconto di Bertani*, Genoa, 1860.

10. Turr: *Da Quarto a Marsala;* Bandi, op. cit.; Vecchi also believed the same and told Dumas so.

11. D'Haussonville in *Revue des deux Mondes*, 15.9.1862; possibly derived from Cavour's own account to Nigra or Talleyrand.

12. Dumas: *Les Garibaldiens*, op. cit.

13. The departure from Quarto is described by eye-witnesses. Bandi, op. cit.; Jack La Bolina (Vecchi's son): *La Vita e le geste di G. Garibaldi*, 1882; Crispi: *Scritti*, op. cit.; and Dumas has Vecchi's version. The subsequent account is based largely on Dumas who, shortly after his arrival in Sicily, obtained Türr's own account, and is confirmed by Türr, op. cit. and Garibaldi's novel, *I Mille*.

CHAPTER XVII

PIECES OF THE ORANGE

1. Cavour: *Carteggi, Mezzogiorno.*
2. Cavour: *Carteggi, supra.*
3. Cavour: *Carteggi: Cavour–Nigra.*
4. Cavour: *Carteggi, Mezzogiorno.*
5. Chiala: *Lettere edite ed inedite di Camillo Cavour.*
6. Cavour: *Carteggi: Mezzogiorno.*

7. Türr, op. cit.

8. Abba: *La Storia dei Mille*, 1904.

9. Bandi, op. cit.

10. Baratieri: *Calatafimi* in *Nuova Antologia*, 1884.

11. Abba, op. cit.; Bandi, op. cit.

12. *The Times*, 8.6.1860; Pecorini-Manzoni: *Storia della 15a Divisione Türr*, 1876.

13. Dumas: *Les Garibaldiens*, op. cit.

14. Odo Russell. Letter to Lord John Russell, 7.6.1860, published by Walpole: *Life of Lord John Russell*, 1889, and Trevelyan G. & *the Making of Italy* where an amusing error is made in transcription. *The Convents are awfully scandalized at this proceeding* should read *The Converts*, i.e. former Anglicans such as Talbot and Wiseman.

Chapter XVIII

A WEB OF INTRIGUE

1. Dumas: *Les Garibaldiens*, op. cit.

2. Cavour to Durando: *Una silloge di lettere del Risorgimento, 1839–73*, ed. 1919.

3. Cavour to Persano, 1.6.1860, *Carteggi: Mezzogiorno*, op. cit.

4. Dumas: *Les Garibaldiens*, op. cit.

5. *Giornale officiale di Sicilia*, 9.7.1860.

6. Trevelyan: *G. and the Making of Italy*, op. cit.

7. Curatulo: *G. Vittore Emmanuele e Cavour*, op. cit.

8. MSS in *Carte Farini* at Ravenna and *Carte Bianchi–Ricasoli* in *Archivio di Stato*, Florence.

9. Teccio to Cavour, 31.5.1860, *Carteggi: Mezzogiorno*, op. cit.

10. Cavour to Farini, 14.7.1860, Chiala: *Lettere*, op. cit.; cf. Rimini: *Mémoires de Griscelli*, Brussels, n.d; MSS Fondo Nelson Gay, *Museo del Risorgimento*, Milan, and MSS police reports, *Archivio di Stato*, Palermo.

11. 7.7.1860, *Archivio Curatulo*.

12. Cavour to Lady Holland, 4.11.1860, *Carteggi: Mezzogiorno*, op. cit.

13. Mancini to Cavour, 21.10.1860; Farini to Cavour, 14.11.1860; *Carteggi: Mezzogiorno*, op. cit.

14. Romano: *Memoire politiche di Liborio Romano*, 1873; that these were Cavour's true sentiments is apparent from his letters to his confidant, Nigra, e.g. 12.7.1860: *Garibaldi is good only for destruction; Carteg: Cavour–Nigra*.

15. Odo Russell to Lord Cowley, 5.12.1860, Cavour's observation quoted Persano: *Diario privato, politico, militare*, 1880.

16. Winspeare to De Martino, 23.7.1860: *Carteggi: Mezzogiorno*, op. cit.

17. Cavour: *Carteggi: Mezzogiorno*, op. cit. cf. Persano: *Diario*, op. cit.

18. For some unexplained reason, de Polnay: *Garibaldi*, op. cit., claims that Dumas was miles away at the time; but later the same day Garibaldi gave Dumas written authority to start *L'Indépendant* (as narrated by Dumas) and this document is reproduced in Dumas: *On Board the Emma*, op. cit. Once again, Dumas's veracity is shown by the documentary evidence.

19. Cavour to Villamarina, 3.9.1860, *Carteggi: Mezzogiorno*, op. cit.

20. Ciampoli: *Scritti*, op. cit.; Cf. Guerrini: *La Missione del Conte Litta* in *Il Risorgimento*, February, 1909.

21. Cavour to Ricasoli, 21.8.1860, *Carteggi: Mezzogiorno*, op. cit.

22. Russell to Corbete, 25.8.1859.

23. Elliott: *Some Revolutions and other Diplomatic Experiences*, London, 1922.

24. Fagan: *Life of Panizzi*, 1880; Trevelyan: *G. and the Making of Italy*, op. cit.; Lacaita: *An Italian Englishman*, London, 1933; Letter from Lord John Russell to Lord Cowley: Cowley, op. cit.

25. 1.8.1860. *Carteggi: Cavour–Nigra*, op. cit. For the events of this period see Mack Smith: *Cavour and Garibaldi, 1860*, Cambridge, 1954.

CHAPTER XIX

THE APOGEE OF A LIFETIME

1. The basis of the conversation and narrative that follows is Dumas: *Les Garibaldiens*, op. cit.; confirmed and checked by Forbes: *Campaign of Garibaldi in the Two Sicilies*, London, 1861; Abba, op. cit.; Bandi, op. cit.; Guerzoni: *Nino Bixio*, 1875; Türr, op. cit.

2. Forbes, op. cit.

3. Werner: *Autobiography*, op. cit.

4. 22.9.1860, Cavour: *Carteggi: Cavour–Nigra*, op. cit.

5. Cavour to Persano, 7.9.1860, Cavour: *Carteggi: Mezzogiorno*, op. cit.

6. Hudson to Russell, 7.9.1860.

7. Cavour to Antonelli, 7.9.1860, Cavour: *Carteggi: Mezzogiorno*, op. cit. There is great mystery about Persano's alleged telegram, although in his *Diario*, 1860–61, op. cit., he seems to acknowledge it as his. Cavour was supposed to have received it on the 7th, and to have sent it on to Nigra in Paris on the 8th; but in a letter of the 8th to Cavour, Nigra appears to be commenting on it. And Persano's own letter of the 8th to Cavour gives a completely different account of affairs in Naples.

8. Mario: *Bertani e i suoi tempi*, 1888.

9. Cavour: *Carteggi: Cavour–Nigra*, op. cit.

10. Cavour: *Carteggi: Cavour–Nigra*, op. cit.

11. MS Randone to Bonham, 6.7.1860, F.O. Public Records Office, London.

12. Elliott, op. cit.

13. Mazzini: *Scritti (Atti della Repubblica Romana)*, op. cit.

14. Crispi: *Scritti e Discorsi Politici*, 1890.

15. *L'Unita Italiana*, Genoa, 26.7 1860.

16. Melena: *Blick*, op. cit.

17. Türr, op. cit.

18. Ciampoli, op. cit.

19. Vecchi: *Garibaldi a Caprera*, op. cit. Garibaldi had on Caprera a bundle of the king's letters tied up with tape, but they appear to have been abstracted after his death.

20. Quoted Sacerdote, op. cit.

21. Mario: *The Red Shirt*, 1865; Mario: *Vita di G. Garibaldi*, Milan, 1882; Castellini: *Pagine Garibaldine*, 1909.

22. Mario: *Supplement,* op. cit.
23. Mundy: *H.M.S. 'Hannibal' at Palermo and Naples, 1859–61.*
24. Persano: *Diario,* op. cit.
25. Cavour to Farini, 2.11.1860, *Carteggi: Mezzogiorno,* op. cit.
26. MSS Panizzi, British Museum.
27. MSS Panizzi, *supra*; Cf. *Lettere ad Antonio Panizzi,* Florence, 1880.

CHAPTER XX

THE WOUNDED LION

1. Vecchi: *Garibaldi e Caprera,* Naples, 1862; shorter English version: *Garibaldi at Caprera,* London, 1862. Morais: *L'Isola Sacra,* Torino, 1907. Curatulo: *Garibaldi agricoltore,* Rome, 1930.
2. Garibaldi: *Scritti,* op. cit.
3. Garibaldi: *Scritti,* op. cit.
4. Mario: *Supplement,* op. cit. Sacerdote: *Vita,* op. cit.
5. de la Rive: *Le Comte de Cavour, récits et souvenirs,* Paris, 1862.
6. Gay: *Lincoln's offer of a Command to Garibaldi,* in *Century Illustrated,* New York, November 1907.
7. Melena: *Recollections,* op. cit.
8. Vecchi: *Garibaldi e Caprera,* op. cit.
9. Quoted by Chambers: *Garibaldi and Italian Unity,* London, 1864, and Mario: *Supplement,* op. cit., c.f. Lassalle's *Briefwechsel,* Berlin, 1923; Blind: *Lücken in Garibaldi's Denkwürdigkeiten* in *Magazin für die Literatur,* 1888; Durando: *Episodi diplomatici,* Turin, 1901.
10. Mario: *Supplement,* op. cit.
11. Cavour: *Scritti,* op. cit.
12. Cavour: *Scritti,* op. cit.
13. Cavour: *Scritti,* op. cit.
14. MS *Notes secrètes de M. Hidalgo* in Vienna State Archives.
15. A Swiss banker named Jecker had lent three-quarters of a million dollars to the falling clerical-reactionary Mexican Government and received in exchange notes of the Mexican Government for fifteen million dollars. He became bankrupt and his assets, including the notes, were acquired for buttons by de Morny, Napoleon III's half-brother and man of affairs; Jecker was promptly made a French citizen and the claim was thereafter persistently supported by the French government, no doubt so that the French Emperor and his brother could make an enormous personal profit. And, after Maximilian was installed as Emperor of Mexico, the French Government demanded sovereignty over the richest silver-bearing province of Mexico.
16. See for Aspromonte and the events leading up to it, Adamoli: *Da Martino a Mentana;* Bruzzessi: *Dal Volturno ad Aspromonte;* Crispi: *Carteggi inediti;* Tosetti: *Garibaldi e Rattazzi.*
17. Sacerdote: *Vita,* op. cit.
18. Werner: *Autobiography,* op. cit.
19. The dispatches of Pallavicini and Cialdini have quite a different story

but neither were eye-witnesses and the Garibaldini versions published in Bruz-zesi, etc. are based on contemporary accounts and are more reliable; as in particular, is E. Cairoli's diary: *Roma ed Aspromonte*.

20. Text in Sacerdote: *Vita*, op. cit. and Chambers, op. cit.
21. Mario: *Supplement*, op. cit.
22. MS d'Azeglio to Panizzi, Panizzi MSS, British Museum.
23. MS *Museo del Risorgimento*, Milan.
24. Mario: *Supplement*, op. cit.

· CHAPTER XXI

PLUM PUDDING AND TURTLE SOUP

1. This was his account to both Speranza and Jessie Mario. Melena: *Recollections*, op. cit. and Mario: *Supplement*, op. cit.
2. Melena: *Recollections*, op. cit.
3. In a letter to *The Scotsman*, 12.1.1887.
4. Tennyson: *A Memoir of Garibaldi*, London, 1864.
5. c.f. Note 7 to Chapter II.
6. Manning: *Letter to Catholics*, London, 1864.
7. *Der Briefwechsel Zwischen Marx und Engels*, Stuttgart, 1921.
8. Queen Victoria: *Letters*, London, 1907.
9. Herzen, *Camicia Rossa*, Lausanne, 1882. For the secret negotiations that were going on at the time, see *Visita del General Garibaldi*, published in newspaper *Avanguardia*, Turin, 1865; copies in *Museo del Risorgimento*, Milan; and *Politica Segreta Italiana*, Turin, 1880.
10. MS *Museo del Risorgimento*, Milan.
11. Garibaldi: *Scritti*, op. cit.

CHAPTER XXII

I OBEY

1. Melena: *Recollections*, op. cit.
2. Melena: *Recollections*, op. cit.
3. Garibaldi, *Scritti*, op. cit.
4. Melena: *Recollections*, op. cit.
5. Werner: *Autobiography*, op. cit.
6. The Official History of the War, *La campagna del* 1866 has a slightly different story: that Garibaldi proposed to descend on Trieste itself but there seems no foundation for this insignificant deviation from the other accounts.
7. The best accounts of Garibaldi's part in the war are to be found in Adamoli: *Da San Martino a Mentana* and Branca, *La campagna dei volontari italiani nel Tirolo*.
8. In a letter to Melena, 11.12.1866, Curatulo: *G e le donne*, op. cit.
9. Mario, *Supplement*, op. cit.

10. Palamenghi–Crispi: *Carteggi Politici inediti de F. Crispi*, Rome, 1912.

11. Garibaldi gave Melena a MS account of his escape, part of which she published in *Recollections*, op. cit; other details from Werner: *Autobiography*, op. cit.

12. The best eye-witness account of Monterotondo and Mentana is Barrili: *Con Garibaldi alle porte di Rome*; from the enemy side, General Kanzler: *Rapporto a Papa Pio IX sull'invasione dello Stato pontificio*. More recent studies are Maravigna: *Mentana*, 1926 and Cesari: *Gli avenimenti del 1867* in *Esercito e Nazione*, 1927.

13. To Melena, *Recollections*, op. cit.; from which the details on the rest of this chapter are derived.

Chapter XXIII

A THUNDERBOLT FROM A CLOUDLESS SKY

1. To Gladstone, 2.1.1870; *Selections from the Correspondence of the First Lord Acton*, London, 1917.

2. See letter to Gueranger in particular and others published in *Acta et Decreta Sacrorum Conciliorum Recentiorum, Collectio Lacenis*, Fribourg, 1890.

3. Mario: *Supplement,* op. cit. from which subsequent conversations with Garibaldi in this chapter are derived.

4. Bordone, *Garibaldi et l'Armée des Vosges,* Paris, 1871.

5. *Nouveau Press Libre,* Dijon, 19.1.1871, copy in *Bibliothèque Nationale,* Paris.

6. Account given to present author by Clelia Garibaldi.

7. Account given to present author by Clelia Garibaldi, who said her father was fond of repeating this story.

Chapter XXIV

WITHOUT AN EPITAPH

1. Account given to present author by Clelia Garibaldi.

2. Melena: *Recollections*, op. cit.

3. MS in *Museo del Risorgimento,* Milan; published by Curatulo: *G e le donne,* op. cit.

4. Mario: *Supplement,* op. cit.

5. Mario: *Garibaldi e i suoi tempi*, Milan, 1905. Source also of subsequent conversation with Orlando.

6. Account given to present author by Clelia Garibaldi.

APPENDIX

GARIBALDI'S OWN ACCOUNT OF HIS
MATRIMONIAL AFFAIRS

As THIS work was going to press, the Dowager Lady Aberconway was good enough to communicate to the author a copy of a letter from Mrs Chambers (see page 298) which is in her possession. Mrs Chambers' letter was addressed to a Mr Ashurst but a copy was sent by her to Mr H. D. Pochin, grandfather of the late Lord Aberconway.

The extracts given below are of interest, not for their historical accuracy (the facts narrated relating to Garibaldi's marriages are demonstrably untrue), but for the stories which the General was wont to tell his women friends about his matrimonial affairs. It is clear from Mario: *Supplement*, op. cit. and Melena: *Recollections*, op. cit. that they also were regaled with similar accounts.

Putney House,
Putney, S.W.,
6th Decr, 1875.

My dear Mr Ashurst,

. . . I nursed the daughter of the General—Teresa Canzio—through two of her confinements . . .

General Garibaldi, at the birth of Lincoln, insisted on his daughter nursing her own child . . . She, on her part, was perfectly determined that nurse she would not . . . and . . . a very strong, healthy, pretty, Piedmontese woman arrived in the Island. This was Francesca . . . She was a widow, her husband had been a sergeant in the Piedmontese Guard and was dead . . . She was most respectable in every way . . .

I was at Caprera during the whole of these events . . . Some sixteen months after, and the people who had praised Francesca up to the skies had now no word in the Italian Language base enough for her . . . She was a thief; she was a swindler . . . she had never been married at all . . .

At this time, to the best of my belief, General Garibaldi had not the slightest idea of marrying Francesca. She was accused of every kind of immoral conduct with every-one at Caprera. Fortunately . . . on the nights she was accused of sleeping out, I was able to prove that she had never left my rooms . . .

Some little time before this, Teresa Canzio had dismissed her from her service . . .

After having charged the poor woman with familiarity with everyone else on the Island, the General himself did not even escape the slander of those wicked tongues . . . he came to me and said that no girl in his house should lose her character thro' false-hoods and to protect it he meant to marry Francesca. If nothing more was said, no one need know anything about the marriage. If these lies . . . went on, she had but one answer to make 'She was his wife'.

I do not think that Francesca understood her position . . . The next year, when I was on Caprera, she never sat down at table unless I told her, although by this time little Clelia had arrived . . . About a year and a half ago, some busy-bodies endeavoured to convince G. Garibaldi that his marriage was illegal and he wrote me letter after letter in the state of greatest distress . . . he requested me to take legal opinions as to the validity of his marriage . . . The poor General never intended to break any laws . . . thus, when he ran away with his first wife, Anita . . . she was a minor and . . . betrothed . . . to another man. Now her betrothal, in the R. C. Church, was the same as a marriage, and this circumstance rendered practically her three surviving children, Menotti, Teresa, and Ricciotti, illegitimate . . .

On his return to Nice in . . . '48 . . . the gentleman who had been betrothed to Anita was dead and the General's mother made him be married over again. But no live child was born after the second ceremony . . .

In '59, during the Campaign on the lakes, he was induced to believe that Raimondi . . . was in love with the cause which he represented . . . The General was easily deceived . . .

On the morning of the marriage he received a letter which stated that, in a few weeks, his destined bride would become a mother . . . he sent for his legal adviser and asked his advice . . .

The advice was this, that the marriage was no marriage until it was consummated; that the General was safe to let the ceremony proceed . . . On returning from the Church . . . the General . . . took possession of his old apartments . . .

The bride, finding herself at liberty, wrote to a young officer, inviting him to spend the night in her apartments; the gentleman's answer, accepting the invitation, was placed in the hands of G. Garibaldi in the presence of her father . . . the marriage was, the General believed, formally annulled. About eighteen months ago . . . he was informed that an important formality had been omitted, which was the publishing of the dissolution of the marriage in some Italian state paper . . . he wrote to me many long and earnest letters and requested me to take legal advice in England for him. I consulted my solicitor, Mr Waller, and requested him to take Counsel's opinion on the whole case . . .

The advice which I received . . . was this—that any fresh marriage now would be to cast a slur on the birth of the children . . . and that there should be some distinct and public recognition both of her and her children . . .

> *Believe me, to remain,*
> *Dear Mr Ashurst,*

The author is grateful to Lord Aberconway for
permission to reproduce the above extracts.

INDEX